Divers Guide
to
Michigan

By Steve Harrington

**Maritime Press in association with the
Great Lakes Diving Council, Inc.**
P.O. Box 759
St. Ignace, MI 49781

Divers Guide to Michigan

Published by Maritime Press in cooperation with the Great Lakes Diving Council, Inc, a private, non-profit organization dedicated to diver education.

Second Edition, First Printing
Copyright 1990, 1998 by Steve Harrington
ISBN 0-9624629-8-5
Printed in the USA

Although every reasonable effort has been made to verify information, no guarantees are made regarding the accuracy of information contained in this book. Divers are encouraged to contact the Great Lakes Diving Council, P.O. Box 759, St. Ignace, MI 49781 with contributions for the next edition.

Cover photo: Steve Harrington prowls a Lake Superior shipwreck. Photo by Mike Kohut.

DEDICATION

A man who has once looked with the archaeological eye will never see quite normally. He will be wounded by what other men call trifles. It is possible to refine the sense of time until an old shoe in the bunch grass or a pile of nineteenth-century beer bottles in an abandoned mining town tolls in one's head like a hall clock. This is the price one pays for learning to read time from surfaces other than an illuminated dial. It is the melancholy secret of the artifact, the humanly touched thing.

--Loren Eiseley
The Night Country

This book is dedicated to those who have "once looked with an archaeological eye...."

Acknowledgements

This book is the product of many hours of research over nearly three decades of diving and research. Still, it would not have been possible without the help of the following: My son, Jason, Dale Purchase, Mike and Linda Kohut, Pete and Linda Lindquist, C. Patrick Labadie, Jim Montcalm, Michelle Whitaker, Jim and Pat Stayer, Karen Rapier, Ken Pott, Mark Rowe, Sleeping Bear Dunes National Lakeshore, Isle Royale National Park, Jed Jaworski, Jack Spencer and staff of Scuba North, Nate Morgan, Ric Mixter, Fred and Betty Shannon, Steve DenBoer, Dan Fountain, Robert Schmitt, Kimm Stabelfeldt, Janene Sonnega, Mike Comsa, Judy Shafir, Lee Barnhill, Chuck and Jeri Feltner, Mike Spears, Valerie Olson, Brian Hartman, Chuck Knowles, Mark and Kathy Roberts, Larry McElroy, Walt Rayl, Scott Peters, Tom Graf, Tom Tanczos, Joyce Hayward, Mark Rowe, and Bear the diving dog.

Contents

Foreword

They say old friends are best because they can see where you are and they know where you've been. I believe that is true and I am glad to count Steve Harrington as one of my friends.

Those who know Steve are frequently surprised to find him a giving person who places a premium on truth and fairness. These qualities make him a natural for writing *Divers Guide to Michigan.*

First, the book enables Steve to share his favorite sport--skin and scuba diving. Readers will find he has made great efforts to make dive sites easy to locate and enjoy. He has gathered information from countless divers, government officials, and retailers to bring to you what no other writer has. Steve has compiled this information in an easy-to-read volume that, to many, has become a "bible" not only for divers but maritime historians as well.

Secondly, Steve provides the most accurate information possible. It would take a lifetime to dive all the sites in this book so to some extent he is at the mercy of other divers. In some cases, divers have purposely provided false information to keep others from favorite shipwrecks. In this second edition, much more accurate information has replaced that provided by unscrupulous divers.

Since 1970, Steve has been exploring the underwater world in the Great Lakes, Michigan's inland lakes and rivers, and in the Caribbean. There is a tendency for those who have been diving so long to turn the sport into work of some sort, as though an excuse is needed to have a good time. To his credit, Steve has avoided that tendency and enjoys diving today as much as he did nearly thirty years ago.

He also enjoys sharing the sport and goes out of his way on docks, air stations, and charter boats to share information certain to help others enjoy their underwater experience. That is why he formed the Great Lakes Diving Council, a private non-profit organization that shares such information with divers throughout the Great Lakes states.

And we are fortunate in Michigan to have so many underwater resources. It would take several lifetimes to explore all the shipwrecks, dock ruins, and geological formations. While he has not dove every site described in this book, Steve has come close. These days he can be found either in the Straits of Mackinac or the Munising areas prowling with his little boat looking for something new or visiting a favorite, familiar place.

Like Steve, I enjoy diving. See you out there!

--Mike Kohut

Preface

It is winter and ice conceals my favorite summer playgrounds. These playgrounds are underwater shipwrecks, dock ruins, weed beds, and rock formations. I cannot share them with others today. I cannot don scuba diving equipment and take new divers by the hand to lead them to vast explorations of a world known only to the adventurous.

Instead, I cower in a warm corner and write. I write about fantastic tales of heroism and rescue and disaster and tragedy. Or I share favorite memories of huge fish or recount the thrill of finding rusted tools discarded by lumbermen of a bygone era.

We who dive are a strange lot. We leave the comfort and safety of the terrestrial world to discover for ourselves the wonder found underwater. Regardless of the number of divers in a team, it is a solitary adventure. Only the individual knows personal challenges and triumphs. And often it is only the individual who knows the sting of failure and the commitment to try again.

My favorite places to dive are often only favorite to me. In my favorite weed bed my eye catches the caudal fin of a prowling pike. Suddenly I realize, again, that I am a transient intruder, an underwater vagabond, who must be careful not to disturb ecological balances that have taken nature centuries to achieve. But the pike turns and hides in vegetation and I feel better, almost invited, to explore.

At my favorite shipwreck, one others scoff, I sift the sand of a debris field and discover a pair of binoculars. Carefully, I clean them off and hold them in my palms. For a moment my mind allows me to stand on the deck of a stricken vessel and search the horizon for a rescue ship that never comes. In his last moments on earth the captain probably held those binoculars in frozen hands until I discover them a century later. In that moment I travelled through time as though I had stepped through a mirror, and discovered a vague notion of my own humanity.

For some divers there comes a time when they simply feel more comfortable underwater than anywhere else. For these divers there exists a bond between themselves and the underwater world. It has everything to do with attitude and cannot be explained beyond that.

For still other divers there exists a bond between themselves and fellow divers. There can develop an unspoken link of spirit forged through shared experiences and desire. These bonds are often the strongest and sustain the human spirit through the storms of life.

I cannot share my favorite playgrounds today. Like some small child I am relegated to a warm corner where a puppy tugs at my socks.

Today, only because of the weather, I write because I cannot dive.

Introduction

This is the second edition of a book that expanded scuba diving and snorkeling for many. Information in the book encouraged divers to explore new areas and discover the thrill of shipwrecks underwater.

The first edition began as an experiment and quickly took on a life of its own. Readers will find this edition significantly changed. Although some chapters, such as the one on Isle Royale, remain largely unchanged from the first edition, other chapters include new dive sites, maps, and illustrations. Whenever possible, drawings of shipwrecks as they are found underwater have been included because they help divers quickly orient themselves and reduce the chances of "surprises."

This edition closely follows the format of the first edition with a few exceptions. Most notably, the designations of sites as "expert", "intermediate," or "beginner" have been removed. This is because such labels can be misleading and it is an individual decision whether to dive a particular site. As a compromise, I have added more site information and attempted to describe conditions as completely as possible.

Another change is the reference to inland lake dive sites specifically around or near underwater preserves. This ensures an opportunity to dive even if the weather or boat malfunctions keep you off the Great Lakes.

Other changes are less dramatic. This edition is considerably larger than the first edition to include new information, such as the Southwest Michigan Underwater Preserve and the DeTour Passage Underwater Preserve. Type size was also reduced slightly to help conserve paper and keep costs down. Loran and latitude/longitude information has been provided in an appendix at the request of divers.

Although the second edition is nearly a "new" dive book altogether, it is not the last word on diving any particular site. Local dive retailers can often provide accurate and important information. I encourage divers to stop in at local dive centers to learn more about local dive sites and diving conditions. It is also a good way to meet new friends and share the excitement of diving.

Loran and latitude/longitude information has been provided in an appendix at the request of divers.

This book is not a training manual and it is presumed that divers have been adequately trained and are not exceeding their individual skill levels. There is no substitute for common sense, good training, experience, and caution.

Finally, it is important to realize that this book is only as accurate as the information gathered. For the most part divers have contributed valuable and accurate information and I have attempted to "field check" as many sites as possible. But there are no guarantees. In a book of this nature it is impossible to be entirely accurate and complete. Please do not hesitate to contact me with information about any dive site--new or old--that you believe divers should have.

Using This Guide

This is the type of book that is nearly outdate the moment it is published. Underwater exploration is ongoing and discoveries are made constantly. That is why some information may be a bit inaccurate. I am happy to report, however, that this book has been reviewed by many expert divers over the years and I have incorporated their comments. The result is a more useful tool for those exploring Michigan's underwater world.

In Michigan there are strict laws governing the removal of artifacts, defacing shipwrecks and other destructive activities. Be aware that there is a double standard at work where museums are free to plunder for profit where individual divers are held to the letter of the law. It is not fair and it is against the law but it is the undeniable practice.

Readers will also notice that this book does not make diving recommendations based on skill levels. That is because it is important for divers to make such decisions for themselves. Also, diving sometimes offers some surprises and what would otherwise be a simple dive could become complicated with cable or fish netting. We have, however, tried to make the decision-making process easier by providing more illustrations and detailed site information.

This book also includes more information about family activities. Most divers are adults (although there is a growing number of young people taking up the sport) and we felt it appropriate to offer suggestions for before or after-diving adventures. Our listings are by no means complete in this regard and more information can be obtained from local chambers of commerce.

> *This book also includes more information about family activities.*

Maps in this book are provided as general guides and should not be used for navigation. They are **not** drawn to scale.

Visibility is always a tough diving factor to describe because it can be so variable. For example, visibility in the Straits of Mackinac area may exceed 30 feet one day but be reduced to 3 feet the following day due to some subtle current change. On the other hand, divers can generally count on 25 feet of visibility in some areas such as Murray Bay in the Alger Underwater Preserve.

Like visibility, depths are also often expressed in ranges to account for the amount of "rise" of a shipwreck or the contour of the bottom around a dock ruin, weedbed, or geologic formation. Because the levels of the Great Lakes vary somewhat, so will the depths but the differences should be slight.

More space is devoted to describing and locating inland skin and scuba sites. That is because there are at least 480 inland lakes in Michigan with public access. These lakes have much to offer.

Finally, we have tried to be brutally honest. For example, black flies are a serious problem at the Whitefish Point Underwater Preserve. While divers can escape the worst infestations on the water, sightseeing can be extremely unpleasant in the early summer. When we become aware of such problems we include them for your trip planning.

Remember there is no substitute for common sense....

Remember there is no substitute for common sense and objective evaluation of each diver's abilities by themselves. This guide is intended to provide general information and should not be relied up to evaluate diving ability.

Michigan Diving

There are about 36,000 miles of streams, 11,000 inland lakes, and 38,575 square miles of Great Lakes water in Michigan. That makes it a diver's paradise not only because the cool, fresh water perfectly preserves shipwrecks and artifacts, but because the water often hosts fascinating dock ruins and geological features.

Another appealing attraction for divers is the aquatic life. In addition to many species of fish, there are fantastic weed beds that host amazing insects. Too often, these are overlooked by divers, except snorkelers who have learned to move slowly and look carefully at the underwater world.

Michigan diving is perhaps best known for shipwrecks. The Great Lakes hosts the best collection of shipwrecks in the entire world and these shipwrecks are time capsules of another era when maritime commerce was the backbone of a developing country.

These shipwrecks include some of the earliest sailing craft to visit the New World as well as modern freighters and pleasure craft. Those who dive Great Lakes shipwrecks know it is much like stepping back into history and glimpsing a time centuries old. They also know about the tragedies that took lives of brave seamen who tried in vain to save their ships and themselves.

Many divers--scuba and snorkelers alike--get their start in warm water, marine environments, such as the Caribbean. Michigan diving is significantly differently. First, the water is colder and often less clear than warm water environments. That means a full wetsuit or drysuit is required for most of Michigan diving. But there are some exceptions. There is a popular shipwreck in a Lake Superior bay, for example, where the water temperature often exceeds 70 degrees in late summer and visibility frequently reaches 50 feet or more.

But for the most part divers should be prepared for colder water and a unique diving environment. For many experienced divers, Michigan diving is not less desirable than warm water diving--just different.

For many experienced divers, Michigan diving is not less desirable than warm water diving--just different.

Michigan divers have established a strong conservation ethic. Through strong diver support, a series of laws have been passed to protect shipwrecks from vandals and thieves. With few exceptions, the shipwrecks of the Great Lakes belong to the state and divers are careful to protect the appeal of dive sites by leaving all artifacts where found. The law regarding collecting artifacts in and out of Michigan's underwater preserve system is included in an appendix of this book. Michigan's underwater preserves are covered in detail later.

Although the state does not have funds to pay for patrols or other protective measures, studies have shown that divers do an excellent job of policing themselves. One study showed, in fact, that more divers on a shipwreck resulted in fewer disturbed artifacts.

One of the most important aspects to consider for Michigan diving is water temperature. It is often cold. But technology has provided sport divers with wet and dry suits to overcome this difficulty (approximately 75 percent of all Great Lakes divers use wetsuits to keep warm).

How cold is cold? In most of Lake Superior, the water temperature rarely exceeds 45 degrees even in the hottest summers. Although shallow bays and other protected water may become considerably warmer.

In shallow water in lakes Huron, Michigan, and Erie, on the other hand, the water temperature can easily exceed 75 degrees during the late summer. The temperature of inland lakes and streams varies considerably due to depth, current, and other factors.

Because of this variability, it is best to plan on cold water. That means wearing wet or dry suits, watching air consumption closely and keeping an eye out for hypothermia-- the cooling of the core body

temperature. The cold water also means that it is especially important to be in good physical condition.

Michigan diving can be exciting because of the variety of aquatic environments available for exploration. Although there are few, if any, lakes and streams that have not been visited by sport divers, many portions of those lakes and streams are unexplored.

Exotic Species

Exotic species are difficult to define. They can be viewed as living organisms that now inhabit the Great Lakes but once did not. But that could include virtually *every* Great Lakes organism.

Recent geological studies have shown that the Great Lakes are much younger that once supposed. Lake Michigan, for example, was probably

Spiny Water Flea

formed about 10,000 years ago and Lake Superior may have been formed 5,000 years ago. These are relatively short time spans in geologic terms.

Because of the relative "youth" of the Great Lakes and man's influence on them through shipping and canal building, it is little wonder that new creatures enter the Great Lakes regularly. And man's activities which introduced certain plants and animals to the Great Lakes include those of Native Americans.

Because of their relationship to the water, divers are often the first to recognize exotic species, plant or animal. Some of these species include the river ruffe, sea lamprey eel, American eel, rusty crayfish, Eurasian watermilfoil, white perch, and zebra mussel.

But divers may also be surprised to learn that other species, such as carp, smelt, and brown trout are also considered exotic species because they were once introduced into the Great Lakes.

For divers, the zebra mussel (*Dreissena polymorpha*) presents particular benefits and challenges.

For divers, the zebra mussel presents particular benefits and challenges.

First, the adult mussels, which frequently form colonies more than a foot thick, filter about a quart of water per day. This filtration removes microscopic plants and animals from the water and leaves the water cleaner. Thus, divers benefit because they enjoy greater visibility.

But the massive colonies of zebra mussels, especially those found in southern lakes Michigan and Huron and lakes Erie and Ontario, obscure shipwrecks, rock formations, dock pilings, artifacts, and many other

Adult life size: 1/4 to 1 inch

Zebra Mussel

underwater attractions.

Scientists are still unsure as to what effect zebra mussels will have on the balance of plants and animals in the Great Lakes. But it is certain that these tough critters can thrive in even the most difficult environments.

Zebra mussels can be found in each of the Great Lakes and in many inland lakes as well. But their ability to form massive colonies in Lake Superior and the colder and less nutrient-rich portions of northern lakes Michigan and Huron is in doubt. Only time will tell if they will be able to find enough food and can tolerate the water temperatures.

There is also some evidence that divers, jet skiers and others who wear wetsuits may unintentionally hasten the spread of zebra mussels. The immature form of the mussels has been found to survive long periods in moist wetsuits so it is a good idea to dry them thoroughly between dives.

It is likely that zebra mussels will remain part of the Great Lakes ecosystem but there is evidence that another exotic species, the round goby, may eat zebra mussels. Gobies are small fish and are believed a natural predator of the mussels. Some divers also report seeing yellow perch apparently eat the mussels from the bottom.

One exotic species that sometimes surprises divers is the American eel. This giant cousin of the sea lamprey can weigh as much as 16 pounds and they have been spotted in southern Lake Michigan.

Lakes food chain and could eventually harm food sources for large trout and salmon.

Like the zebra mussel, these exotic species are likely to remain in the Great Lakes ecosystem. At first their populations are expected to "blossom" but through competition,

American Eel

These eels are harmless to divers and migrate from the Sargasso Sea in the Atlantic Ocean where they spawn. They are harvested by some Canadian fishermen along the St. Lawrence Seaway and sent to Europe where they are considered a delicacy.

Another exotic species divers may find is the river ruffe or ruffe. This small, perchlike fish has been discovered around Duluth, Minn. Like the zebra mussel and other exotics, the ruffe is believed to have been introduced by way of discharged ballast of freighters entering the Great Lakes from brackish ports.

The spiny water flea is another exotic species that is expected to have a profound effect on the Great Lakes fishery. This small, transparent creature is similar to the freshwater species but has an obvious spine that makes it unpalatable to yellow perch and other gamefish. Unfortunately, the niche occupied by the spiny water flea interferes with the Great

predation, and environmental factors, their populations will eventually be reduced.

Divers can do little but help avoid the more rapid spread of these species. Thoroughly drying wetsuits and cleaning boat hulls are two important measures that can be taken.

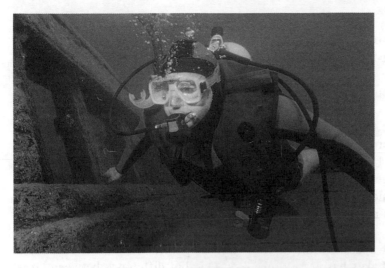

Shipwreck Diving

The Great Lakes are famous for having the finest collection of shipwrecks in the world. The shipwreck legacy begins with the French explorer LaSalle who launched the *Griffon* at Niagara Falls in 1679. The ship was lost, loaded with pelts, in a snow squall near the Straits of Mackinac the same year.

Some estimate that, since the *Griffon*, more than 4,000 other vessels have been lost in the Great Lakes. Of those, only about half have been discovered.

The ships lost include schooners and yachts to modern steel freighters, like the *Edmund Fitzgerald*. Many include the loss of life, such as the Lady Elgin, which went down in 1860 off the coast of Illinois with 297 souls.

Some of these maritime disasters involve heroic rescues but nearly all ended with the tragic loss of a proud vessel.

Today, divers have the opportunity to swim back into time and see these vessels on the bottom. But more than the vessel itself, divers find themselves eerily close to the tragedy and the lost lives. As divers, we must never forget that these are special places worthy of our respect.

Shipwrecks are found in various stages of decomposition. Some are upright and intact while others are upside down and debris may be scattered for miles. Many shipwrecks succumb to the ravages of waves and ice and are nothing more than a pile of boards and anchor chain on the bottom.

But even a pile of boards on the bottom of the Great Lakes has a story to tell. The pieces and artifacts

---

But even a pile of boards on the bottom of the Great Lakes has a story to tell.

---

are clues about daily life on the ship and its demise. Scattered remains also help divers understand the often complex construction of these vessels.

For novice shipwreck divers it is often best to start on scattered remains as long as disorientation is not a problem. From there it is a quick jump to intact shipwrecks.

It is important to explore carefully as divers can become lost inside shipwrecks so dive with experienced buddies and challenge yourself in small increments. Special courses in shipwreck diving are frequently available at local dive centers.

Just as with any outdoor activity there are risks. For diving, entanglements are a primary concern but so is disorientation and panic.

Don't push yourself without thinking. We want you diving for a long time!

Collections of especially noteworthy shipwrecks are found in Michigan's underwater preserves, a topic that is covered later in this book.

Inland Lakes

The Great Lakes is not the only place where exciting diving can be found in Michigan. There are at least 480 lakes with public access sites as well as public access sites on rivers.

One big difference between Great Lakes and inland lake diving is water temperature. Inland lakes tend to warm faster than the Great Lakes although even in the warmest weather inland lakes will develop a "thermocline" where water temperature cools greatly. Still, divers will find that warm water lake margins frequently host colorful gamefish such as bluegill, sunfish, bass, and pike.

Inland lakes can also provide superior visibility depending upon the amount of nutrients in the water. Generally, lakes with many nutrients are less clear than lakes with few nutrients. A good example of a lake with few nutrients is Higgins Lake in Roscommon County. Here, visibility often reaches 40 feet or more.

But lakes with few nutrients are generally shy on gamefish. Lakes with much vegetation tend to support larger populations of fish and other aquatic life.

More about inland lakes is provided later but it is important for divers not to overlook these diving opportunities. This is especially true when foul weather prevent divers from exploring the Great Lakes.

Divers prepare to submerge.

Besides a variety of diving environments, there are a variety of activities for divers to enjoy. Those activities include photography, videography, orienteering, archaeology, drawing, or just plain enjoyment of the underwater environment.

Technology and new designs by equipment manufacturers have made many underwater activities easier and safer. A good example is videography. Smaller recorders and more convenient housings now make it possible for even novice divers to capture excellent images of their underwater adventures.

For many divers a good part of the experience is sharing it with nondiving friends. There is a universal interest in the unknown and many nondivers pick up the sport after watching a neighbor's slide show or video. Practice makes perfect and it usually isn't long before amateur videos approach professional quality.

Fortunately, there are special classes available through dive centers which teach divers how to shoot underwater photos or videos or even participate in archaeological projects. Check out the classes available at your local dive center for more information.

Eco-Diving

One way an increasing number of divers are enjoying their sport is through eco-diving. This is a diving method usually used in relatively shallow water and involves careful observations of plants and animals.

Instead of swimming far ahead to explore shipwrecks, more and more divers are taking it slow and watching the antics of sticklebacks, burbots, and even sculpins. It is a way to learn first hand about the underwater ecosystem.

There are classes available to learn how to become an "underwater naturalist" but it is easy enough to simply go slow and stop on the bottom among weeds. Eventually fish become curious and it can be similar to having your own freshwater aquarium.

And all the excitement is not found with visiting fish. There are crayfish, snails, clams, and a large variety of insects that can entertain observant divers for hours.

Bluegill

Also, eco-diving can be performed in the Great Lakes or in inland lakes and streams.

To get a taste of eco-diving find a suitable dive buddy and set of goal of visiting only one or two shallow water sites. Take a slate to make notes and drawings of what is seen. Soon you will see how the smaller components of the Great Lakes or inland lakes ecosystems affect larger components--even shipwrecks.

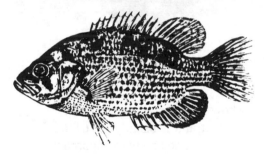

Rock Bass

When learning eco-diving it is important to stay shallow at first and concentrate on a relatively small area. Although it may appear that there is little or no action, careful observation will reveal a whole world of living creatures most simply swim past.

This is an exciting underwater world that escapes most divers who prefer to challenge themselves by diving deeper and deeper or explore only shipwrecks. Eco-diving is fun, inexpensive (it can be done while snorkeling) and requires little energy.

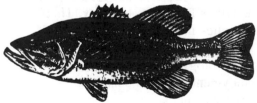

Largemouth Bass

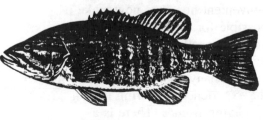

Smallmouth Bass

The Great Lakes

The Great Lakes comprise the largest collection of freshwater in the world. Lakes Michigan, Huron, Superior, Ontario, and Erie are valuable resources but they are also environmentally fragile.

The Great Lakes collect water from throughout the Midwest and portions of Canada. Contaminated water from those areas too frequently finds its way to the Great Lakes. That is important to divers because water quality affects visibility, health risks, and plant and animal life found in and near the water. It is little wonder that Great Lakes divers are emerging as strong advocates of water quality.

Besides the introduction of exotic species, such as the zebra mussel, divers are concerned about toxic chemicals, increased salinity diversion, turbidity, and sedimentation. Environmental issues are complex but divers are making their voices heard through the political process.

The Great Lakes offer a variety of underwater environments. Generally, the water is colder than inland lakes and streams and a dry suit maximizes comfort, although wetsuits are often adequate and are worn by most divers. Divers should be aware of underwater currents, unpredictable weather, and boat traffic.

Underwater currents are variable.

One day may be still and the next could bring a current not unlike that found in a river. Although generally not a problem, even for the novice diver, currents should be considered to avoid drifting away from a tending boat or nearby shoreline.

Unpredictable weather and boat traffic warrant a topside observer. Some divers get careless and fail to leave someone topside to watch for trouble. This can be a fatal mistake.

Topside observers can warn boaters to maintain their distance and watch weather conditions. If a boat

Topside observers can warn boaters to maintain their distance and watch weather conditions.

drifts on its anchorage, a topside observer can account for that situation and prevent an unwelcome surprise for divers in the form of a derelict.

Not all Great Lakes diving requires a boat. Some very interesting dives can be had at old dock sites accessible from shore. More and more skin and scuba divers are finding that dock ruins provide a tremendous exploration opportunity.

When venturing into open water,

however, it is best to know the area. Some divers first use a dive charter before exploring on their own. This gives them a chance to learn unusual features of the area and become familiar with local diving conditions. Most charter operators welcome questions and offer advice for later visits.

Smart divers use boats large enough to handle the Great Lakes. Small fishing boats may be great for inland lakes, but waves can build quickly on the Great Lakes. Inflatables are becoming increasingly popular on the Great Lakes because of their economy, stability, and convenience for diving. And don't overlook the value of having a vhf radio on board in the event help is needed.

The best advice is to err on the side of safety. If divers question weather conditions and the capability

so be careful to keep your pockets clean.

While Canada has a strict set of no-collecting regulations similar to Michigan's, other Great Lakes states are still considering such laws. Some believe it will not be long before other states become aware of the value of keeping shipwrecks intact where they rest.

Whenever enjoying Great Lakes diving, remember that the Great Lakes are immense, but nonetheless fragile. Divers, as direct observers of the underwater environment, can have tremendous impacts on the policies that affect water quality.

In the section that follows, readers will find descriptions of Great Lakes dive sites that are not within underwater preserves. Those sites within preserves are covered in other chapters.

> ### The best advice is to err on the side of safety.

their boats, it is best to try an inland dive site and save the Great Lakes for another day.

Michigan has a unique set of laws that prohibit most "souvenir collecting" in the Great Lakes. Those laws are covered later in this book but divers should be aware that it is not "finders keepers" in the Great Lakes. A completely different set of laws apply to inland lakes and streams where collecting is based on property rights.

Other divers often report divers who do not observe collecting laws

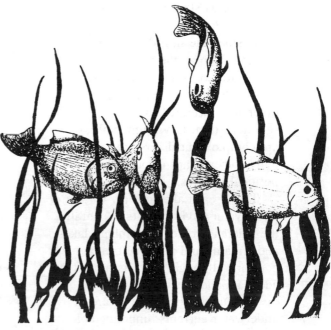

IRONSIDES

The *Ironsides* was a 231-foot, twin-screw steamer that carried passengers and freight up and down Lake Michigan until it foundered four miles west of Grand Haven in Lake Michigan.

The *Ironsides* was carrying a cargo of general merchandise when it was lost on Sept. 15, 1873. It was built in Cleveland, Ohio, in 1864.

The *Ironsides* remains a popular West Michigan dive site. Although there is no penetration diving at this site, divers can find many interesting shipbuilding features. Arches used to strengthen the wooden hull of the vessel are well-preserved.

Although the *Ironsides* is visited frequently throughout the summer, the weather is usually most cooperative and visibility the best in October. The wreck rests on a sandy bottom so visibility is variable and often a function of wave action and underwater currents. Local divers try to visit this wreck in the morning before westerly breezes build waves and make diving uncomfortable.

Dive charters serving this wreck are difficult to find and private boats are most often used. Small buoys sometimes mark this site during the summer and fall but there generally is no mooring buoy present so an anchor must be set.

Location:	Four miles west of Grand Haven in Lake Michigan.
Loran:	32525.1/49494.5
Depth:	110-120 feet
Visibility:	5 to 15 feet
Tips:	Visibility and underwater currents could make this a challenging dive for some. First divers down should check anchorage.

IDA

The *Ida* was a three-masted schooner that capsized in an autumn, northwest gale in 1908. The ship, which was built in 1867, had seen a long life as a Great Lakes freighter.

The crew of the *Ida* abandoned ship about 12 miles north of Frankfort in Lake Michigan and the remains, including its cargo of lumber, drifted to within two miles of the city where it was declared a total loss.

This wreck is accessible by boat or shore and is completely broken up on a sandy bottom in only 12 feet of water. This wreck is typical of those found grounded along the Lake Michigan coast in shallow water. Ice and waves tends to break them up quickly and completely.

A massive anchor chain and other large artifacts can be seen at this site. Because of the shifting sands in this area, some parts of the wreck are more visible at times than others.

Divers can access the *Ida* from shore from the Congregational Church Assembly located in the tiny community of Pilgrim off Pilgrim Highway (M-22), a few miles north of Frankfort. It is best to obtain permission from the Assembly office before using their walkway to the beach.

Divers will find the remains of the *Ida* in about 12 feet of water 75 yards from shore directly out from the Assembly walkway. It is believed that some of the Assembly cabins were constructed from lumber salvaged from the wreck.

In addition to the wreck, divers are likely to spot sculpins, crayfish, and small gamefish such as yellow perch in the area.

Visibility will be greatly reduced during periods of heavy seas and rains.

Location:	About two miles north of Frankfort, 75 yards from shore out from the Congregational Church Assembly beach access.
Depth:	10 to 15 feet
Visibility:	Variable, 5 to 20 feet unless adverse weather conditions persist.
Tips:	This makes a great snorkel dive in calm weather. Turbulence makes it an extremely difficult dive when heavy seas are present. Ask permission first and keep the area clean.

NWMMM Graphic

IDA

F.T. BARNEY

The *F.T. Barney* was a two-masted schooner headed through the Straits of Mackinac with a load of coal in 1868 when it collided with another ship.

The remains of the 354-gross ton *F.T. Barney* were discovered north of Rogers City in Lake Huron. How the ship that was involved in an accident so many miles away came to rest upright and intact where it did is a mystery.

Location:	Four miles north of Rogers City in Lake Huron. This site is usually buoyed with a small marker buoy.
Loran:	30984.1/48390.7
Lat/Lon:	45 29.27/83 50.51
Depth:	150 to 160 feet
Visibility:	5 to 20 feet.
Tips:	Do not disturb fragile artifacts. Narrow passages make penetration of cabin areas treacherous. Be certain anchorage is secure.

Although the *F.T. Barney* has been visited by relatively few sport divers, it is considered an important archaeological study site because of the condition of the wreck. The masts and cabin are still intact suggesting that the ship sank slowly despite a hefty cargo.

There are many small artifacts, including personal items, still at this site. This is proof that Michigan sport divers are committed to preserving the integrity of shipwrecks they visit.

In 1989, the *F.T. Barney* was explored with the use of a remote-operated vehicle (ROV). The ROV was used to obtain high-resolution video images of the wreck for archaeological study and education programs. Scuba divers also contributed video for these purposes.

The rope rigging of the *F.T. Barney* has disintegrated so there is no significant danger of entanglement associated with the exterior of this wreck. But the cabin area of the ship can be dangerous because of narrow passages. Most hatches of the ship are clogged with the load of coal. Experienced divers prefer to explore the wreck site from the outside and penetrate only small portions of the wreck.

Divers may be surprised to find a crows nest still intact on one mast of the ship, which was built in Vermilion, Ohio in 1856.

The *F.T. Barney* was granted special preserve status to ensure conservation of artifacts at the site. The Rogers City community is concerned about the removal of artifacts and the site is watched closely.

Divers can usually find sport fishing charter operators in Rogers City willing to take them out to the site.

SAGAMORE

The *Sagamore* is an excellent example of the whaleback steamer-barges that were once common bulk freighters on the Great Lakes. Their design is unique but was short-lived. Although capable of shedding water in heavy seas, the hull was simply not large enough to run economically.

The 308-foot, steel-hulled *Sagamore* was at anchor on a foggy day in the shipping channel near the entrance of the St. Mary's River in Lake Superior on July 19, 1901. The *Sagamore*, just inside the U.S./Canada border, was loaded with a cargo of iron ore when it was struck on her starboard side by the *Northern Queen*.

The *Sagamore* sank almost immediately taking the captain and two crew members with her. When the ship sank, the pilot house was separated from the steel hull. Otherwise, the ship is intact and is a popular dive destination because it is accessible and protected.

The hatches of the *Sagamore* are open and provide easy penetration diving. A ladder is located in the bow. The wreck is located in 70 feet of water and rises about 25 feet from the gravel bottom.

Divers also find large schools of perch and other gamefish around the *Sagamore*. Burbot are also common.

This site is not buoyed because it is located in the shipping channel. Before visiting the *Sagamore*, it is a good idea to contact the U.S. Coast Guard Station at Sault Ste. Marie to let them know that a boat will be anchored at the site. They will advise ships entering the shipping channel of your presence. Regular "security calls" from the dive boat are also recommended.

Charter services to this wreck can be found on both sides of the border.

Location:	Near the entrance to the St. Mary's River in Lake Superior off Gras Cap Reef.
Loran:	31072.9/47771.9
Depth:	45-75 feet
Visibility:	15-30 feet, sometimes less
Tips:	Be sure to keep the U.S. Coast Guard informed of your activities at the site and keep someone topside to avoid problems with large ships in the shipping channel. Monitor vhf channel 16.

The whaleback Sagamore sank in 1901 after being rammed by another ship.
Three men died in the mishap

GOSHAWK

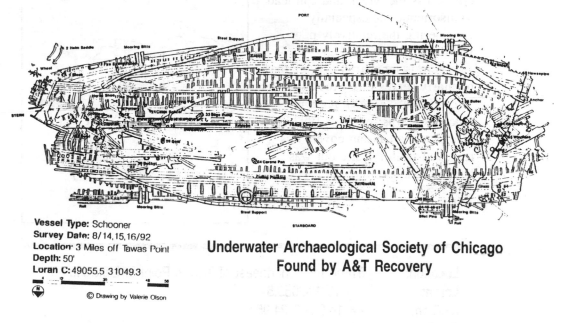

Vessel Type: Schooner
Survey Date: 8/14,15,16/92
Location: 3 Miles off Tawas Point
Depth: 50'
Loran C: 49055.5 31049.3

© Drawing by Valerie Olson

**Underwater Archaeological Society of Chicago
Found by A&T Recovery**

The *Goshawk* was built at Cleveland, Ohio in 1866. It was a three-masted, wooden schooner of 550 gross tons, 180 feet long, 32 feet wide, and had a 13-foot draft. The vessel was primarily used as a lumber schooner for the Blodgett fleet until 1902 when it was converted to a tow barge.

During a storm on June 16, 1920, after a remarkable 55 years of service, the *Goshawk* foundered in Lake Huron about three miles northeast of Tawas Point. At the time of her loss, the vessel was being towed by the tug *P.J. Ralph* (later lost near South Manitou Island) and was carrying a cargo of salt from Port Huron, Mich. to Duluth, Minn.

No lives were lost in the disaster, the crew abandoned the stricken ship via lifeboats. The vessel is noted for being the oldest working vessel when it sank. It was discovered in 1992 by A&T Recovery of Chicago, Ill.

Today, the *Goshawk* lies in 50 feet of water with the sides of its hull broken at the turn of the bilge. This means a dive site approximately 180 feet long and 80 feet wide on a sand bottom. The decking, if present at the time of the disaster, was probably lost in the sinking process. The wreck is mostly flattened on the bottom, rising only four or five feet.

A 1992 survey by the Underwater Archaeological Society of Chicago revealed concentrations of small artifacts near the bow and stern with many large pieces of machinery, including the capstan, bilge pump, boiler, four anchors, and a windlass scattered throughout the site.

Although badly broken up, the site is interesting because of the number of artifacts that include tools, ship features, and machinery. Timbers criss-cross the wreck and can lead to disorientation, especially considering the relatively poor visibility (usually 10 feet).

There is no charter service that regularly serves this wreck site. As a result, the *Goshawk* remains much as it was found in 1992. One piece, a capstan cover, was removed from the site but was later returned voluntarily.

Location:	Three miles northeast of Tawas Point in Lake Huron.
Loran:	31049.3/49055.5
Lat/Lon:	44 14.96/83 24.95
Depth:	50 feet
Visibility:	5 to 15 feet
Tips:	Avoid disorientation by paying attention to position underwater. This site is usually not buoyed.

NEWELL A. EDDY

The *Newell A. Eddy* was built in West Bay City, Mich. in 1890. It was a 242-foot, three-masted schooner with eight deck hatches and aft cabin housing quarters, kitchen, dining room and storage. There was an eagle figurehead on the bow and nameplates on either side of the figurehead.

The *Newell A. Eddy* was hauling a cargo of corn from Chicago, Ill. to Buffalo, N.Y. when it foundered in a spring storm on April 20, 1893. It was being towed by the steamer *Charles A. Eddy* when the tow line broke and the vessel disappeared in the gale. The following day the entire stern of the *Newell A. Eddy* was found on the north side of Bois Blanc Island near Round Island.

The storm claimed many vessels in lakes Michigan and Huron that day and the remains of the *Newell A. Eddy* lay on the bottom until a University of Michigan research vessel stumbled upon them in 1992 in 168 feet of water.

A survey by the research team showed that the vessel was fully rigged--

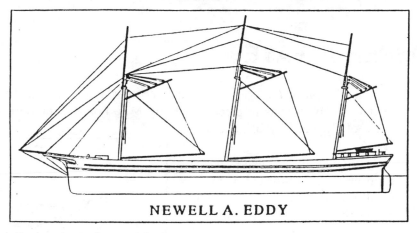

NEWELL A. EDDY

standing and running--with the deck rising 24 feet above the bottom (depth to the deck is 144 feet). All eight hatches are open, one bow anchor on deck and the cabin was blown off during the sinking process. The stern section is heavily damaged.

Today, the wreck is sometimes marked with a small buoy attached to one of the masts. Divers usually set their own anchor and then descend the small buoy line and mast to the deck. Divers must be cautious to avoid entanglement in the rigging.

Academicians predicted heavy diving on the wreck with loss of artifacts. But they failed to consider the remoteness of the site. Relatively few divers have visited the wreck and it remains in pristine condition on the bottom.

There are no regular dive charter services to this wreck. Private boats can be conveniently launched at Cheboygan.

Location:	Northeast of Bois Blanc Island, .3 nautical miles north of Raynolds Reef.
Loran:	31067.0/48194.9
Lat/Lon:	45 46.89/84 13.75
Depth:	168 feet to bottom, 144 feet to deck
Visibility:	5 to 15 feet
Tips:	Bring a light and be prepared for the depth as it is beyond normal recreational dive limits.

JOSPEH F. FAYE

The *Joseph F. Faye* was a wooden steamer that sank sometime in the 1920s. Today, it rests in pieces off Forty Mile Point Lighthouse six miles north of Rogers City in Lake Huron.

Although ice and waves have torn the vessel apart and many small artifacts are no longer found at the site, two very large and interesting pieces of the *Joseph F. Faye* remain.

The wreck is located directly off a point in about 15 feet of water, 250 to 300 yards offshore. The location presents some potential hazards because divers must be certain they can swim to the wreck and back and currents sometimes make diving difficult, especially for novice divers.

This is a popular night diving site because there are many fish, such as lake chubs, yellow perch, burbots, and suckers. Although, the lighthouse itself is a tourist destination and a museum is in the works. It is not unusual to find local caretakers who can direct divers to the wreck (it is visible from the surface) and provide interesting background information. The lighthouse has a changing area.

Snorkelers as well as scuba divers enjoy this site, especially in recent years as currents have removed some of the sand overburden. Visibility here is generally good but is reduced during periods of heavy seas.

Location:	Off the point at Forty Mile Lighthouse about six miles north of Rogers City, Mich. in Lake Huron.
Depth:	About 15 feet.
Visibility:	Usually about 15 feet or more but less during periods of heavy seas.
Tips:	This makes a good snorkel as well as scuba dive. Bring a dive light, night diving is excellent. Watch currents.

Although ice and waves have torn the vessel apart and many small artifacts are no longer found at the site, two very large and interesting pieces of the *Joseph F. Faye* remain.

The wreck is located directly off a point in about 15 feet of water, 250 to 300 yards offshore. The location presents some potential hazards because divers must be certain they can swim to the wreck and back and currents sometimes make diving difficult, especially for novice divers.

This is a popular night diving site because there are many fish, such as lake chubs, yellow perch, burbots, and suckers. Although, the lighthouse itself is a tourist destination and a museum is in the works. It is not unusual to find local caretakers who can direct divers to the wreck (it is visible from the surface) and provide interesting background information. The lighthouse has a changing area.

Snorkelers as well as scuba divers enjoy this site, especially in recent years as currents have removed some of the sand overburden. Visibility here is generally good but is reduced during periods of heavy seas.

Location:	Off the point at Forty Mile Lighthouse about six miles north of Rogers City, Mich. in Lake Huron.
Depth:	About 15 feet.
Visibility:	Usually about 15 feet or more but less during periods of heavy seas.
Tips:	This makes a good snorkel as well as scuba dive. Bring a light, night diving is excellent. Watch currents.

Northern Pike

White Sucker

KEUKA

The *Keuka* was a three-masted schooner barge that was built in 1889 in Mt. Clemens, Mich. It was 172 feet long and had a beam of 32 feet and was originally named the *A. Stewart.*

This vessel was specifically built for the lumber hauling trade, although it did carry other cargoes in its life on the Great Lakes. From its launching until 1915, it was primarily used to haul lumber on a run that took it from Buffalo, N.Y. to Chicago, Ill., and Manistique, Mich. It was towed by the steamer *F.R. Buell.*

In 1916 it became part of the Hines Lumber Fleet out of Chicago but this service was shortlived and in 1918 it was sold again and renamed the *A.J. McAvoy* and made a run between Buffalo and Thessalon, Ont.

In 1925, the vessel was sold to the R.T. Jones Lumber Company of Tonawanda, N.Y. and named the *Keuka.* In 1929, it was sold to the Wolverine Steamship Co. of Escanaba and was used primarily as a party boat for the company's owner who lived in Charlevoix, Mich. The *Keuka*, over the next several years, sometimes visited Boyne City in addition to Charlevoix and there are rumors that the vessel was used as a floating speakeasy.

In the early 1930s the *Keuka* was no longer used and was deemed an eyesore. It was taken out into Lake Charlevoix where it was scuttled in 50 feet of water.

Today, the *Keuka* rests upright where the bow cabins can be entered and machinery inspected. The stern cabins are not present. Divers can also investigate the cargo hold of the vessel by entering a forward cargo hatch. Other cargo hatches are sealed off by a hardwood dance floor that was constructed on the deck of the vessel.

The deck of the vessel rises to within 35 feet of the surface and makes a popular ice dive because it is only a half-mile from shore.

Visibility here is best in spring, fall, and winter when it reaches 10 to 20 feet. In the summer, the nutrient-rich Lake Charlevoix grows much algae, which obscures vision. Summer visibility is typically 2 to 10 feet.

Location:	In Lake Charlevoix, ½ mile from shore (2½ miles from the lake's entrance)
Loran:	31495.6/48304.4
Lat/Lon:	45 18.40/85 14.34
Depth:	35 feet to deck, 50 feet to bottom
Visibility:	2 to 10 feet in summer, 10 to 20 feet other seasons
Tips:	Bring a dive light to inspect the interior.

HENRY CORT

The *Henry Cort* began her life as the *Pillsbury* when it was launched in the McDougall Shipyard at Superior, Wis. in 1892. The *Henry Cort* was a whaleback steel-hulled freighter that was 315 long with a 42-foot beam.

While it was originally thought that the vessel would be put to grain hauling for the Pillsbury Company, it was sold to the Soo Line and hauled package freight throughout the Great Lakes.

In 1895 the vessel was purchased by the Bessemer Steamship Company and renamed the *Henry Cort*.

The whaleback design was concocted by a naval architect named Capt. Alexander McDougall. The thought was that it would be streamlined so as to cast off heavy seas. While the design eventually proved impractical for hauling freight economically, its design was perfect for ice breaking duties.

In December of 1917, the *Henry Cort* had begun layup preparations but was called out to help ice-bound ships of the same line. In the process of freeing the 600-foot freighter *Midvale*, the *Henry Cort* was struck and sank in about 35 feet of water. It was salvaged the following season and saw a complete rebuilding.

> *While the design eventually proved impractical for hauling freight economically, its design was perfect for ice breaking duties.*

In 1927, the *Henry Cort* was again sold and saw significant modifications so that she could be unloaded or loaded by crane. While owned by the Lake Ports Shipping and Navigation Company of Detroit, Mich., the *Henry Cort* saw more accidents and suffered considerable damage.

Finally, on Nov. 30, 1934, while attempting to enter the Muskegon harbor during a gale, the *Henry Cort* was smashed against the north breakwall. The crew spent the night in the vessel and in the morning were rescued by a local U.S. Coast Guard station. No lives (except one

**The HENRY CORT against the north
Muskegon breakwall.**

guardsman from a night rescue attempt) were lost in the disaster.

Today, the *Henry Cort* lies in 50 to 55 feet of water off Muskegon's north breakwall. Sometimes divers mark the site with a small buoy. The once-proud ship is now smashed and lies in pieces over a large area. Sand sometimes obscures pieces of the wreck. Some of the ship's machinery was salvaged but much remains for divers to explore. The *Henry Cort* was one of the last whalebacks on the Great Lakes at the time of her loss.

Location:	Near the north Muskegon breakwall.
Depth:	50-55 feet
Visibility:	10-20 feet, less with heavy seas from the north or northwest
Tips:	Plan on exploring a wide area because wreckage is scattered.

SALVOR

The *Salvor* was an ocean freighter that was built as the *Turret Chief* in 1896. It was 253 feet long and had a beam of 44 feet. The 300-gross ton vessel served the ocean trade until 1907 and then entered the Great Lakes trade where it saw several name changes. She was named the *Salvor* in 1923.

The vessel saw many adventures including a grounding near Copper Harbor, Mich., during the Great Storm of 1913. The ship was used as an ammunition carrier for a short period during WWI but quickly returned to the Great Lakes.

In 1927, the *Salvor* was grounded in the DeTour Passage (see separate chapter on DeTour Underwater Preserve) while owned by the Durocher Company. Her engines were stripped and she became a steel barge and was towed by various other steamers.

On Sept. 16, 1930, the *Salvor* was being towed by the *Richard Fitzgerald* near Muskegon when the tow line broke. The ship sank with a load of stone and all 11 crewmen were lost in the disaster.

The vessel lies intact and upright in about 25 feet of water but is partially obscured by sand and its stone cargo. Shifting sands in this area sometimes cover and uncover portions of the ship.

Expect to see many species of fish, especially yellow perch and largemouth bass, on this wreck. Watch for slight yet troublesome underwater currents in this area.

Location:	2 3/4 miles north of the Muskegon lighthouse.
Loran:	32467.0/49355.8
Depth:	25-30 feet
Visibility:	10 to 20 feet, sometimes less if heavy seas have been running from the north or northwest
Tips:	Expect to see fish. Bring a dive light to look into narrow openings where fish like to hide.

STATE OF MICHIGAN

The *State of Michigan* was a typical steamer in her day in that she had a wooden hull supported by a pair of arches to prevent "hogging" in heavy seas. The ship was built in 1873 in Manitowoc, Wis. as the *Depere*. It was 165 feet long with a beam of 29 feet and draft of 10 feet.

The steamer served the Great Lakes trade long and well, hauling passengers and package freight. But on August 18, 1901, during a routine run between Chicago, Ill. and Muskegon, Mich., the *State of Michigan* sprang a leak and sank.

Today, the ship rests upright and mostly intact in about 75 feet of water. She suffered some stern damage with the collision with the bottom.

There is much to see here despite colonies of zebra mussels. Divers can enjoy the thrill of seeing such an old and "classic" vessel that once was common on the Great Lakes. Visibility is sometimes a problem, however, and slight underwater currents make it important to properly "orient" oneself to the wreck and ascent line.

Location:	About two miles northwest of Whitehall, Mich.
Loran:	32453.8/49263.3
Depth:	75-80 feet, deck rises to 60 feet
Visibility:	10 to 20 feet
Tips:	Try to avoid anchoring into the wreck. The bottom is sandy so a good anchorage next to the wreck is best.

Report Shipwreck Thefts
1-800-292-7800

Petoskey Diver Memorial

A few hundred yards east of the Petoskey marina is a diver memorial that has come to have special meaning because some of diving's most notable characters are remembered here.

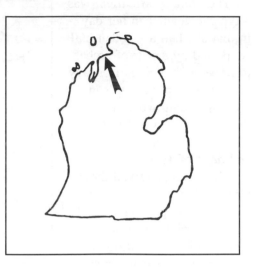

According to local divers, an Italian marble crucifix was being shipped to a local church but the crucifix arrived with minor damage. Instead of shipping it back, the company allowed local divers to use it as a centerpiece for a diver memorial. Now, in addition to the crucifix, there are brass and other placques placed in the immediate area to honor divers who contributed to the sport.

The site is maintained by local divers and there is no organization that purchases and places the memorials. Rather it is simply a place where friends remember friends doing what they loved most--diving. One of the most recent additions is a placque honoring Dr. Bill Kenner who was instrumental in writing and passing legislation to protect Michigan shipwrecks.

The diver memorial is located in about 30 feet of water about 1,000 yards from shore so it is quite a swim. Most divers, however, access the site by boat. The memorial is marked on the surface with a mooring buoy.

Location:	A few hundred yards east of the Petoskey municipal marina, north of Bay Front Park.
Loran:	Straight north from 31385.84/48305.21
Lat/Lon:	North of 45 22.744/84 57.222
Depth:	About 30 feet
Visibility:	Usually 20+ feet
Tips:	There is plenty of parking in a great coastal park off Lake Street Boulders make shore entry challenging. Watch for conflicts with boaters entering and leaving the marina--fly a dive flag.

Miscellaneous Dive Sites

While it is impossible to write about every Great Lakes dive site in Michigan's waters, it is possible to provide basic information on some of the more popular ones. What follows, in outline form, is information about other shipwrecks that may be of interest to divers. Additional information is often available in local libraries.

Anna C. Minch

The *Anna C. Minch* was a steel steamer that collided with another ship on Nov. 11, 1940. The 387-foot ship was built in 1903 in Cleveland, Ohio and was carrying a load of lumber. It lies about 1½ miles south of Pentwater, Mich., in 35 to 40 feet of water in Lake Michigan. **Loran:** 32326.3/49029.9 (bow); 32327.1/49030.7 (stern).

Carl D. Bradley

The *Carl D. Bradley* was a 623-foot steel freighter that foundered in a storm on Nov. 18, 1958 about 12 miles southwest of Gull Island in northern Lake Michigan. It was not carrying a cargo at the time of the disaster. The ship was built in 1927 in Lorain, Ohio and lies in about 355 feet of water. **Loran:** 32427.2/49190.4.

William Home

The 141-foot schooner *William Home* foundered on Sept. 25, 1894 near Point Seul Choix in Lake Michigan with a cargo of iron. The ship was built in 1871 in Clayton, N.Y. **Loran:** 32482.5/48732.4.

Kate Winslow

The *Kate Winslow* was a 202-foot schooner that stranded off Point Seul Choix in Lake Michigan in October 1897. It was hauling a cargo of iron. The ship was built at East Saginaw, Mich. in 1872. Its remains lie in 84 feet of water. **Loran:** 31356.4/48026.4.

Albert Miller

The *Albert Miller* was a 141-foot steam barge that burned on Aug. 30, 1882. The ship was loaded with a cargo of lumber and sank one mile off AuSable Point in Lake Superior. It was built in 1889 in Algoma, Mich. **Loran:** 32242.9/48166.7.

Novadoc

The *Novadoc* was a 248-foot steel freighter that stranded on March 17, 1947 off Jupiter Beach near Pentwater, Mich. It was carrying a cargo of furnace coke. Its remains are found in Lake Michigan in 12 to 15 feet of water. **Loran:** 32365.4/49063.5.

Perseverance

The *Perseverance* was a schooner that sank in Lake Huron off Cheboygan after a collision with another vessel, the *Gray Eagle*. The vessel is badly broken up in 65 feet of water but some portions are intact. Many smalll artifacts remain at this site. **Lat/lon:** 45 42.08/84 26.34.

Persian

The *Persian* was a schooner that sank after a collision in Lake Huron off Forty Mile Point in 1868. Ten lives were lost in the mishap. **Loran:** 31055.1/48246.2

Additional information, including location data, is found in an appendix to this book.

Yellow Perch

Crappie

(Speckled Bass)

Isle Royale

Diving at Isle Royale National Park in Lake Superior is unique. Visibility ranges from 30 to 100 feet and ten major shipwrecks offer a variety of diving opportunities.

But water clarity and attractive shipwrecks come with a price -- cold water.

Lake Superior is cold at all times except for an occasional protected cove. The temperature at the surface usually hovers around 50 degrees even in late summer. Below 50 feet, divers can expect temperatures close to 38 degrees. That means a good wetsuit is required at a minimum for virtually all diving. Dry suits are standard for divers who regularly visit Isle Royale.

Each year, about 500 divers visit the island and make an average of six dives each during their stay. That shows that Isle Royale is a popular place for extended visits. Or said another way, once you take the time and effort to get there, make the most of it!

Because Isle Royale is located in the middle

...once you take the time and effort to get there, make the most of it!

---

of Lake Superior, it "attracted" ships--those that simply failed to navigate properly and others that sought refuge in rough weather.

Although visibility outside of shipwrecks is excellent, visibility within those wrecks deteriorates when fine silt is disturbed. Entanglement in cables and lines is a real danger. A diving line and redundant lights are recommended for interior exploration of the shipwrecks here.

Because Isle Royale is a national park, there is an unusual set of regulations intended to protect fragile underwater sites of particular

---

Divers without a compressor can often make arrangements to have their tanks filled by charter operators.

---

archaeological value. Do not succumb to the temptation of disturbing or "collecting" artifacts. There are also many regulations regarding boating and camping. And beware the rules that forbid the mere presence of innocent dogs!

Charter operators must be licensed by the National Park Service so unless divers have their own boats capable of handling the Great Lakes, the selection of commercial dive charters is limited. Because air tanks cannot be refilled (no commercial facilities), many dive charter operators have on-board compressors. And there are rules regarding when and how long these compressors can be operated.

Divers without a compressor can often make arrangements to have their tanks filled by charter operators. Those arrangements should be made prior to leaving for the island. A simple telephone call is usually sufficient.

Besides shipwrecks, Isle Royale offers

interesting underwater natural features. Large, untouched copper veins are popular attractions. Divers also enjoy collecting greenstones--Michigan's official gem.

Rules

It is difficult to list all the rules of Isle Royale National Park here so below are general rules that affect boaters and divers. It is an excellent idea to write or stop in at the national park headquarters in Houghton, Mich., to obtain literature that details rules for all anticipated activities on or near the island. (Note: The National Park Service has jurisdiction some three miles from shore.)

- Visiting and diving is permitted only between April 16 and Oct. 31.
- All divers must register at a ranger station and obtain a free permit before diving. Before leaving, the permit must be returned. The system is used to gain important information about diving activities in the area.
- Do not remove or disturb any artifacts. Collecting **any** "souvenirs," no matter how small, may mean stiff fines and imprisonment.
- No spear guns or metal detectors are permitted.
- Use mooring buoys whenever available. If no such buoys are provided, tie off to a **stable** piece of wreckage. Do not anchor in a wreck area. Note: The most popular dive sites have mooring buoys available. If not, anchor near the wreck site, send a diver down to secure a line on a stable piece of wreckage or rock, and then retrieve the anchor line. Avoid disturbing any shipwreck debris with an anchor.
- The following areas are closed to sport diving:
  Passage Island small boat cove, inland lakes, land-associated underwater cultural and archaeological sites--"known or unknown."
- Compressors may be used at certain hours at the Scuba Cache in Rock Harbor, Windigo Information Center, public docks, and on board private vessels. Compressors must not violate the island's noise regulations. Note: Island management is undergoing considerable changes and it is best to check on this particular regulation as it is subject to change with little notice.
- Divers are prohibited from diving the *America* at certain times during the day. This is because ferries pass over the wreck to show passengers (a small price to pay for sharing maritime heritage with nondivers).
- Divers are subject to all other regulations on Isle Royale. Copies of those regulations are available in advance by writing to the National Park Service and divers are strongly urged to do so.

Because there are many regulations, it is important to put effort into advance planning. This is considered by many divers as "a trip of a lifetime" so make the effort to plan carefully. Don't let some "innocent" violations spoil an otherwise profound diving experience.

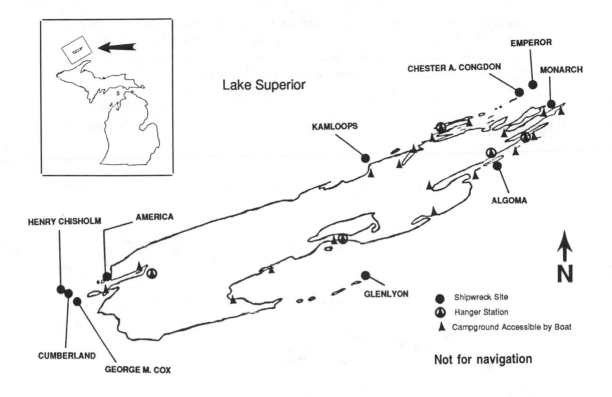

Lake Superior

EMPEROR

CHESTER A. CONGDON

MONARCH

KAMLOOPS

ALGOMA

HENRY CHISHOLM

AMERICA

GLENLYON

N

● Shipwreck Site
◉ Ranger Station
▲ Campground Accessible by Boat

CUMBERLAND

GEORGE M. COX

Not for navigation

Isle Royale National Park

Boating

All boats visiting the island must register at one of the ranger stations.

Overnight docking is permitted only at certain designated campgrounds and docks. A map of those facilities and a brochure detailing boating regulations is available from the National Park Service.

Fuel is available from mid-May to late September at Windigo and Rock Harbor, although diesel fuel is not available at Windigo. Pre- and post-season service is available at Windigo and Mott Island. Pump out facilities are available at Rock Harbor and Windigo.

The Mott Island and Windigo ranger stations monitor vhf channel 16. The Windigo station monitors the channel from 8 a.m. to 5 p.m. each day and the Mott Island station monitors the channel from 8 a.m. to 4:30 p.m. on weekdays. Marine weather forecasts are available from all ranger stations.

Great Lakes Chart No. 14976 is recommended for all boaters cruising waters around Isle Royale. This chart is available at Windigo, Rock Harbor, and on the mainland at the park headquarters in Houghton. The chart can also be ordered from the Isle Royale Natural History Association.

Be aware that the bottom in this entire area is rocky and often drops off quickly, making it difficult to secure an anchor. Whenever divers are below, it is a good idea to have at least one person topside to monitor weather and lake conditions, watch for other boats, and to be sure the boat does not drift. Please be sure the topside observer knows how to run the boat!

AMERICA

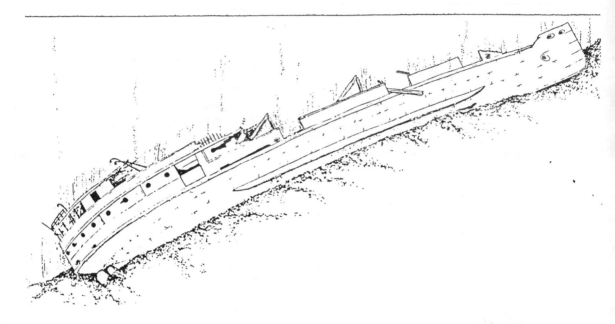

An artist's view of the AMERICA shows the stern intact. (NPS Graphic)

The *America* was a 183-foot, steel-hulled passenger and package freighter that sank in 1928. The steamer was built in 1898 and was a familiar sight in the region because it served many Lake Superior communities. It is one of the most popular dive sites at Isle Royale.

The ship sank after it struck a reef in Washington Harbor. No lives were lost in the accident. An unsuccessful salvage effort was mounted in 1965 by a Duluth, Minn. group.

The bow of the ship has been damaged by ice and waves. The midships and stern are intact, including the engine room, galley, social hall, and some cabins.

A silt-laden storeroom near the galley has been dubbed the "forbidden room" after a 1976 diving fatality which occurred there. As a result of that death, the door to the room was removed to increase the size of the opening.

Many divers start at the bow of the vessel and work their way deeper toward the intact stern. But the passageways were not designed for scuba divers' tanks so proceed with caution. This is not an area to penetrate with an uncertain supply of air.

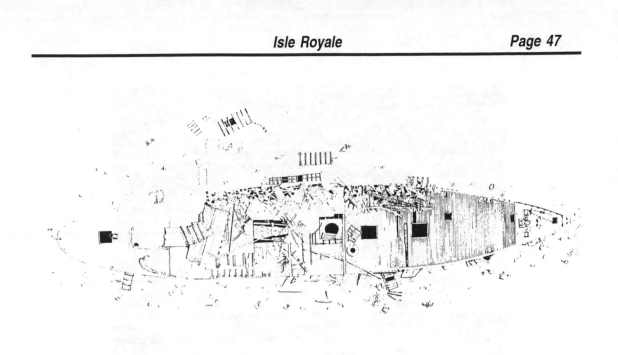

This overhead view of the AMERICA shows damage to some of the superstructure of the vessel, especially toward the bow. (NPS Graphic)

Location:	North Gap of Washington Harbor
Loran:	31909.2/46082.3
Depth:	2-80 feet
Visibility:	Usually 30+ feet
Tips:	Penetrate the stern cabin area with caution.

CUMBERLAND
HENRY CHISHOLM

Although these shipwrecks occurred 21 years apart, they are so closely associated that they can be considered a single dive site.

Divers describe the site as a "mass of confusion" or a "jumble of timbers" because wreckage from both shipwrecks is scattered and overlaps. The site provides a fascinating glimpse into the nature of wooden ship construction of the late 1800s.

Divers cannot see all of the widespread wreckage from a few vantage points so several dives and "exploring" is required to see all that is there.

Parts of the paddle wheel from the CUMBERLAND provide a glimpse into marine architecture of the 1880s. (NPS Photo)

The *Cumberland* was a 214-foot side wheel steamer built in 1871 to carry passengers for a rapidly developing excursion trade in northern Lake Superior. It had a number of close calls before it struck Rock of Ages Reef on July 25, 1877 with enough force to push half the ship onto the reef.

After several weeks of attempting to pull it free, the shipwreck was abandoned and autumn storms eventually sent it to the bottom.

At 270 feet, the *Chisholm* was the largest steam barge on the Great Lakes at the time of its construction in 1880. The *Chisholm* also had a history of close calls--running aground and collisions.

On Oct. 21, 1898, the *Chisholm* struck the Rock of Ages Reef at full speed-- about 9 knots. Crewmen quickly realized that the ship was a total loss and three days later, the ship broke up and sank during a gale. No lives were lost in either disaster.

Divers visiting the site can expect to find a mass of timbers, boilers, an engine, other machinery, rudders, and propellers. Careful inspection of the remains reveals that the *Cumberland* is broken into distinctly smaller pieces than the *Chisholm*.

The *Chisholm* engine should be considered a single dive site and is buoyed separately. The maximum depth of this dive is 140 feet. The buoy is tied off on the top of the engine at about 110 feet deep. The *Chisholm* engine should be visited cautiously because of the depth. There are no intact portions or major "overhangs" at this site.

The paddle wheel of the *Cumberland* is a popular spot for underwater photography. This type of propulsion was once common among steamers of the era.

Location:	Near Rock of Ages Lighthouse
Loran:	31935.9/46068.9
	31936.0/46068.0 (*Chisholm* engine)
Depth:	20-140+ feet
Visibility:	Usually 30+ feet
Tips:	This is a good area for exploration as some machinery from the *Cumberland* is still unaccounted. The remains of the 30-foot *Cumberland* paddle wheels, which lie in about 80 feet of water in the north-northeast section of the wreck site, are especially interesting.

GEORGE M. COX

**The GEORGE M. COX hard aground at the
Rock of Ages in 1933. (NPS Photo)**

The 259-foot steel passenger steamer was originally named the *Puritan* when it was constructed in 1901. The ship made many trips between Chicago and other Lake Michigan port cities before it was recruited for service in WWI. After the war, it returned to Great Lakes passenger service.

Early in 1933, the ship was renamed after the owner of the transportation company that purchased it. The *George M. Cox* was elegantly refitted and the subject of much attention when it began its maiden voyage under the new name. But that trip was the first and last for the *George M. Cox.*

In a heavy fog on May 27, 1933, the ship struck a portion of the Rock of Ages Reef about one mile from the lighthouse. The ship was traveling at 17 knots at the time of the collision and four people were injured. No lives were lost in the disaster.

The *George M. Cox* remained on the reef for a month until it broke up and sank stern first. When the ship came to rest on the bottom, much of the superstructure was flattened and there is little opportunity to penetrate the once-stately cabins and pilot house. A small portion of the stern can be accessed by divers.

Divers can expect to find scattered wreckage of all sorts and much machinery.

The *George M. Cox* is a popular dive site but small artifacts were removed long ago. Divers can expect to find scattered wreckage of all sorts and much machinery. A large rip in the ship's steel hull is believed to have resulted when it dropped off the reef.

Location:	Southwest of Rock of Ages Lighthouse
Loran:	31934.9/46069.8
Depth:	10-100 feet
Visibility:	30+ feet
Tips:	Some debris has migrated, including some remains of the *Chisholm* and *Cumberland* into the *George M. Cox* wreck site. There may be some unaccounted for remains between the two wreck sites.

GLENLYON

The 328-foot *Glenlyon* was built as the *William H. Gratwick* in 1893. The *Glenlyon* was a steel-hulled package freighter but also served passengers and hauled bulk grain. Few Great Lakes ships saw such a diversity of duties as this vessel.

On Nov. 1, 1924, the *Glenlyon* was loaded with 145,000 bushels of wheat when it sought refuge from a fierce storm in Siskiwit Bay. But upon entering the bay, the steamer ran hard aground on a submerged reef off Menagerie Island.

The captain ordered the ship scuttled to secure it to the reef to wait out the storm and for salvage later. No lives were lost in the disaster.

**This late view of the package freighter GLENLYON shows freight
elevators and gangway hatch cranes.**

But the *Glenlyon* could not be salvaged and it disappeared from the reef that winter attesting to the power of moving ice in the area.

The *Glenlyon* is one of the shallowest of the "metal wrecks" at Isle Royale and it is completely broken up from waves and ice. Except for a small forward deck cabin, there are opportunities for penetration diving.

Divers can find much machinery, including the ship's triple-expansion steam engine, exposed for easy inspection. This type of steam engine was commonly used on Great Lakes freighters but rarely is there such a good opportunity to view them.

Location:	Glenlyon Shoal north of Menagerie Island
Loran:	31808.3/46188.5
Depth:	15-100+ feet
Visibility:	30+ feet
Tips:	Wreckage is strewn about an area 900 feet long. There is easy exploring with some large sections intact. The area is protected from north and northwest winds.

ALGOMA

The *Algoma* was a 263-foot steamer capable of transporting more than 800 passengers. The steel-hulled ship was built in England in 1883. It was one of the first ships on the Great Lakes with electric lights.

The *Algoma* was one of a fleet of ships known for their swiftness. But on Nov. 7, 1885, the *Algoma* became lost in a fierce storm and ran aground on Isle Royale. About 45 lives were lost in the disaster and there were 14 survivors.

During salvage efforts, only a few bodies were discovered. It was believed by some that island residents robbed the dead and sunk the bodies to conceal the thefts. This was later proven false but the practice was not uncommon in some coastal communities.

> **It was believed by some that island residents robbed the dead and sunk the bodies to conceal the thefts.**

Machinery from the *Algoma* was recovered. The bow of the *Algoma* has yet to be found and sport divers frequently search for it, hoping it will be intact. But archaeologists believe it broke up in the wreck and fragments lie to the west of the wreck site.

The *Algoma* is completely broken up. There are no major overhangs. Archaeologists are anxious to learn of discoveries of new fragments, especially west of the wreck site.

Location:	South of Mott Island
Loran:	31738.3/46177.8
Depth:	10-100+ feet
Visibility:	30+ feet
Tips:	Wreckage is widely scattered with few large pieces intact. Report new finds west of the site to park officials.

MONARCH

The wreck of the wooden-hulled steamer *Monarch* is shrouded in mystery. It is unknown why the 240-foot ship crashed at cruising speed into The Palisades, a rocky cliff at Blake Point on Dec. 6, 1906. Some speculate that weather of -20 degrees and blowing snow contributed to the accident. Others suggest a faulty compass.

The *Monarch* was a passenger and package freight vessel loaded with grain and "general merchandise" when it crashed into the rocks. One life was lost when an

The MONARCH after alterations that included the addition of cabins aft of the pilot house. The vessel had this configuration when lost.

18-year-old watchman fell into the icy water. The exact number of passengers and crew is not known, but two passengers were considered heroes in the disaster.

One man risked his life to make it to shore to secure a line from the stricken ship. A woman fashioned meals from canned salmon and flour salvaged from the ship to boost morale and provide much-needed nourishment. Some survivors had to hike eight miles across the island for rescue several days later.

Two years after the shipwreck, the engines and boilers were salvaged. The *Monarch* sank shortly after the accident and additional remains were discovered recently north of the wreck site in about 150 feet of water.

Divers can expect to see massive sections of hull, decking, and machinery.

Location:	Immediately offshore from The Palisades on the north side of Blake Point.
Loran:	31702.5/46171.2
Depth:	10-150 feet
Visibility:	30+ feet
Tips:	Watch for cable which could present an entanglement hazard. Although broken up, this site provides an excellent opportunity for divers interested in marine architecture. There is a rapid dropoff at this site.

Many small artifacts have been removed, but there are still some beer bottles filled with grain and stoppered with cotton at the site.

The remains of the *Monarch* are massive but there are no intact portions for exploration by curious divers.

EMPEROR

The 525-foot steel bulk freighter *Emperor* was launched late in 1910. It had a history of productive seasons until it ran aground at Canoe Rocks on June 4, 1947.

A navigational error is blamed for the wreck. The ship stayed afloat for about 30 minutes after the accident but it began to take on water quickly.

The ship, loaded with 10,000 tons of iron ore, sank so quickly that some lives were lost when crew members were sucked beneath the water. At least one lifeboat was capsized by the turbulent waters stirred by the sinking. Twelve lives were lost from a crew of 33.

The *Emperor* is split but remains in a single major piece. It is one of Isle Royale's most popular dive sites. Most divers prefer to explore the Emperor with two dives--one to investigate the bow and one on the stern. Although the bow has been severely damaged by ice, the stern is nearly intact. The bow is in water ranging from 30 to 80 feet and gives divers a chance to explore cargo holds. The bow is a good dive for beginners and the stern section should be reserved for more experienced divers.

> *Most divers prefer to explore the Emperor with two dives--one to investigate the bow and one on the stern.*

The intact stern section starts in about 80 feet and goes to a depth of 150 feet at the propeller. The engine room is about 140 feet deep.

The buoy is attached to a pad eye near the forward edge of the stern cabin roof. Descending the buoy line is the best method of accessing the shipwreck. The stern may be entered through windows--glass is believed to have been blown out during the sinking process. The engine room may be entered by a blown-out skylight. Doors are open or missing, which provides for easy access.

The engine room is well preserved with the emergency wheel and throttle still intact. Some cabins are also intact and can be entered. On the port side, the forward cabin contains six bunks and was the quarters for the deck hands. Proceeding to the stern, divers can see the crew's dining room, kitchen, and pantry areas.

The *Emperor* was not the first ship to collide with Canoe Rocks. In 1910, the steel package freighter *Dunelm* ran aground. It was freed a few weeks later but evidence of the accident is still present.

The remains of the stranding of the 250-foot *Dunelm* are located about 100 yards east of the *Emperor* bow in about 60 feet of water. Those remains include wreckage of a lifeboat and anchors and chain.

**An artist's view of the EMPEROR shows the stern
intact in deep water. (NPS Graphic)**

Location:	Northeast end of Canoe Rocks
Loran:	31712.1/46150.0 (stern buoy)
	31711.8/46150.6 (bow buoy)
Depth:	30-175 feet
Visibility:	30+ feet
Tips:	Extreme caution must be used when exploring the interior because of the depth and reduced visibility from silt.

CHESTER A. CONGDON

The *Chester A. Congdon* was a 532-foot steel bulk freighter. It was built in 1907 and frequently carried grain and iron ore throughout the Great Lakes.

The *Chester A. Congdon* ran aground at Canoe Rocks in a thick fog on Nov. 6, 1918. It was loaded with about 400,000 bushels of wheat and at first it was believed that removing the cargo would save the ship. But a storm blew up and broke the ship in two

...at first it was believed that removing the cargo would save the ship.

**The CHESTER A. CONGDON rested shortly on Canoe Rocks before
breaking into two pieces and sliding off into deeper water.**

pieces on the rocks only two days after the wrecking incident.

The loss, at $1.5 million, was the most costly on the Great Lakes at the time. Extensive salvaging was accomplished on the bow section of the wreck.

The bow section sank upright at the base of a steep cliff. The stern section of the ship received minor damage but much of that section lies in water more than 130 feet deep. A portion of the stern section is accessible in about 70 feet of water. The stern is usually not buoyed.

Divers can enjoy exploring the bow section of the ship, which includes an intact pilot house. The wreck lies on a steep angle and questions remain as to how the two sections came apart. Much of the wreck can be explored in 50 to 130 feet of water on the north side of the reef.

Wreckage on the reef between the two sections offers an exploration opportunity in shallow water.

Location:	Congdon Shoal south of Canoe Rocks
Loran:	31717.4/46147.8 (bow section)
Depth:	70-110 feet on the bow; 50-200 feet on stern; 10 feet on reef
Visibility:	30+ feet
Tips:	Because of its depth, much of the stern section is unexplored. But the most interesting features are found on the shallower bow section.

KAMLOOPS

The 250-foot package freighter *Kamloops* was lost without a trace in early December 1927. The ship failed to survive a fierce, early winter storm as it rushed to complete the shipping season. Twenty-two lives were lost in the shipwreck which is believed to have occurred when the ship capsized in heavy seas near shore.

The *Kamloops* was constructed in 1924 and hauled grain to and from many Great Lakes ports.

The ship's remains were discovered by sport divers in 1977. A few artifacts have been removed and some artifacts, such as the emergency steering wheel, have been padlocked in place by sport divers to prevent further looting. In recent years bodies of crewmen were removed from the engine room compartments.

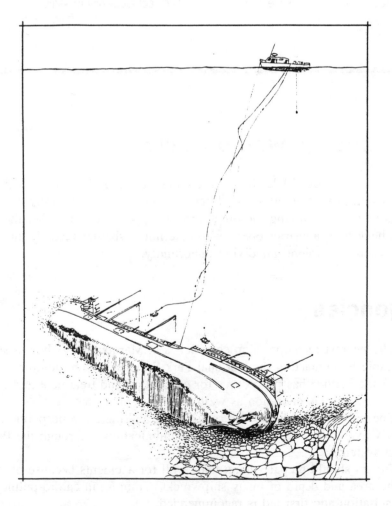

The KAMLOOPS was investigated using an ROV. (NPS Graphic)

Although the *Kamloops* lies mostly intact with some damage to the bow, it is an extremely dangerous site for sport diving because of its depth. Much of the ship lies in more than 200 feet of water only 75 yards west of 12 O'Clock Point. Because of the depth, the wreck was explored by ROV (remote-operated vehicle) soon after its discovery.

The National Park Service discourages divers from visiting this site because of the dangers posed in such deep diving.

Location:	About 75 yards west of 12 O'Clock Point on the northwest side of the island.
Loran:	31786.1/46124.4
Depth:	260 feet
Visibility:	20 feet--dive light required
Tips:	Use extreme caution and technical diving skills.

Lake Trout Spawning Reefs

The reefs around Isle Royale are known as natural spawning habitat for large lake trout. Divers report seeing large schools of lake trout around these spawning areas and careful diving (no quick moves) appears to not bother the fish.

Check with a charter operator to determine whether Lake Trout are spawning and where to explore this diving opportunity.

Emergencies

The nearest recompression chamber is at Marquette, Mich. Assistance is available by contacting the National Park Service, which monitors vhf channel 16. The Park Service has procedures for evacuation and treatment and can activate a search and rescue operation as well.

The park is a wilderness area, however, and there are no public telephones readily available. The most reliable communication is through the Park Service radio system.

Divers should prepare themselves well for accidents because of the remoteness of the area and depth of many shipwrecks. Training in cardio-pulmonary resuscitation and first aid is recommended.

Getting There

Statistics show that nearly twice as many divers use charters than private means to explore Isle Royale's shipwrecks.

Visitors can get to Isle Royale by ferry from Houghton, Mich., Copper Harbor, Mich., and Grand Portage, Minn. The cost ranges from $56 to $70 for round trip passage (adult tickets). Additional fees are generally charged for boats, canoes, outboard motors, and air tanks.

Seaplane service is available to Isle Royale at a cost of $120 for a round trip.

Current information about transportation to Isle Royale is available by asking for a brochure entitled "Getting There" from the National Park Service. Note that only federally licensed vessels are permitted to run charters to Isle Royale so the selection is somewhat limited and it may pay to plan far ahead to book your trip early.

Accommodations

There are many campgrounds on Isle Royale accessible from the water. Rock Harbor Lodge offers spacious rooms and cottages on Isle Royale. Lodge rooms cost about $65 per person per day based on double occupancy. Housekeeping cottages cost about $36 per person per day based on double occupancy.

More information about Rock Harbor Lodge is available by contacting the National Park Service or National Park Concession, Inc., P.O. Box 405, Houghton, MI 49931. The telephone number for the concessionaire is: (906) 337-4993.

Important Addresses/Phone Numbers

Isle Royale National Park and
Isle Royale Natural History Association
87 N. Ripley
Houghton, MI 49931
(906) 482-0986

Dive Charter Operators:

Superior Diver, Inc.
P.O. Box 388
Grand Portage, MN 55605
(612) 773-8710
(313) 426-4276

Royale Diver
3444 White Bear Ave.
White Bear Lake, MN 55110
(612) 773-8710

Superior Trips
Ken Merryman
7348 Symphony St. NE
Fridley, MN 55432
(612) 635-6438

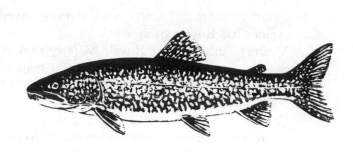

Lake Trout

Coho Salmon

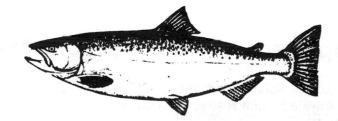

Chinook Salmon

Underwater Preserves

The Michigan Underwater Preserve system is the result of efforts by sport divers to protect shipwrecks from "souvenir" hunters. Too many divers saw their favorite dive sites disappear piece by piece.

Also, the underwater preserves are areas where there are concentrations of shipwrecks making it easier to identify key areas for divers.

Designation of an area as an underwater preserve costs state taxpayers nothing. But it tells sport divers that a Great Lakes area has a particularly interesting collection of shipwrecks or natural features on the bottom. In most cases, designation also means that support services, such as air stations and dive charters, are readily available in the area.

Underwater preserves also attract tourists--a fact not lost on local businesses. As a result, sport divers generally receive warm welcomes to the preserves and nearby communities. Restaurants, motels, and resorts may offer special prices for divers visiting their areas. Some preserves also host special events, such as film festivals and treasure hunts, for divers to enjoy.

But there is a set of expectations for sport divers. They are expected to respect the resources--natural or man-made--that brought them to the underwater preserve. That means **no collecting** of any kind in a preserve without a permit from the state. All the resources, from geologic formations to abandoned vessels, are the property of the State of Michigan, according to state and federal laws. And while state enforcement is weak when it comes to collecting by maritime museums, those protection laws are strictly applied to individual sport divers. Divers should keep their "goody" bag topside or risk criminal prosecution that could mean imprisonment, stiff fines, and even confiscation of boats, cars, and scuba equipment.

The chances of seeing law enforcement officers patrolling underwater preserves are slim. But the chances of being reported by other divers, even in the same group, are great. Some sport divers have "turned in" members of their own diving parties for

Divers largely drafted Michigan's tough laws establishing and protecting underwater preserves.

pilfering even small artifacts.

Charter operators are equally strict abut their enforcement of laws that prohibit the removal of artifacts. Not only do they risk stiff penalties that include confiscation of their boats and equipment, but they also realize that even the most complete shipwreck sites can be stripped clean in a single season. That is not good for future charter business and they recognize this financial stake in keep shipwrecks as pristine as possible.

Why is Michigan so conservation oriented? The reason lies with the sport diving community. Divers largely drafted Michigan's tough laws establishing and protecting underwater preserves. They respect and enjoy sport diving so much that they wanted to preserve it for others, including future generations.

They have done their job well. Michigan is recognized as a leader in shipwreck conservation despite wholesale looting without permits by some maritime museums. Teams of volunteer sport divers have been trained in maritime archaeology and are a vital part of ongoing research that is teaching us about our maritime heritage. Their work also allows nondivers to enjoy shipwreck exploration. Divers are providing valuable data, including video and still photos, that help archaeologists

The state has had little or no funds to dedicate to the underwater preserves. That has left management to local preserve support groups.

interpret our past.

Other states are watching Michigan. Although sport divers in those states have yet to take the lead in passing preservation laws, many are also concerned about the future of sport diving in the Great Lakes. The future may see a system of underwater preserves where divers and nondivers alike can enjoy shipwrecks, fish, and

geologic features that were once only read about. Already there are two glass-bottom boats that serve the Alger Underwater Preserve and take tourists on a narrated shipwreck tour.

The state has had little or no funds to dedicate to the underwater preserves. That has left management to local preserve support groups, generally consisting of interested citizens and divers. These groups place buoys on shipwrecks, publish brochures, and provide a variety of information to divers. They are generally the first to report trouble or new discoveries to state officials.

Local support groups have donated thousands of hours of volunteer time and the use of expensive boats to keep underwater preserves safe and enjoyable.

For sport divers, underwater preserves have come to mean ready access to the world's finest collection of shipwrecks. And studies have shown that the more divers dive on shipwrecks, the better protected they are.

Currently there are nine "official" preserves with two more recently proposed. The DeTour Passage and Southwest Michigan proposed preserves are expected to become reality soon and are included in this section for that reason.

It takes many volunteers to manage underwater preserves. Divers who live near a preserve may want to consider becoming involved in a local support group. The names and addresses of preserve contacts are provided here.

State and federal laws regarding ownership of shipwrecks and the underwater preserves are found in an appendix to this book and may answer questions about the formation of underwater preserves and the permit system.

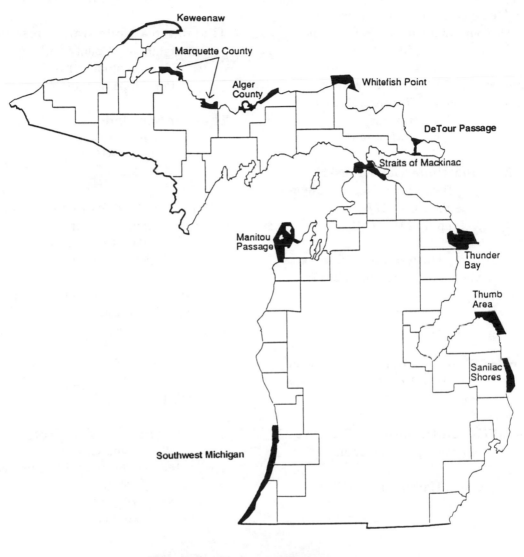

Michigan's Underwater Preserve System

Alger Underwater Preserve
P.O. Box 272
Munising, MI 49868

DeTour Underwater Preserve
c/o DeTour Area Chamber of Commerce
DeTour, MI 49725

Keweenaw Underwater Preserve
c/o Keweenaw Tourism Council
P.O. Box 336
Houghton, MI 49931

Manitou Underwater Preserve
c/o Sleeping Bear Dunes Nat. Lakeshore
P.O. Box 277
Empire, MI 49630

Marquette Underwater Preserve
c/o Marquette Area Chamber of
Commerce
501 S. Front St.
Marquette, MI 49855

Sanilac Shores Underwater Preserve
P.O. Box 47
Port Sanilac, MI 48469

SW Michigan Underwater Preserve
c/o Michigan Sea Grant
333 Clinton
Grand Haven, MI 49417

Straits Underwater Preserve
c/o St. Ignace Chamber of Commerce
680 N. State St.
St. Ignace, MI 49871

Thumb Area Underwater Preserve
Lighthouse County Park
7320 Lighthouse Road
Port Hope, MI 49468

Thunder Bay Underwater Preserve
P.O. Box 65
Alpena, MI 49707

Whitefish Underwater Preserve
c/o Paradise Area Chamber of Commerce
P.O. Box 82
Paradise, MI 49768

General information about diving
Michigan's Underwater Preserves is
available by contacting:

Michigan Travel Bureau
P.O. Box 30226
Lansing, MI 48909

**Michigan Underwater
Preserves Council**
c/o St. Ignace Chamber of Commerce
680 N. State St.
St. Ignace, MI 49781
(800) 338-6660

Alger Underwater Preserve

The Alger County Underwater Preserve consists of 113 square miles of Lake Superior bottomlands. Within its boundaries are eight major shipwrecks.

Also, in or near the underwater preserve are underwater natural features for divers to explore.

The Alger Preserve includes the area off the City of Munising, once a major Upper Peninsula port for smelting iron ore. Ships came to this harbor to load and unload cargoes of raw iron ore, refined iron, wood, charcoal, lumber, and limestone.

But bad weather and unseen shoals combined to cause ships to run aground, collide or founder in heavy seas. Many ships were battered by north winds against the steep cliffs that form the Pictured Rocks National Lakeshore.

Today, Munising is the unofficial "host" community for the underwater preserve. Signs boast of the city's relationship to the preserve and divers often receive the "red carpet" treatment at motels and restaurants.

The area is popular because of a variety of attractions. Divers can explore unusual rock formations--including caverns--or many shipwrecks. Two shipwrecks, the wooden steamer *Smith Moore* and an intact schooner found in Murray Bay near Grand Island are the most popular dive sites. But a recent addition, the 71-foot tugboat, *Steven M Selvick*, is now offering competition to the old "standbys."

Local divers have established a ritual with local fish. The divers provide food and the fish eat it.

Large schools of rock bass, whitefish, burbots, and yellow perch can be found around many shipwrecks in this area. Divers frequently bring dog food, cheese and other food, which attracts even more fish. One popular food, although it cannot be used in deep water, is cheese from an aerosol can.

Visibility in the Alger Underwater Preserve is among the best found anywhere in the Great Lakes.

Visibility in the Alger Underwater Preserve is among the best found anywhere in the Great Lakes. The bottom is generally composed of resistant sandstone and limestone. There are relatively few small particles that remain suspended to cloud the water.

Visibility is so great, two glass-bottom boats provide tourists with a first-hand view of shipwrecks. A narrator tells passengers about this history of the area and how the vessels came to rest on the bottom. In this way, state-owned maritime resources are being shared with the nondiving public.

Although there are several intact shipwrecks, there are also some "piles of boards" that are currently under study by archaeologists. Divers must be certain not to move artifacts, regardless of size. Moving artifacts, even very small ones, can affect studies that have been underway for years. It is best to inspect artifacts where they lie.

Locating dive sites in this area is easy. Virtually all shipwrecks are buoyed with white mooring buoys with a blue stripe. Instructions on the buoys will inform boaters how to attach to the mooring lines provided.

The northern boundary of the Alger Underwater Preserve extends to the 150-foot depth contour. Part of the area is under the jurisdiction of the National Park Service as the Pictured Rocks National Lakeshore is located just east of Munising. Their jurisdiction extends one quarter mile on the surface of the water only.

Unlike Isle Royale, divers will find no federal restrictions or registration requirements.

Grand Island, which is a prominent feature of Munising Bay, is owned by the U.S. Forest Service, which has no surface water jurisdiction.

Unlike Isle Royale, divers will find no federal restrictions or registration requirements. But divers may want to visit the Park Service visitor center on the north side of Munising to learn more about this fascinating area.

Because the shipwrecks are readily accessible and the visibility excellent, many of the shipwrecks have been picked over by early divers. Still, there are many large artifacts to discover and some divers of long ago are now bringing back artifacts for replacement on the shipwrecks.

And don't worry if you don't have a boat. In addition to some of the best dive

There are two excellent shore dives certain to keep divers coming back again and again.

charter operators on the Great Lakes, there are two excellent shore dives certain to keep divers coming back again and again. Also, divers will find that some dive centers down state will offer special charter packages so do not forget to check with your local dive center when planning a trip to this underwater preserve.

There is only one air station in Munising and it is a gathering place for divers. It provides a good opportunity to share experiences, learn about new dive sites, and make new friends. Michigan divers may be surprised to find that this area is especially popular among divers from Wisconsin and Illinois.

Munising and the Pictured Rocks areas have much to offer in the way of family activities. Those other attractions are covered separately in this chapter. But when planning, do not forget the family for a memorable vacation.

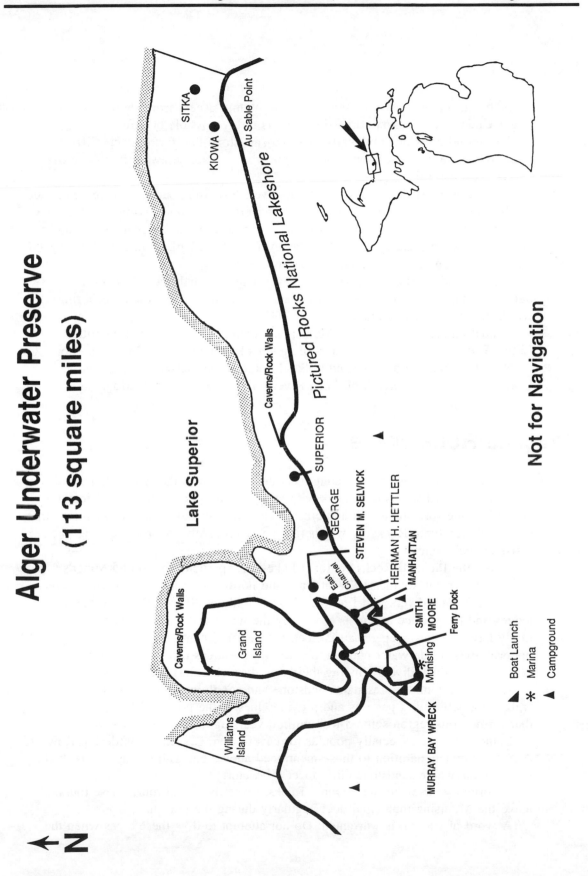

Alger Underwater Preserve
(113 square miles)

Not for Navigation

Boating

Although there is a strong temptation to attempt access from shore at some Alger Underwater Preserve dive sites, that is rarely possible or safe.

The shoreline is predominantly resistant sandstone that forms steep cliffs. Although some dive sites appear accessible from a map, be aware that the cliffs can be extremely dangerous.

Boats can be used to access all of the dive sites. And boaters may be comforted by the thought that rough weather rarely interferes with sport diving in these relatively protected waters. Boaters should keep an eye out for changing weather patterns, however, and they should note several natural harbors in the Munising and Grand Island areas that can provide refuge.

Mooring buoys should be used whenever available and major wrecks are buoyed annually. The rocky substrate makes anchoring difficult and anchoring within the wreck causes undue damage.

A boat launch is available in Munising, which also hosts marina facilities. Limited support services for boaters are available outside of the Munising area.

Boat launches are also located at Sand Point in the Pictured Rocks National Lakeshore and at the mouth of Anna River one mile northeast of Munising.

Caverns/Rock Walls

The resistant sandstone and conglomerates common to the Alger Underwater Preserve area provides sport divers with an opportunity to explore usual features created by the force of waves and erosion caused by water. It was these forces that created the Pictured Rocks by weathering away relatively soft rock leaving resistant rock behind.

Along the Pictured Rocks National Lakeshore, particularly around Miner's Castle, and on the southeast (Trout Bay) and northwest (southwest of Gull Point) on Grand Island, divers will find rock ledges at about 30 feet. Between these ledges and the surface are areas eroded by the water and waves. These caverns rarely have cavities deeper than 20 feet, but they offer interesting sport diving opportunities. Underwater photographs from these areas have been remarkable because they show divers winding their way through colorful formations.

Associated with this resistant sandstone and conglomerates are rock walls. The walls have interesting patterns and provide clues to the powerful forces of nature that formed this region some 5 to 8 million years ago.

Some areas are especially popular for cavern diving, such as Battleship Row off AuSable Point in addition to those mentioned above, but wall diving can be had virtually anywhere sandstone cliffs meet the water.

To orient yourself to the Pictured Rocks, invest in a boat tour. These tours leave the Munising municipal dock regularly during the season.

A word of caution is warranted: Do not attempt to dive these areas when the

**The resistant rock of this area provides divers with an
opportunity to explore caverns.**

Location:	Southwest of Gull Point and in Trout Bay along Grand Island, Battleship Row off AuSable Point, and around Miner's Castle.
Depth:	0-30 feet (most diving is done in about ten feet of water)
Visibility:	20-30+ feet, less if heavy seas have been running
Tips:	Do not dive if waves (even relatively small ones) are running from the north or northwest.

waves are coming from the north or northwest. It is an easy matter for these waves to literally pick up divers and cast them against the rocks.

Ferry Dock/Weedbed

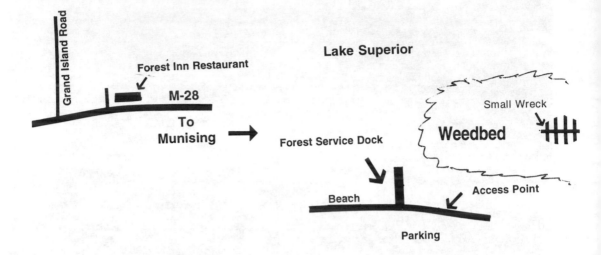

When Cleveland-Cliffs owned Grand Island they created a ferry dock north of Munising at the end of Grand Island Road, which runs east off M-28 about 1.5 miles from town. Today, it is owned by the U.S. Forest Service (which now owns Grand Island) and ferries use it regularly throughout the summer season.

This shore-access dive site was once known only to local divers who enjoyed fish watching in the area. But other divers have recently discovered this terrific place and it is becoming increasingly popular.

There are three areas to explore at this site. First, the area around the ferry dock itself offers the opportunity to spot old tools, bottles, and machinery that are the legacy of activity on the dock. Also, many small fish, and an occasional lake trout, can be seen in the area. It is the massive schools of small minnows that often encircle divers that makes this dive exciting. The bottom is comprised of clean sand. Maximum depth at this site is about 45 feet.

A second dive site is the weedbed, which is found about 75 yards south of the ferry dock. A variety of aquatic vegetation attracts yellow perch, northern pike, suckers, and a variety of other fish. Swimming through the area in late summer is

Location:	About 1.5 miles north of Munising at the end of Grand Island Road. Locals can direct you.
Loran:	31657.56/47437.91
Lat/Lon:	46 26.704/86 39.867
Depth:	30 to 95 feet
Visibility:	25 feet, somewhat less if waves are running from the east.
Tips:	Watch for ferry boat traffic!

almost like swimming through a kelp bed. It is a great place for underwater photography because of the colorful vegetation and excellent visibility. A small wooden fishing boat rests on the sandy bottom in this area. Maximum depth for exploration is about 35 feet.

Finally, divers report a series of underwater caverns, much like those found around Miner's Castle. Although visibility is less than the shallower caverns of the area, the caverns still provide an interesting exploration opportunity. The caverns are reported to be directly east of the weedbed in 60 to 95 feet of water.

Dock Ruins

Divers who have never explored dock ruins are missing out on a great diving opportunity. It is difficult to explain the feeling one has when winding through massive wooden pillars. On the bottom one often finds tools, bottles, machinery, and other items that were cast from or fell off the dock.

The dock ruins north of Munising High School, on M 28, are no exception. This is a massive collection of upright timbers and a fun place to explore. Because the dock was once used for loading logs and lumber, tools, such as cant hooks, can be found here. Also, largemouth bass, lake trout, and salmon are known to prowl between the pilings.

This is either a boat or shore access dive. The end of the dock is in about 20 feet of water and it is easy to snag a line around one of the pilings for a secure anchorage. For shore access, park in the high school parking lot and follow a narrow, tricky trail down to the water. There is a small beach for donning scuba equipment. It is a long, 300-yard swim to the dock ruins, however, so be certain you are up to the swim.

The bottom here is gravelly with some silt but visibility is generally excellent.

Location:	You can't miss this one! East of Munising High School--very obvious.
Depth:	10 to 25 feet
Visibility:	Generally 25 feet
Tips:	Park in high school lot. This site makes an excellent snorkeling place.

Report Shipwreck Thefts
1-800-292-7800

MANHATTAN

During a storm on Oct. 25, 1903, the *Manhattan* sought refuge in Munising Bay. The 252-foot steamer was carrying a cargo of wheat and was headed for Buffalo, N.Y. from Duluth, Minn.

On Oct. 26, the storm subsided and the *Manhattan* headed out the East Channel of the harbor when a steering malfunction caused the crew to lose control of the wooden-hulled ship. The *Manhattan* struck a reef and a fire broke out, apparently from a fallen lantern on board.

The ship burned to the waterline and sank without a loss of life. After the sinking, some of the ship's machinery was recovered. Much of the remains were removed as a hazard to navigation.

Today, divers can find timbers from the hull of the ship and miscellaneous pieces of machinery and equipment on the north side of the East Channel. The remains are completely broken up and sometimes local divers run cable or line between large sections of the shipwreck.

Location:	North side of East Channel, off south end of Grand Island
Loran:	31648.3/47438.1
Depth:	20-30 feet
Visibility:	Usually 30+ feet
Tips:	There are several large hull sections here. Take time to view construction techniques.

Murray Bay Wreck

This shipwreck has been the focus of much maritime research over several decades and no one is still quite sure which vessel it is. It has been called the *Bermuda, Arnold, Dreadnaught*, and *Grenada* among others. To play it safe, it is referred to here as the "Murray Bay Wreck" because it is located in Murray Bay off the south side of Grand Island.

This is probably one of the most visited shipwrecks in the Great Lakes. The shallow depth (30 feet maximum) and intactness of this 145-foot schooner is appealing to all. Also, large schools of rock bass are often found on this wreck and divers frequently feed these fish. Other fish found on the wreck include largemouth bass, burbot, splake, and menominee.

The vessel, which has a beam of 26 feet, was designed to fit snugly in

**A diver inspects the starboard rail
of the Murray Bay Wreck.**

the Welland Canal and ships of this type are often referred to as "canallers." Local historians say there is evidence that this vessel has been resting in Murray Bay since 1860, making it one of the earliest intact schooners in the Great Lakes.

The vessel was carrying high-grade iron ore when it sank and part of the deck was destroyed during a salvage operation. But there is still much of the white oak deck remaining. Although the cabins are missing, the starboard rail is complete and the port rail is nearly complete. There is some evidence of a fire but the hull is intact and it appears as though it could float today if raised.

Although this is a popular shipwreck, it is disheartening to hear divers say they saw everything in only a half hour. They simply aren't looking closely.

Divers who explore slowly and carefully will find rare freshwater sponges, a one-celled colonial animal called bryophytes, as well as Plimsoll marks along the bow stem, and sculpins everywhere.

Although there were two salvage attempts, much of the iron ore cargo remains along the keelson and in the bow area. The vessel had two masts, which are both missing, as well as anchors and anchor chain. But red, green, and white paint on the hull remain after more than a century on the bottom.

Although the maximum depth here is 30 feet, the remains rise to within ten feet of the surface. From the surface, hatches, bow stem, stern rail, and sometimes even the rudder are visible. Because the wreck is intact and so much is visible from the surface, this is a prime stop on the shipwreck tour. For that reason it is a good idea to keep a watchful eye out for the tour boat. Cooperation between divers and nondivers have preserved this wreck so be prepared for a brief interruption of your dive if the tour boat comes by.

Sculpin

Please keep dive knives away from the hull. Some unscrupulous divers have carved names and initials in the hull but the wreck is watched closely and future vandals are likely to be caught. Also, an old wooden barrel was recently found near the wreck and placed on the deck. Please keep it where others can enjoy it.

The cargo hold is virtually intact and divers can see well enough to explore this area without a light, although a light permits viewing of fish and other small features. Take a moment to see how shipbuilders used timbers and knees to support the deck and how the hatch was framed. And do not forget an underwater camera if you have one. Even a waterproof, disposable camera can take good photos on the deck.

Finally, no exploration of this wreck is complete without a trip to the rudder. Here, divers can see the massive structure and appreciate the fine lines of the vessel.

The bottom here is sandy with a fine layer of silt.

Location:	East side of Murray Bay at the south side of Grand Island, just inside Muskrat Point.
Lat/Lon:	46 27.88/86 38.80
Depth:	10 to 30 feet
Visibility:	25+ feet
Tips:	Surface occasionally to watch for shipwreck tour boat or call "Shipwreck Tours" on vhf channel 16 to determine their schedule. Boaters: Note the sandy shoal off Muskrat Point. Nature Lovers: Eagles and osprey are commonly seen in this area.

**The Murray Bay Wreck looked much
like this before sinking.**

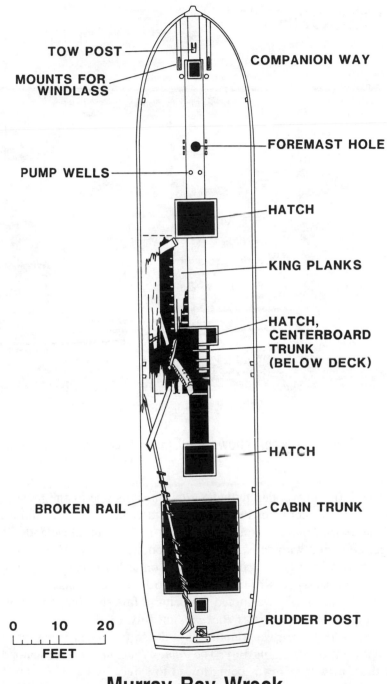

TOW POST

COMPANION WAY

MOUNTS FOR
WINDLASS

FOREMAST HOLE

PUMP WELLS

HATCH

KING PLANKS

HATCH,
CENTERBOARD
TRUNK
(BELOW DECK)

HATCH

BROKEN RAIL

CABIN TRUNK

RUDDER POST

0   10   20

FEET

Murray Bay Wreck
Deck Configuration

SMITH MOORE

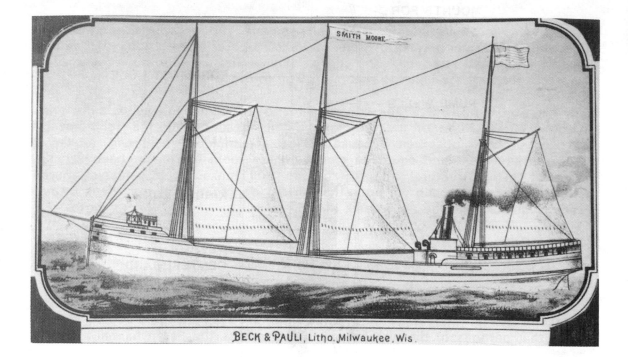

This lithograph shows the Smith Moore under full sail.

The 226-foot wooden-hulled *Smith Moore* is one of the most popular dive sites in the Alger Underwater Preserve. It has a beam of 35 feet and a depth of 18 feet.

The *Smith Moore* was a steamer built in 1880 in Cleveland, Ohio. The steam barge, equipped with sails, was a common sight in the Munising and Marquette harbors. It primarily hauled iron ore but on at least one occasion is known to have transported passengers from Marquette to Pictured Rocks.

The *Smith Moore* was noted for being a fast ship but it sank when it collided with the steam barge *James Pickands* on July 13, 1889.

The *Smith Moore* was running in a dense fog when it was struck in the East Channel out of Munising Bay. The *James Pickands* was unscathed in the incident and the *Smith Moore* was being towed to safety by the *M.M. Drake* when it suddenly began to sink. All crewmen were saved. The *Smith Moore* was loaded with low-grade, soft iron ore and was declared a total loss. At the time of its sinking, the masts of the ship protruded 15 feet above the surface of the water.

The cabins were blown off the deck when it went down but the deck of the vessel remains and offers divers a chance to penetrate portions of the cargo hold. This site is different each year due to shifting sands. In recent years it appears as

A diver inspects the engine above the spar deck.

though the sand is again moving away from the wreck, which will make it easier to explore.

Today, divers generally find the wreck marked with stern and bow mooring buoys. The deck is virtually intact except in the bow area where the collision occurred. Six cargo hatches provide easy access to the cargo hold during periods when sand does not fill the hold.

Much machinery remains on the deck. Divers can see steam winches, capstans, mooring bitts, pinrails, pumps, boom saddles, and tackle. Divers can also see the tops of the twin cylinder steam engine. Smaller artifacts were removed many years ago. Although the anchors have also been removed, it is believed that the anchor chain remains in the wrecked bow section. Also, the masts of the vessel are covered with sand next to the wreck.

...a dive light is recommended to look inside many small openings....

Although visibility at this site is usually 15 feet or more, a dive light is recommended to look inside many small openings where fish hide. Schools of whitefish, perch, and an occasional lake trout or salmon are commonly seen on this wreck.

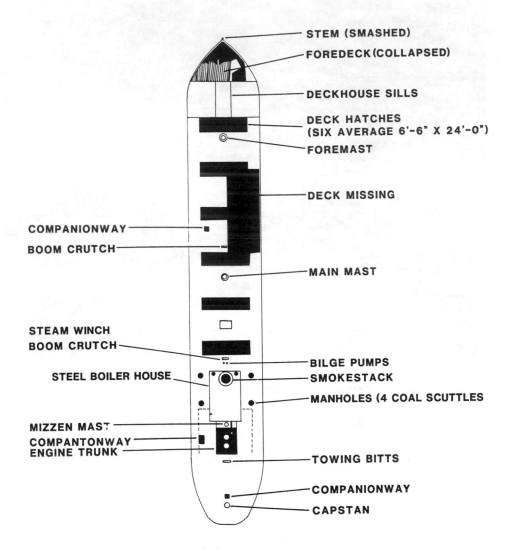

SMITH MOORE
Deck Configuration

0 10 20 30 40 FEET

PETE LINDQUIST, 1988

Location: In the East Channel between Grand Island and the mainland. Usually has two buoys.
Loran: 31642.2/47442.2
Visibility: 15 to 30 feet
Tips: Bring a dive light.

HERMAN H. HETTLER

The HERMAN H. HETTLER Hauling a cargo of lumber.

The *Herman H. Hettler* was built as the *Walter Vail* at West Bay City, Mich. in 1890. It was a three-masted steam barge with a single deck, a common configuration for vessels known as "lumber hookers."

The ship was 200 feet long, had a beam of 35 feet, and a depth of 13 feet. It was built of oak and heavily reinforced so that it could carry as much as one million board feet of lumber at one time. The vessel also carried cargoes of coal, grain, and salt. It also towed barges from port to port.

In 1913, the *Walter Vail* was sold to the Herman H. Hettler Lumber Co. of Chicago, Ill. and was finally purchased by a Michigan City, Ind. shipping firm in 1923.

During a snowstorm on the night of Nov. 23, 1926, the *Herman H. Hettler* attempted to find shelter behind Grand Island when it piled up on a shoal near Trout Point. The ship pounded on the rocky shoal all night, which opened some leaks in her hull but it was believed that it could be safely pulled off. Before a tug could be summoned for the job, however, another storm came in and demolished much of the vessel. The U.S. Coast Guard dynamited portions of the wreck because it was a hazard to navigation. No lives were lost in the disaster.

Today, divers will find portions of the ship's hull and decking in shallow water on a rocky bottom near Trout Point. This is an interesting dive because of the large sections that can be seen and local divers sometimes use cable or line to construct a "trail" between the pieces. The wreck is usually marked with a single mooring buoy.

Location:	Off the east end of Trout Point off Grand Island.
Loran:	31632.2/47431.4
Depth:	20 to 35 feet
Visibility:	Usually 30+ feet
Tips:	Look around, there is a widespread debris field.

STEVEN M. SELVICK

The 71-foot city class tugboat, *Steven M. Selvick* began her life as a steam-driven tugboat called in the *Lorain.* It was launched in 1915 in Cleveland, Ohio and had beam of 17 feet and draft of 11 feet.

The *Cabot* saw various duties around the Great Lakes, primarily working on construction projects. In 1953 the vessel was sold to a marine construction company and renamed the *Cabot.* At that time she was refitted with a diesel engine and continued working on the Great Lakes including the building of the Mackinaw Bridge in 1956 and 1957.

In 1988, the *Cabot* was sold to Selvick Marine and Towing of Sturgeon Bay, Wis. Again, the vessel's engine received an upgrade, this time in the form of a massive Fairbanks-Morse diesel. The *Cabot* was renamed the *Steven M. Selvick* in honor of the owner's son.

After several years working in the Sturgeon Bay area, the *Steven M. Selvick* was allowed to rest a season at dock. There, the owners realized that the vessel's rusting hull could not be repaired. The hull was made of riveted steel but had the hull been made of welded steel, she could have been repaired.

In 1994, the *Steven M. Selvick* was donated to the Alger Underwater Preserve as a vessel to intentionally sink as a sport diving attraction. Pete Lindquist and Mike Kohut transported the tugboat from Wisconsin to Munising where it was cleaned and prepared for sinking. After much volunteer time and effort was

**The STEVEN M. SELVICK moments before
it was intentionally sunk.**

expended to clean up the tugboat, the vessel was ready for sinking on June 1, 1996. Pumps were used to flood the engine room and it sank quickly and without problems north of Trout Point off Grand Island. This was the first intentional vessel sinking in the U.S. side of the Great Lakes.

Today, divers will find the *Steven M. Selvick* in about 60 feet of water laying on her port side. Although currents have moved the vessel somewhat on the rocky bottom, divers can still inspect the pilot house as well as the engine room. Some deck plates from the stern section have been removed to make for easier and safer diving. Doors have been permanently blocked open for the same reason. The large rudder broke off during the sinking and lies near the stern of the wreck.

This is a fun dive because the vessel is in excellent condition and many artifacts were intentionally left on the vessel for divers to enjoy.

Location:	Off Grand Island north of Trout Point
Loran:	31629.3/47427.0
Lat/Lon:	46 29.53/86 35.03
Depth:	40 to 60 feet
Visibility:	20 to 40 feet
Tips:	Note the size of the diesel engine!

GEORGE

The *George* was one of a class of 200-foot sailing vessels built for the Great Lakes grain trade between 1869 and 1874. The vessel was 203-feet long and was built at Milwaukee, Wis. in 1873 and was one of the largest on Lake Michigan at the time of her construction.

The *George* hauled many grain cargoes throughout the Great Lakes in that lucrative trade until it became the victim of a fall gale. It was enroute to Marquette with a cargo of 1,330 tons of coal when it ran into a snowstorm on Oct. 23, 1893. The next day the vessel was in sight of Grand Island but the wind shifted to the northwest and grew in intensity.

The captain attempted to make the lee of Grand Island and wait out the storm but the wind was too much for the *George*. Anchors were set but the vessel, in heavy seas, dragged on the anchors until it hit a rocky bottom off Pictured Rocks about two miles east of Miner's Castle.

After much effort, the crew of eight and one woman were able to launch a yawl and row through heavy seas to Grand Island. No lives were lost in the disaster. Some tackle was salvaged after the incident but much of the vessel was left to break up against the rocks.

Some tackle was salvaged after the incident but much of the vessel was left to break up against the rocks.

Today, divers will find the *George* lying in the shadow of the soaring Pictured Rocks. One large section of the ship's bottom lies just outside a 300-foot cove in the stone wall while other, smaller pieces, lie against the shore and under rocks eroded from the cliff face. The large section of the vessel is about 120 feet long. Six keelsons make up the hull of the *George* and the centerboard trunk is found among the remains.

Smaller pieces of the wreck are found in the area and may be seen from the surface. Deadeyes, chain plates, clevises, chain, treenails, and spikes are lodged between the rocks or lying among shifting sand.

Location:	About two miles east of Miner's Castle very near a rock wall that is part of Pictured Rocks Lakeshore.
Loran:	31604.5/47430.6
Depth:	15 feet
Visibility:	30+, less if heavy seas have been running from the north or northwest
Tips:	Bring a light and look between frames and keelsons for fish. This is a good snorkeling site.

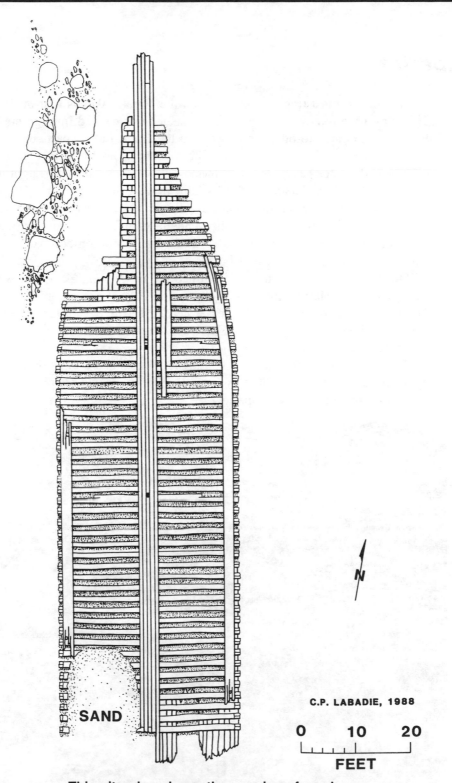

C.P. LABADIE, 1988

SAND

0   10   20

FEET

This site plan shows the remains of much
of the GEORGE. Many smaller artifacts are located
among rocks and shifting sands nearby. (NPS Graphic)

Superior

One of the most tragic shipwrecks on the Great Lakes is that of the *Superior*. This was a well-known passenger sidewheeler that carried immigrants from the Buffalo, N.Y. area to other areas west on the Great Lakes, particularly Chicago.

The *Superior* was 191 feet long with a beam of about 28 feet. It had two decks, the upper deck for passengers and the lower deck for package freight, crew's cabins, and offices. The steamer was built in 1845 in Perrysburg, Ohio.

During its service on the Great Lakes, the *Superior* was known for its speed and capacity. But the vessel was also known for minor mishaps, particularly collisions. In 1854, the vessel was sold to a transportation company that served both the upper and lower Great Lakes.

On Oct. 29, 1856, a routine trip turned tragic. The *Superior* was westbound from Sault Ste. Marie with passengers and cargo when it encountered heavy seas. The seas began to build and the vessel headed for the lee of Grand Island until the storm subsided. But the ship's rudder was suddenly torn away and a resulting lurch shifted cargo and panicked passengers.

The *Superior* was left to drift helplessly amid much confusion until it came upon rocks near Spray Falls at Pictured Rocks. Forty-two people died, the third-worst loss of life on Lake Superior.

Spray Falls where the SUPERIOR sank in 1856.

There were some salvage attempts and steel, the ship's safe, and engine were recovered.

Divers can generally find the vessel's three boilers fairly easily as they lie in only 8 feet of water just west of Spray Falls. Portions of the hull are more difficult to find but can also be seen from the surface. Two of the boilers are complete. A 35-foot section of keelsons and frames rest on the bottom in 15 feet of water approximately 100 feet off shore and 300 feet west of Spray Falls among large rocks.

In addition to these remains, other machinery can be found by exploring the area. Considering the relatively shallow depth and proximity to shore and large rock, this may be an area to avoid during periods of heavy seas from the north or northwest.

Location:	West of Spray Falls in Pictured Rocks National Lakeshore.
Lat/Lon:	46 33.45/86 24.91
Depth:	8 to 20 feet
Visibility:	15 to 30+ feet, less if heavy seas have been running from north or northwest
Tips:	This is a good snorkeling site. Use snorkels to look around for various machinery and other debris from the wreck.

Kiowa

The *Kiowa* was an ocean-going freighter built in 1920 at Wyandotte, Mich. It was 261 feet long with a beam of 43 feet. It was one of many "lakers" built around WWI for war time service but the war was over when the *Kiowa* was completed so it was purchased by a private shipping company.

In 1927, the vessel was purchased by O.W. Blodgett of Bay City, Mich. Although Blodgett was involved in the waning lumber trade, the vessel also carried cargoes of salt, coal, and limestone. After owning the *Kiowa* for little more than a year, it grounded on Parisienne Island near Whitefish Bay. The damage was serious and cost the company $30,000 to repair.

A little more than a year after that grounding, the *Kiowa* grounded again for her last time. The ship was bound to Chicago, Ill. from Duluth, Minn. with a cargo of flax seed when it got caught in a gale on Nov. 30, 1929. It finally came to rest in 30 feet of water about 4 miles west of AuSable Point Light. One crewman was lost in the disaster.

Although the superstructure of the vessel fell victim to the scrap metal drives of WWII and was dynamited from the wreck. It appears as though the vessel was

A diver examines remains of the KIOWA's steam pumps.

salvaged to the waterline. Still, about 80 percent of the vessel remains for divers to explore.

The *Kiowa* and its machinery are broken up in large pieces (most from 50 to 80 feet long). The wreck is about 400 yards from shore and lies just west of the middle stairway of the swimming beach below the Twelve Mile Beach campground. The bottom here is sandy and there is a slight west-to-east current that sometimes obscures parts of the wreckage. The poop deck rises to within 10 or 12 feet of the surface. Much of the shipwreck layout can be seen from the surface.

Although parts of the wreck and machinery are twisted, the midships portion is the most interesting. It is here that much of the machinery was placed. The ship's engine is mostly broken up but its components can be easily discovered.

> *Much of the shipwreck layout can be seen from the surface.*

Although some distance from Munising, the *Kiowa* is a popular dive site because of the variety of artifacts found here. The fragments and twisted metal attest to the power of ice and waves on Lake Superior.

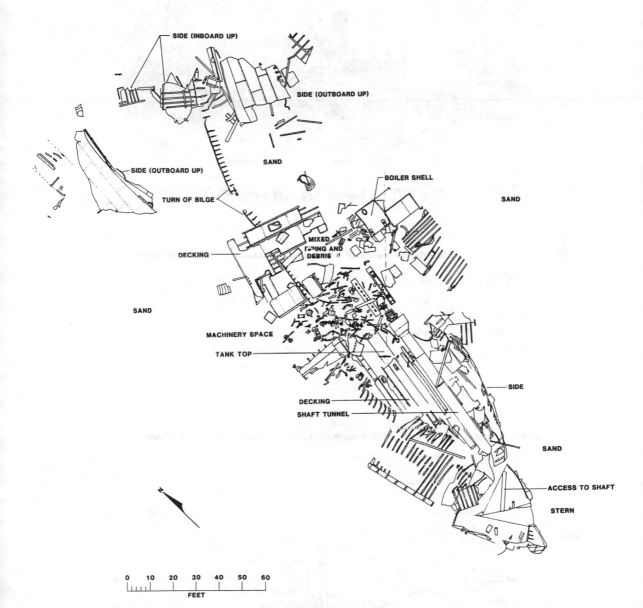

This partial site plan shows how wreckage is scattered. (NPS Graphic)

The KIOWA before her last grounding.

Location:	Directly off (400 yards) the middle stairway to the beach of Twelve Mile Beach campground.
Loran:	31499.8/47425.1
Depth:	10 to 20 feet
Visibility:	10 to 30 feet, less if heavy seas have been running from the north or northwest
Tips:	Explore slowly, use snorkel to orient self to wreck layout.

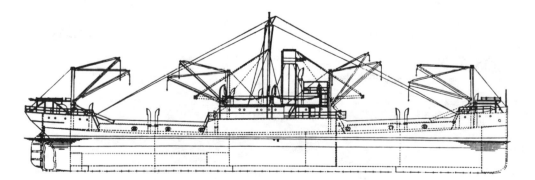

The basic layout of the KIOWA.

East Channel Lighthouse Wreck

The East Channel Lighthouse

Shifting sands make a diver's life interesting! In late 1997, a group of divers decided to explore the area directly in front of the East Channel Lighthouse. The bottom is sandy and the group hoped to find artifacts or other debris associated with the construction or operation of the lighthouse.

What they found was a shipwreck that had been uncovered by shifting sands. The wreck is believed to be that of a schooner and enough wreckage remains to make an interesting dive. Only a handful have dived this wreck and if currents continue to push sand away who knows what will be discovered.

Simply go to the lighthouse and head straight out into about ten feet of water. Look around in this area--shifting sands are likely to alternately cover and uncover the wreck.

Sand Point Wrecks

Around Sand Point, northeast of Munising, there is a collection of shipwrecks in relatively shallow water. Although this collection is off a sandy beach in only 10 to 15 feet of water, it is best to investigate this site with a boat. Distances can be deceiving and it is too far to swim to this site from shore. Besides, a boat will allow divers to search large areas of Sand Point for wreckage.

Although some of the wreckage is unidentified, it is known that the wreck of the steamers *Michael Groh* (46 27.70/86 75.87) and *Elma* (46 47.57/86 35.53) are located here. Look for dark masses contrasted against the white sand. It is easy to anchor here and explore by snorkeling.

Inland Dive Sites

There are 11 inland lakes in Alger County that have public access sites. Of these, however, only Beaver Lake, in the state forest is sufficiently deep and without an overly silty bottom to warrant diving. Unfortunately, the access to Beaver Lake is through Little Beaver Lake at Little Beaver Lake campground. Divers and snorkelers must first swim through Little Beaver Lake. The campground is off H-58 in Alger County.

Emergencies

The nearest recompression chamber is located in Marquette, about 45 miles west of Munising. Search and rescue is handled by the Alger County Sheriff's Department. Most sheriff's deputies are scuba divers and have emergency medical training. An ambulance, operated out of Munising, is staffed by deputies.

The Alger County Sheriff's Department monitors vhf channel 16. The department has a diver emergency medical treatment program.

A U.S. Coast Guard Auxiliary station at Munising has a few small boats available for search and rescue on a limited basis. The National Park Service has a small boat available for search and rescue upon request during the summer.

A U.S. Coast Guard station at Marquette can provided search and rescue operations if required.

Accommodations

The Munising area attracts many visitors because of the Pictured Rocks National Lakeshore and other attractions. Many cabins, campgrounds, and motel rooms are available. During July and August, it is best to make reservations to avoid lodging disappointments. More information is available from the Alger Chamber of Commerce in Munising, (906) 387-2138.

There are "chain" motels, such as Best Western, Comfort Inn, Days Inn, and Super 8, but some of the best values are found at the many small "mom and pop" operations, such as the Sunset Motel on the east side of Munising Bay. For a complete list of motels and suggestions, contact the Alger Chamber of Commerce.

Other Attractions

Munising is really a family vacation destination. In addition to diving, there are resorts, waterfalls, nature trails, scenic overlooks, lighthouses, sand dunes, fishing, canoeing, and kayaking to enjoy. Don't overlook the opportunity to share this area with the entire family. Contact the Alger Chamber of Commerce for more information about sightseeing and family activities. The telephone number for the Chamber of Commerce is: (906) 387-2138.

Important Addresses/Phone Numbers

Alger County Sheriff's Department
Munising, MI 49862
(906) 387-4444

U.S. Coast Guard Station Marquette
400 Coast Guard Road
Marquette, MI 49855
(906) 226-3312

Munising Memorial Hospital
Munising, MI 49862
(906) 387-4110

Pictured Rocks National Lakeshore
P.O. Box 40
Munising, MI 49862
(906) 387-2607
(906) 387-3700 (general information)

Alger County Chamber of Commerce
P.O. Box 139
Munising, MI 49862
(906) 387-2138

Charter Operators:

Shipwreck Tours (diving and sightseeing)
1204 Commercial
Munising, MI 49862
(906) 387-4477

Pictured Rocks Cruises, Inc. (sightseeing)
P.O. Box 355
Munising, MI 49862

Fun Time Diving Charters
3120 Branwood Drive
Wisconsin Rapids, WI 54494
(715) 424-0181
(800) 582-7817

Catfish

DeTour Underwater Preserve

The Lake Huron bottomlands near the DeTour Passage hosts a diverse collection of cultural and natural resources. This area is especially important because commercial maritime activities were diverse and span many decades.

The DeTour Passage area has long been known to host an impressive collection of submerged cultural resources. These resources are in the

The DeTour Passage area has long been known to host an impressive collection of submerged cultural resources.

form of dock ruins, cribbing, and shipwrecks and in recent years have begun to attract the attention of an increasing number of sport divers.

This collection was amassed over two centuries of human activity in the region. The DeTour Passage was an important crossroads for European explorers, missionaries, and those involved in maritime commerce.

The extent of human activity in this region is combined with a variety of navigational hazards. In addition to many irregularly shaped islands and coastlines, there are many dangerous shoals in this part of northern Lake Huron.

Natural features were not the only factors that created the collection of submerged cultural resources in the DeTour Passage area. Sudden storms, high waves, and low visibility conspired to litter the bottom with a variety of vessels, tools, and debris.

But the human activity unique to the DeTour Passage area was also an important factor. Specifically, at least five large fueling docks were constructed in the region. The location of the passage at the north end of Lake Huron and convenience as a crossroads made it a logical choice for major fueling operations.

These facilities attracted many commercial vessels and when no longer operating, the facilities themselves became important collections of historical artifacts.

The remains of fueling stations

include cribbing, tools, propellers, and a variety of other items intentionally discarded or accidentally lost in the water The DeTour Passage area is somewhat

---

The freshwater environment of the region can be expected to preserve these otherwise fragile resources for decades to come.

---

unique because many shipwrecks are found relatively close to shore. In fact, the remains of at least two vessels can be easily seen partially emerged near DeTour Village.

The activities of the Durocher Marine Company are an important factor in the number and location of shipwrecks in this region. The company was in the business of salvaging old vessels and after useable items were removed, some were left to sink at docks or near shore.

In addition, at least one business operating a ferry between the mainland and nearby islands was in the practice of purchasing older vessels near the ends of their maritime lives. The ferry company would use the vessels for only a few years and then permit them to sink at their moorings.

Some may be critical of the practice of using the Great Lakes as a virtual dumping ground for old vessels but it must remembered that this was a common practice during the heydays of Great Lakes maritime commerce. Also, the practice has left a remarkable collection of resources that have become exciting sport diving attractions.

The cold freshwater environment of the region can be expected to preserve these otherwise fragile resources for

decades to come because rust stabilizes itself and there are no organisms that readily attack wood underwater.

Although this area is not officially designated an underwater preserve at this time, that designation is expected within a few years, depending on local support.

The DeTour Passage area is generally sheltered from bad weather, although this area is known for its morning dense fog. Islands and bays shelter many of the dive sites described here making this an appealing dive destination because divers will be virtually assured of enjoying their sport regardless of wind and wave conditions.

The *John B. Merrill,* located on the unprotected Holdridge Shoal, is a notable exception to this general rule. This site is extremely vulnerable to westerly and southerly winds. Divers and dive charter operators should note this vulnerability and have alternative dive sites planned in the event of unfavorable weather.

Visibility

Underwater visibility is widely variable in this area. Water from the St. Mary's River generally carries a heavy sediment load as clay from Munuscong Bay tends to cloud the water. This is especially true during and shortly after periods of heavy rain.

Secchi disk readings during the summer of 1994 revealed a general visibility of 6 to 8 feet in the channel between DeTour Village and Drummond Island. This visibility is generally the norm but can increase dramatically depending upon currents and weather conditions. For example, visibility at the site of the *J.C. Ford* near Little Trout Island is often greater than 15 feet. The fact that freshwater sponges grow here is also an indication that water clarity is

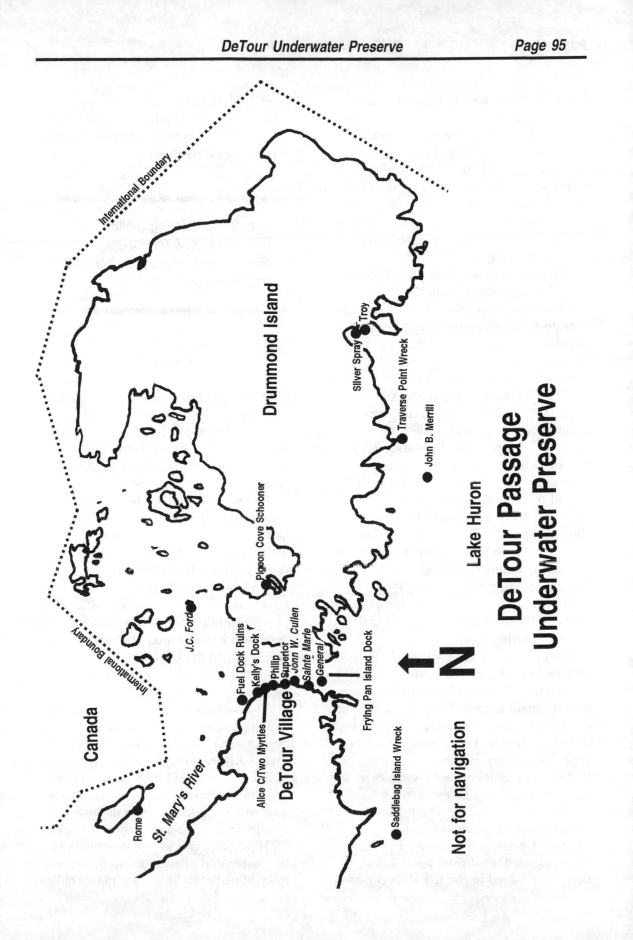

International Boundary

Canada

International Boundary

Rome

St. Mary's River

J.C. Ford

Drummond Island

Pigeon Cove Schooner

Fuel Dock Ruins
Kelly's Dock
Philip
Superior
John W. Cullen
Sainte Marie
General
Alice C/Two Myrtles
DeTour Village

Frying Pan Island Dock

Saddlebag Island Wreck

Silver Spray   Troy

Traverse Point Wreck

John B. Merrill

Lake Huron

N

**DeTour Passage
Underwater Preserve**

Not for navigation

generally better here than at other areas of the passage.

Similar, but less pronounced, variability was observed at the site of the *General*. Here, visibility was measured at 9 feet and on the same day, visibility at the sites of the *Sainte Marie* was 3 feet. This variability is remarkable considering the fact that these sites are only a few hundred yards apart.

No mooring buoys are generally placed at any dive sites in this area yet. Occasionally local divers or dive charter operators will place marking buoys at popular dive sites. These marking buoys are generally milk jugs secured to wreckage by light line.

The DeTour Passage remains an important route for commercial vessels. In addition to vessels travelling to and from the mouth of the St. Mary's River and Lake Superior, there is a limestone quarry on Drummond Island that is served by commercial freighters.

While there are reportedly some shipwrecks and other submerged resources in the shipping route, those resources, as reported in historical documents, do not appear significant. There should be no apparent conflicts between scuba divers and commercial shipping traffic.

Commercial fishing activity in the area includes treaty gill netting by Native Americans. These nets pose potential entanglement hazards for sport divers but commercial fishermen value these nets and strive to avoid shipwrecks and other areas where they may be lost. Thus, there is a natural conflict avoidance as a result of the nature of these two uses.

Sport fishing in the region has declined in recent years but is still an important activity in the area. For example, an annual trout and salmon derby conducted in the fall attracts many

sport anglers to the DeTour Passage.

Use of the existing facility in the fall by an influx of sport divers could cause minor, temporary conflicts.

> **Use of the existing facility in the fall by an influx of sport divers could cause minor, temporary conflicts.**

Currents

Although currents can be caused by wave action, the type of currents considered here are caused by uneven heating of the water column. When water molecules vibrating at different frequencies meet movement occurs.

Prevailing winds are believed to be a major cause of mixing differentially heated water masses. As a result, underwater currents are often present throughout much of the year.

Underwater currents in the Great Lakes are notoriously unpredictable. It is possible for divers to experience a current in one direction at the beginning of a dive and discover the current had completely reversed itself by the end of the dive.

The currents in this region appear to be fairly consistent with some variability attributable to the outflow of the St. Mary's River. In relative terms, currents in this area are mild with most less than 2 knots. Currents in the DeTour Passage area will not cause adverse diving conditions or pose any particular hazards.

However, currents can contribute to the suspension of various biological and mineral particles. This resulting turbidity can reduce visibility and in turn present diving hazards or affect overall diving pleasure.

Entanglements

Entanglements can take many forms and pose a considerable hazard to scuba divers. One of the most troublesome entanglements is monofilament nylon line--from gill nets or fishing. It must be remembered that commercial fishermen will generally seek to avoid shipwrecks and other submerged features that pose hazards to their nets.

Monofilament fishing line, however, may pose a very real threat to sport divers. Sport fishing is a very popular activity in this region and fish commonly congregate around shipwrecks and certain geologic features for cover. Fishing line that becomes snagged and is then broken

---

Underwater visibility is widely variable in this area.

---

off often forms a "nest" in these areas. These nests are sometimes difficult to see and sport divers can become entangled.

Once entangled, novice sport divers may panic and become increasingly entangled. Diver should keep cool and carry a knife to cut their way out of such entanglements.

The bottomland of this region is comprised of sand, gravel, and rock with some overlying silt. This varied composition presents a variety of benefits and detriments to sport divers. Sand will alternately cover and expose artifacts, especially in this region where underwater currents cause sand to drift on the bottom.

This dynamic characteristic enhances diving because it encourages divers to visit sites repeatedly to discover changes. Another advantage to sand is the fact that it is an undesirable substrate for zebra mussels. This variety can be appealing to divers.

A disadvantage of this bottom composition is that fin action can easily stir up sediments that will remain suspended in the water long enough to confuse divers and detract from the diving experience. Experienced divers, adept at buoyancy control, will not experience any particular problems of this nature.

Gravel bottoms are frequently used by game fish for spawning and concentrations of gamefish are always exciting for divers to see. Unfortunately in this area, zebra mussels may attach themselves to gravel, depending upon the size of rocks and the behavior of sand in the area.

Sand and gravel bottoms are favorable for anchoring, which is both a convenience and safety consideration for sport divers. Large rocks are favorite targets for zebra mussels. In this area zebra mussels have not yet presented any problems.

The DeTour Passage area also hosts large limestone blocks. These blocks are sometimes confused as shipwrecks during remote sensing operations. Blocks and the limestone bottomland can present anchoring difficulties.

What To See

This area hosts a remarkable collection of a variety of important cultural resources in the form of dock ruins, shipwrecks, debris fields, and items discarded through a variety of coastal human activities, including barrel making, plaster making, ferrying, and shipbuilding.

Submerged cultural resources may be found virtually anywhere in this region. The abundance, duration, and nature of human activity make it possible to discover artifacts from Native American, pre-Colonial periods to contemporary times. These artifacts may reflect such activities as fishing, fortification,

> **Tools, pieces of ships, hardware, and other artifacts are commonly discovered in this area and are the result of Durocher's salvage activities.**

fabrication, quarrying, ferrying, shipbuilding, commercial shipping, logging, and even rum running.

A significant contributing factor to the number and diversity of submerged cultural resources in this region is the Durocher Company. Throughout the 1900s this company has been involved in a variety of maritime activities.

The DeTour Passage area was a focus of Durocher activity as the company operated both a salvage operation and passenger service here. Much of the salvage work was in association with Frying Pan Island, which lies very near the mainland in the channel between the mainland and Drummond Island.

Tools, pieces of ships, hardware, and other artifacts are commonly discovered in this area and are the result of Durocher's salvage activities.

Finally, it must be noted that many divers have boycotted the DeTour Passage area in recent years to protest legislation sponsored by Michigan Rep. Patrick Gagliardi, a Drummond Island real estate salesman turned politician. Gagliardi is responsible for legislation that has restricted some diving activity and has supported the shipwreck furniture making.

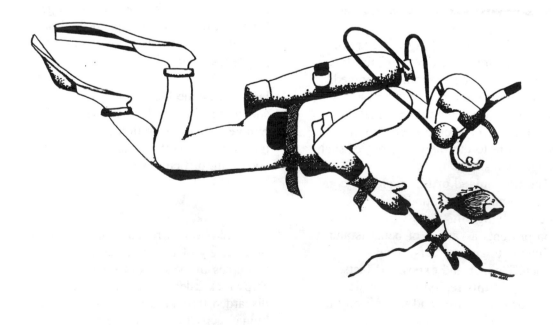

Boating

Boat launching facilities in the DeTour Passage area are marginally acceptable for the type of vessels commonly used by sport divers. The DNR boat launch just west of DeTour Village offers sufficient parking but the waterway is relatively narrow. In the past, this problem has been overcome with makeshift buoying. Another boat launch is available on Drummond Island.

In the autumn, fishing tournaments put an extra strain on boating facilities and divers should note that it will be difficult enough just to get a boat in the water. Be prepared for lines and many anxious anglers who like to start early and fish late.

Fuel can be purchased at the DeTour Marina as well as at Nate's Marina on Drummond Island.

Overnight slips are often not regarded as vital to diving parties. Most recreational divers using their own boats simply trailer them in the evenings. Still, the availability of slips, pumpout facilities, and other support services at the DeTour Marina may be important to some.

SAINTE MARIE

The *Sainte Marie* was a railroad car ferry that once ran between the Straits of Mackinac before it was purchased by a DeTour operation. After several years of service as a barge that ran materials between Drummond Island and the mainland, it was left to "molder" in 1927 and some of the remains can be seen above water. The *Sainte Marie* was built in 1893 at Wyandotte, Michigan. It was 288 feet long with a beam of 53 feet and depth of 19.5 feet.

The vessel was built with massive timbers and served the Straits of Mackinac ferry trade well. It was such a good ice breaker that Russian shipbuilders came to the Straits to see the ship and eventually patterned some of their own ships after it.

The vessel lies on a sandy bottom where some scouring has occurred. No small artifacts can be found at this site. Beginning divers should be cautioned that many spikes protrude from wreckage and could pose an entanglement hazard. There is some minor penetration here among the wreckage. The boiler is marked with an orange flag.

This site poses no apparent law enforcement concerns but may catch beginning divers by surprise if they are not familiar with the wreck, thus it may be a safety hazard to the novice diver. Some ice diving may occur at this site. This site is accessible from shore if divers ask permission first. Although the wreck lies several hundred feet offshore, shallow water makes it possible for divers to walk much of this distance.

One of the sidewheels of the *Michigan Central*, a different vessel, is located next to the emerged wreckage of the *Sainte Marie*. The sidewheel is interesting but no small artifacts or pieces of the wheel itself are found here.

The SAINTE MARIE breaking ice in the Straits of Mackinac.

Sainte Marie

Location:	Between DeTour VIllage and Frying Pan Island.
Loran:	30922.24/48136.68 (anchoring point)
Lat/Lon:	N 45° 59.30'
	W 83° 53.64'
Depth:	0-40 feet
Visibility:	4-8 feet
Level:	Beginner/Intermediate
Comments:	Divers should be warned of protruding spikes in wreckage and cable. A slight easterly current is sometimes found here. Overhangs are present and some penetration is possible.

JOHN W. CULLENS

This site is located about 100 yards eastward of the boiler of the *Sainte Marie*. The *John W. Cullen* was a dredge that was allowed to molder after its useful life was completed. This shipwreck is generally visited in conjunction with the *Sainte Marie*. There are large timbers here and, like the *Sainte Marie*, beginning sport divers should be cautioned about the entanglement hazard posed by protruding spikes. There are no small artifacts at this site.

Like the *Sainte Marie*, the *John W. Cullen* was near the end of its lifespan when it was purchased by a DeTour operation. The vessel was built in 1883 at Milwaukee, Wisconsin and was abandoned in 1933. The vessel was 141 feet long, had a beam of 28 feet, and a depth of 10.5 feet.

> **There are large timbers here and, like the Sainte Marie, beginning sport divers should be cautioned about the entanglement hazard posed by protruding spikes.**

Because of its proximity to the *Sainte Marie*, diving conditions are similar. Thus, the *John W. Cullen* can be considered a shore-access dive. Although a beginner-level dive, all divers should approach both this and the *Sainte Marie* with caution to avoid the entanglement hazards posed by protruding spikes and timbers.

Location:	About 100 yards east of the *Sainte Marie* boiler, between DeTour Village and Frying Pan Island.
Loran:	30922.24/48136.68 (anchoring location)
Lat/Lon:	N 45° 59.30'
	W 83° 53.64'
Depth:	5-40 feet
Visibility:	4-8 feet
Tips:	Novice divers should be aware of the entanglement hazard posed by protruding spikes and cable. A slight easterly current is sometimes present.

Report Shipwreck Thefts
1-800-292-7800

GENERAL

The *General* was a 97.5-foot tugboat that served the Great Lakes until it sank on April 7, 1930 at the northwest end of Frying Pan Island. The *General's* boiler and machinery were removed but some interesting remains are left to attract divers.

The *General* was built in 1900 in West Bay City, Michigan. It had a beam of 24 feet and depth of 10 feet. It is interesting to note that the General sunk

> *Much of the structure of the vessel remains and divers often visit the General as part of multi-dive experiences.*

off Lime Island on November 30, 1910 following a collision. The tugboat was raised ten years later by the Durocher Company of DeTour. Three lives were lost when the vessel sank in 1910.

Today, the *General* can be located using readily visible landmarks near Frying Pan Island. Large boulders mark a convenient anchoring location and divers can find the remains nearby.

Much of the structure of the vessel remains and divers often visit the *General* as part of multi-dive experiences. It is common, for example, for divers to visit other wrecks in the outer reaches of the DeTour Passage and then dive the *General* as they return. The *General* is also a popular dive destination when weather conditions make it difficult to visit other sites in this area.

This is a good beginner dive as there are no apparent entanglement hazards, it is relatively shallow, and visibility is often better here than in many places in the region. There are no penetration diving opportunities at this site.

Location:	At the northwest end of Frying Pan Island.
Loran:	30923.5/48137.0
Lat/Lon:	N 45° 59.20'
	W 83° 53.83'
Depth:	15-20 feet
Visibility:	4-15 feet
Tips:	It may be possible to use the large rocks nearby to secure a vessel.

Pigeon Cove Schooner

A relatively intact canal schooner is found in the eastern bay of Pigeon Cove on the north side of Drummond Island. Although there are no small artifacts, the integrity of the vessel makes it an interesting dive.

The remains of this unknown vessel lie north of a sand bar in about 15 feet of water. The wreck rises to within 4 feet of the surface. Local boaters sometimes grapple accessible portions of the wreck and break them off claiming it to be a hazard to navigation. Very often, however, local boaters place a plastic milk or detergent jug onto the wreck so that it can be easily avoided.

The hull of the vessel is generally intact and the decking has slid off to the north. The vessel lies in an east-west orientation with damage to both the stern and bow.

This is a good beginner dive but divers should be watchful for fishing line on this wreck. There are no penetration opportunities at this site. The port rail and much of the hull is intact. Near the bow divers will find a boiler that appears to be part of a donkey boiler system.

> *This is a good beginner dive but divers should be watchful for fishing line on this wreck.*

This vessel has not been popular among sport divers but could become a popular destination because it is protected from the weather. Also, there are a number of relatively small and interesting artifacts at this site and fish, such as bass, are often observed. This wreck could be especially interesting for its archaeological potential.

The original dimensions of this vessel are unknown and debris is scattered over an area approximately 190 feet by 50 feet. Additional research on this wreck could reveal much about its origin and demise.

Location:	In the eastern bay of Pigeon Cove north of a sand bar and south of Nick's Marina.
Loran:	30888.22/48130.48
Lat/Lon:	N 46° 01.45'
	W 83° 48.42'
Depth:	4-16 feet
Visibility:	6-15 feet
Tips:	Except for damage by local boaters, this vessel is remarkably intact. It appears to escape wave and ice damage. This site is sometimes marked by a small buoy placed by local boaters. Conflict with boaters is unlikely but watch for fishing line on the wreck.

J.C. FORD

This wreck, located east of Little Trout Island, is among the big surprises of this area. Although badly broken up, this site offers much for divers of all levels. The *J.C. Ford* was a steamer that caught fire and exploded off the island on November 26, 1924. It was a 172-foot steamer that was built in Grand Haven in 1889. It had a beam of 32.75 feet and a depth of 12 feet.

The area containing debris is large. Portions of the hull are generally in three sections. A large (8-foot) bronze propeller is found intact at this site complete with shaft and connected to the shaft and the engine remains. It appears as though some efforts to remove the propeller have been made in the past. It also appears that the propeller shaft has been used to secure

It is reported that one diver recovered a gold coin here.

mooring and/or marking buoys in the past, although this site is generally not buoyed.

There are many, many small artifacts including tools, spikes, and hardware. There are also unusual formations of freshwater sponges and bryophytes.

Although this site has not been popular among divers recently, it could easily become one of the most visited sites in the area. The relatively shallow depth and clear water make this an excellent place for underwater photography.

Many small artifacts that can be easily removed and concealed are located at this site but do not succumb to the temptation to remove artifacts without a permit. It is reported that one diver recovered a gold coin here. Talk about temptation! There is nothing wrong, however, in sifting through the sand and gravel to see what else may lie here.

Location:	East of Little Trout Island, visible from the surface.
Loran:	30894.88/48116.95
Lat/Lon:	N 46° 02.66'
	W 83° 50.17
Depth:	5-15 feet
Visibility:	8-20 feet
Tips:	Although an excellent beginner dive, this site will appeal to the experienced diver as well. Rare freshwater sponges and bryophytes are found at this site. Burbots and crayfish are found among wreckage. The propeller shaft may make a good anchorage. Many small artifacts are found here, sift through the sand and gravel.

ROME

The remains of the *Rome* are located at the northwest end of Lime Island. The *Rome* was a wooden-hulled steamer that was built in 1879 in Cleveland, Ohio. It was 265-feet long, had a beam of 36.75 feet, and a depth of 16.3 feet.

The *Rome* had just been purchased by a Canadian firm when it burned at Lime Island on November 17, 1909. When it burned, the vessel was bound for Sault Ste. Marie, Ontario, with a cargo of cement and hay. The vessel burned to the waterline and was a total loss. No lives were lost in the disaster and the *Rome* had two barges in tow at the time.

While the insurance company considered the *Rome* a total loss, enterprising islanders did not. The hull of the vessel was filled with limestone blocks and used as a breakwall in the harbor. Today, the *Rome* continues to act as a breakwall at the entrance to the harbor. It is readily accessible from shore.

The stern of the *Rome* is badly broken up but the bow is intact. There are many overhanging timbers and pilings also found at this site. Divers should also watch for entanglement in protruding spikes. Divers may find a broad debris field nearby worth exploring. In addition to shipwreck artifacts, there may be bottles and other items discarded from the island long ago. This could pose hazards, however, if divers venture toward the harbor entrance so use caution here.

Because of visibility and the inability to penetrate the interior of the wreck, the *Rome* is unlikely to become a popular scuba diving destination. However, recent development on Lime Island could make the *Rome* a popular snorkeling site. The future use of this site is likely highly dependent upon the nature and scope of development on Lime Island by the Michigan Department of Natural Resources.

> *Divers may find a broad debris field nearby worth exploring. In addition to shipwreck artifacts, there may be bottles and other items discarded from the island long ago.*

Today, the stern of the *Rome* is badly broken. The bow is intact as is much of the hull. Large limestone blocks, however, prevent interior investigation. The wreck rises approximately 9 feet from the bottom and portions of the vessel can be seen from the surface. Visibility at this site is often limited to two feet.

It is important to note the potential for significant artifacts to be found in the waters around Lime Island. Lime Island may have known human occupation for as long as 6,000 years. It is an area rich in human history and archaeologists and historians are just beginning the process of understanding the role of Lime Island in colonial development. One of Lime Island's key resources is limestone that was used for the production of plaster.

Large kilns are still found on the island and are the focus of archaeological research. Limestone blocks from the island are also believed to have been used for fort construction on St. Joseph and Drummond islands. Some of these features are interpreted on the island.

The island has hosted a variety of human activities. This is probably attributable to its location near the mouth of the St. Mary's River and juncture of several trading routes. The waters around the island are likely dumping grounds for a variety of "junk" that, through time, has acquired historical significance. One local diver, for example, has discovered artifacts from a cooper's operation, which may date to colonial times.

Location:	Northwest of Lime Island at the entrance to the harbor.
Loran:	30946.30/48073.00
Lat/Lon:	N 46° 05.21'
	W 84° 00.76'
Depth:	15 feet
Visibility:	1½-10 feet
Tips:	This could be an important snorkeling site because of proposed development of Lime Island. On Lime Island there is interpretation of some of the many and varied human activities that have occurred there. It is a good picnic spot.

JOHN B. MERRILL

The *John B. Merrill* is an important resource for this region. The wreck was discovered in 1992 and was quickly documented by volunteer divers. The *John B. Merrill* was a three-masted schooner that was built in 1873 in Milwaukee, Wisconsin. It had a length of 189 feet, beam of 34 feet and was 13.3 feet deep.

The *John B. Merrill* spent most of its career hauling coal and grain on the Great Lakes. It ran aground at Holdridge Shoal in a storm on October 15, 1893. No lives were lost in the disaster but the crew was stranded for 24 hours before DeTour area fishermen saved them.

The vessel was hauling coal from Buffalo, New York to Marquette, Michigan at the time of the wreck. The *John B. Merrill* was being towed as a barge by the steamer *F.E. Spinner* at the time of the sinking. It was common practice, however, for such vessels to remain rigged even when towed.

Today, the *John B. Merrill* is among the most popular dive sites in the area. The fact that the wreck was recently discovered and has been featured in presentations to divers have combined to focus attention on the site. There are many small artifacts at this site because it was so recently discovered.

When visiting this site, divers generally start at the anchor, which is found in 30 feet of water. Following the chain takes divers to the forward keelson section in about 65 feet of water. Below this section lies the starboard side of the hull with the outside facing upward. In 75 feet of water lies the port side of the hull with the inside facing upward. Near the bow area the decking has been turned upside down and lies in about 80 feet of water.

The debris area is approximately 100 by 200 feet. Although there is no penetration here, there are some overhangs near the bow area that warrant caution. This is an intermediate skill dive and visibility here is often 5 to 10 feet but is sometimes greater.

Location:	On the west side of Holdridge Shoal south of Drummond Island.
Loran:	30880.3/48192.0
Lat/Lon:	N 45° 55.05' W 83° 43.93'
Depth:	20-70 feet
Visibility:	10 to 20 feet
Tips:	The debris field here includes many small artifacts and it may take divers more than a single dive to investigate this site. Divers should be watchful for fishing nets tangled on the wreck. Another wreck on Traverse Shoal makes a good snorkel and surface interval.

Agnes W

The *Agnes W* was a 267-foot steamer that was built in 1887 in Milwaukee, Wisconsin. It had a beam of 38 feet and a depth of 17.5 feet. The steamer was, at one time, the largest wooden vessel on the Great Lakes. The *Agnes W* became stranded on Traverse Point south of Drummond Island in a storm on July 2, 1918. It broke up in the waves and became a total loss.

Today, little remains of the once-proud vessel. The main keelson structure lies on the bottom with only the bottom of the hull. Machinery was removed during a salvage operation. The debris field is about 240 feet long and many small artifacts remain.

This is a relatively shallow dive (2 to 12 feet) and is often used as a surface interval for divers visiting the *John B. Merrill*. Snorkelers enjoy this shipwreck, which is usually not buoyed but can be seen from the surface.

Location:	Off Traverse Point south of Drummond Island.
Loran:	30869.87/48191.41
Lat/Lon:	N 45° 55.45'
	W 83° 42.50'
Depth:	2-12 feet
Visilibility:	6-15 feet
Tips:	This is a popular surface interval dive when visiting the *John B. Merrill*. Divers can enjoy this wreck, with its wide debris field, by snorkeling.

TWO MYRTLES

The *Two Myrtles* was an 80-foot steamer that was converted to a lighthouse tender. It was built in Manitowoc, Wisconsin in 1889 and was abandoned at Watson's Dock in the 1930s.

This vessel was a common and well-known vessel of the region and like many vessels in this area was simply left to "molder" after its useful life had passed. Unfortunately, one local resident reports that this wreck was "raised" by a crane during construction activities in the 1970s. The hull broke apart when it was lifted above water and the remains were scattered.

This explains the current condition of the badly broken and scattered wreck. Some believe that the remains of the *Two Myrtles* may even be mixed with the remains of one or more other vessels left to molder at the dock.

Location:	North of the east-west DeTour Harbor breakwall about 90 yards from shore.
Loran:	30922.5/48131.6
Lat/Lon:	N 45° 59.84'
	W 83° 53.94'
Depth:	10-15 feet
Visibility:	4-12 feet
Tips:	Access to this site can be obtained from shore, either from the breakwall or from the marina property. Divers should plan their activities so that they do not interfere with marina operations.

Despite the poor condition of this shipwreck, it is not an insignificant dive site. There are no small artifacts but divers will discover a hodge-podge of timbers and debris. In addition, the dock ruins are also worth investigating. Visibility here is somewhat variable and may range from less than 2 feet after extended periods of rain to more than 10 feet. Novice divers should use caution in low visibility to avoid entanglements.

Access to this site can be gained from shore from either the DeTour Village Harbor breakwall or from private property (Boundary Waters Resort).

SUPERIOR

The *Superior* was a wooden-hulled scow steamer that was built in 1881 at Fort Howard, Wisconsin. The steamer was rebuilt in 1916 in Marine City, Michigan and had a length of 138 feet. The *Superior* burned on June 11, 1929 near DeTour and was considered a total loss. The remains of the vessel can be found near the south entrance to the DeTour Harbor.

This site is accessible from shore and is sufficiently distant from the recreational boaters' route to avoid conflicts. Unfortunately, this site has only large timbers remaining with some of the wreck buried. It is not a particularly viable dive site in that there is relatively little to see and visibility is rarely greater than three feet.

Location:	Near the entrance to the DeTour Harbor
Loran:	30922.9/48133.3
Lat/Lon:	45 59.63/83 53.92
Depth:	10-15 feet
Visibility:	1-3 feet
Tips:	This is not a great dive site but will do in a pinch.

Kelly's Dock Ruins/Frying Pan Island Dock

These dock ruins provide divers with an opportunity explore and discover many small artifacts that tell the tale of human activity in the region over many decades. Divers will find tools, bottles, ship parts (including a propeller), machinery, and other items that, for one reason or another, found their way off docks and decks and into the water.

Kelly's Dock Ruins are found a short distance from shore and are usually buoyed with a small marker that serves as a local navigation aid. The ruins consist of cribs interspersed with large timbers. The cribs are filled with rocks but in some cases divers can explore the interior. Timbers on top of cribs can create an atmosphere of penetration so beginning divers should go slow and exercise caution in this unfamiliar environment.

Kelly's Dock Ruins are in relatively close association to the shore of the mainland but private property makes this a boat-access dive. The site can be readily seen from a street so law enforcement personnel can easily monitor diver activities. This may be important because of the number and nature of artifacts found here. Divers will enjoy exploring about 100 yards of dock ruins, which extend to a depth of approximately 18 feet. Visibility here is variable and is greatly reduced during periods of heavy rain.

The Frying Pan Island Dock Ruins offer divers an opportunity to explore similar debris fields as those found at the Kelly Dock Ruins. At the island ruins, however, divers are more likely to find hardware discarded from vessels that were salvaged at this site by the Durocher Company.

In addition, divers should be aware that there are steep dropoffs, the first occurring at the dock ruins and dropping to 45 feet. A shelf at this depth "catches" artifacts and there is another dropoff that goes to a depth of 90 feet. This area has not been thoroughly explored and significant discoveries may await divers who investigate these ruins.

Visibility at this site is widely variable but is generally better than in many areas in the DeTour Passage. Divers can generally expect visibility in the 8 to 10-foot range. Divers should be aware that large vessels sometimes come very close to the island and it is prudent to display a diver down flag properly. Divers should also be aware that the island is privately owned.

Location:	Kelly's Dock Ruins are located north of DeTour Village about 100 yards from shore. This is not a shore-access dive because of private property but it is visible from the road. The site is often marked to facilitate recreational boat navigation.
	Frying Pan Island is located offshore from DeTour Village and divers will be able to see emerged wreckage, including a paddlewheel. Divers will find artifacts on the north, south, and east sides of the island, which is privately owned.
Loran:	30922.89/48126.56 (Kelly's Dock Ruins)
Lat/Lon:	N 46° 00.38' (Kelly's Dock Ruins) W 83° 54.25'
Depth:	At Kelly's Dock Ruins divers will find debris, artifacts, and cribs at 4 to 15 feet. At Frying Pan Island, divers will find artifacts at 4 to 90 feet.
Visibility:	6-12 feet, sometimes close to 20 feet

Saddlebag Island Wreck

These remains of an unknown, small freighter lie south-southeast of Saddlebag Island. Although divers have been known to access this site from shore (from a park off M-134), this should be considered a boat-access site. The swim is simply too long and risky.

Little remains of this wreck. A few large objects, such as farm machinery and twisted remnants of the vessel itself have attracted divers' attention through the years. Local residents are unsure of the name of this wreck but believe some farm machinery, carried as cargo, was salvaged shortly after the vessel went down more than 30 years ago. The site is usually not buoyed and can be difficult to locate even under good conditions.

A few large objects, such as farm machinery and twisted remnants of the vessel itself have attracted divers' attention through the years.

The best way to locate this site is visually working the south-southeast side of Saddlebag Island in 10-20 feet of water. Portions of the wreck will be visible from the surface. Few divers visit this site. This is because of its relatively remote location and limited amount of artifacts and vessel remains. It appears as though natural coastal forces (ice and waves) have damaged and distributed much of the shipwreck and its cargo.

Location:	Southeastern end of Saddlebag Island.
Loran:	30973.3/48137.2
Lat/Lon:	N 45° 57.08'
	W 84° 01.50'
Depth:	10-25 feet
Visibility:	8-15 feet
Tips:	This site is not a primary site because little remains of the wreck. It is also sometimes difficult to locate but can often be found from the surface on clear, calm, sunny days.

Inland Dive Sites

While there are eight inland lakes in Chippewa County with public access sites, only Caribou Lake is close enough to this preserve to be a viable alternative to diving the DeTour Passage or Lake Huron. And even though it is unlikely that the wind will make diving difficult in this area, fog is common and can create a real boating hazard considering the number of commercial shipping traffic.

Caribou Lake is located north of DeTour. The public access site is located on the north side of the lake and can be found by taking Hwy. 48 north to N. Caribou Drive. In just over 4 miles divers reach the lake and access site. The lake is 825 acres and hosts a healthy population of gamefish such as bluegills, bass, and northern pike. Exploring this area could be a fun alternative if fog keeps you away from Great Lakes diving.

Emergencies

Divers with emergencies should call for the U.S. Coast Guard on vhf channel 16. If local law enforcement agencies are monitoring their vhf radios, they, too, will assist. An ambulance is located in DeTour and the nearest recompression chamber is located in Marquette. Due to flying restrictions, however, divers who are air transported by the Coast Guard may find themselves in Milwaukee, Wis.

Emergency assistance may be extremely slow for an on-the-water situation. DeTour is remote so it will take time for whatever assistance arrives.

The DeTour Ambulance service can be reached at (906) 297-2700; the DeTour Police Department can be reached at (906) 297-5411; the U.S. Coast Guard at Sault Ste. Marie, Mich. can be reached at (906) 635-3217; and the Chippewa Co. Sheriff's Department can be reached at (906) 635-6355.

Potential Problems

Finding an air station in this area is somewhat difficult at times. In the past, air fills have been available through North Country Sports in the small village of DeTour. But sometimes divers have had a difficult time locating an air station.

The best bet is to first check with North Country Sports or Capt. Allen Allen who has sold air out of his home on Plaisance Street. If neither has an air compressor, plan on a trip to Sault Ste. Marie (there are air stations on both sides of the international border) or St. Ignace. Regardless, you can expect air to be more difficult to obtain during the week than the weekend.

Also, it may be a good idea to avoid this area in the last part of August and first week of September because of the fishing tournaments. While it is possible to avoid conflicts by starting later in the morning and finishing up in the afternoon, parking remains a problem.

Accommodations

DeTour Village, Drummond Island, and the surrounding area has a notable lack of motel accommodations available during the summer months. This means that divers will likely seek overnight accommodations in nearby communities, such as Sault Ste. Marie, Cedarville, and St. Ignace. Divers can avoid disappointments by making reservations early.

There appears to be an adequate number of state, federal, and private campgrounds available for visiting divers.

Also, there are several excellent restaurants in DeTour that are open all year. Some specialize in local fare, such as extra-beefy hamburgers. Divers will not go hungry in this town!

Gasoline is expensive in this remote area so divers may want to fill up in St. Ignace or Sault Ste. Marie before heading to DeTour or Drummond Island.

Getting There

The DeTour Passage area is easily accessible via M-134. A ferry service operated by the Eastern Upper Peninsula Transit Authority provides transportation between the mainland and Drummond Island. Chippewa County International Airport is located approximately one hour from DeTour Village near Kinross, Mich., and a smaller airport providing passenger service is located on Drummond Island.

Other Attractions

Locally, divers will be able to enjoy fishing, exploring local historic and scenic attractions, casino gambling, swimming, beachcombing, stage entertainment, and boating. The DeTour Passage provides an opportunity for divers to get extremely close to large commercial vessels as they negotiate the narrow shipping channel in this area. This makes an ideal opportunity for photographs.

The DeTour Area Chamber of Commerce has brochures detailing the entertainment options. Visitors may also want to obtain similar information from St. Ignace, Sault Ste. Marie, Mich., and Sault Ste. Marie, Ont. The DeTour Area Chamber of Commerce can be reached at: (906) 297-5987.

Important Addresses/Telephone Numbers

DeTour Area Chamber of Commerce
P.O. Box 161
DeTour Village, MI 49725
(906) 297-5987

Paradise Point Resort
 (camping/boat launch)
DeTour Village, MI 49725
(906) 297-3178

DeTour Marine, Inc.
(boat launch)
(906) 297-3181

DeTour Harbor
(85 slips)
(906) 297-5947

North Country Sports
(some dive gear, charts)
M-134--Main Street
(906) 297-6461

Drummond Island Chamber of Commerce
(906) 493-5245

Nate's Marina
(Drummond Island)
(906) 493-5352

Chippewa Co. Sheriff's Dept.
Court St.
Sault Ste. Marie, Mich. 49783
(906) 635-6355

St. Ignace Chamber of Commerce
560 N. State St.
St. Ignace, MI 49781
(800) 338-6660

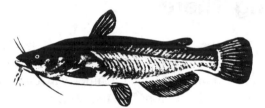

Bullhead

Muskellunge

Keweenaw Underwater Preserve

The Keweenaw Peninsula offers the most striking geologic formations in Michigan. As a result, divers can find unusual diving opportunities in this 103-square mile underwater preserve.

The Keweenaw Underwater Preserve follows 65 miles of shoreline. Most of the preserve is less than 200 feet deep and there are 12 major shipwrecks within its boundaries. The preserve area includes an area around Manitou Island (not to be confused with the Manitou islands in Lake Michigan), which is found at the tip of the Keweenaw Peninsula.

The Keweenaw Preserve offers much more than shipwreck diving. Mineral formations can be explored in relatively shallow water--20 feet or less--and are

Mineral formations can be explored in relatively shallow water--20 feet or less--and are accessible from virtually anywhere along the shore.

accessible from virtually anywhere along the shore. That makes the Keweenaw an ideal skin and scuba diving destination.

The combination of pre-historic volcano action and glaciers created a geological and mineral wonderland. Divers can expect to find virgin copper and silver veins extruding from conglomerate rocks. Occasionally, other minerals such as silver, greenstones, agates, and datolite, can be found in shallow water.

Clear water comes with a price--cold temperatures.

Because the bottom is resistant rock (primarily a conglomerate), there are relatively few sediments to cloud the water in this region. That means exceptional clarity--and visibility. Diving in this area provides an opportunity for outstanding underwater photography.

Clear water comes with a price--cold temperatures. Like most Lake Superior sites, divers can expect frigid water, even in the hottest summers.

Some studies have shown that about 75 percent of all Lake Superior divers use wetsuits as opposed to drysuits. While drysuits are indisputably more comfortable, a good wetsuit is generally adequate.

Because it has only been relatively recent that technology has made extensive sport diving possible in such cold water, many of the shipwrecks in this region have retained many artifacts. Divers can find many brass fittings, equipment, machinery, bottles, and other items still scattered in debris fields. With Michigan's stiff penalties for removing such artifacts, however, future generations are assured quality sport diving in the Keweenaw Underwater Preserve.

Unfortunately, law enforcement problems are prevalent in this region. For example, local divers routinely dynamite portions of unique copper formations to obtain raw copper to sell. State authorities have turned a blind eye to such violations owing to the remoteness of the region.

Many of the shipwrecks of this region are within 150 feet of shore, which makes it convenient for skin and scuba divers to visit these sites.

Winters are especially long and hard in this area. As a result, ice builds up in great quantities. The force of large "icebergs" moving in relatively shallow water has crushed abandoned ships and scattered debris.

That means fewer penetration diving opportunities, but great exploration for basic and intermediate divers. There are exceptions to the rule, however, and the wreck of the *Mesquite* is one such exception. More about that special shipwreck is found later in this chapter.

Whenever diving in the Keweenaw Underwater Preserve, it is a good idea to be alert for discoveries of shipwreck debris. And divers should not be

---

Even with modern navigational aids, the rocky reefs pose a formidable hazard.

---

surprised to find large schools of gamefish, especially salmon and lake trout, sharing the pure Lake Superior water.

The Keweenaw Peninsula, jutting out into Lake Superior, was a logical place

for ships to seek refuge from fierce storms that often arose suddenly on the largest body of freshwater in the world.

In addition to outstanding underwater geologic formations, there are many terrestrial sites worth visiting.

But even with modern navigational aids, the rocky reefs pose a formidable hazard. The 1989 wreck of the 180-foot U.S. Coast Guard cutter *Mesquite* is an example of the dangers posed by the geologic formations of this region.

The Keweenaw Peninsula was once busy with shipping activity. During the logging era, ships carried millions of board feet from its harbors. During the mining era, ships carried millions of tons of rich copper and iron ore.

Although the region was never densely populated, the lack of agriculture required frequent shipments of food-- another reason for ships to visit the Keweenaw Peninsula's harbors.

The maritime heritage of this region is preserve by several organizations that strive to remind residents and visitors of the sacrifices others made to settle this area.

In addition to outstanding underwater geologic formations, there are many terrestrial sites worth visiting. There are remnants of once-productive mining operations. In addition, six lighthouses in the region offer tours and a glimpse of the dangers that threatened the shipping industry.

And where you have harbors and a long history of human activity, you are likely to find bottles, tools, and a variety

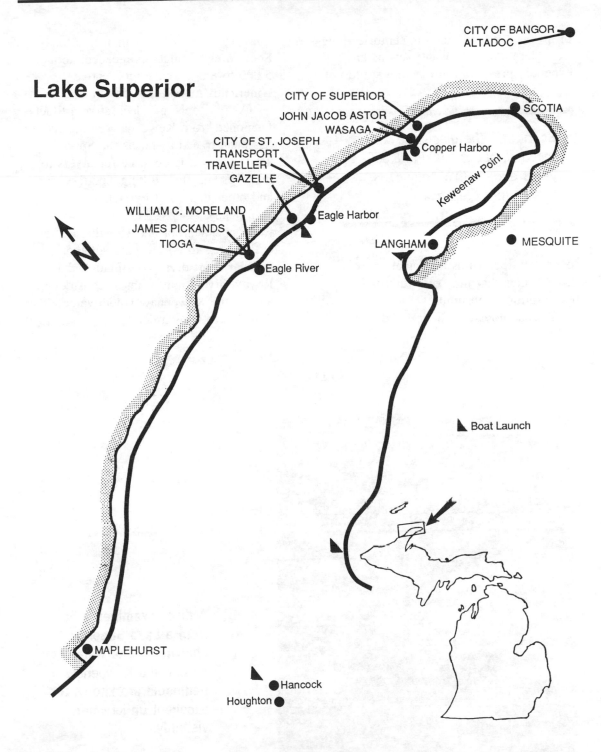

Lake Superior

CITY OF BANGOR
ALTADOC

CITY OF SUPERIOR
JOHN JACOB ASTOR
WASAGA
SCOTIA
Copper Harbor

CITY OF ST. JOSEPH
TRANSPORT
TRAVELLER
GAZELLE

Keweenaw Point

WILLIAM C. MORELAND
JAMES PICKANDS
TIOGA

Eagle Harbor

LANGHAM
MESQUITE

N

Eagle River

Boat Launch

MAPLEHURST

Hancock
Houghton

Keweenaw Underwater Preserve

(103 square miles)

of artifacts discarded from centuries long ago. Here, the cold water acts as an excellent preservation medium so do not

> **Soon after the glaciers receded, about 5,000 to 8,000 years ago, Native Americans moved into the area.**

overlook dock ruins and other shore-access sites that may offer unusual exploration opportunities.

Archaeologists believe Lake Superior was once much lower than it is today. Soon after the glaciers receded, about 5,000 to 8,000 years ago, Native Americans moved into the area.

Copper tools and decorative artifacts fashioned from Keweenaw Peninsula ore has been traced as far as the Southwest. That means it is possible for divers to discover ancient workings, pottery, tools, and other items left by Native Americans.

Copper Harbor and Houghton offer easy access to Isle Royale, another popular sport diving destination. Isle Royale divers may want to consider adding the Keweenaw Underwater Preserve to their itineraries.

A diver examines a boiler from a Lake Superior shipwreck. The waters around the Keweenaw Peninsula are known for excellent underwater visibility.

Boating

Boaters in this region should have a good navigational chart that shows reefs and shoals. The resistant conglomerate rock commonly found in this area is unforgiving and can be very destructive to hulls of any material.

Boaters in the Copper Harbor and Portage Lake Ship Canal should be aware of the regular ferry service to Isle Royale in addition to commercial shipping traffic. Divers should avoid exploring in these busy shipping channels and always display a diver down flag to avoid conflicts.

Marinas with fuel and transient accommodations can be found in the Houghton-Hancock area, Eagle and Copper harbors, Boat launches are found near Hancock, Eagle and Copper harbors and at Little Traverse and Bete Grise bays.

This is not a place to be caught in a small, open boat.

Although sport fishing is popular in this area, it is best not to rely on others for assistance. Lake Superior is a vast body of water and the Keweenaw Peninsula is remote. If trouble arises, other boaters may not be able to hear distress calls. So enter this area with a well-tuned engine and other marine equipment in good working order. The best bet is prevention.

Another potential problem for boaters is rapidly changing weather. Be sure to keep track of weather developments. Be sure your vessel is sufficiently sea worthy to handle the unpredictable conditions of Lake Superior. In addition to waves, fog can suddenly fall upon boaters. This is not a place to be caught in a small, open boat.

If on-water assistance is needed, there is a U.S. Coast Guard Station at Hancock, which monitors vhf channel 16.

MAPLEHURST

The *Maplehurst* was a 230-foot steel steamer that was built in 1892. It served the mining trade and was part of the Cleveland-Cliffs fleet.

On Dec. 1, 1922, the ship was southeast of Isle Royale and battered by a powerful storm. It was headed to a western Lake Superior community with a load of coal when the storm struck. The 29-year-old captain decided to head for the Portage Canal for safety but was unable to guide the ship between breakwalls.

The *Maplehurst* suffered severe damage almost immediately but the U.S. Coast Guard made it to the scene quickly after having spotted signal flares. Although nine crewmen left the stricken ship, the captain and ten others decided to wait out the storm on board. Those eleven perished in the disaster.

No salvage attempt was made because the vessel was so badly damaged.

Eventually the upper structure of the ship was dynamited as a hazard to navigation.

Today, the *Maplehurst* provides divers with an interesting shore-access dive site. Much of the remains are covered with sand, but shifting sand makes it a "new" dive each year. Debris that is visible is widely scattered owing to the dynamite and the forces of waves and ice.

Location:	Houghton side of the upper entry of the Portage Canal, 75 yards west of the 1,350 mark of the southwest pier.
Depth:	15-20 feet (some scouring around the wreck is likely to be found)
Visibility:	20-30 feet, less if north or northwest heavy seas have been running
Tips:	This makes a good snorkeling site. Avoid it, however, if heavy seas are running.

COLORADO

The *Colorado* was a 1,471-ton wooden steamer that was built in Buffalo, N.Y. in 1867. The vessel was loaded with 1,500 tons of flour bound for Port Huron from Duluth when it was driven ashore in heavy seas. The 254-foot ship came to rest on Sawtooth Reef near Eagle River on Sept. 19, 1898.

The ship's crew and the crew of the U.S. Coast Guard removed 600 tons of flour and tried to pull it off the reef for three days when another storm came and she began to break up. Although heavy seas were running at the time of the disaster, some speculate that dense smoke from a forest fire led to a navigational error.

Although much of the ship's machinery remains at the site, it is basically flattened due to the force of ice. Also, the remains of this vessel are scattered with the remains of a ship that sank three years later, the *Fern*. The site is usually buoyed.

Location:	On Sawtooth Reef near Eagle River
Loran:	31825.1/46553.2
Lat/Lon:	47 25.46/88 18.02
Depth:	20-35 feet
Visibility:	20-30 feet
Tips:	There is a large field of debris so plan on spending time here to see everything.

FERN

The 65-foot tugboat, *Fern*, was anchored near the wreck of the *Colorado* from which it was salvaging scrap iron. Before nightfall on June 29, 1901, the captain and his four-man crew could see a storm building over the lake but decided to weather it and remain on site. The entire crew was lost.

Today, the remains of the *Fern* are found intermingled with those of the *Colorado*. The remains of both vessels are broken up, scattered, and flattened by that action of waves and ice.

Location:	On Sawtooth Reef near Eagle River.
Loran:	31825.1/46553.2
Lat/Lon:	47 25.46/88 18.02
Depth:	15-20 feet
Visibility:	20-30 feet
Tips:	There is a large debris field for exploration.

JAMES PICKANDS

Forest fires were once common around Lake Superior. Slashings from timbering operations would dry out after several years and lightning would touch off a fire that spread quickly. The resulting smoke followed the prevailing winds out over Lake Superior and would cause serious navigational errors.

This was the case of the *James Pickands*, a 232-foot wooden steamer that was bound for Chicago, Ill. from Duluth, Minn. with a load of iron ore. The ship, which had been built as a twin stacker in Cleveland, Ohio in 1886, ran into heavy smoke on Sept. 22, 1894. The smoke was from forest fires in Minnesota and northern Wisconsin.

The crew was blinded by the thick smoke and the vessel ran aground hard on Sawtooth Reef (sometimes called Eagle River Reef) off Eagle River. The captain and crew abandoned the ship to notify the owner of the grounding. But before the vessel could be lightened and pulled off, a storm came up and broke the vessel into pieces.

Interestingly, it was the *James Pickands* that collided with the *Smith Moore* in a fog near Munising only five years earlier (see Alger Underwater Preserve, page 76).

Today, divers will find wreckage scattered high on the reef. The boilers and rudder are intact. Like other shallow shipwrecks on this reef, the remains are scattered, broken, and flattened by the force of winter ice.

Location:	On Sawtooth Reef at the mouth of the Eagle River. This wreck is usually buoyed.
Loran:	31824.4/46553.3
Lat/Lon:	47 25.53/88 17.88
Depth:	20-35 feet
Visibility:	20-30 feet
Tips:	Wreckage here may be scattered and intermingled with wreckage from these other shipwrecks: *Fern, Colorado*, and *Tioga*. Boilers make for good underwater photography.

TIOGA

The *Tioga* was a 286-steel package freighter belonging to the Massey Steamship Company Fleet, of Superior, Wis. The vessel was built in 1888 and was among the early steel steamers on the Great Lakes.

On Nov. 26, 1919, a snowstorm with high winds drove the *Tioga* onto Sawtooth Reef. All hands were rescued by the U.S. Coast Guard but the ship, with a load of 110,000 bushels of grain bound for the lower lakes.

Unfortunately, the ship broke up only three days later, before a salvage effort could be mounted. Thus ended the ship's 31-year career on the Great Lakes.

The remains of the *Tioga* are much like those of the other vessels wrecked on Sawtooth Reef. They are broken, scattered, and flattened but still make an interesting dive. The boilers and engine are interesting to explore. Remains from the other vessels may be intermingled with the wreckage of the *Tioga*.

Location:	On Sawtooth Reef. This site is usuall buoyed.
Loran:	31824.4/46553.3
Lat/Lon:	47 25.53/88 17.88
Depth:	20-35 feet
Visibility:	20-30 feet
Tips:	Although badly broken up, this is still an interesting dive. Be sure to check out the boilers and rudder. Wreckage is scattered.

The TIOGA was an early steel package freighter.

WILLIAM C. MORELAND

The *William C. Moreland* was a 580-foot steel steamer constructed in 1910. It was only two months old, serving the iron trade, when it ran into trouble.

On Oct. 18, 1910, the *William C. Moreland* was downbound with a cargo of 10,772 tons of iron ore. The vessel ran into a cloud of dense smoke from a forest fire and while the captain thought they were more than a mile from shore, the ship ran hard aground on Sawtooth Reef.

The ship took on water and broke in two. A salvage effort was made and during the effort the vessel broke again. Realizing that they could not salvage the entire vessel, the wreckers settled for a 254-foot section of the stern and took it to Sarnia for salvage work. Eventually the stern section was fitted with a new bow section and served the Great Lakes shipping industry for another 60 years as the *Sir Trevor Dawson*.

Despite the loss of the stern section at this site, much remains to be seen. The bow section's hull has been flattened by ice but much machinery is still present. The hull is an impressive sight and divers enjoy exploring the scattered remains.

The stern section of the *William C. Moreland* under tow.

Location:	Sawtooth Reef just west of Eagle River. This site is usually buoyed.
Loran:	31833.2/46551.0
Lat/Lon:	47 24.84/88 19.73
Depth:	20-35 feet
Visibility:	20-30 feet
Tips:	The hull is impressive and large artifacts remaining make good underwater photography subjects.

GAZELLE

The 158-foot *Gazelle* was a sidewheel steamer that was constructed in 1858 in Newport, Mich. The vessel was attempting to enter Eagle Harbor when a storm blew up and caused her to run aground on rocks on Sept. 8, 1860. The vessel served Great Lakes ports for only two years before her demise.

Many of the remains of the vessel were salvaged in 1864. What remains are sections of the wooden hull and some unidentified wooden pieces that could be part of the decking.

Note that underwater visibility is often reduced in harbors. Also, to avoid conflicts with boaters, be sure to display a diver down flag and leave someone topside to warn boaters of divers below.

Location:	In Eagle Harbor.
Lat/Lon:	47 27.45/88 09.28
Depth:	10 -20 feet
Visibility:	10-20 feet
Tips:	This site can be used as an "orientation" dive so that divers can become accustomed to diving in this region.

A diver inspects a boiler discovered on Sawtooth Reef near Eagle River. (Mark Rowe Photo)

TRAVELLER

The *Traveller* was a 179-foot sidewheeler that burned and sank in Eagle Harbor on Aug. 17, 1865.

The ship was a frequent visitor to Eagle Harbor, hauling passengers and freight, including an occasional cargo of copper ore. The *Traveller* had just arrived at a wharf when it was discovered to be on fire--a common malady among early wooden steamers. Passengers and crew managed to remove most baggage before the ship sank in about 20 feet of water.

The *Traveller* was built in 1852 at Newport, Mich. It was rated at 603 gross tons.

Today, the *Traveller* is among the most visited dive sites in the area. The hull and keel are torn apart but are visible on the sandy bottom.

This wreck is sometimes buoyed by local divers. This is a shore-access dive.

Location:	Start from the grassy area near the life boat house and head into harbor until the edge of a reef. Follow the base of the reef along a sandy bottom northwest until the remains are found against the reef. Wreck is sometimes buoyed.
Lat/Lon:	47 27.57/88 09.12
Depth:	15-20 feet
Visibility:	10-20 feet
Tips:	Sand shifts here so the remains discovered may depend on movement of the substrate.

CITY OF ST. JOSEPH/TRANSPORT

A diver examines bitts on the CITY of ST. JOSEPH. (Mark Rowe Photo)

**A diver explores machinery found on the
CITY OF ST. JOSEPH. (Mark Rowe Photo)**

The *City of St. Joseph* and the *Transport* were two ships cut down to bargers and were both lost at the same time (within 30 minutes of each other) and place (with 110 yards of each other). So while it is prudent to consider this a single dive site, the vessels comprising the two shipwrecks led distinct and distinguished careers upon the Great Lakes.

The *City of St. Joseph* was a 254-foot steel-hulled steamer that was built in 1889. For 45 years, under that name and as the *City of Chicago*, the ship served the passenger trade on the Great Lakes.

The *Transport* was a 254-foot iron-hulled steamer that served the railroad ferry trade in the Detroit area for 55 years. In 1942, both were working barges for the Roen Steamship Company of Sturgeon Bay, Wis. It remains a common practice to cutdown large steel and iron-hulled vessels into barges that are towed by tugboats. In this case, on September 21, 1942, both were towed by the 104-foot tug *John Roen* and carrying large cargoes of pulpwood from Grand Marais, Minn. to Port Huron, Mich.

It remains a common practice to cutdown large steel and iron-hulled vessels into barges that are towed by tugboats.

As the trio approached the Keweenaw Peninsula, a storm blew up across the lake. The *John Roen* attempted to find shelter but the rudder went out on the *City of St. Joseph*. And if that were not enough, the towline broke sending the barges free to run aground on a reef near the entrance to Eagle Harbor.

The U.S. Coast Guard at Eagle Harbor was alerted to the disaster by signal flares. The Coast Guard crew decided to save those aboard the *Transport* first, leaving the crew of the *City of St. Joseph* on their own, even though a large wave had knocked down the pilot house of the doomed ship.

The captain and two crewmen (and two crewmen of the Coast Guard) managed to hang onto pieces of pulpwood and make it to shore for a long hike to Eagle Harbor. The only casualty was the captain's wife who drowned after the ship went aground. In later years much machinery was salvaged from both vessels.

Today, the hulls of the once-proud working vessels are flattened by ice and twisted metal is scattered throughout a wide area. At the site of the *City of St. Joseph* divers will find the bow windlass, chain, rudder, and stern towing machinery. Anchor chains are present but the anchors have not been located. The wreck of the *Transport* is found about 110 yards toward shore from the *City of St. Joseph.*

Location:	¼ mile off the mouth of Little Grand Marais Harbor. The *Transport* is located 110 yards toward shore from the *City of St. Joseph.*
Loran:	31777.8/46581.5 (*City of St. Joseph*)
Lat/Lon:	47 28.15/88 06.82 (*City of St. Joseph*)
	47 28.10/88 06.58 (*Transport*)
Depth:	10-35 feet
Visibility:	20-30 feet
Tips:	The *Transport* can make a good snorkel. Divers usually visit both sites as a single dive.

JOHN JACOB ASTOR

The *John Jacob Astor* is one of the oldest shipwrecks of the Keweenaw Peninsula and the state. The 78-foot brig was used extensively in the fur trade of the region. Missionaries and explorers also relied on the ship, which was owned by the American Fur Company.

The *John Jacob Astor* was blown into a Copper Harbor reef during a storm on Sept. 21, 1844 after its main anchor failed. Although the ship was in once piece after the storm, efforts to free it before winter storms took their toll and were unsuccessful.

Much of the rigging and equipment were saved before the ship broke up that winter. The *John Jacob Astor* was originally built as a two-masted schooner in 1835. Her main anchor was recovered in 1976 and is now part of the underwater orienteering trail covered later in this chapter.

Divers can expect to find many small pieces of hull and timbers at this site. This wreck is an important historical site but leaves little for divers to explore.

Location:	Just west of the Copper Harbor Lighthouse dock near Fort Wilkins.
Depth:	10-12 feet
Visibility:	10-30 feet
Tips:	This site is worth visiting for its historical significance. All that is left are timbers.

CITY OF SUPERIOR

The average age of a typical Great Lakes schooner was seven years. A wooden-hull vessel of any type was considered "old" at 10 years. Generally, shipowners had to have three good years of service to pay for the vessel. The owners of the *City of Superior* likely groaned when they heard the vessel sank after only three months of service.

The ship was launched on July 18, 1857 as a 190-foot wooden-hulled propeller. It was built in Cleveland, Ohio and made only five runs between that city and Superior City on the west end of Lake Superior. The ship carried passengers and freight and was on her sixth trip toward Copper Harbor with a load of barrels of copper when the captain, who was a part owner of the vessel, made a navigational error in a blinding snowstorm.

The mistake, on Nov. 10, 1857, was costly and sent the *City of Superior* onto the rocks directly in front of the Copper Harbor Lighthouse. Despite efforts by the crew of the steamer *Michigan*, the vessel could not be pulled off and broke up in a storm the following day. The loss totaled $50,000 but the vessel was insured for only $32,000. No lives were lost in the disaster. The rudder was recovered in the 1970s.

Wreckage on the bottom includes large timbers and sections of the hull, which may be intermingled with wreckage from the *John Jacob Astor*.

Location:	In front of the Copper Harbor Lighthouse.
Lat/Lon:	47 28.43/87 51.73
Depth:	10-12 feet
Visibility:	10-30 feet
Tips:	This shoreline could make a good snorkel.

WASAGA

The *Wasaga* was a 238-foot Canadian steamer that burned and sank in Copper Harbor on Nov. 6, 1910.

The ship was carrying a cargo of farm equipment and general freight when it sought refuge in Copper Harbor from a rising northwest storm. Without an apparent reason, the forward section was discovered engulfed in flames. The crew managed to escape and the *Wasaga* burned to the waterline. Most of the cargo and the ship's engines and machinery were salvaged.

Divers can find portions of the *Wasaga's* keel at this site.

Location:	150 yards northeast of the Harbour Haus Restaurant in Copper Harbor. It is sometimes buoyed.
Lat/Lon:	47 28.25/87 52.94
Depth:	25-35 feet
Visibility:	10-30 feet

SCOTIA

The *Scotia* was built in Buffalo, N.Y. in 1873 and was considered a fast steamer of the era. The ship was bound for Duluth, Minn. when it ran into an autumn snow storm on Oct. 24, 1888. Before tugboats could arrive to pull the ship off the rocks, it broke in two.

The *Scotia's* boilers, engines, and machinery were recovered and part of the hull was salvaged for scrap. In the early 1970s divers recovered one of the steamer's propellers, which is on display at Fort Wilkins. The other remains of the ship--hull, machinery, prop--are widely scattered. This is a shore-access dive.

Location:	About 100 feet out in a northwesterly direction from the old rocket launch pad at Keweenaw Point.
Lat/Lon:	47 25.87/87 42.29
Depth:	15 feet
Visibility:	10-30 feet

LANGHAM

The TOM ADAMS was later named the LANGHAM.

The *Langham* was a wooden steamer that was built in 1888. It was 281 feet long and rated at 1,810 tons.

On Oct. 23, 1910, the captain of the *Langham* sought refuge from a prolonged storm in Bete Grise Bay. The ship was loaded with coal for Port Arthur. While the ship was at anchor in 120 feet of water waiting for the weather to settle down, it suddenly caught fire. The fire kept the crew from the anchors so they escaped in a yawl and watched from shore as the ship burned to the waterline. No lives were lost in the disaster.

Today, divers will find the ship's boilers, engines, rudder, anchors, and machinery intact.

Today, divers will find the ship's boilers, engines, rudder, anchors, and machinery intact. The decks were burned off but much of the hull is still visible. The top of the engines can be reached in 85 feet of water and the vessel rests in 105 feet of water.

Location:	Bete Grise Bay. This site is usually buoyed at the stern of the shipwreck.
Loran:	31758.3/46676.0
Lat/Lon:	47 22.29/87 55.57
Depth:	85 feet to top of engines, 105 feet to keel.
Visibility:	10-30 feet
Tips:	Bring a light to inspect machinery. There is much to explore here despite the fire that sank her.

MESQUITE

The *Mesquite* was a 180-foot U.S. Coast Guard buoy tender that was built in Duluth, Minn. in 1942. It was one of a class of cutters that had a 37-foot beam and draft of 14 feet. The cost of construction was about $900,000.

The ship was part of the seventh fleet of the U.S. Navy during WWII and was stationed in the Pacific Ocean. After the war, the ship returned to the Great Lakes for buoy tendering and was stationed at Charlevoix, Mich.

At about 2 a.m. on December 4, 1989, the *Mesquite* ran aground off Keweenaw Point while removing a navigational buoy. At first, the crew thought they could maneuver off the shallow reef because damage was minimal. But the vessel began to rock in heavy seas and began to take on water quickly.

> *At first, the crew thought they could maneuver off the shallow reef because damage was minimal.*

The crew was rescued by a passing commercial freighter, the *Mangal Desai.*Some valuable equipment was removed soon after the grounding but much was left aboard during the long winter debate about what to do with the vessel. The U.S. Coast Guard estimated that it would cost $44 million to replace the *Mesquite.*Finally it was decided that the ship would be removed from the Keweenaw Point and placed in the underwater preserve as a sport diving attraction.

The ship's superstructure was removed during the moving operation and placed on a barge. The superstructure and remainder of the vessel were moved to Keystone Bay and placed in about 120 feet of water in a protected area off the Keweenaw Peninsula.

Today, divers enjoy prowling the decks of the once-proud *Mesquite.* Although equipment was removed shortly after the grounding, much remained aboard, including tools, file cabinets with files, pictures, personal belongings, and many

The MESQUITE as she looked five days after running aground off Keweenaw Point. (U.S. Coast Guard Photo)

other items. Local divers recovered some of these useful items but many are still intact on the vessel.

The main structure of the vessel is intact and upright. The superstructure has been placed on the bottom nearby. This site is generally buoyed with an official mooring buoy or two although an embarrassed U.S. Coast Guard sometimes removes the buoys.

The main decks can be reached in 100 feet of water. Bring a dive light to enter the interior of the vessel. There is no silt to kick up and disrupt visibility but some of the passages are narrow. The interior is not a place for the claustrophobic diver.

Location:	Keystone Bay--it is usually marked with one or two mooring buoys.
Loran:	31758.3/46676.0
Lat/Lon:	47 22.29/87 55.57
Depth:	100 to 120 feet
Visibility:	15-35 feet
Tips:	Do not penetrate this wreck unless you are sufficiently skilled and equipped. It is better to play it safe and explore only the exterior if you are unsure.

Underwater Orienteering Trail

Local sport divers have developed an underwater orienteering trail. With a good compass and knowledge of how to use it, divers can find a variety of artifacts by Lake Fanny Hooe in Copper Harbor. The trail includes the anchor of the *John Jacob Astor*.

To access this trail and learn about the various underwater check points, see the kiosk in the picnic area of Fort Wilkins State Park. The trail is shallow (no more than 20 feet) and visibility is 10 to 30 feet.

Inland Dive Sites

There are few inland lakes in this area accessible to the public. Divers who seek inland sites generally find abandoned iron or copper mines that have flooded. This type of diving is extremely risky because while the water is clear to start, but an errant fin stroke can quickly reduce visibility to nothing.

Also, there are several interesting shore-access dive sites along the Keweenaw Peninsula. Accessibility varies year to year so it is advisable to check with local dive retailers before trespassing on private property. Information about mine and shore-access diving is available by contacting Narcosis Corner Dive Center at (906) 337-3156.

Emergencies

The only U.S. Coast Guard Station on the Keweenaw Peninsula is located at Hancock. Because some dive sites are remote, vhf radio signals may not reach this station if help is sought. For that reason, it is best to use extreme boating caution, especially because reefs that claimed large ships can also damage dive boats. Divers should note, however, that it may be possible to relay a message through other boaters who can reach the Coast Guard.

The U.S. Coast Guard monitors vhf channel 16 and is responsible for search, rescue and handling of on-water emergencies. Arrangements for medical care can be made by the Coast Guard.

The Keweenaw County Sheriff's Department is a small department, often with a single officer on duty. The department does not monitor vhf channels but the dispatcher can arrange for emergency transportation.

> *It may be possible to relay a message through other boaters who can reach the Coast Guard.*

The nearest recompression chamber is located at Marquette General Hospital in Marquette, Mich.

The telephone number for the Coast Guard Station at Hancock is: (906) 482-1520. The telephone number for the Keweenaw County Sheriff's Department is (906) 337-0528.

Accommodations

Because the Keweenaw Peninsula is sparsely populated, overnight accommodations are limited so be sure to make reservations early to avoid disappointments. Major cities, primarily Houghton, Hancock, and Calumet, offer some hotel and motel accommodations.

Campgrounds are also uncommon. But the Copper Country State Forest provides many trails and quiet areas where campers willing to "rough it" can spend several nights undisturbed. Good campsites for rustic camping can also be found in many areas along the Lake Superior shore. But consider the nuisance of mosquitos and black flies wherever you end up!

Information about camping, hotels, and motels can be obtained from the Keweenaw Tourism Council, (906) 482-2388.

Other Attractions

There is more to see in the Keweenaw Peninsula than mosquitos and black flies! Divers and their families may be interested in a tour of a working copper mine. The Arcadian Mine in Hancock offers underground tours of a horizontal copper mine. They can be reached at (906) 482-7502. Delaware Copper Mine, 11 miles south of Copper Harbor, also offers tours, call: (906) 289-4688.

Coppertown USA is located in Calumet. Here, exhibits trace the history of copper mining in the Keweenaw Peninsula. They can be contacted at (906) 337-4354.

The Seaman Minerological Museum is on the campus of Michigan Technological University in Houghton. They can be contacted at: (906) 487-2572. And if you are looking for more mining culture, contact the Quincy Mine Hoist for a tour near Hancock, call (906) 482-3101.

For interesting attractions in the Copper Country State Forest call: (906) 353-6651.

Getting There

Highways 26 and 41 are the primary roadways up and down the Keweenaw Peninsula. Divers should note that no roadway serves Keweenaw Point. Hwy. 26 feeds visitors into the area from the west while Hwy. 41 feeds visitiors from the east.

In Houghton there is a medium-size airport with several commercial carriers that run small aircraft regularly from Chicago and down state cities. A commercial bus (Indian Trails) also serves Houghton.

Important Addresses/Phone Numbers

U.S. Coast Guard Station
Hancock, MI 49930
(906) 482-1520

Keweenaw Tourism Council
P.O. Box 336
Houghton, MI 49931
(906) 482-2388
(800) 338-7982 (outside Michigan)

Keweenaw County Historical Soc.
Eagle Harbor, MI 49951

Fred's Charters
(Charters)
P.O. Box 89
Copper Harbor, MI 49918
(906) 289-4849

Keweenaw Co. Sheriff's Dept.
Eagle River, MI 49924
(906) 337-0528

Keweenaw Peninsula Chamber of Commerce
P.O. Box 336
Houghton, MI 49931
(906) 482-5240
(906) 337-4579

Narcosis Corner Dive Shop
(air station, equipment, charters, information)
474 Third St.
Centennial Heights
Calumet, MI 49913
(906) 337-3156

Ruffe

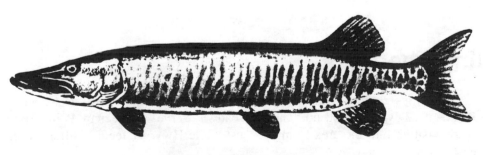

Muskellunge

Manitou Passage Underwater Preserve

When French explorers first came to this region, they learned of how the Manitou islands and Sleeping Bear Dunes were created according to Chippewa legend.

The Indians told the explorers that a mother bear and her two cubs fled a Wisconsin forest fire by swimming across Lake Michigan. When the mother bear reached the Michigan shore, she climbed a steep bluff to watch for her young.

Within sight of shore, the cubs tired and drowned. The mother waited and waited, but her young never arrived. Eventually, the mother bear died of sorrow atop the bluff.

The Great Manitou, a spirit Indians believed governed the natural world, was touched by the mother bear's devotion to her young. As a tribute, he created a great mound of sand, Sleeping Bear Dune, where the mother died in her sleep. The Manitou Islands mark the spots where the cubs drowned.

The Manitou Passage Underwater Preserve hosts a variety of shallow shipwrecks and natural features. It is also believed to contain the remains of many shipwrecks yet to be discovered.

The most striking aspect of the Manitou Underwater Preserve is sand. The Sleeping Bear Dunes National Lakeshore virtually surrounds the preserve and it is the volume of sand that makes this area unique for visiting divers.

The sand is always in motion. As a result, shipwrecks and reefs are periodically covered and uncovered. That makes the Manitou Passage (that area between the mainland and the islands) especially attractive for divers looking for exploration opportunities. Each year, "new" shipwrecks are discovered and "old" shipwrecks are covered. That means that any dive can yield new discoveries--even in shallow water.

Recently, one of the most active dive sites for exploration in the preserve has been areas south and east of North Manitou Island. Maritime archaeologists, with the help of many volunteer sport divers, are documenting shipwreck remains and searching for wrecks known to be in those areas. One recent discovery is the wreckage of the *William T. Graves*, the first bulk freighter on the Great Lakes, which foundered on North

Manitou Shoal in 1885. More recently than that are the discoveries of the *Alva Bradley* on North Manitou Shoal and the *Three Brothers,* on South Manitou Island.

Because most of the shipwrecks in the Manitou Underwater Preserve are in shallow water, there is little opportunity for divers to penetrate cabins and cargo holds. Waves and ice have broken up the wrecks or, such as in the case of the *Francisco Morazan* off South Manitou Island, are in the process of breaking up.

Besides shipwrecks, the Manitou Passage hosts many shoals of rock and sand that attract large schools of fish around massive boulders. Massive carp feed and spawn in these areas and sometimes surprise unwary divers.

The Manitou Passage has a long and colorful history. Much of that history is tied to the docks that once lined the coasts to service schooners and steamers that transported goods throughout the Great Lakes.

Today, those docks are little more than pilings, but they are home to schools of fish and unusual artifacts and skin and scuba divers often find dock ruins a fun attraction.

Because many shipwrecks are in shallow water in the Manitou Passage, it is an area popular with skin divers. This is a preserve where a minimum of equipment is required. Even nondivers can marvel at wrecks in only 25 feet of water.

Another feature of the Manitou Passage Underwater Preserve is its association with the Sleeping Bear Dunes National Lakeshore. The National Park Services offers a variety of interpretive programs for all visitors.

Some charter operators make arrangements with the Park Service for group tours of the lighthouse on South Manitou Island. The tour explains how hidden shoals and bad weather conspired to make the Manitou Passage an especially treacherous area for ships. Although the passage appears broad, there is only a three-mile wide channel for ship passage. That, combined with fog and storms and a confusing coastline make commercial shipping difficult through the passage to this day.

The lighthouse tour includes a visit to the top of the lighthouse tower, which offers a splendid view of the passage. Careful observation will reveal light blue patches of water where shoals lie.

> **Although the passage appears broad, there is only a three-mile wide channel for ship passage.**

The Park Service has jurisdiction over much of the mainland associated with the Manitou Underwater Preserve and a portion of the surface water. Park Service rangers monitor diving activity and are available to assist in emergencies.

Free registration is required before camping on the pair of Manitou Islands. Be certain to obtain brochures about those islands before planning trips. Park Service rules are designed to protect natural and cultural features as well as ensure visitor safety. Plenty of information is available from park headquarters in Empire.

Divers should plan their trip in a manner that allows them to visit the interpretive portion of the park headquarters. Here, they can learn about the geologic processes that shaped the region as well as local conditions that may affect diving. Weather forecasts are also available at Park Headquarters.

Boating

Although boats are not required to visit some of the most interesting dive sites in the Manitou Underwater Preserve, boats can provide quick and easy access to others.

Boaters should be prepared for rapid weather changes. There are currents of cold water in the Manitou Passage that can cause dense fog without warning. A good compass and chart--and the ability to use both--are vital. Boaters should reference NOAA Chart No. 14902 for navigational information of the area.

The depth of the Manitou Passage fluctuates greatly and quickly. Small boats drafting less than four feet rarely have any problem navigating. But nearly every year small boats run into problems through inattention.

Gull Point at South Manitou Island, North Manitou Shoals, and reefs in Platte Bay are potential problem areas. Boaters should also use caution when exploring the southwest shore of North Manitou Island and any area around dock ruins.

A shipping channel runs through the passage and is used frequently by ocean-going ships and Great Lakes freighters of all types. The channel follows very deep water, however, and should pose no threat to sport divers. There are no dive sites within the shipping channel.

> *Gull Point at South Manitou Island, North Manitou Shoals, and reefs in Platte Bay are potential problem areas. Boaters should also use caution when exploring the southwest shore of North Manitou Island and any area around dock ruins.*

Many boaters "beach" their vessels on the sandy shores that are commonly found throughout the preserve area. Some also anchor in quiet bays found throughout the area. Note that anchoring in South Manitou Harbor can be particularly tricky because the water becomes extremely deep a short distance from shore. Be aware that open fires on beaches are forbidden by the National Park Service, which patrols the Sleeping Bear Dunes National Lakeshore, which includes both islands. Before camping, check park regulations.

U.S. Coast Guard stations at Traverse City, Charlevoix, and Frankfort monitor vhf channel 16 for distress calls. On occasion, direct radio communication with the Coast Guard in some areas of the preserve is limited. In that circumstance, other boaters can often assist by relaying emergency messages. Note that the Manitou Passage is a favorite place for trout and salmon fishing so boats of all sorts are found here.

A permanent, concrete boat ramp is available at the municipally operated marina in Leland. There is a small fee for using the ramp, but the facility can handle even very large boats. Boaters should note that the ramp is steep and water makes it slippery. Removing a large boat can mean traction problems, but assistance is usually available. Divers should note that local anglers frequently complain about divers visiting the area. A gentle smile and quick use of launching

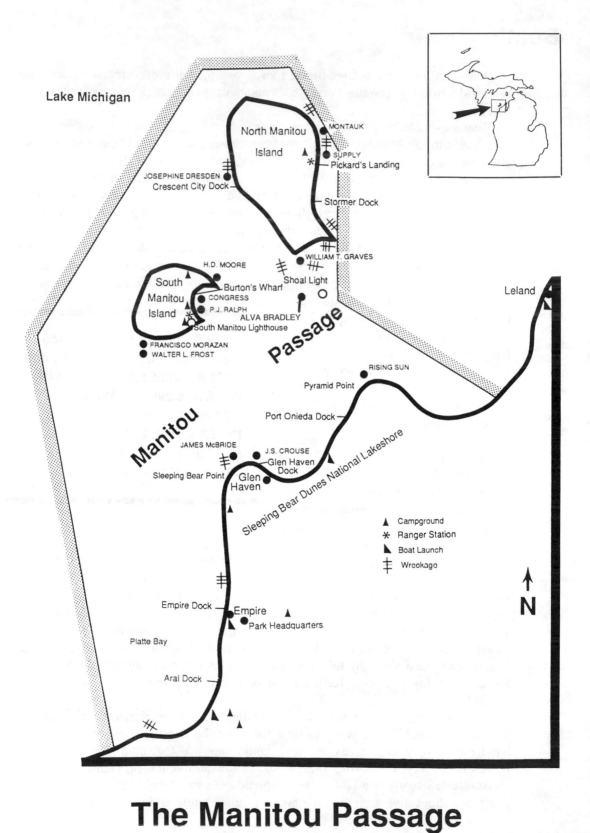

Lake Michigan

North Manitou
Island

MONTAUK

SUPPLY
Pickard's Landing

JOSEPHINE DRESDEN
Crescent City Dock

Stormer Dock

WILLIAM T. GRAVES

H.D. MOORE

South
Manitou
Island

Burton's Wharf
CONGRESS
P.J. RALPH
ALVA BRADLEY

Shoal Light

South Manitou Lighthouse

FRANCISCO MORAZAN
WALTER L. FROST

Passage

Manitou

Leland

RISING SUN
Pyramid Point

Port Onieda Dock

JAMES McBRIDE

J.S. CROUSE
Glen Haven
Dock

Sleeping Bear Point

Glen
Haven

Sleeping Bear Dunes National Lakeshore

▲ Campground
✳ Ranger Station
◣ Boat Launch
╪ Wreckage

N

Empire Dock
Empire
Park Headquarters

Platte Bay

Aral Dock

The Manitou Passage
(282 square miles)

facilities can go a long way in smoothing tensions.

Boaters must also be aware that sand periodically fills large portions of the Leland Harbor, which is protected by a limestone breakwall. Early in the season (April and May), it is a good idea to proceed through the harbor cautiously. Dredging, if done at all, is usually accomplished late in the season.

July is generally the peak month for this marina so reservations should be made for slip space or plan on trailering your watercraft.

The marina offers a variety of services for boaters and nearby Fishtown offers tourists other attractions. Grocery stores, a gas station with mechanics, restaurants, and lodging are available in the village--a short walk from the marina.

July is generally the peak month for this marina so reservations should be made for slip space or plan on trailering your watercraft.

Leland offers direct access to the Manitou Underwater Preserve. But it is also a popular fishing area so be watchful of other boat traffic.

One of the best-located boat ramps is found in Glen Haven, south of Leland off County Road 209. The ramp is located at the end of a residential street, next to a restaurant. It is privately maintained and boaters should respect the maintenance costs and contribute by paying the nominal fee requested. A metal box is found at the ramp for the deposit of money or boaters can pay at a sport shop in nearby Glen Haven. A parking fee, which can be used as credit for a meal, can be paid at the restaurant.

The Glen Haven ramp is used far less than the Leland facility and there is no discrimination against divers. Also, the Glen Haven ramp provides a shorter route to South Manitou Island and North Manitou Shoal where most diving occurs.

Small boats can use the launch at Empire, off M 22. It is a seasonal facility not suitable for very large boats. There is no charge for using the launch, which is located at the village park on Lake Michigan.

Empire is a small, friendly community. There are several "homey" restaurants, motels, an art gallery, historical museum with maritime artifacts, and an extensive play area for children at the village park. Empire also hosts the headquarters of the Sleeping Bear Dunes National Lakeshore. The headquarters features an interpretive center that focuses on geologic processes and maritime heritage. It is certainly worth a visit.

A paved boat ramp is located at the mouth of Platte River at the southern end of Platte Bay. This is a no-cost ramp located at the end of Lake Michigan Road but it should be used only by small boats because of shallow water at the mouth of the river. Once in Platte Bay, look for rocky reefs extending from the southern shore of the bay.

The headquarters features an interpretive center that focuses on geologic processes and maritime heritage. It is certainly worth a visit.

Although the distance between Sleeping Bear Point, foreground, and South Manitou Island is seven miles, there are many shoals and coves that make navigation tricky.

For a nominal fee, boaters can launch even large boats from the municipal boat launch in Frankfort. This paved facility is located considerably south of the Manitou Preserve but Frankfort offers many amenities, including a full-service marina.

The Frankfort boat launch is located south of Main Street on Betsie Bay. Frankfort is a popular sport fishing area so boaters should be watchful of boat traffic and avoid conflicts with others.

Note: Fuel is not available on South Manitou Island!

Dock Ruins

Dock ruins are among the most popular--and accessible--dive sites in the Manitou Underwater Preserve.

The Manitou Passage was one of the first areas settled west of the Straits of Mackinac. As a result, many docks and wharves were constructed to serve schooner and steamships using the passage and to transport goods to and from fledgling coastal communities.

Many of those communities disappeared early in the 1900s as the lumbering industry moved north. Left behind were massive pilings that are the remains of once-busy docks. Today, those docks provide shallow dive sites that are especially attractive to snorkelers.

Dock ruins were often considered a "junk yard" of sorts. It was a common practice for ships' crewmen to dispose of unwanted items, such as bottles, by simply tossing them into the water. Old machinery and carts used to transport goods on docks were often cast into the water when they outlived their usefulness. That makes dock diving especially appealing. The shifting sands of the Manitou Passage constantly cover and uncover such artifacts so every year is a "new" dive.

Some dock ruins offer a glimpse into the lives of those who used the structures more than a century ago. Be aware, however, that the same rules regarding souvenir collecting apply to dock ruins as shipwrecks.

The same rules regarding souvenir collecting apply to dock ruins as shipwrecks.

Year after year, docks were rebuilt. Often, docks were rebuilt atop old pilings. That may give some dock ruins a "calico" appearance where some features are relatively new while others are decades old.

Dock ruins are also popular with fish. They often gather around protective pilings searching for food or cover. Divers can expect to see yellow perch, carp, trout, and salmon.

The temptation to use an underwater metal detector to locate tools, machinery, and other metal items is great. But National Park Service rules forbid even the possession of such devises in the park or within ¼ mile of park land. Park rules also require the use of a diver down flag.

Major dock ruins in the Manitou Passage are buoyed with mooring buoys for the convenience of divers and for the safety of boaters. The major dock ruins are covered here. No boats are required--these are shore-access dives, although some sites on the islands are sufficiently remote to make a boat useful.

Aral Dock

Aral was once a thriving lumber town. It boasted a sawmill and other facilities that made it a frequent stop for freighters around the turn of the century.

As lumbering faded, so did Aral. It ceased to exist around 1907. A historical marker at the access point tells of the boom town that once bloomed at the now remote site.

Topside, the only evidence of a once-extensive dock is three pilings near shore. Underwater, however, are remains of pilings extending to about 200 yards from shore. Most pilings appear to have been cut or broken off near the sandy bottom.

Anchor chain has been discovered at the end of this dock and archaeologists believe an anchor lies nearby. Also found at this site is a propeller from an old

**Steamers, such as the ILLINOIS, made frequent stops
at docks in the Manitou Passage.**

steamer. Divers may want to explore south of this site to discover wreckage from vessels that sought refuge from storms in Platte Bay.

Otter Creek is nearby, which makes this a fine site for a family outing. Nature trails start and end at Aral, more information about them is available from the National Park Service Headquarters in Empire. This site makes an excellent snorkel but avoid it during periods of heavy seas.

Location:	At the end of Esch Road (County Road 610) in Benzie County.
Loran:	31899.93/48488.80
Lat/Lon:	44 45.50/86 03.35
Depth:	12-15 feet
Visibility:	8-20 feet, less if heavy seas have been running.
Tips:	This site is easily accessible with ample parking. It is also a popular swimming beach. For security reasons, divers may not want to leave equipment on the beach unattended.

Empire Dock

The Empire Dock was used extensively for the lumber trade. It was used somewhat for the shipping of produce. Except for concrete structures on shore, there is little evidence of the ruins topside.

Divers can use remains on shore to guide their exploration of the area. Shifting sand in this area may uncover machinery. Information about the history of the village and maritime activities is available at the historical museum in Empire off M-22.

Divers recently discovered an underwater "forest" where trees believed to be 3,000 years old once grew.

Recently, divers exploring just north of this dock site (off the sandy beach) discovered an underwater "forest" where trees believed to be 3,000 years old once grew. The stumps are found in about 12 feet of water.

Location:	At the municipal park at the west end of the village.
Loran:	31895.46/48482.05
Lat/Lon:	44 46.25/86 04.00
Depth:	12-20 feet
Visibility:	8-20 feet
Tips:	This is a popular swimming beach. It is easily accessible and there is plenty of parking. The beach is rock-laden directly off the park so enter south of the rip rap. Folks here are notoriously friendly and helpful.

Glen Haven Dock

The Glen Haven Dock was used extensively for lumber and produce shipping. Small freighters frequently used this harbor because it offered some protection from west and southwest winds.

Groups of pilings make these ruins easy to locate.

Divers will find the remains of the wreck *J.S. Crouse,* and wreckage of perhaps two other ships at the base of pilings in about 12 feet of water. A horse-drawn cart that once ran on rails to transport

A horse-drawn cart that once ran on rails to transport goods on the dock is located in seven feet of water.

goods on the dock is located in seven feet of water. Machinery may also be found by curious divers. More on the wreck of the *J.S. Crouse* is found later in this chapter.

Location:	Off County Road 209 just east of the U.S. Life Saving Service Station in Leelanau County. Look for an old fruit storage building, dock ruins are directly offshore.
Loran:	31840.71/48401.69
Lat/Lon:	44 55.30/86 01.30
Depth:	12-25 feet
Visibility:	8-20 feet
Tips:	See more about the *J.S. Crouse* later in this chapter.

Port Oneida Dock

An unknown shipwreck can be found by divers exploring the Port Oneida dock ruins. There is a record of a small schooner running aground on rocks in about 14 feet of water.

Location:	At the end of Kilderhouse Road north of Glen Arbor in Leelanau County.
Loran:	31807.43/48397.08
Lat/Lon:	44 57.10/85 56.45
Depth:	8-20 feet
Visibility:	8-20 feet
Tips:	Many Petoskey stones can be found here.

This was once a thriving port that serviced small freighters. Today, there is little evidence of the dock ruins remaining topside. Shifting sands in this area make discoveries possible each diving season.

Shifting sands in this area make discoveries possible each diving season.

**Warves like this one were used to load lumber
on small steamers and schooners.**

Burton's Wharf

Burton's Wharf was the main dock for South Manitou Island. And because
virtually all goods arriving or leaving the island were transported by freighters, it .

was a busy facility. Through the years, the wharf underwent several major rebuildings. As a result, it is a massive underwater structure--one of the most popular for sport divers.

Since Burton's Wharf was used so extensively, there is a significant collection of artifacts associated with it. Divers can find these artifacts with relative ease because the wharf's position in South Manitou Harbor makes it somewhat stable.

Burton's Wharf served many large vessels though the years so its remains lie in water as deep as 45 feet. Directly out from the ruins in 65 feet of water, divers will find an old Jeep to explore.

Location:	In the middle of the crescent that forms South Manitou Harbor at the end of an old roadway that takes you through the Bay Campground.
Loran:	31833.37/48334.08
Lat/Lon:	45 01.32/86 05.00
Depth:	5-45 feet, 65 feet to Jeep
Visibility:	10-20 feet, depending upon depth
Tips:	The bottom slopes steeply in this area. Divers must watch depth closely when exploring.

Crescent City Dock

Although only the tops of a few pilings can be seen protruding from the water, the Crescent City Dock was a substantial structure at the turn of the century.

The dock served a lumbering boom town that had its heyday from 1907 to 1917. The town boasted a 200-room hotel, butcher shop, post office, mill, and other businesses. A railroad was constructed from Crescent City north through the forests to haul lumber the locomotive and much mill machinery was brought in via freighters that used the dock.

Beachcombers frequently discover new wreckage from several ships known to have foundered in the area. Perhaps the best-known ship to have wrecked at the dock is the *Josephine Dresden*. More about the ship is found later in this chapter.

Divers can explore an extensive system of underwater pilings that extend several hundred yards into Lake Michigan. The remains attract a variety of fish.

Divers can expect to find almost anything at the Crescent City Dock ruins. An anchor off the *Josephine Dresden* was once found in shallow water but it was quickly covered by shifting sand before its exact location could be noted by maritime archaeologists.

Timbers of the ship and other ships litter the shoreline.

> *Divers can explore an extensive system of underwater pilings that extend several hundred yards into Lake Michigan.*

**The JOSEPHINE DRESDEN ran hard aground
at Crescent City Dock in 1907.**

Location:	On the west side of North Manitou Island where the remains of Crescent City can be found (site of the "big barn").
Loran:	31802.15/48288.43
Lat/Lon:	45 06.57/86 03.35
Depth:	3-25 feet
Visibility:	10-20 feet, much less if westerly or northwesterly seas have been running.
Tips:	If arriving by boat, proceed into the area slowly because of many large boulders several hundred yards from shore. Once the dock ruins are located, come straight in from west to east. This is a good snorkeling site.

Stormer Dock

Little evidence of this unbuoyed dock remains. It was one of two main docks that served North Manitou Island after 1920. The Stormer Dock was preferred by some ships because it offered slight protection from northern winds and the bottom was stable and sloped off quickly.

Divers can expect to find old pilings and machinery at this site. Exploration may yield significant discoveries because many shipwrecks known to have been lost on the east side of North Manitou have yet to be found. The bottom here consists of gravel.

Location:	Almost directly across from the old cemetery on North Manitou Island.
Loran:	31784.39/48316.15
Lat/Lon:	45 05.00/85 48.59
Depth:	5-20 feet
Visibility:	10-25 feet
Tips:	Look for evidence of pilings topside. The bottom is relatively stable so visibility is generally very good. A slight current may carry divers northward.

Pickard's Landing

Pickard's Landing includes several dock ruins that served North Manitou Island for more than 100 years.

This site was chosen for a dock because sand bars do not build up directly east of it. Less than 100 yards either way, sand bars create shoals that must be avoided by those arriving by boat.

Pickard's Landing consists of an extensive matrix of pilings, many of which are visible from the surface. The site attracts many game fish and the sandy bottom may yield exciting discoveries.

Location:	About 200 yards north of the National Park Service dock on the east side of North Manitou Island.
Loran:	31773.72/48296.53
Lat/Lon:	45 07.15/85 58.30
Depth:	0-25 feet
Visibility:	8-20 feet
Tips:	This is a popular skin diving site. Docking at the Park Service dock is permitted only for short periods.

**Although the Manitou Passage had warning devices
such as this lighthouse on South Manitou Island
built in 1840, ships still ran aground on unseen
shoals. Tours of this lighthouse are offered daily
by the National Park Service.**

J.S. CROUSE

The *J.S. Crouse* was a small steam freighter of 90 feet. It was built in 1898 in Saugatuck, Mich. for the coarse freight and lumber trades.

The wooden-hulled *J.S. Crouse* was purchased by Charles Anderson in 1907 and was used extensively in the Manitou Passage. In later years, he operated the small ship out of South Manitou Island, where he owned a farm.

This boat was called a "rabbit" boat--one that had a covered hold, exposed freight deck, and machinery, crew quarters and pilot house at the stern. Eventually, the upper deck of the *J.S. Crouse* was removed to accommodate cargoes of lumber and posts.

On Nov. 15, 1919, the *J.S. Crouse* was loaded with lumber and potatoes at the Glen Haven dock. Shortly after departing for Traverse City, it caught fire and sank near the dock. Today, the remains of the *J.S. Crouse* can be seen at the Glen Haven Dock (see page 145).

Wreckage from this ship, and perhaps as many as two other, unidentified ships, is strewn throughout the Glen Haven dock area. Burn marks are evidence on some of the wreckage. Sport divers are likely to find a variety of machinery, in the area.

Location:	At Glen Haven dock off County Road 209 in Leelanau County.
Loran:	31840.71/48401.69
Lat/Lon:	44 55.30/86 01.30
Depth:	10-20 feet
Visibility:	8-20 feet
Tips:	Roadside parking is available. This is a good snorkeling site.

JAMES McBRIDE

The *James McBride* was a 121-foot brig built in New York in 1848. The *James McBride* carried many loads of grain between Chicago, Ill. and Buffalo, N.Y., but its most notable cargo was of salt from the British West Indies. This load was delivered to Chicago late in 1848 and was touted as the first shipment direct from the Atlantic Ocean.

The ship collided with another and sank near Milwaukee, Wis. in 1855. It was raised and rebuilt and continued service for two more years.

On Oct. 19, 1857, while returning from a trip from Chicago to the Manitou islands, the *James McBride* was driven ashore at Sleeping Bear Bay by a gale.

The James McBride can be seen from the top of dunes at Sleeping Bear Point.

Today, the *James McBride* can be seen from the top of dunes at Sleeping Bear Point. Its hull, stern-first, protrudes from the base of a sand dune in about 15 feet of water. The sternpost is about five feet below the water's surface and is sometimes marked with a small buoy.

This shipwreck, as one of the oldest in the Manitou Underwater Preserve, has been studied extensively by maritime archaeologists. It is well-preserved by a layer of sand that sometimes obscures virtually all of the wreck.

This is a good wreck for snorkelers to explore, especially if access is from the mainland. It is a long walk to the site from the nearest roadway. Visitors can walk from the U.S. Life Saving Service interpretive center at Glen Haven or the dune climb a few miles south.

To avoid a long walk, a boat is required. But it is worth a climb to the top of the nearest sand dune to look for other wreckage in the area. The *James McBride* is not the only ship lost at Sleeping Bear Point.

Location:	Off Sleeping Bear Point.
Loran:	31864.87/48408.68
Lat/Lon:	45 02.30/86 00.00
Depth:	5-15 feet
Visibility:	2-20 feet (visibility is greatly reduced when heavy seas are running)
Tips:	If this wreck is not visible on one trip try it again. The sand shifts rapidly in this area and can uncover yet-undiscovered artifacts.

RISING SUN

The *Rising Sun* was a 133-foot steamer used by the House of David colony on High Island near Beaver Island to transport people and produce between the colony and the religious order's headquarters in Benton Harbor, Mich.

The wooden-hulled *Rising Sun* was built in Detroit, Mich. in 1884 and was originally used as a passenger and freight vessel. It spent much of its time on the Great Lakes making trips between Cheboygan, Mich. and Sault Ste. Marie, Mich.

In 1913, the ship was sold and served the colony until a storm blew up on Oct. 29, 1917. The ship left High Island loaded with potatoes, rutabagas, and lumber and headed for a safe mainland port. But the captain became confused in a blinding fog and the Rising Sun ran aground at Pyramid Point.

It spent much of its time on the Great Lakes making trips between Cheboygan, Mich. and Sault Ste. Marie, Mich.

The ship was abandoned with no loss of life. It was not salvaged, probably because of the remote location, and much of the wooden structure has broken up.

The RISING SUN ran aground off Pyramid Point in 1917.

A single-piston steeple tower engine lies on its side and heavy machinery and bilge framing remain. Occasionally, unusual artifacts emerge from the sandy bottom. On clear days, the remains of the *Rising Sun* can be seen from the beach at Pyramid Point. Some years, the top of the boiler is emerged.

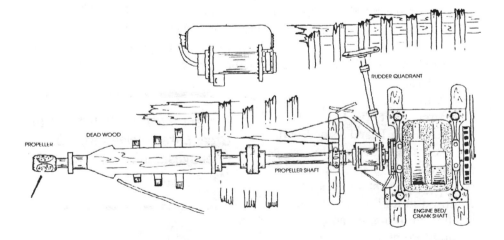

Remnants of the RISING SUN's steam engine remain.

Location:	North of Pyramid Point about 100 yards.
Loran:	31799.6/48386.8
Lat/Lon:	44 58.23/85 55.97
Depth:	7-12 feet
Visibility:	10-20 feet
Tips:	The top of the boiler is in about 7 feet of water. This is a good site for snorkeling but access is best by boat. It is also a good place for underwater photography but fish are scarce here.

WALTER L. FROST

The WALTER L. FROST aground during the winter of 1903-04.

The *Walter L. Frost* was a 235-foot steamer built in Detroit, Mich. in 1883.

The wooden-hulled ship stranded on the south end of South Manitou Island in a dense fog on Nov. 4, 1903. It was headed north with a load of package freight.

The U.S Life Saving Service saved the crew of 19 and attempted emergency salvage efforts but high seas turned all boats back. The *Walter L. Frost* began to break up on Nov. 7 and was given up as a total loss.

The wreckage of the ship is scattered because in 1960, the *Francisco Morazan* crushed the *Walter L. Frost* when it ran aground a few hundred yards north.

Today, the hull of the wreck is intact to the turn of the bilge. There are many small spikes and pieces of metal on the bottom at this site. A smashed boiler is testimony to the power that crushed the *Walter L. Frost* in 1960. Although many metal items were salvaged by islanders through the years, some small machinery parts and pipe remain at the scene. An anchor chain leads from the wreckage into the sand but it is unknown if an anchor is found at this site.

A smashed boiler is testimony to the power that crushed the Walter L. Frost in 1960.

Divers will find this site generally buoyed with an official mooring buoy at the stern of the vessel. Few fish are generally seen in this area but it is an interesting place to explore to discover how steamers of this class were constructed.

From the *Walter L. Frost* it is a good swim to the *Francisco Morazan* but many divers prefer to explore both in one dive. Those who do usually miss important discoveries. Take time and spend a tank of air at each site.

Location:	About 200 yards directly south of the *Francisco Morazan,* which is partially emerged on the shores of South Manitou Island. Much of the main structure, including the keelsons, can be seen from the surface.
Loran:	31859.1/48339.4
Lat/Lon:	44 59.65/86 08.68
Depth:	10-15 feet
Visibility:	Usually 10 to 20 feet
Tips:	A slight current from the west should be noted by divers. The wreck of the Francisco Morazan attracts boaters so watch for boat traffice and display a diver down flag.

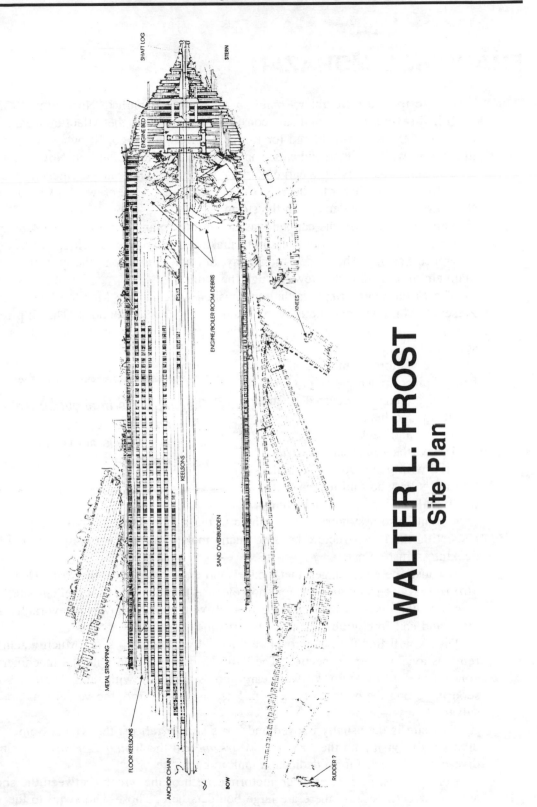

WALTER L. FROST
Site Plan

FRANCISCO MORAZAN

The 246-foot steel freighter *Francisco Morazan* was built in Norway in 1922.

It had several owners and saw considerable service in the Atlantic Ocean. The *Francisco Morazan* was bound for Rotterdam from Chicago, Ill. when it wrecked in shallow water on the southwest end of South Manitou Island on Nov. 29, 1960.

The ship was carrying a cargo of shampoo, hides, and canned chicken when it ran into an early blizzard. The U.S. Coast Guard saved the crew of 14 before the ship sustained heavy damage in the storm.

Some accounts say the captain was ordered to "plant" the *Francisco Morazan* because it was too late in the season to make it through the ice-clogged St. Lawrence Seaway. The owners, some say, did not want to pay the cost of maintaining the ship and crew through the winter.

The *Francisco Morazan* is the most visited wreck of the Manitou Underwater Preserve. Many visitors come by boat and simply cruise around it. The ship rests in about 20 feet of water and much of the superstructure is above the water's surface.

Some visitors swim the 300 yards from shore to reach the ship. One death of a teenager occurred when he overestimated his ability to swim to the wreck and back.

Today, the *Francisco Morazan* is covered with guano from ring-billed herring gulls who find it a perfect perch and nesting area. Double crested

The ship rests in about 20 feet of water and much of the superstructure is above the water's surface.

cormorants also nest here and contribute to the stench. Divers should avoid inspecting the superstructure because guano makes surfaces very slippery and the decking is rusting out.

Because there are ragged metal edges and enclosed places, the *Francisco Morazan* is not recommended for snorkelers. It is, however, an excellent site for careful scuba divers. During periods of high water levels, however, hydraulic oil leaks and can form globs that stick to wetsuits.

Divers will find the hull broken and partially filled with sand. Much machinery remains available for inspection. The hull can be penetrated with the machinery concentrated in the stern. Forward cargo holds are filled with sand. There is some scouring along the bottom of the ship. Except for its cargo, the vessel was not salvaged.

This site is not usually buoyed and boats simply raft off the wreck. Some divers try to visit both the *Francisco Morazan* and the *Walter L. Frost* in a single dive but it is more fun to dedicate a tank to each site.

Boaters must be careful when motoring north of the wreck (between the shore and the wreck) because there are large boulders here. Those who swim to the wreck are taking a substantial risk and are often disappointed because of the guano on the deck.

The FRANCISCO MORAZAN ran aground in 1960.

Location:	The wreck can be seen from the southwest end of South Manitou Island.
Loran:	31859.2/48339.3
Lat/Lon:	44 59.07/86 08.09
Depth:	15-20 feet
Visibility:	10-20 feet
Tips:	Watch for sharp metal edges and narrow passages. This site is not recommended for snorkeling.

P.J. RALPH

The P.J. RALPH served many Great Lakes ports.

The *P.J. Ralph* was built in 1889 at Marine City, Mich. It was a 211-foot wooden-hulled steamer that hauled a variety of cargoes on the Great Lakes. It primarily hauled grain and lumber and was named after its Detroit-based owner.

On Sept. 8, 1924, the ship was bound for Filer City, Mich. with a load of pulpwood when it began taking on water near North Manitou Island. The captain headed for South Manitou Harbor where it sank near shore.

During the wrecking process, the pulpwood destroyed much of the decking and cabins. The remains were dynamited by the U.S. Coast Guard shortly after the sinking as a navigational hazard. No lives were lost in the disaster.

About all that is left today is some of the hull sections and the large steam engine. It is believed that much of the rest of the vessel is buried in the soft sand found here.

Location:	In the southern end of South Manitou Harbor.
Loran:	31839.47/48333.50
Lat/Lon:	45 01.10/86 06.00
Depth:	10 feet to top of engine, 45 feet to scattered wreckage on dropoff.
Visibility:	8-15 feet

CONGRESS

The CONGRESS burned at South Manitou Harbor in 1904.

The *Congress* was built in 1867 and at 265 feet, was the longest propeller on the Great Lakes for eight years.

The wooden-hulled ship made many trips between Buffalo, N.Y., Milwaukee, Wis., and Chicago, Ill. In its early years, it was rebuilt several times.

In 1903, the *Congress* was rebuilt into a coarse freighter and was used extensively in the lumber trade. On Oct. 4, 1904, loaded with lumber, the *Congress* caught fire at a dock at South Manitou Harbor. The ship was cut loose to save the wharf.

> *On Oct. 4, 1904, loaded with lumber, the Congress caught fire at a dock at South Manitou Harbor. The ship was cut loose to save the wharf.*

The *Congress* sank in 165 feet of water--the deepest part of South Manitou Harbor. It is possible to penetrate some of the forward cabin area, which escaped the flames. The hull is intact with machinery, anchors and boilers still in place. This wreck has been dubbed the "burbot hotel" because of a high concentration of the fish here.

Through the years the wreck has sustained anchor damage from ships using the harbor for refuge. One such vessel lost its anchor in the midships portion of the wreck. Anchor drags through the wreck can also be seen.

Visibility here is extremely poor. Many fine sediments drift down to the site in the funnel-shaped harbor and remain suspended. Caution is warranted.

Location:	In South Manitou Harbor on the east side of South Manitou Island. The site is usually not buoyed.
Loran:	31834.3/48330.4
Lat/Lon:	45 01.50/86 05.44
Depth:	165 feet
Visibility:	0 to 10 feet
Tips:	This wreck is usually not buoyed so it may be necessary to anchor in the wreck. Use extreme caution here because of lack of visibility.

H.D. MOORE

The *H.D. Moore* was a two-masted, 103-foot schooner that was built in Saugatuck, Mich. in 1874. The vessel served many years on the Great Lakes considering the average lifespan of a wooden-hulled schooner was about seven years.

In the middle of the night on Sept. 10, 1907, the vessel was struggling to make the South Manitou Harbor for refuge from a thunderstorm. A navigational error was made and the *H.D. Moore* stranded on the north side of Gull Point on South Manitou Island.

The U.S. Life Saving Service on the island came to the rescue of the four crewmen and over the next several days recovered personal belongings and 45,000 board feet of lumber. The schooner *Josephine Dresden*, which became a shipwreck herself off North Manitou Island a few months later, assisted in the salvage operation.

Today, the *H.D. Moore* lies in about 12 feet of water. There is little to see except for the bottom of the hull section. Keelsons are intact and some machinery can be found here. This site is

> *There is little to see except for the bottom of the hull section. Keelsons are intact and some machinery can be found here.*

usually not buoyed but makes a good snorkel about 100 yards from shore. Hikers are sometimes prohibited from walking on Gull Point so check with South Manitou rangers before attempting a shore access.

Shifting sands periodically cover and uncover this shipwreck so it may be impossible to find one season and fully exposed the next. It is believed that more of the wreck may be visible if the sand shifts away.

Location:	On the north side of Gull Point off South Manitou Island, about 100 yards off shore.
Lat/Lon:	45 02.01/86 04.45
Depth:	10-12 feet
Visibility:	10-25 feet
Tips:	This may make a good snorkel but check with park rangers first if accessing this site by shore.

WILLIAM T. GRAVES

The *William T. Graves* was the largest vessel on the Great Lakes when it was launched in Cleveland, Ohio in 1867. It was a three-masted barkentine and primarily hauled grain. Later, in 1870, the vessel was converted to a twin propeller steamer and had a deck added in the rebuild.

On Oct. 31, 1885, the *William T. Graves* was towing the *George W. Adam* and both were loaded with a cargo of corn bound to Buffalo, N.Y. from Chicago, Ill. About midnight a gale blew up and the two ships were stranded on North Manitou Shoal. The U.S. Life Saving Station at South Manitou Island responded to a distress call and attempted to free the vessels with the help of the wrecking tug, *Mocking Bird*.

Although the tug was successful in freeing the *George W. Adams* after unloading 3,000 bushels of corn from her hold, the *William T. Graves* would not budge. After several days the *Mocking Bird* abandoned its efforts and the *William T. Graves*, with its 30,000 bushels of corn, was left as a total loss.

Some machinery, including the engines, were salvaged after the disaster. Today, the site offers divers an opportunity to inspect about 128 feet of her stern section. Little else has been noted at this site but machinery could be nearby.

After several days the Mocking Bird abandoned its efforts and the William T. Graves, with its 30,000 bushels of corn, was left as a total loss.

This site is usually not buoyed and could make a good snorkel but access is only by boat. Although the wreck rests in 10 feet of water, it is still about three miles from North Manitou Island.

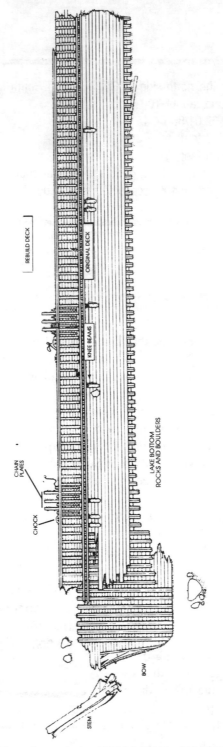

Site plan of the WILLIAM T. GRAVES.

Location:	On North Manitou Shoal, about three miles from shore.
Loran:	31802.80/48330.75
Lat/Lon:	45 02.95/86 00.44
Depth:	10 feet
Visibility:	10-20 feet
Tips:	This site is usually not buoyed and finding a good anchorage may be difficult.

SUPPLY

The *Supply* was a 132-foot brig that was built in Buffalo, N.Y. in 1855. Little is known about the relatively small vessel except that it stranded off Vessel Point on North Manitou Island in mid-November of 1869.

At the time of the disaster, the ship was carrying 300,000 bricks to be used to construct a blast furnace at Carp River, which is now Leland.

Because the vessel rests in only eight feet of water and can be easily spotted from the surface, its cargo and some artifacts were recovered. Still, some small rigging artifacts remain as well as piles of bricks in the cargo hold.

The sand is dynamic here and sometimes the vessel is completely covered. In recent years, however, it has been increasingly exposed. The wreck is sometimes buoyed with a small marker buoy and makes a good snorkel and can be easily reached from shore. Park rangers discovered the wreck several years ago and can help visitors locate it for diving.

Location:	Off Vessel Point on North Manitou Island, about 75 yards from shore.
Loran:	31769.77/48285.03
Lat/Lon:	44 58.23/85 58.50
Depth:	8-10 feet
Visibility:	10 to 20 feet
Tips:	Rangers may assist in locating this wreck. It makes a great snorkel.

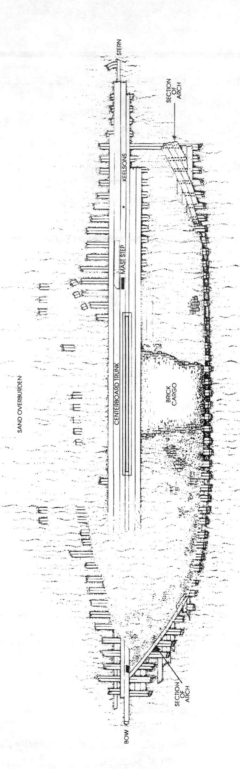

Site plan of the brig SUPPLY.

THREE BROTHERS

On April 30, 1996, National Park Service Ranger Chris Johnson was moving a small boat in South Manitou Harbor when he looked into the water. Johnson, an experienced diver, immediately recognized what he saw--a shipwreck only five feet below!

So begins the tale of the rediscovery of a lumber hooker named the *Three Brothers*. Since then, a number of individuals have sought command of the vessel. Ironically, artifacts from the discovery only became "missing in action" after the state relinquished control of the *Three Brothers* to amateur archaeologists. Those archaeologists screamed every time an artifact was missed. But what they forgot to tell the newspapers is that the artifacts were neatly buried in the sand by the archaeologists themselves!

It is little wonder, then, that the archaeologists began seeking diver restrictions on the wreck. Command of a sunken ship is a heady venture. Real archaeologists have stayed clear of the fracas having played the game with these amateurs before.

Recreational divers made other shipwreck discoveries in the area in 1996 and 1997 but have elected to keep the sites secret because of the irrational conduct of archaeologists and the laziness of state officials.

The *Three Brothers* was a 162-foot ship designed to haul lumber throughout the Great Lakes region. It was built in 1888 in Milwaukee, Wis. and had a 422 horsepower steam engine. The vessel was a common sight in northern Michigan as it hauled milled hemlock and hardwood out of Boyne City, Mich.

On Sept. 29, 1911, the *Three Brothers* was upbound with a load of lumber when it encountered an autumn gale. The captain sought refuge from the storm in South Manitou Harbor but the waves were so high they were coming in over the bow and threatened to sink the ship. Once near the lighthouse, the captain decided to run the vessel aground on Sandy Point to avoid loss of life and perhaps saving the ship and cargo.

The storm did not abate and several days later, with damage to her bow, the *Three Brothers* was declared a total loss. Lumber from the disaster was salvaged by island residents and was used to build homes and cottages in the small community.

Through the years, the site was covered by shifting sand and vegetation covered the sand. But during the winter of 1995-96 winter

> *Lumber from the disaster was salvaged by island residents and was used to build homes and cottages in the small community.*

currents eroded more than eight acres of land from the point leaving the vessel exposed again. Although the hold of the vessel is filled with sand, the site has attracted hundreds of divers because of publicity about the discovery. Also, the convenience of a regular charter (Manitou Island Transit) encouraged divers to make the long (18 mile) voyage to South Manitou Island.

Today, the stern cabin structure is still intact, although filled with sand, and the

The THREE BROTHERS running empty.

bow cabin is missing. Also, it appears as though the sand-filled cargo hold is causing the vessel to break up near the bow but state officials have refused to allow sport divers to voluntarily remove the sand. They said it is better to allow the wreck to go the way of so many other Manitou Passage wrecks and degrade into a pile of boards naturally.

In addition to the stern deck, much machinery is found in the stern area. Divers also enjoy exploring the exterior of the wreck, including the stern name plate which positively identifies this wreck as that of the *Three Brothers.*

The bow of the vessel lies in only five feet of water while the stern lies in 45 feet of water. Local sport divers often place an official buoy on the stern of the wreck but local archaeologists in command of the vessel often remove the buoy and then complain about dive boats sending anchors into the wreck-- yet another reason to prohibit diving on the *Three Brothers*, they argue!

The bow of the vessel lies in only five feet of water while the stern lies in 45 feet of water.

Dive charters to the wreck are available through the two dive centers in Traverse City. Also, divers can take the regular ferry service to the island on a first-come, first served basis. Manitou Island Transit does not charge for the first tank but does for the second. Most divers, however, are satisfied with spending a single tank at the site.

When diving the *Three Brothers,* do not fail to check out the sandy bottom. You may discover hidden artifacts! The National Park Service monitors the site and asks divers to participate in a free registration program. Park rangers here are generally friendly and helpful and are more into interpretation than regulation.

Location:	Directly off Sandy Point on South Manitou Island a few yards from shore.
Loran:	31839.3/48339.3
Lat/Lon:	45 00.55/86 05.59
Depth:	5 to 45 feet
Visibility:	10 to 25 feet, depending upon currents and weather conditions.
Tips:	Search the sandy bottom near the wreck for small artifacts. Register at the ranger station before diving to learn more about local conditions.

MONTAUK

The *Montauk* was a 137-foot schooner built in 1863 in Oswego, N.Y. Its homeport was Chicago, Ill. and primarily hauled cargoes of grain throughout the Great Lakes.

On Nov. 23, 1882, the *Montauk* was caught in a northerly gale and ran aground on North Manitou Island. The vessel was loaded with coal bound for Chicago from Buffalo, N.Y. The captain was blinded by a fierce snow storm and struck the northeast point of North Manitou Island. Local fishermen discovered the stranded vessel the next morning and alerted the U.S. Life Saving Service on the island.

Visibility here is generally good with a rocky bottom with a light clay overlay.

All eight crewmen were saved and the ship broke up. Interestingly, a fishermen's camp nearby shows that parts of the vessel were salvaged and lumber from the ship may have been burned to gain access to metal fasteners.

There are times when this vessel can be spotted from the surface of the water but it is not buoyed. Visibility here is generally good with a rocky bottom with a light clay overlay. Two large sections of the vessel are diveable and a third section is often buried by sand.

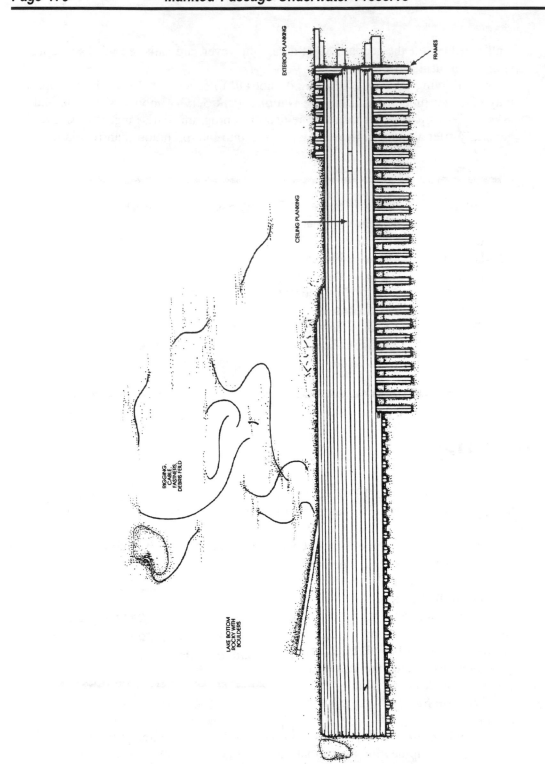

EXTERIOR PLANKING

FRAMES

CEILING PLANKING

RIGGING,
CABLE,
FASTNERS,
DEBRIS FIELD

LAKE BOTTOM
ROCKY WITH
BOULDERS

Drawing of one section of the MONTAUK.

Location:	Off the northeast end of North Manitou Island several hundred yards off shore. It is generally not buoyed.
Loran:	31759.59/48270.62
Lat/Lon:	45 09.55/85 59.48
Depth:	35 feet
Visibility:	10-25 feet
Tips:	Look for a debris field with small artifacts northeast of the main section of this wreck. Anchorage may be difficult in clay/rock bottom.

ALVA BRADLEY

The *Alva Bradley* shares a history with the *Three Brothers* in that after it was discovered on North Manitou Shoal in 1990, it became the focus of a flurry of bureacratic activity, attempts to restrict divers from the site, and artifacts buried by amateur archaeologists.

The vessel was a three-masted schooner barge built and stationed at Cleveland, Ohio. The *Alva Bradley* was used to haul a variety of cargoes throughout the Great Lakes during its 24 years of service, which began when the vessel was launched in 1870.

The 192-foot ship had a beam of 20 feet and had many brushes with disaster. In 1875 the ship sank while docked at Buffalo, N.Y. It was raised and in 1883, while hauling a load of coal, was stranded off Shot Point near Marquette. A

The ship had many close brushes with disaster during its 24 years of service on the Great Lakes.

rebuild of the stout vessel was completed in 1888 and included a donkey boiler. Later that year the ship hit a submerged rock in Lake Huron. The next year it hit a bridge in Milwaukee.

As a schooner barge, the *Alva Bradley* was generally towed by steamers. In mid-October of 1894, the ship became separated from her escort, the *Joseph S. Fay,* during an autumn gale and ran aground on North Manitou Shoal in about 26 feet of water. The crew was saved by the U.S. Life Saving Service stationed on North Manitou Island. The famous tug, *Favorite,* was dispatched to the scene of the

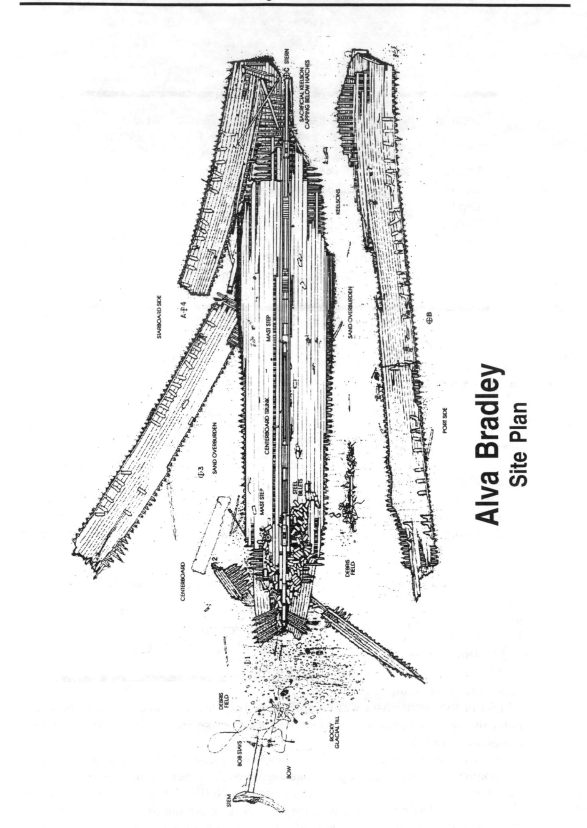

Alva Bradley
Site Plan

disaster and reached the *Alva Bradley* on Oct. 16.

At first it was thought that the stricken ship could be raised once again but only 50 feet of her bow was visible. Waves had broken up the remainder of the ship and it was left to the salvagers who arrived two weeks later. In only two hours of work, more than 40 tons of steel billets were recovered as well as machinery and rigging. During the salvage process, and from more than a century of wave and ice forces, the *Alva Bradley* broke up completely leaving only parts of the deck and hull and many small artifacts.

Today, divers will find many steel billets remaining at the site. In addition, small artifacts such as dead eyes, cable, tools, bolts, and hardware have been left at the site. Through years of sport diving, many artifacts have been moved for better underwater photography and out of curiosity, but much of the wreckage is intact.

This is another area where dead eyes and other small artifacts may be found buried in sand found nearby. Also, a hundred yards northeast of the wreck lies a bundle of cable rigging, which includes additional artifacts. Sometimes burbots, yellow perch, and sculpins are found prowling the wreck.

Location:	Off the south end of North Manitou Island on the shoal. This site is usually buoyed with an official mooring buoy placed by local divers. Sometimes, local "archaeologists" remove the buoy.
Loran:	31798.5/48339.2
Lat/Lon:	45 02.27/85 59.26
Depth:	22-26 feet
Visibility:	10-25 feet
Tips:	Be sure to check out the debris field northeast of the main wreck.

J.B. NEWLAND

The *J.B. Newland* was a three-masted schooner built in Manitowoc, Wis. in 1870. It served the Great Lakes much as the *Alva Bradley* and other schooners in its class.

On Sept. 8, 1910, the *J.B. Newland* was bound for Sturgeon Bay, Wis. from Milwaukee, Wis. when it became lost in a dense fog and a strong southwest wind. The schooner strayed across Lake Michigan and became stranded on North Manitou Shoal in about eight feet of water.

The U.S. Life Saving Service from South Manitou Island responded but it was quickly realized that the ship was stuck fast. Heavy seas began to run due to a northwest gale and the crew managed to save personal belongings as well as rigging, sails, and running gear.

The J.B. NEWLAND in an oil painting.

Today, the *J.B. Newland* rests in a deep scour surrounded by large boulders. It is too far from shore to be a shore access site, but it makes a great place for snorkeling. The rudder is located about 100 feet southwest of the main wreck. Although completely broken up by the forces of waves and ice, much of the deck and hull remain for divers to explore. Boaters should approach this site cautiously to avoid collisions with large boulders.

Location:	Off the southern end of North Manitou Island on North Manitou Shoal.
Loran:	31803.34/48338.13
Lat/Lon:	45 02.30/86 00.00
Depth:	4-10 feet
Visibility:	15-25 feet
Tips:	Enter this area with caution to avoid collisions with boulders.

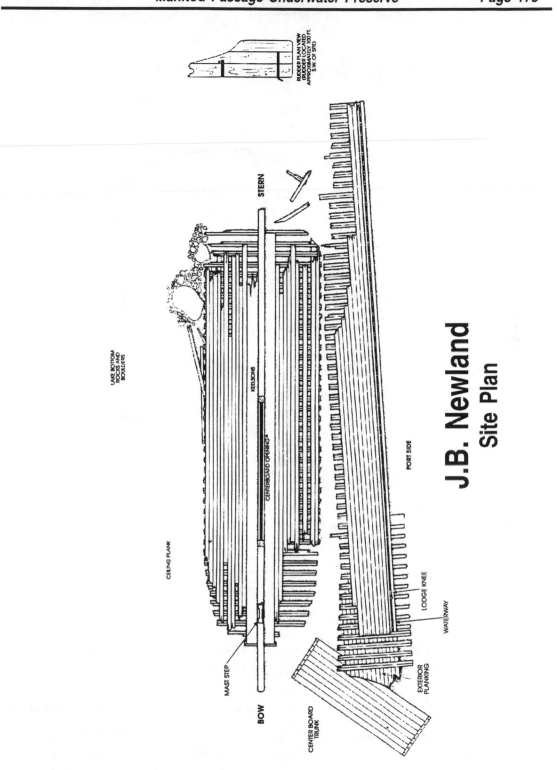

RUDDER PLAN VIEW
(RUDDER LOCATED
APPROXIMATELY 100 FT.
S.W. OF SITE)

STERN

LAKE BOTTOM
ROCKS AND
BOULDERS

KEELSONS

CENTERBOARD OPENING

CEILING PLANK

PORT SIDE

MAST STEP

BOW

CENTER BOARD
TRUNK

LODGE KNEE

WATERWAY

EXTERIOR
PLANKING

J.B. Newland
Site Plan

Shoal Wreckage/North Manitou Shoal Light

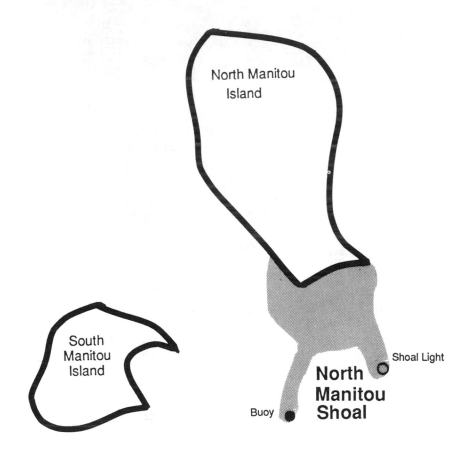

North Manitou Shoal, located on the south end of North Manitou Island, is littered with wreckage from a variety of ships. Some of the wreckage, like that of the *William T. Graves,*has been identified but many of the scattered, broken pieces are not.

Some of the pieces are fairly large and offer insight into the construction techniques used to build the schooners and steamers that once travelled the Great Lakes but met their final fate on North Manitou Shoal. Newspaper accounts from the

Newspaper accounts from the past tell of how the islands were "littered" with wreckage after major storms.

past tell of how the islands were "littered" with wreckage after major storms.

Some pieces of wreckage can be spotted from the top of "Old Baldy," a sand dune on North Manitou Island. Many pieces are a short swim from shore and, occasionally, beachcombers find pieces of shipwrecks--one even found an anchor!

The bottom on the shoal is generally rock with some very large boulders that make it tricky for even small watercraft. The shoal can be an excellent place for snorkelers willing to share it with large schools of carp.

The North Manitou Shoal Light, referred to locally as the "crib," is also a good exploration site for sport divers. There are many, very large boulders here, too, and large schools of gamefish, such as yellow perch. The manixmum depth around the lighthouse is about 25 feet.

Inland Dive Sites

There are many inland dive sites for scuba diving and snorkeling in this area. Of particular note are North and South Sand Bar lakes off M-22 near Empire for snorkeling. For scuba diving, Glen Lake, also off M-22, is popular but there is little to see here in either section of the lake although the western portion is notably warmer and a better place for snorkeling.

Also popular are the unusually clear waters of Boardman River near Traverse City for both scuba diving and snorkeling. And divers may want to check out the public access sites on Lake Leelanau for snorkeling. Many gamefish are found here but watch for conflicts with anglers.

Some divers enjoy prowling the short stretch of the Carp River in Leland for fishing lures and equipment. The water is clear but watch for incoming and outgoing boat traffic. Divers here may see trout, salmon, carp, and even lake sturgeon.

Most lakes in this region have sandy bottoms and little silt, which makes for excellent visibility.

Most lakes in this region have sandy bottoms and little silt, which makes for excellent visibility.

For additional information, check with the two dive retailers in Traverse City for recommendations.

Emergencies

In the event of a diving emergency, call the Leelanau County Sheriff's Department at (616) 256-9829. If you are away from a telephone but have access to a vhf radio, call the U.S. Coast Guard on channel 16. Describe the nature of the emergency and follow instructions. Assistance can also be obtained from the National Park Service.

The U.S. Coast Guard Air Station at Traverse City has helicopters that can respond to emergencies if commercial medical care is unavailable or insufficient. Because there is a variety of medical help available in the area, it is best to first call the Leelanau County Sheriff's Department. If you are unsuccessful or unable to call, contact the Coast Guard directly by radio or telephone: (616) 922-8210.

If you are unable to contact either, try the ranger stations on North and South Manitou Islands, headquarters in Empire, or ranger stations on the mainland. Rangers have access to emergency radio frequencies and are also trained in handling medical emergencies.

Generally, diving emergencies will be handled by sheriff departments or staff from the Coast Guard stations at Frankfort or Charlevoix.

Accommodations

Lodging in the form of campgrounds and hotels/motels is available in Frankfort, Empire, Glen Arbor, Leland, Northport, and surrounding communities. There is no shortage of rooms or camping spaces much of the year but in July and August this area becomes a popular tourist destination and availability may be limited. It is best to obtain reservations during those months to avoid disappointments.

Camping is permitted on several mainland campgrounds associated with the Sleeping Bear Dunes National Lakeshore. There are also several private campgrounds near Empire, Frankfort, and Leland.

Camping is permitted on most of North Manitou Island but there are virtually no amenities. Limited services are available on South Manitou Island, which has three campgrounds. Only the Bay Campground a mile from the South Manitou Island Ranger Station is close to wrecks.

Check with the National Park Service to determine what campgrounds and facilities are available in the park.

Information about overnight accommodations can be obtained by contacting the West Michigan Tourist Association, 1253 Front St. NW, Grand Rapids, MI 49504/(616) 456-8557.

Other Attractions

Northwest Michigan is a popular tourist destination during the summer. Visitors come to enjoy quaint Fishtown in Leland and the entertainment found in Traverse City. There are casinos near Traverse City as well as luxurious overnight accommodations.

The area also abounds with golf courses and the Sleeping Bear Dunes National Lakeshore, with dune climbs, hiking, and other interpretive programs, attracts visitors from throughout the U.S. The clear waters of Lake Michigan and Grand Traverse Bay appeal to boaters and anglers and unusual shops in Glen Haven,

Empire, Northport, and Traverse City do a brisk business for three months of the year.

All this means there is plenty in this region for a family vacation or a weekend getaway. The best way to obtain information about the region is through the West Michigan Tourist Association, 1253 Front St. NW, Grand Rapids, MI 49504/(616) 456-8557. Because it is such a busy area it is important to plan ahead well ahead.

Getting There

Traveling to northwest Michigan is easy. There are major highways from Grand Rapids (US 131), the western lakeshore (US 31), and even I-75 from the Detroit area will take visitors to connecting highways westward, such as M-72.

Once in the area, the primary lakeshore highway is M-22. Many small communities are found here as well as access to many of the dive sites described in this chapter. A state map is sufficient to meet most people's needs and local maps are available from the National Park Service headquarters in Empire (M-72 and M-22).

Commercial airlines serve Traverse City and there are many small airports such as the ones at Empire and Frankfort. Be aware, however, that the airports on North and South Manitou Islands are closed.

Important Addresses/Phone Numbers

Sleeping Bear Dunes National Lakeshore
P.O. Box 277
Empire, MI 49630
(616) 326-5134 (headquarters)
(616) 334-3976 (S. Manitou Island)

Leelanau Co. Sheriff's Dept.
112 Chandler
Lake Leelanau, MI 49653
(616) 256-9829

Benzie Co. Sheriff's Dept.
7157 Crystal Ave.
Beulah, MI 49617
(616) 941-7940

Scuba North
13380 West Bay Shore Dr.
Traverse City, MI 49684
(616) 947-2520

Manitou Island Transit
Fishtown
Leland, MI 49654
(616) 256-9061 or
(616) 271-4217

U.S. Coast Guard Air Station
Traverse City, MI 49684
(616) 922-8210

Great Lakes Scuba
US 31 South
Traverse City, MI 49684
(616) 943-3483

Marquette Underwater Preserve

Marquette has been a major shipping port on Lake Superior since the discovery of iron ore in 1844.

This area is important historically because Marquette, the largest city in the Upper Peninsula, played a crucial role in the development of the region. Marquette was a busy port and served as the loading site for tons of iron ore.

Marquette also served as a trans-shipping port where large ships would unload their cargoes onto smaller vessels for delivery to other Lake Superior ports.

Heavy vessel traffic to and from the port, along with Superior's gales and fogs, made shipwrecks here inevitable in the early days of navigation.

The Marquette Underwater Preserve was established in 1990 to promote conservation of the area's submerged historic resources. The preserve offers outstanding scuba diving along Lake Superior's shoreline in two areas of Marquette County, the Marquette Unit and the Huron Islands Unit.

The Marquette Unit includes 24 miles of shoreline around Marquette and extends to the 200-foot depth contour. In this area divers can explore the wrecks of wooden schooners, steamers, and commercial fishing vessels as well as unique geological formations.

Because this was a busy shipping area, there are many unmarked docks that can provide excellent skin and scuba diving experiences. Diving from shore may also yield discoveries of remains from many schooners that were blown ashore during storms. Many of these ships were looted and then left to the elements a century or more ago.

Although Marquette was a busy harbor and port, unmarked shoals made navigation difficult and left little room for error. One schooner captain refused to enter the harbor and anchored offshore.

Because there are few harbors in this region, many ships caught in rough seas raced to Marquette for refuge--a race they sometimes lost.

The Huron Islands Unit includes some of the most impressive coastline in the state. The shore ranges from sandy beaches to towering cliffs, backed by the scenic Huron Mountains. Much of the diving is done in the clear waters surrounding the Huron Islands, a group of rugged granite knobs rising out of Lake Superior's depths.

The Marquette County Underwater Preserve has a strong support group of local divers who generally keep popular dive sites buoyed with mooring buoys. Divers should remember that Lake Superior remains very cold even in the hottest summers, so a good wetsuit or drysuit is recommended.

The impact of its maritime heritage is not lost on the citizens of Marquette. The Marquette Maritime Museum offers exhibits displaying the maritime heritage of the region. It is located on Lakeshore Boulevard.

The U.S. Coast Guard Station is located across from the maritime museum. This station features a

lighthouse that was erected 1866. Group tours of the lighthouse can be arranged by contacting the U.S. Coast Guard. McCarty's Cove, a city park and beach adjacent to the station off Lakeshore Boulevard, is a good place to photograph the lighthouse.

Visitors to the Marquette area will also find a variety of cultural activities scheduled for summer months. It is an area that offers many non-diving attractions. More information about those activities is available from the Marquette Chamber of Commerce, (906) 226-6591.

Boating

Boaters can reach the Huron Islands from the Big Bay Harbor of Refuge at Big Bay, or from Witz's Marina at Skanee in Baraga County. In either case, it is a cruise of more than 12 miles to the islands so boaters must take appropriate precautions.

Access to the Marquette Unit dive sites is by boat from launch ramps at Marquette's upper and lower harbors. Small boats can also be launched at the Chocolay Township launch ramp on the Chocolay River and can reach the *Charles J. Kershaw* and *Queen City* wrecks by navigating the shallow channel at the river mouth.

A public marina and boating service facilities are found in Marquette, which is usually not crowded even in late summer. The Marquette Cinder Pond Marina is located at 300 W. Baraga Ave., and has ten transient slips available. The marina can be reached at (906) 228-0469 or on vhf channels 9, 16, or 71.

The Marquette Presque Isle Marina is also located at 300 W. Baraga Ave. and has more than four transient slips. The marina can be reached at (906) 228-0464 or vhf channels 9 or 16.

It is vital for boaters to be aware that Lake Superior and the waters in this preserve area foster considerable wave energy. That means it is important to have a craft capable of handling heavy seas. This is not a place for light boats.

Marquette hosts a U.S. Coast Guard Station, which can be reached on vhf channels 9 or 16 in case of an on-water emergency. The telephone number of the Coast Guard Station is (906) 226-3312.

For navigational assistance, boaters should have NOAA Chart No. 14970.

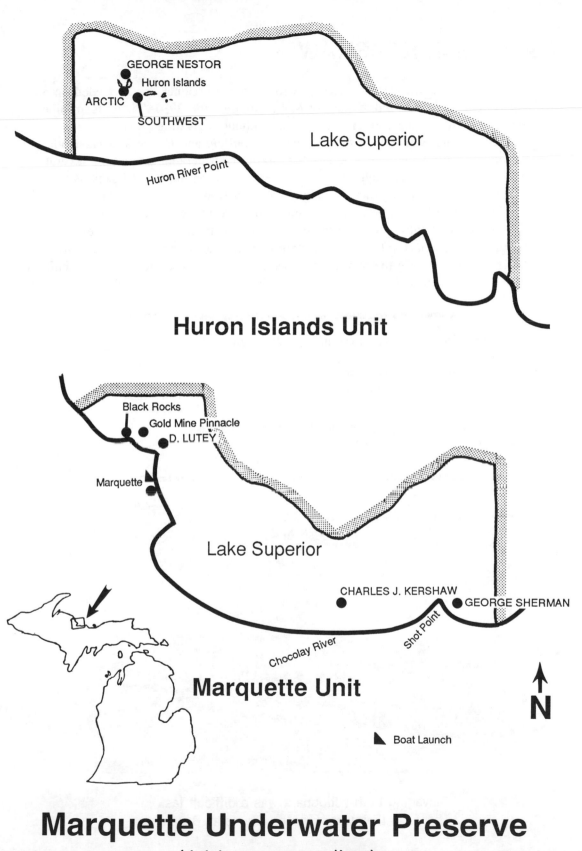

Huron Islands Unit

Marquette Unit

Marquette Underwater Preserve
(144 square miles)

CHARLES J. KERSHAW

The *Charles J. Kershaw* was a 223-foot wooden steamer that grounded on a rocky reef about two miles south of Marquette on Sept. 29, 1895. A steam pipe burst on that evening and left the steamer without navigating power.

The steamer was towing the schooners *Moonlight* and *Henry A. Kent.* Both schooners were blown onto the beach and after considerable effort over several months, were refloated and continued to see service on the Great Lakes. But the *Charles J. Kershaw* was not so lucky. It quickly went to pieces on the reef.

The steamer's massive boiler lies just inside the western end of the reef providing excellent photo opportunities. A short distance to the south lies a large section of the *Charles J. Kershaw*'s starboard stern quarter and part of her iron boiler house. Outside the reef, another section of hull can be found, along with one of her bilge pumps. Small artifacts can be found all around the reef.

Location:	Abuot two miles south of Marquette on a rocky reef.
Lat/Lon:	46 30.56/87 21.81
Depth:	25 feet
Visibility:	20-40 feet
Tips:	Scout around the reef to find smaller artifacts.

**Salvaging both schooners was a difficult task
because they were high on Chocolay Beach.**

D. LEUTY

The *D. Leuty* was a wooden steamer of 647 tons and 179 feet. The vessel was caught in a blinding snowstorm on Oct. 31, 1911 while trying to enter the Marquette Harbor. Instead of making the harbor entrance, the ship ended up on a reef just outside the harbor. The remains of the steamer are located about 250 yards off Marquette's Lighthouse Point.

A large piece of the hull is located in about 30 feet of water inside the rock reef, while the reef itself is covered with broken pieces of metal. This appears to be all that is left of the ship's machinery and attests to the power of moving ice.

The rudder of the *D. Leuty* lies in about 40 feet of water a few hundred feet north of the hull wreckage.

Location:	About 250 yards off Marquette's Lighthouse Point.
Lat/Lon:	46 32.76/87 22.44
Depth:	30-40 feet
Visibility:	10-40 feet
Tips:	Search the area for small artifacts that may have broken loose over time.

GEORGE SHERMAN

The *George Sherman* was a 140-foot wooden-hulled schooner that wrecked at Shot Point. It is the easternmost wreck of the Marquette Underwater Preserve.

The schooner was carrying a load of coal to Marquette when it was caught in an autumn gale on Oct. 23, 1887. The vessel, and the schooner *Alva Bradley* (see page 171), were left stranded on Shot Point. While the *Alva Bradley* was later salvaged, the *George Sherman* went to pieces.

Three pieces of hull lie in shallow water along the east side of the point and small pieces of wreckage can be found all along that side of Shot Point.

Location:	On the east side of Shot Point east of Marquette.
Lat/Lon:	46 29.89/87 09.63
Depth:	10-12 feet
Visibility:	10-20 feet

QUEEN CITY

The schooner *Queen City* was rated at 365 tons and was hauling a cargo of firebrick, stone, and machinery for the Collins Iron Company's Collinsville blast furnace when it ran into a gale in November 1864. The ship was blown ashore while approaching Marquette.

Today, the wreck is about 150 feet offshore in shallow water and is often nearly buried in sand. When the wreck is exposed, a large part of the port side and the centerboard trunk can be seen. Part of her cargo is still intact and brick are still neatly stacked in the hold. Massive stone blocks lie nearby. This is one of the oldest shipwrecks in the preserve and can be accessed from shore and makes a good snorkel when sand isn't covering it up.

Location:	About 150 feet offshore of Chocolay Beach in 13 feet of water.
Lat/Lon:	46 29.42/87 18.64
Depth:	10-13 feet
Visibility:	10-20 feet

DeSOTO

The *DeSoto* was a wooden bark which spent nearly her entire career hauling iron ore from Marquette to lower lakes ports. The vessel was built in 1856 and was rated at 411 gross tons. On Dec. 4, 1869, a severe gale broke the *DeSoto* loose from her moorings and drove her aground on a sand beach at the south end of the Marquette Harbor.

The bones of the *DeSoto* can be found in shallow water a few hundred yards north of the Shiras Steam Plant just inside the submerged ruins of an old dock. Her cargo of 480 tons of iron ore is still in the hold, and other pieces of wreckage lie hidden in the shifting sands.

Location:	In Marquette Harbor near the Shiras Steam Plant.
Lat/Lon:	46 32.07/87 23.55
Depth:	8-10 feet
Visibility:	10-20 feet

FLORIDA

Just north of the remains of the *DeSoto* lies the wreck of the schooner *Florida*, which was blown onto the docks south of Whetstone Brook on Nov. 17, 1886. It is believed that the captain of the *Florida* misjudged the distance to shore and set an anchor too late to avoid a collision with docks in the Marquette Harbor. One crewman was lost in the disaster.

Standing frames and planking are partly buried in sand just outside the remains of an old timber-cribbed dock.

Location:	At the mouth of Whetstone Creek in Marquette Harbor.
Lat/Lon:	46 32.11/87 23.53
Depth:	6-8 feet
Visibility:	10-20 feet
Tips:	Little remains are found here but the wreck is historical.

F-106B

Not all dive sites in the Marquette Underwater Preserve involve shipwrecks. Near the Shiras Steam Plant there are the remains of an aircraft accident.

On June 12, 1974, an F-106B fighter plane from K.I. Sawyer Air Force Base lost power and crashed into Lake Superior after the pilot ejected and parachuted to safety. Although the engine and all large pieces of the airframe were salvaged, divers can still find many small pieces of the airplane buried in the sand under 22 feet of water.

Location:	Near the Shiras Steam Plant in Marquette Harbor.
Lat/Lon:	46 31.71/87 23.75
Depth:	20-22 feet
Visibility:	10-20 feet
Tips:	Probe and sift the sand to discover more small artifacts from this accident.

The FLORIDA wrecked when it ran up
against docks in the Marquette Harbor.

J.H. SHEADLE

Midway between Picnic Rocks and Presque Isle and about a quarter mile offshore is a green buoy marking a rocky reef that comes within three feet of the surface. Lying on this reef is evidence of the grounding of the steel ore freighter *J.H. Sheadle*.

The *J.H. Sheadle* was backing away from the Lake Superior & Ishpeming Railroad ore dock and making a turn to head into the lake when it struck the reef on Nov. 20, 1920. The vessel lost her rudder and at least one blade from her propeller, and remained on the reef for more than a month before being raised, patched, and towed to Detroit for extensive repairs.

Her rudder and a bucket broken from her propeller lie on the reef in 15 feet of water and the bottom nearby is strewn with iron ore dumped overboard during the salvage operation. Just inshore from the reef sits the massive water intake for the long-closed Cliffs Dow Chemical Company charcoal Plant, known to divers as the "Iron Man" for its humanoid shape.

Location:	Between Picnic Rocks and Presque Isle, about a quarter mile offshore near a green buoy.
Lat/Lon:	46 34.08/87 23.17
Depth:	15 feet
Visibility:	10-25 feet

Presque Isle Cove

This cove is a popular shore dive at Presque Isle, a city park in a wilderness setting on the north side of Marquette. The site provides a sheltered entry from a clean pebble beach. Underwater, divers can swim over some of the oldest rock on earth. The dark basalt here is criss-crossed with lighter colored mineral veins, including seams of pyrite and galena, which were mined for silver in the 1840s.

The "Gold Mine" Pinnacle

The "Gold Mine" is a pinnacle of granite rising from Lake Superior's depth to within 12 feet of the surface. It got its name from the wealth of fishing gear lost by lake trout anglers who snagged the rock.

For divers, the pinnacle offers a wall dive starting at 60 feet and dropping nearly vertically to the sand bottom at 150 feet. There are dramatic cliffs, cracks, and overhangs all around the rock at shallower depths. It is 3/4 of a mile offshore and surrounded by deep water. Visibility is usually outstanding because the site is away from shore.

Location:	About 3/4 of a mile from shore in Lake Superior northeast of Presque Isle Black Rocks.
Lat/Lon:	46 35.38/87 21.75
Depth:	12-150 feet
Visibility:	20-40 feet
Tips:	Look for lake trout in this area.

SUPERIOR & MARION L

Just as with most ports, some vessels were allowed to "molder" at their docks. Such was the case with the fish tugs *Superior* and *Marion L*. Both vessels are found inside Marquette's Lower Harbor.

The bare hull of the *Marion L* lies in about 20 feet of water along the south side of Thill's dock. Across the slip on the north side of the Association dock lies the hulk of the *Superior*. Divers should be aware of heavy boat traffic in the area.

Location:	Near Thill's Dock in Marquette's Lower Harbor.
Lat/Lon:	46 32.50/87 23.35
Depth:	18-22 feet
Visibility:	10-20 feet
Tips:	Be sure to fly a diver down flag to avoid conflicts with boat traffic.

Docks

Since Marquette has been a busy port city since the discovery of iron ore in the region in 1844, the harbor has seen dozens of docks, wharves, and piers. From the surface, it seems that most of these structures have disappeared. But underwater, the remains of the old ore, merchandise, and passenger vessel docks can be found throughout the city's waterfront.

Iron ore, pig iron bars, old bottles, and nearly anything else thrown or dropped off the docks and moored vessels may still be found on the bottom. Divers should remember, however, that artifact collecting is forbidden in Michigan's Underwater Preserves.

SOUTHWEST

The schooner *Southwest* was running in heavy fog and smoke on Sept. 18, 1898 when it ran aground 1.5 miles southeast of the largest of the Huron Islands. The captain charged that the fog whistle was not sounding at the time of the accident.

The 137-foot *Southwest* was returning from a run to the lower lakes with a load of stone. The wreck was discovered in 1978 by local divers who were guided by a fisherman, who, as a boy in the early 1900s, had seen the masts sticking out of the water.

The remains of the wreck have settled in about 100 feet of water. Pieces of the hull are scattered but many artifacts can be found. Many fittings are still within a 100-foot radius of the main hull sections. At the bow, one of the anchors and the windlass can be seen. The deck lies on top of the keel and bottom framing.

Location:	Southeast of the easternmost of the Huron Islands.
Lat/Lon:	46 56.42/87 56.11
Depth:	90-100 feet
Visibility:	20-40 feet

ARCTIC

The steamer *Arctic* was a 237-foot sidewheeler that wrecked at Huron Island in a fog on May 28, 1860 while loaded with passengers and freight.

The *Arctic* struck the rocks with great force and was quickly abandoned. A storm the following day damaged the ship beyond hope of pulling it off. The ship's machinery was recovered.

The remains of the ship are badly broken up by waves and ice but there are many artifacts still at the site. Sand sometimes covers parts of the wreck in shallow water. The remains are scattered along the east side of the island but a great deal of wreckage remains at the point of impact. Artifacts, including parts of her engine and paddle wheels, can be found on a steeply sloping field of boulders dropping from 5 to 60 feet. Much of her framing lies at the bottom of the slope.

A large section of the *Arctic*'s starboard bow can be found in about 20 feet of water in the channel just south of Lighthouse Island. The steamer's massive single-cylinder steam engine was removed frm the wreck and brought to shallow water for partial salvage. Much of the engine and its massive framing can be found just northwest of the boathouse.

Location:	In shallow water at the northernmost of the Huron Islands.
Lat/Lon:	46 57.74/87 59.85
Depth:	5-100 feet
Visibility:	10-30 feet

GEORGE NESTER

The *George Nester* was a 207-foot schooner-barge that broke her tow in a storm on April 30, 1909. The ship was in the tow of the steamer *Schoolcraft*.

The schooner was driven onto the Huron Islands where it broke up against sheer cliffs within five minutes. Seven of the ship's crew, including her captain, were lost in the disaster.

The *George Nester* was constructed in Baraga, Mich. in 1887 for the lumber and iron ore trades.

Sections of the hull are scattered over a 100-yard radius and because this wreck is relatively remote, many small artifacts remain. Note that the debris field here is about 1/4 mile north of the wreck of the *Arctic*.

Location: Near the lighthouse on Huron Island.
Lat/Lon: 46 57.99/88 00.20
Depth: 20-100 feet
Visibility: 20-40 feet

HURON ISLAND

Just north of the rocks on the north side of the channel between Lighthouse Island and the next island lie the remains of a 40-foot wooden launch. The collapsed hull lies on its side, with its two-cylinder engine partly buried in the sand. It is believed that this may be the wreck of the lighthouse launch *Huron Island*, lost in 1922. The depth here is about 15 feet and visibility is usually excellent.

Big Bay Lumber Dock

If divers get "weathered out" of a dive at the Huron Islands, or if divers just want to enjoy a nice shore dive, the old dock, a few hundred yards north of the Big Bay Harbor of Refuge can provide an interesting dive. The dock was linked to the sawmill at Big Bay by a rail line, and one of the old rail cars can be seen off the north side of the dock. Other artifacts can also be found among the old timber cribs and ballast stones.

Black Rocks

This site is popular among divers interested in unusual geologic formations. Some of the oldest rock formations in Michigan are at this site at the northernmost tip of Presque Isle Park.

Black Rocks is accessible from shore and offers spectacular snorkeling. It is also a popular night-diving site. The depth here is 10 to 50 feet with 20 to 40 feet of visibility. Gamefish are often spotted here.

The lighthouse at Marquette warned many sailors of the dangers of the area.

Inland Dive Sites

As with the Keweenaw Underwater Preserve, this area contains flooded iron ore mine shafts that are sometimes dove. But these sites are extremely dangerous because they are deep and visibility is often reduced.

There are at least 12 inland lakes with public access sites. Most of these lakes have rocky bottoms and, as a result, water clarity is excellent. Of these lakes, consider diving in Bass Lake, Big Shag Lake, and Little Shag Lake. Schools of friendly gamefish are found in these lakes, which also make for good snorkeling.

Other Attractions

Marquette was once an industrial city. It was a place for loading iron ore and little else. But the city has changed and readily adapted to the tourist industry. In addition to fine restaurants, the city offers a maritime museum and excellent shopping in unique shops downtown, which is a short walk from the harbor.

Excellent art galleries are found at the Marquette County Historical museum on North Front Street and at other locations downtown. Visitors will find that Marquette residents value history and, as a result, have taken great pains to restore magnificent historic homes that overlook the harbor.

One of the main features of the city is Presque Isle Park, which juts northward into Lake Superior. This 300-acre park is one of 23 in the city and offers a great place to relax or picnic. Also, two shore-access dive sites are found here.

Unique adventures are available through Marquette Country Tours, (906) 226-6167.

Be sure to mark your calendar for the *Henry B. Smith* Memorial Weekend when a variety of activities are planned for divers and maritime history buffs. More information about this fun event is available by contacting Diver Down Scuba at (906) 225-1699.

Emergencies

Marquette hosts a U.S. Coast Guard Station, which can be reached on vhf channels 9 or 16 in case of an on-water emergency. If stricken divers reach shore, then the Marquette County Sheriff's Department should be contacted to coordinate emergency medical services. The telephone number of the sheriff's department is: (906) 228-6980. Divers should be aware that Marquette General, the major hospital of the region, has a recompression chamber to handle diving medical emergencies. The hospital is only 1.5 miles from the Coast Guard Station.

Extra patrols through the preserve area are performed during the summer months, holidays, and on weekends.

Getting There

Marquette lies on the shores of Lake Superior appoximately in the center of the Upper Peninsula. Main highway serving Marquette is US 41, sometimes referred to as M-28. This highway, as M-28, runs approximately east and west through the Upper Peninsula. Although it is a two-lane roadway, traffic moves swiftly.

Marquette also has a modern airport that is served by commuter airlines.

Accommodations

Because Marquette is a major city with many tourist attractions, overnight accommodations in the form of motels, hotels, and campgrounds, are plentiful. But as with any popular tourist destination, it is best to make reservations early to avoid disappointments. Contact the Marquette Visitors and Convention Bureau at (906) 228-7749 for complete information about lodging options in this area.

Important Addresses/Telephone Numbers

U.S. Coast Guard Station (Marquette)
(906) 226-3312

Cinder Pond Marina
300 W. Baraga Ave.
Marquette, MI 49855
(906) 228-0469

Marquette Country Convention & Visitors Bureau
(906) 228-7749

Marquette General Hospital
515 W. College Ave.
Marquette, MI 49855
(906) 228-9440
(800) 562-9753

Diver Down Scuba
717 N. Third St.
Marquette, MI 49855
(906) 225-1699
(Air station, equipment, instruction)

Marquette County Sheriff's Dept.
(906) 228-0464

Presque Isle Marina
300 W. Baraga Ave.
Marquette, MI 49855
(906) 228-0464

Marquette Country Tours
(906) 226-6167

Upper Peninsula Travel &
Recreation Association
P.O. Box 400
Iron Mountain, MI 49801
(906) 774-5480
(800) 562-7134

Underwater Rapture
N5383 M-95
Iron Mountain, MI 49801
(906) 779-1101
(charters)

Sanilac Shores
Underwater Preserve

The Sanilac Shores Underwater Preserve includes 163 square miles of Lake Huron bottomland. The area contains a collection of ten major shipwrecks in 15 to 100 feet of water.

Ships went down in this area primarily as a result of accidents or rough weather. The Sanilac Shores Underwater Preserve is enjoying increasing popularity because of its proximity to the bulk of the state's population and the discovery of new shipwrecks in the area.

Two of the shipwrecks in this preserve are the result of the Big Storm of 1913. This was arguably one of the worst storms on Lake Huron and perhaps the entire Great Lakes. In all, before the storm had blown itself out, forty ships and 235 lives were lost on the Great Lakes.

Some say the staggering loss was the result of captains' negligence and failure to heed storm warnings. But others and history remember the Nov. 10-13 storm as simply one of the most fierce and devastating events in Great Lakes history. To maritime historians, then, the storm of 1913 is always referred to as the "Big Storm" and an appropriate amount of reverence for the destruction it wrought.

The preserve was established following the discovery of the *Regina*, a 250-package freighter that went down in the Big Storm of 1913. The wreck had eluded wreck finders for several decades before it was discovered by an ardent group of expert scuba divers.

Initially, state officials considered designating only that single wreck site as an underwater preserve but interested sport divers recognized the need to have a much broader area designated so that other valuable dive sites could be protected.

Visibility in this area is variable because the bottom is frequently comprised of fine silt. Wave action and currents sometime disturb these fine sediments and cause reduced visibility. But visibility is rarely reduced to less than four feet and sometimes, visibility is as much as 25 feet.

A group of local sport divers and charter operators are amateur maritime archaeologists. Much of the information known about the shipwrecks in this area is the result of their research. That group hopes to establish an interpretive center so that divers and nondivers alike will be able to learn about and enjoy the maritime heritage represented by the shipwrecks of this region.

August through October are the best months to dive this area because of increased visibility during that period.

An informative book, "Shipwrecks of Sanilac," contains many historical and underwater photos of the wrecks found in this preserve. The book is available through book stores, dive centers, or directly from Lakeshore Charters and Marine Exploration, Inc., 4658 S. Lakeshore, Lexington, MI 48450.

Boating

Aside from commercial shipping traffic using an established, busy route, boaters in this region have no unusual concerns. With some exceptions, Lake Huron in this area is not particularly riddled with hidden shoals, confusing bays, and other navigational hazards. As always on the Great Lakes, boaters must be aware of other boat traffic and sudden weather changes.

Marinas with complete services are available in Lexington and Port Sanilac. They offer transient accommodations, gas, water, electricity, pump outs, restrooms, showers, and monitor vhf channel 16.

Boat launching facilities are available at or near both marinas as well as at the Sanilac State Park in Forestville.

Most of the shipwrecks in this preserve are buoyed with mooring buoys maintained by local divers.

COLONEL A.B. WILLIAMS

The *Colonel A.B. Williams* was a 110-foot schooner that became lost in a storm in 1864 while carrying a cargo of coal. It is the oldest shipwreck of the Sanilac Shores Underwater Preserve.

The wreck was discovered in 1957 when a diver went down to investigate tangled commercial fishing nets. The *Colonel A.B. Williams* was found in about 85 feet of water, sitting upright and in excellent condition.

Although the stern has fallen away and the masts and cabin are missing, the rest of the wreck is intact with a variety of equipment still on the deck. In the 1960s, divers removed anchors, wheel and steering gears. One of the anchors off the Colonel A.B. Williams is displayed at the Sanilac Historical Museum in Port Sanilac.

Divers enjoy exploring the cargo hold and other portions of the wreck. This vessel was typical of the small schooners that were once the backbone of Great Lakes commerce.

Location:	About 12.5 miles northeast of Port Sanilac.
Loran:	30779.1/49407.2
Lat/Lon:	43 36.470/82 30.670
Depth:	75-85 feet
Visibility:	5-25 feet
Tips:	Because the stern has fallen away, part of the aft cargo area is exposed and provides interesting diving.

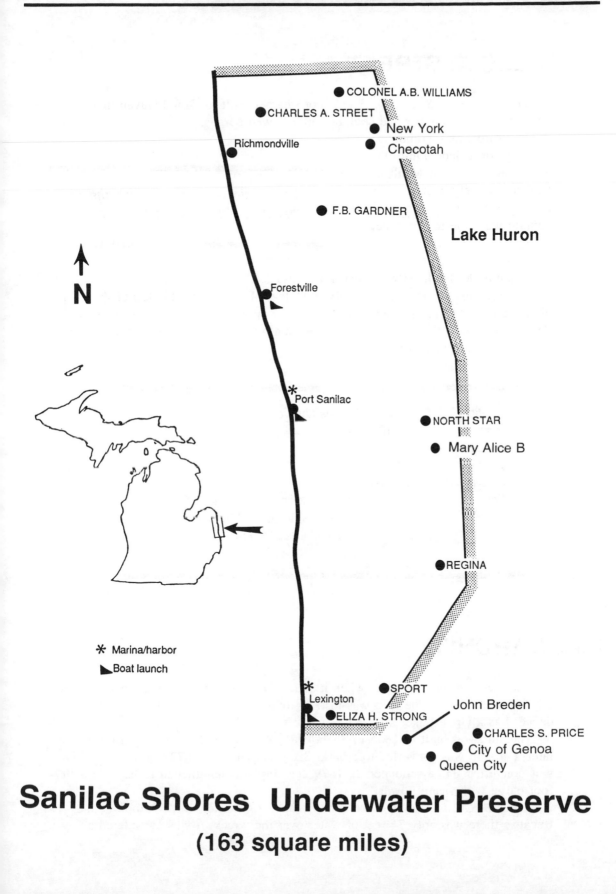

Sanilac Shores Underwater Preserve
(163 square miles)

CHARLES A. STREET

The *Charles A. Street* was a 165-foot steamer built in Grand Haven in 1888. The ship carried lumber and coal and often towed barges.

The ship was southbound, heading for Toledo, Ohio on July 20, 1908, when it suddenly caught fire--a relatively common malady among these early steamers. The captain was able to bring the *Charles A. Street* up on a reef about a mile north of Richmondville. No lives were lost in the disaster.

> **The captain was able to bring the *Charles A. Street* up on a reef.**

The remains of the ship lie in about 15 feet of water with the top of the engine about four feet from the water's surface. The boiler is missing but some ribs and decking remain. Like most shipwrecks in shallow water, it has been badly broken up by the forces of waves and ice.

Location:	About 11.5 miles north of Port Sanilac.
Loran:	30818.2/49413.1
Lat/Lon:	43 35.50/82 27.50
Depth:	4-15 feet
Visibility:	5-25 feet
Tips:	This is a good snorkeling site. Because it is shallow and there is ample light, underwater photographers find it appealing.

F.B. GARDNER

The *F.B. Gardner* was lost when it suddenly caught fire while in tow on Sept. 15, 1904. But before the ship was lost, it saw many changes during its nearly five decades as a Great Lakes vessel.

The ship was built in 1855 in Sheboygan, Wis. as a 139-foot brig. Eleven years later, the ship was converted to a bark. Six years later, in 1872, the *F.B. Gardner* was converted into a schooner. In 1879, the ship was lengthened to become a 177-foot barge with steam power.

The *F.B. Gardner* burned and sank in 50 feet of water in the shipping lane. Because there was only 34 feet of water over the wreck, it was considered a hazard to navigation and dynamited.

Today, the *F.B. Gardner* is scattered but equipment at the site makes diving interesting. The equipment includes a large windlass with chain.

The remains of the vessel are badly broken up but it is a good dive site for those who like to prowl the bottom and make discoveries.

Location:	6.5 miles northeast of Port Sanilac
Loran:	30802.4/49407.2
Lat/Lon:	43 31.63/82 31.77
Depth:	50-55 feet
Visibility:	5-25 feet
Tips:	Wreckage is scattered. Search the area to find a variety of equipment and artifacts.

NORTH STAR

The *North Star* was a 300-foot steamer that was built in Cleveland, Ohio in 1888. It had a steel hull and in its first year on the Great Lakes was involved in a collision with the *Charles J. Shefield*, which sank without loss of life.

In 1898, the *North Star* ran aground to avoid another collision in the St. Mary's River. The vessel was pulled off successfully.

On Nov. 25, 1908, the *North Star* was headed to Buffalo, N.Y. from Duluth, Minn. with a load of grain and shingles when it ran into a thick fog. In this fog, the package freighter *North Star* struck its sister ship, the *Northern Queen*. The *North Star* took the blow on her starboard bow and sank quickly, but there was no loss of life.

The ship lies upright, in two pieces, with the pilot house intact on the bow and the engine and boiler on the stern. Divers can explore the pilot house and cargo holds of the *North Star*. The ship is basically broken in half and wreckage extends for about 400 feet.

Location:	About 5.5 miles southeast of Port Sanilac, 10 miles northeast of Lexington.
Loran:	30787.3/49508.1
Lat/Lon:	42 23.954/82 26.524
Depth:	85-100 feet
Visibility:	5-20 feet
Tips:	Visibility is variable on this wreck, a line reel is advised so that divers can locate the ascent line. Divers should be aware of gill netting on certain parts of the wreck.

REGINA

**The REGINA was a 250-foot freighter that sank
in the Big Storm of 1913.**

The *Regina* was a 250-foot, steel-hulled package freighter built in Scotland in 1907. Although the *Regina* served Great Lakes ports without incident for many years, its demise caused wide speculation that continues today.

The *Regina* was caught in the Big Storm of Nov. 10-13, 1913. The ship was lost with all hands and, days later, bodies washed ashore from the *Regina* and other ships, including the *Charles S. Price* (see page 207). Speculation began when it was reported that at least one body of a *Charles S. Price* sailor washed ashore wearing a *Regina* life belt.

Some theorized that the two ships collided during the storm and sailors from the *Charles S. Price* managed to grab *Regina* life belts during the

> *Some theorized that the two ships collided during the storm and sailors from the Charles S. Price managed to grab Regina life belts during the collision.*

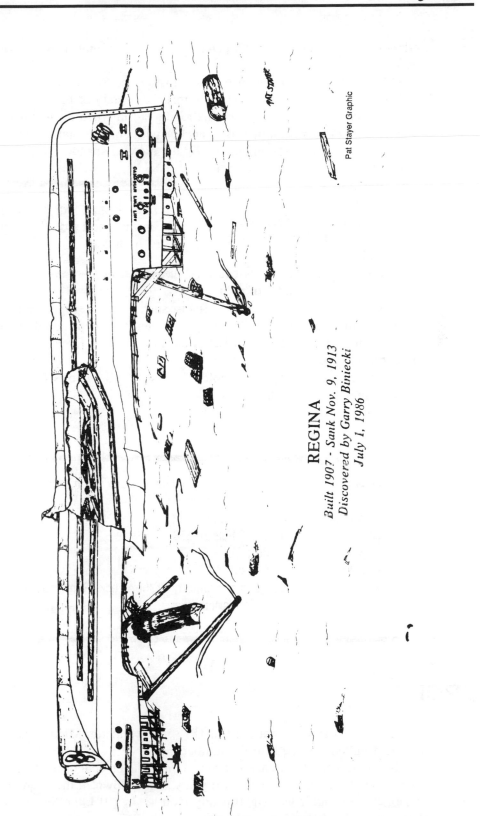

REGINA
Built 1907 - Sank Nov. 9, 1913
Discovered by Garry Biniecki
July 1, 1986

Pat Stayer Graphic

collision. The condition of the *Regina* was a mystery until it was discovered in 1986.

Although there is no evidence of a collision, there is a hole in the bottom of the ship's hull. Some divers now speculate that the captain of the *Regina* tried to run close to shore to find shelter from the raging storm when it ran aground.

When the *Regina* sank, it was at anchor with engines and electrical systems shut down. This indicates an attempt by the crew to abandon ship.

The *Regina* rests on the bottom upside down in about 80 feet of water. The keel is about 55 feet from the surface. There is a 56-foot hole in the *Regina*'s port side that exposes the cargo holds.

There is a 56-foot hole in the Regina's port side that exposes the cargo holds.

A permit to salvage was issued for part of the cargo, but little of value was removed from the ship. Key artifacts, such as the *Regina*'s bell, were removed for display in area museums. The *Regina* is generally considered one of the most attractive dive sites in the Great Lakes because it was a large ship that was conserved for sport divers.

Divers can explore the cargo hold of the ship and a debris field nearby offers the opportunity for new discoveries.

Location:	About 6.5 miles northeast of Lexington, about 7.5 miles southeast of Port Sanilac.
Loran:	30801.7/49534.9
Lat/Lon:	43 20.434/82 26.878
Depth:	55-80 feet
Visibility:	5-25 feet
Tips:	Cargo is scattered near the wreck. Remember that collecting is forbidden.

SPORT

The *Sport* was a tugboat built in 1873 in Wyandotte, Mich. It was 57 feet long and steel-hulled designed for the lumber industry.

The *Sport* started her career towing lumber-laden schooners around the Ludington, Mich. harbor. After two years, a slowdown in the economy forced the sale of the tug and it was significantly rebuilt. In 1913, the *Sport* was sold to a Port Huron, Mich. towing company.

On Dec. 13, 1920, after years of reliable service from Detroit to southern Lake

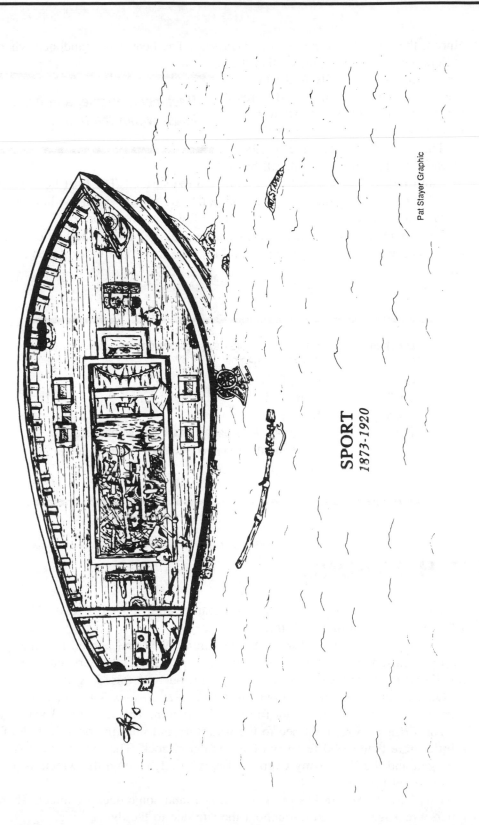

SPORT
1873-1920

Pat Stayer Graphic

Huron, the *Sport* found herself in heavy seas. The boat was abandoned when its boilers went out, which meant that the water was rising steadily in the bilge. The captain and crew managed to row three hours in a lifeboat to shore near Lexington.

Machinery, engine, and boiler are intact within the hull.

The *Sport* was discovered in 1987 in about 50 feet of water with all but its cabin intact. The port rail is 33 feet from the surface. The boat lies upright with a starboard list. Machinery, engine, and boiler are intact within the hull. Many artifacts are on the *Sport*'s deck or within a few feet on the bottom.

The *Sport* is a popular dive sites because of its relatively shallow depth and great underwater photography opportunities. The *Sport* can be explored on a single tank.

Location:	About three miles east of Lexington
Loran:	30824.9/49569.2
Lat/Lon:	43 15.98/82 27.93
Depth:	45-60 feet
Visibility:	5-25 feet
Tips:	The propeller, steering chain and wheel lie a few feet from the wreck. A historical marker is found at this site.

ELIZA H. STRONG

The *Eliza H. Strong* was a 205-foot steamer built in Marine City, Mich. in 1874. It was a ship that sunk three times.

On May 3, 1895, the *Eliza H. Strong* ran aground and burned in Lake Erie. The ship was raised and refitted in Buffalo, N.Y. in 1899. Two years later, the ship foundered in rough weather in Lake Superior, but was raised again.

On Oct. 26, 1904, luck ran out for the *Eliza H. Strong*. The ship had a schooner in tow when it caught fire near Lexington. The crew of 13 was saved.

The *Eliza H. Strong* burned to the waterline and sank in about 25 feet of water, a little more than 4,000 feet from the Lexington dock. The machinery was salvaged and the U.S. Army Corps of Engineers dynamited the wreck as a navigational hazard.

The *Eliza H. Strong* lies upright with keel and some decking intact. There is much wreckage scattered throughout the site due to the dynamiting.

Location:	Less than one miles east of Lexington dock.
Loran:	30847.0/49570.4
Lat/Lon:	43 15.709/82 30.581
Depth:	25-30 feet
Tips:	This is a good dive for beginners but visibility can be reduced depending on weather conditions.

CHARLES S. PRICE

The *Charles S. Price* was a 504-foot freighter that was built in 1910. It became one of many victims of the Big Storm of November 1913.

The ship was caught in the storm that began brewing on Nov. 9 and continued for 76 hours. At this time, steel hulls were relatively new to Great Lakes shipbuilding and many captains placed too much confidence in what they believed were "indestructible" hulls. But for many that autumn, 90 mph winds and 40-foot waves were too much.

After the storm subsided, the hull of a capsized ship was spotted off the Port Huron lighthouse station. For several days, the ship drifted in the shipping lanes unidentified and was dubbed "the mystery ship". Finally, a diver was able to determine that the black hull was that of the *Charles S. Price.*

For several days, the ship drifted in the shipping lanes unidentified and was dubbed "the mystery ship".

A few days after the ship was identified, the *Charles S. Price* rolled on her side and sank in about 65 feet of water. Today, the ship lies upside down on the bottom. Twenty-eight crewmen and her captain were lost in the disaster.

The bow of the *Charles S. Price* faces south and there are several large holes in the hull, which permit divers to explore the interior of the cargo holds.

Location:	About 11 miles southeast (141 degrees) of Lexington Harbor.
Loran:	30799.6/49622.5
Lat/Lon:	43 09.174/82 21.174
Depth:	35-70 feet
Visibility:	5-25 feet
Tips:	Use caution if exploring inside the hull.

CHECOTAH

The *Checotah* is one of the more recent discoveries in the Sanilac Shores Underwater Preserve. Local divers have done an excellent job of research and documentation of the wreck.

The *Checotah* was a scow schooner built in 1870 in Toledo, Ohio. It was a ship that hauled bulk freight and sank more than once. In 1882, the ship sank in the St. Mary's River with a loss of three lives. Six years later, the *Checotah* was raised and used as a schooner barge to haul lumber.

On Oct. 30, 1906, while being towed, the heavily loaded vessel began to founder in rough seas. It was separated from other vessels and the crew of seven managed to launch a yawl and save themselves. It was not unusual for the captain of the steamer towing schooner barges to simply cut the towing howser with a knife and leave the occupants on the barge to fend for themselves.

The location of the shipwreck was discovered in 1988. The stern of the wreck is broken and scattered but the rest of the wreck is mostly intact. Much of the equipment remains on the bow and there are many small artifacts associated with this site. Visibility is sometimes very low here so caution should be exercised.

The wreck of the *New York* lies close to the wreck of the *Checotah*.

Location:	Approximately 12.2 miles from Port Sanilac on a bearing of 22 degrees.
Loran:	30761.3/49413.5
Lat/Lon:	43 36.08/82 28.16
Depth:	90-115 feet
Visibility:	2-10 feet
Tips:	Visibility is not great on this wreck. Consider using a dive reel and line.

NEW YORK

The wreck of the *New York* lies relatively close to that of the *Checotah*.

The *New York* was built in 1856 and started out her life on the Great Lakes as a luxurious passenger ship running between Buffalo, N.Y. and Toledo, Ohio. This Lake Erie run occupied much of the vessel's 20 years of service, which saw several serious accidents with other ships.

In 1874, the *New York* ran aground and was considered a total loss by her owners. But the insurance company sold the wrecked vessel to a new owner who

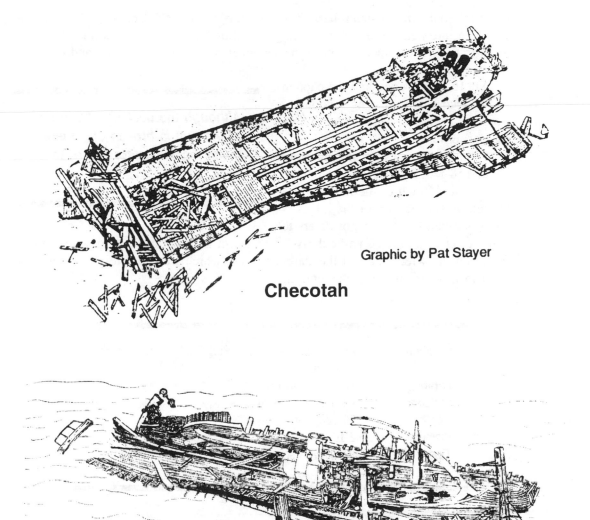

Graphic by Pat Stayer

Checotah

NEW YORK
1856 - Oct. 13, 1876
Found Aug. 12, 1988

Drawing by Pat Stayer

had her rebuilt into a steam barge for the lumber trade. On Oct. 13, 1876, the *New York* ran into heavy seas while hauling a load of lumber from Georgian Bay, Ont. to Buffalo. The steamer cut loose the schooner barges it was towing and began to take on water rapidly.

All 16 of the crew and the captain were saved by the passing schooner, *Nemesis*, which lost one of her crew in the daring rescue.

Although the decking and much of the hull is broken up, there is much machinery for divers to explore.

Today, the *New York* lies upright in about 118 feet of water. Although the decking and much of the hull is broken up (at the turn of the bilge), there is much machinery for divers to explore. Divers may be particularly interested in the twin oscillating steam engines found on the wreck. Part of the starboard arch, which was used to give strength to the 185-foot steamer, remains upright.

Location:	About 12.3 miles from Port Sanilac on a bearing of 22 degrees.
Loran:	30761.0/49411.9
Lat/Lon:	43 36.23/82 28.24
Depth:	90-120 feet
Visibility:	2-10 feet
Tips:	Visibility is sometimes very low. Use caution.

QUEEN CITY

The *Queen City* was a 292-foot steamer that was built in 1848 in Buffalo, N.Y. The ship was one of the earliest steamers on the Great Lakes and sported a side paddle wheel.

The *Queen City* saw much trouble in her first six years on the Great Lakes. She experienced groundings and sinkings and was eventually converted into a steam lumber barge.

On Aug. 17, 1863, the ship was in tow of the tug *Eagle* when the *Queen City* struck a reef off Lexington. The tow line snapped and the crew managed to escape without loss of life before the ship quickly broke up and went to the bottom.

Today, divers find the wreck in 50 feet of water in a broken up condition. The length of the remains is 142 feet and portions of the wooden arch are found. Some miscellaneous equipment and artifacts are found here as well. This is a good site for beginning wreck divers.

Location:	About 9.3 miles south east from Lexington Harbor.
Loran:	30831.2/49622.3
Lat/Lon:	43 09.18/82 25.77
Depth:	45-51 feet
Visibility:	10-20 feet
Tips:	Take time to look around and see the early construction techniques used on the Great Lakes' first steamers.

JOHN BREDEN

The *John Breden* was a three-masted schooner built in 1862 at Port Dalhousie, Ont. It was 130-feet long and had a beam of 25 feet.

The ship had a history of neglect and rough use as its owners were barely solvent much of the time. Still, the vessel managed to serve the Great Lakes shipping industry for 37 years, a long time for a sailing vessel of the period.

On July 21, 1899, the ship was heading up Lake Huron toward Bay City, Mich. with a load of 600 tons of coal when it was hit by a northernly gale. The ship began to break up quickly as it neared Lexington. Heavy seas eventually claimed the vessel and three of her crew.

Today, the *John Breden* is little more than a wide debris field on the bottom of Lake Huron. Wreckage is spread over an area 600 feet long and divers will find the ship's wheel, windlass, and anchors here. Little remains of the decking and hull structure.

Location:	About 5.4 miles southeast of Lexington Harbor.
Loran:	30823.4/49595.7
Lat/Lon:	43 12.26/82 26.31
Depth:	About 50 feet
Visibility:	10-20 feet
Tips:	The debris field here is long and wide. Consider using a line or long tape measure to cover it thoroughly.

CITY OF GENOA

The *City of Genoa* was a 301-foot steamer built in 1892 in West Bay City, Mich. This was a period when many shipbuilders were changing over to steel hulls but this builder, James Davidson, constructed this vessel from wood.

The *City of Genoa* caught fire in 1892 and received a rebuild that increased its cargo capacity. In November 1911, the ship was bound for Buffalo with a load of 125,000 bushels of wheat when it ran into a dense fog on the St. Clair River. It had a collision with the steamer *Gilbert* and sank. Later that year it was raised and the cargo was salvaged.

Two years later, in 1913, the engines and boilers of the *City of Genoa* were removed while at her docks in Port Huron. In the fall of 1915, vandals set the ship on fire and it was eventually scuttled in Lake Huron.

> *This wreck was known by some as the "Wheelbarrow Wreck" because of a wheelbarrow that was found resting on the deck.*

Today, the wreck, which was burned to her waterline, lies in 64 feet of water southeast of Lexington Harbor. Divers will find some of the decking intact and parts of the remains rise 12 feet from the bottom. The propeller, shaft, and associated machinery is also intact.

This wreck was known by some as the "Wheelbarrow Wreck" because of a wheelbarrow that was found resting on the deck. This is a good wreck for beginning wreck divers.

Location:	About 11.4 miles southeast of Lexington Harbor.
Loran:	30805.1/49624.9
Lat/Lon:	43 08.78/82 22.31
Depth:	50-65 feet
Visibility:	10-20 feet

MARY ALICE B

The *Mary Alice B* was a 65-foot tugboat built in 1931 in Duluth, Minn. The steel-hulled tug was built specifically for the U.S. Army Corps of Engineers but was owned by several others during her 44 years of service on the eastern Great Lakes.

The tug was used for a variety of purposes and was constructed much like the *Steven M. Selvick*, which was intentionally sunk in the Alger Underwater Preserve as a sport diving attraction (see page 80). City class tugs, such as the *Mary Alice B,* are still used today for marine construction and salvage purposes. They generally tow or push barges with construction material. Interestingly, the tug was used in the salvage operations of the *Nordmeer* (see page 314 and *Monrovia* (see page 313).

In 1975, the *Mary Alice B* was bound for Detroit from Rockport, Mich. and was being towed by another tugboat. The crew decided to stop in Port Sanilac for the evening and to check on the tug when they discovered that it was taking on water rapidly.

Some caution is warranted when in the engine room because silt tends to cloud the area if divers are not careful with their fins.

The *Mary Alice B* was cut loose from her tow as pumps would not keep her afloat. It sank quickly and rests upright on the bottom of Lake Huron in about 90 feet of water.

The divers who visit this wreck will find her in excellent condition with much of her still intact, including the wheel, pilot house, and engine compartment. All of these areas can be explored by divers although some caution is warranted when in the engine room because silt tends to cloud the area if divers are not careful with their fins.

Location:	About 6.2 miles east-southeast of Port Sanilac.
Loran:	30790.8/49520.5
Lat/Lon:	43 22.34/82 26.31
Depth:	60-95 feet
Visibility:	10-20 feet
Tips:	Use fins carefully in engine room to avoid visibility reduction.

MARY ALICE B.
Built 1931-Sank Sept. 5, 1975
Discovered July 8, 1992

Drawing by Pat Stayer

Note: The wrecks of the *Aztec, Province,* and *Sachem*, collectively known as the "Ghost Fleet of St. Clair River," are not covered in this chapter. Many dive charter operators serving the Sanilac Shores Underwater Preserve also serve the Ghost Fleet. See page ??? on the St. Clair River for information on the Ghost Fleet.

Accommodations

Because this area does not attract many tourists, overnight accommodations are somewhat limited.

Campers can find a private campground in Lexington and the Lakeport State Park north of Port Huron offer campsites.

Limited motel and resort accommodations are located in Lexington and Port Sanilac. Some such facilities are found in Croswell and Sandusky. For more information, contact the Lexington Chamber of Commerce at (810) 359-2262.

Emergencies

Divers with medical emergencies can contact the U.S. Coast Guard Station at Harbor Beach, (517) 479-3285. Another contact is the Sanilac County Sheriff's Department in Sandusky, (810) 648-2000. Both agencies have patrol boats capable of responding to on-water emergencies.

The Sanilac County Sheriff's Department dispatches ambulances in Lexington and Port Sanilac.

Important Addresses/Phone Numbers

U.S. Coast Guard Station
Harbor Beach, MI 48441
(517) 479-3285

Sanilac County Sheriff's Department
65 N. Elk St.
Sandusky, MI 48471
(810) 648-2000

Greater Port Sanilac Business Assn.
P.O. Box 402
Port Sanilac, MI 48469

Lexington Chamber of Commerce
Lexington, MI 48450
(810) 359-2262

Fatham Four (air station)
Port Sanilac, MI 48469
(810) 622-3483

Charter Operators:

Lakeshore Charters & Marine Exploration, Inc.
4658 S. Lakeshore
Lexington, MI 48450
(810) 359-8660

Macomb Scuba
13465 E. 12 Mile Road
Warren, MI 48093
(810) 558-9922

Fathom Four
Port Sanilac, MI 48469
(810) 622-3483

Sport

The tug *Sport*, one of the nation's earliest steel-hulled vessels, was built for lumber and steel entrepreneur Eber Brock Ward in 1873 by the Wyandotte Iron Ship Building Works in Wyandotte, Michigan. For forty-seven years the tug towed, salvaged, and aided vessels in distress. Frank E. Kirby designed the tug and later became a nationally known navel architect recognized for designing large, elegant sidewheel passenger steamers and ice-breaking car ferries such as *Chief Wawatam*. In 1913, *Sport* was purchased by Captain Robert Thompson of Port Huron.

BUREAU OF HISTORY, MICHIGAN DEPARTMENT OF STATE
REGISTERED STATE SITE NO. 636
PROPERTY OF THE STATE OF MICHIGAN, 1992

Sport

Sport's final voyage began on the afternoon of December 13, 1920, when it departed Port Huron bound for Harbor Beach. The tug fought heavy seas and by 6:00 p. m. was taking on more water than the pumps could handle. Near Lexington, the seasick fire-tender crawled to his bunk. The unattended fire died, the boat lost steam, and the pumps quit. The six-man crew abandoned ship in a lifeboat around 11:00 p.m. when waves crashed over the deck. The crew washed ashore near Lexington, cold and exhausted but alive. *Sport* sank and was not discovered until 1987.

BUREAU OF HISTORY, MICHIGAN DEPARTMENT OF STATE
REGISTERED STATE SITE NO. 636
PROPERTY OF THE STATE OF MICHIGAN, 1992

Southwest Michigan Underwater Preserve

The maritime heritage of southwest Michigan is especially rich because of the variety and duration of human activity. Native Americans, for example, likely found the region's network of rivers and lakes a convenient means of transportation.

Because rivers eventually flow into Lake Michigan, it is reasonable to expect that the near-shore waters were used by Native Americans on relatively calm days. Dugout and birch bark canoes and similar small craft were likely the only means of water transportation available to them.

European settlement came to southwestern Michigan in the early 1800s. Land was cleared and tilled and

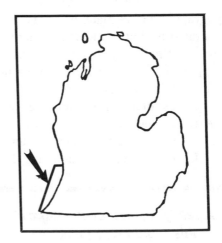

> **Because there were few natural harbors and river mouths often filled with sand, piers were constructed on Lake Michigan bottomland.**

Native Americans soon found opportunities for trading a greater variety of goods. By 1835, Native Americans were nearly completely displaced and small coastal communities sprang up and grew into agricultural and industrial centers.

In addition to agricultural activities, the region was also an important source of timber and tanbark. It was necessary to clear the land of trees before planting could begin and entrepreneurs found a ready market for lumber.

Because there were few natural harbors and river mouths often filled with sand, piers were constructed on Lake Michigan bottomland to accommodate growing shipping activity. Also, South Haven, St. Joseph, Holland, Saugatuck, and other coastal communities enjoyed a steady shipbuilding industry. Historical photos of area harbors depict busy ports jammed with lumber hookers, scow schooners, and steamers.

Several saw mills were once located

on the Black River near its mouth in the mid to late 1800s. Millions of board feet of lumber were loaded from the mills onto waiting lumber hookers, which were relatively small steamboats designed to carry lumber on its deck for delivery to Great Lakes ports. Schooners and larger steamboats were also used to transport lumber from South Haven and other coastal communities.

Fruit growing was an early practice in southwestern Michigan. The soil, topography, and climate, which is moderated by Lake Michigan, offers prime fruit-growing conditions. Orchards of apples, pears, and peaches in the mid to late 1800s were later supplemented with grapes, blueberries, and other crops.

A ready market for fruits growing in this region was found in Chicago and other Lake Michigan communities. In

A ready market for fruits growing in this region was found in Chicago and other Lake Michigan communities.

addition to the fruit, related industries arose, such as basket factories. A large basket factory was founded in South Haven in 1879 and canning companies were established in and near South Haven in the 1890s.

Commercial shipping, particularly small package freighters, were used to transport various fruit products across the Great Lakes to markets in rapidly growing coastal communities. With this fruit travelled accounts of the region's beauty, parks, entertainment, resorts, and natural resources. These accounts gave rise to the region's important resort industry.

Piers were constructed to keep the mouth of the Black River from becoming too shallow from drifting sand and served this purpose well. Freighters carried goods to and from South Haven readily and this ease of navigation also facilitated passenger travel to and from the port.

Chicago was the primary market for the region's resorts. Large passenger steamers made regular runs between Chicago and South Haven for several decades beginning in the 1880s. Once in South Haven, passengers had the option of taking smaller vessels up the Black River to a variety of parks and pavilions. Passengers could also remain in South Haven where there were several large dance pavilions and hotels to accommodate fun seekers.

There were several passenger lines that offered rapid service between Chicago and South Haven. These lines included goodrich, East Shore, Dunkley Williams, and South Haven. A regular visitor to South Haven was the *Eastland*. This steamer often competed with others on the South Haven-Chicago route. In 1915, while waiting in the Chicago River Harbor to depart for a day trip to Michigan City, the *Eastland* capsized and more than 800 lives were lost in the

The Eastland tragedy did not dampen enthusiasm for South Haven resorts.

worst Great Lakes maritime disaster in history.

The *Eastland* tragedy did not dampen enthusiasm for South Haven resorts. Many docks were constructed at the

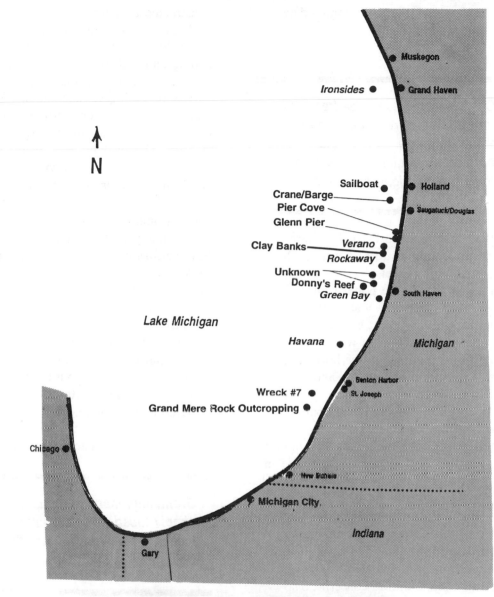

Southwest Michigan Underwater Preserve

South Haven Harbor to accommodate the bustling resort trade.

Although the glory days of schooners

> **Calm summer evenings frequently find scores of red, green, and white lights dancing on the horizon as boaters leisurely cruise the Lake Michigan shoreline.**

and steamships is past, southwestern Michigan continues to host a large fleet of recreational vessels. Trout, salmon, and perch fishing are popular and so is water skiing, personal watercraft, and cruising. Calm summer evenings frequently find scores of red, green, and white lights dancing on the horizon as boaters leisurely cruise the Lake Michigan shoreline.

In addition to fishing and boating, a growing number of scuba divers have begun using these waters. Divers come to enjoy the variety of shipwrecks found in the region. Special attention was focused on the area with the discovery and subsequent documentation of the scow schooner *Rockaway*, a few miles north of South Haven.

Southwestern Michigan hosted several important shipbuilding concerns. The first commercial vessel to have been built in South Haven was the two-masted schooner *South Haven.* This vessel was constructed in 1865 by George Hannah who operated a lumber yard, lime kiln, and sawmill.

Approximately 55 commercial vessels were constructed in South Haven. These vessels were primarily schooners and construction occurred from 1865 to the turn of the century. More than 1,000 vessels are reported to have been

constructed at Saugatuck and Douglas.

Many small communities sprang up along the Lake Michigan coast as timber and agricultural industries flourished. Each community became a port as a variety of sailing vessels and steamers made their rounds. For virtually all major coastal communities in this region, such as South Haven, long piers were constructed to control moving sand that would block access to harbors. These communities grew and enjoyed a long and rich maritime history.

For many other communities, however, a long pier or dock extending to deep water was constructed. Very often these structures were temporary because they could not withstand the powerful forces of waves and ice. Each year these piers and docks would require repairs and even a lapse of a year to two without maintenance could threaten the viability of these structures.

Eventually, many communities simply faded away as other means of transporting goods became available.

> **Eventually, many communities simply faded away as other means of transporting goods became available.**

Without a strong need, piers and docks quickly fell into disrepair. Despite many decades of neglect, however, evidence of these structures often remains. Large pilings on or near shore and broken pilings underwater mark these sites. In addition, tools, carts, bottles, and other items litter the Lake Michigan bottomland near these sites.

Piers and docks in this region are significant because in many cases they

**Harbors such as South Haven were once
jammed with schooners and steamers.**

are the only evidence of a once-bustling community. They act as memorials to generations long since gone and provide historians and archaeologists an opportunity to explore the past.

For sport divers, pier and dock ruins provide exciting opportunities for discovering artifacts and exploring among pilings. Large fish, such as trout and salmon, often find these ruins suitable for hunting prey species and divers enjoy close encounters with these sleek predators.

Shipwrecks

The Lake Michigan bottomland off southwestern Michigan hosts a variety of shipwrecks--primarily schooners and steamers. Most were lost during the most

active commercial periods of the region; basically the late 1880s through the 1930s. In a single storm off St. Joseph, more than 30 commercial vessels were reported lost. During the years, several tugboats were lost off South Haven and a great variety of recreational vessels have been lost.

These shipwrecks are both intact and broken up, although many are the latter considering the high-energy coast that tends to break up wooden structures. They vary from the broken remains of the *Rockaway* to the intact *Francie*. Whether intact or broken up, these sites have much to offer sport divers. Intact vessels have long been favorites among divers because they offer many places to explore and provide an atmosphere of mystery. But intact shipwrecks can be intimidating to some divers, especially when the site is deep and visibility is poor.

Broken and scattered remains are often referred to as "piles of boards." But these piles of boards can be extremely interesting because they offer sport divers an opportunity to learn how vessels were constructed. Broken wrecks are also less threatening to unsure divers.

It is important to remember, especially in this area where there are sometimes strong currents and drifting sand, that even shipwrecks visited very often can offer surprises as shifting sand can alternately cover and reveal artifacts.

Natural Resources

In this area divers have reported seeing many perch, burbot, carp, suckers, and alewives. Trout and Salmon are more wary and not generally seen by divers in large schools. In addition, divers have reported at least one close encounter with an American eel. Other aquatic life, such as crawfish, can enhance sport diving experiences and are commonly found in this region.

The geologic features of Lake Michigan bottomland in this area are of two general types: clay banks and ridges and "canyons."

Clay banks are anomalies found north of South Haven.

Clay banks are anomalies found north of South Haven. They appear to be formations of resistant clay differentially weathered by wave action during previous lake levels. The banks are found at a depth of about 40 feet and rise as

much as 15 feet from the bottom. Holes through formations are as large as two feet in diameter.

Some geologists from Western Michigan University believe these formations may be important clues as to the age of the Great Lakes. This substrate

A long ridge south of South Haven was discovered on the bottom.

is sufficiently solid to support colonies of zebra mussels, which are common here. This colonization, combined with the form of the clay banks themselves, provides divers with a unique diving experience.

A long ridge south of South Haven was discovered on the bottom. This ridge is comprised of a variety of materials presumably deposited by retreating glaciers. Landward of the ridge is a 15 to 20-foot depression that locals call "canyons." The nature, location, and form of this underwater structure indicates that some powerful geologic forces were at work. For sport divers, this ridge and canyon formation offers a unique opportunity to explore an unusual bottom feature.

Zebra Mussels

Zebra mussel form dense colonies in this area. The clay substrate forms an ideal habitat for them in addition to the currents and relatively warm water.

Although zebra mussels are attributed to dramatically improving visibility from two feet to 20 feet or more, they also have detriments. Small shipwreck artifacts covered by zebra mussel colonies are so concealed that they may be unrecognizable to divers.

Colonies do not restrict themselves to small artifacts, either, and large timbers can become so encrusted with the critters that divers may pass by a shipwreck not knowing it was ever there.

This area has several unique aspects that could affect divers. First, are waves.

Prevailing winds from the west and

This area has several unique aspects that could affect divers.

---

northwest often create considerable waves as they sweep across Lake Michigan. By the time these waves reach the southwestern Michigan shoreline, they can build in size and energy.

While even large waves have little or no effect on sport divers once they descend below 15 feet, waves can create hazardous conditions for divers on the surface and can make it very difficult for boats to remain anchored. These factors make it extremely important for sport divers and boaters to monitor weather conditions here closely.

Although currents can be caused by wave action, the type of currents of concern here are caused by uneven heating of the water column. When water molecules vibrating at different frequencies meet, movement occurs. Prevailing winds are believed to be a major cause of mixing differentially heated water masses. As a result, underwater currents are often present throughout much of the year.

Underwater currents in the Great Lakes are notoriously unpredictable. It is possible for divers to experience a

current in one direction at the beginning of a dive and discover the current had completely reversed itself at the end of the dive.

While currents in the Great Lakes are fairly common, there is evidence that the currents in this region are consistently strong and are found at depth. For example, small sand ridges are found on the bottom as deep as 70 feet near the site of the *Rockaway*. These ridges were created by currents moving sand particles creating "waves" on the bottom.

Currents found in this area can create very difficult conditions for certain activities, such as underwater archaeology. These currents themselves generally pose little hazard to divers but divers and boat captains must be aware of their existence and carefully plan entrance and exit points.

Generally, visibility in this area ranges from two to 20 feet and it is often four to 10 feet. Sediments are easily stirred on the bottom and quickly reduce visibility although conditions are not as severe as "blackouts" found when fine organic material is present.

This visibility does not compare well with other underwater preserves but is on

---

This visibility does not compare well with other underwater preserves.

---

par with other dive sites in southern Lake Michigan.

Entanglement hazards can take many forms and pose a considerable risk to scuba divers. One of the most troublesome entanglements is monofilament nylon line--from gill nets or sport fishing. Gill nets in this region are not particularly common because there is little commercial fishing activity.

Monofilament fishing line, however, may pose a very real threat to sport divers here. Sport fishing is a very popular activity in this area and fish commonly congregate around shipwrecks and certain geologic features for cover. Fishing line that becomes snagged and is then broken off often forms a "nest" in these areas. These nests are sometimes difficult to see and sport divers can become seriously entangled.

Once entangled, novice sport divers may panic and become increasingly entangled. Although divers are trained to keep cool and carry a knife to cut their way out of such entanglements, some are likely to forget this training.

Overall, the Southwest Michigan Underwater Preserve has no major attractions as found in the other preserves in the state. But it is a good place for quick dives for those who live nearby.

Boating

Southwest Michigan is a boater's paradise. There are plenty of boat launches, marinas, and service facilities all along the coast. There are many major communities along the coast and each provides expert service for boats and motors as well as boat launches, cellular telephone service, pumpouts, slips, and other amenities.

Of particular note are the following communities that have developed a thriving economy based, in large part, on the boating tourist. They are: Douglas, Saugatuck, South Haven, Holland, Grand Haven, St. Joseph, and Muskegon. Boat launches are found at Muskegon State Park in Muskegon, Grand Haven, Port Sheldon, Holland, Douglas, South Haven, St. Joseph, and New Buffalo.

A U.S. Coast Guard Station is found at Grand Haven. They monitor vhf channels 9 and 16 and there are no "holes" in radio coverage of the area. They also can be reached by telephone at (800) 492-2583.

ROCKAWAY

The *Rockaway* was a scow-schooner, a workhorse of the Great Lakes, that was lost about 2.5 miles northwest of South Haven in Lake Michigan on Nov. 19, 1891. The ship was 106 feet long, 24 feet wide, and had a depth of seven feet. It was rigged as a schooner and rated at 164 gross tons. The *Rockaway* was built in 1866 at Oswego, N.Y.

The wreck of the *Rockaway* was discovered by accident when a perch fishing charter boat's anchor became entangled in the anchor chain of the ship. Since that time, it has been the focus of extensive archaeological work sponsored by the Michigan Maritime Museum in South Haven.

The wreck of the Rockaway was discovered by accident when a perch fishing charter boat's anchor became entangled in the anchor chain of the ship.

The *Rockaway* carried grain, wood products, coal, salt, produce, and packaged goods on lakes Ontario and Erie for much of her sailing life. In 1880, the vessel was sold to be used in the lumber trade on Lake Michigan; primarily hauling lumber from the port of Muskegon.

The *Rockaway* was lost in a fierce autumn storm while transporting a load of lumber from Ludington, Mich. to Benton Harbor, Mich. The crew of five stayed with the stricken vessel until it became waterlogged. All hands were rescued.

Today, the *Rockaway* is broken into three major pieces on a level plain in 70 feet of water. The stem structure and centerboard trunk remain upright. The upper decks are gone and there are no cabins.

The keelson and centerboard, with port and starboard sides, are attached. The ship's centerline assembly, including its keel, keelsons, and centerboard trunk are intact. The end of the centerboard trunk begins about 30 feet after the stem. The trunk measures 22.5 feet long and stands more than 5.5 feet high, representing the site's most visually prominent feature.

The vessel has settled into the bottom approximately parallel to the shore. The starboard section is broken at the turn of the bilge and lies parallel and immediately adjacent to the inner starboard section. The 106-foot long outer port section has pivoted away from the central port structure at the bow and lies about 30 feet out. The *Rockaway*'s windlass lies about 35 feet forward of the bow. A turnbuckle and small spar are also located forward of the bow. The length of the wreckage is about 100 feet and the architectural remains of the vessel are distributed over an area approximately 75 x 140 feet.

There is an interesting chain pile lying in the starboard bow quarter and a hand lever for operating the ship's windlass projects from under the keel on the port side. Mast steps can be seen in the keelson.

Poor visibility (two to four feet at times) and currents are frequently cited as difficulties at this site. But these problems have not prevented the *Rockaway* from becoming one of the most popular diving attractions in the region.

There is much sand in the area and as much as half of the wreckage is covered but many interesting artifacts remain. Sand "waves" on the bottom indicate strong currents that may cause the sand to cover and expose various parts of the vessel. The bottom is clay with an overburden of sand, silt, and small stones.

> *There is an interesting chain pile lying in the starboard bow quarter and a hand lever for operating the ship's windlass projects from under the keel on the port side.*

Perch anglers sometimes use this site for fishing so divers must be aware of the potential for entanglements in monofilament line. also, divers must ascend carefully as other boats may be in the area. Perch, sculpins, and burbot are frequently found at this site.

A layer of zebra mussels covers all exposed parts of this shipwreck but divers continue to visit it and have made it one of the main attractions in the underwater preserve. This site is usually buoyed with an official mooring buoy.

Location:	About 2.5 miles northwest of South Haven and nearly 2 miles from shore.
Loran:	42264.4/86184.5
Lat/Lon:	42 26.37/86 18.48
Depth:	65-70 feet
Visibility:	2-15 feet (4-6 feet average)

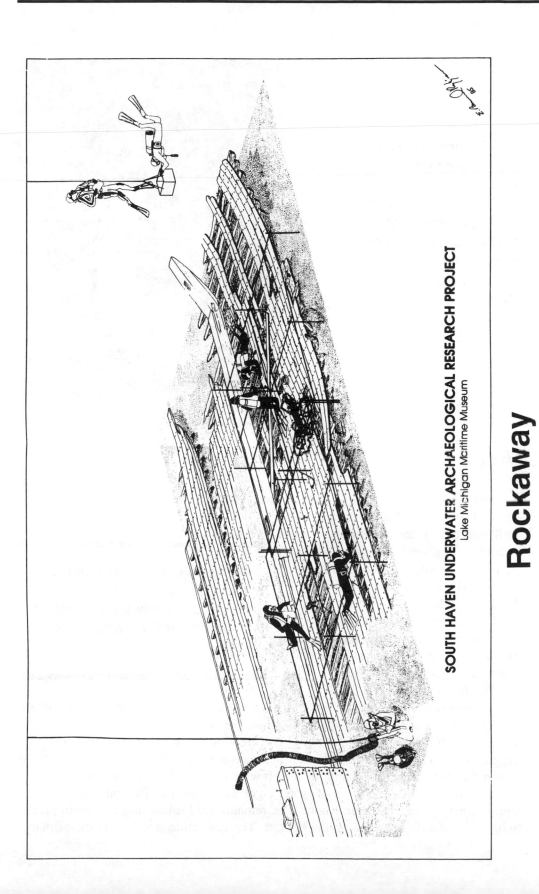

SOUTH HAVEN UNDERWATER ARCHAEOLOGICAL RESEARCH PROJECT

Lake Michigan Maritime Museum

Rockaway

Small schooners, such as the *Moonlight* seen here, once carried much of the goods shipped on the Great Lakes. They paved the way for large lakes freighters now a common sight on the lakes.

HAVANA

The *Havana* was a 306-ton, two-masted schooner built at Oswego, N.Y. in 1871. The *Havana* hauled a variety of bulk cargoes on the Great Lakes before it foundered in a gale on Oct. 3, 1887. The ship was bound for St. Joseph with a load of iron ore from Escanaba, Mich.

During her career, the 135-foot *Havana* ran aground near the thumb in Lake Huron and was salvaged and repaired at Port Huron, Mich.

The *Havana* anchored off St.

Unable to signal a tug with the hold filling with water, the Havana eventually drifted north of St. Joseph and the vessel was lost.

Joseph and was apparently unable to enter the harbor due to heavy seas. Unable to signal a tug with the hold filling with water, the *Havana* eventually drifted north of St. Joseph and the vessel was lost. The crew of seven scrambled into the rigging but three were drowned when the mainmast fell. The remaining four were saved through the heroic efforts of the crew of the tug *Hannah Sullivan*.

The *Havana* lies in 52 feet of water eight miles north of Benton Harbor, approximately one mile from shore. The remains are broken into two main pieces with much debris scattered on the bottom. The centerline structure is the primary visual feature of this wreck with the keelsons intact. Portions of the wreck rise 5 to 6 feet from the bottom. Although broken and scattered, most of the remains can be seen in a 20 x 60-foot area.

Because of shifting sands, the potential for finding new artifacts in this area is great. Some experienced divers have attempted to find the vessel's anchors but have been unable to do so despite the fact they located anchor chains.

Divers will enjoy exploring the large sections that remain. Architectural features are generally recognizable and can be examined by peeling off the 1 to 2-inch layer of zebra mussels. Good diving gloves are recommended to protect hands from sharp mussel shells.

> *Because of shifting sands, the potential for finding new artifacts in this area is great.*

Fine sediments are easily stirred by divers' actions at this site, which greatly reduces visibility momentarily. Because of these visibility concerns, this site may not be suitable for many divers at one time. Anchoring at this site may be difficult so divers should be sure their boat is secure before diving. This site is usually buoyed with a mooring buoy.

Location:	About six miles north of St. Joseph, about one mile from shore.
Loran:	32888.1/50024.9
Lat/Lon:	42 11.71/86 25.74
Depth:	48-52 feet
Visibility:	2-15 feet (2-6 feet average)
Tips:	Exploring the sandy bottom may result in the discovery of new, small artifacts.

CITY OF GREEN BAY

The *City of Green Bay* enjoys one of the most colorful histories of all Great Lakes vessels. The ship was a three-masted schooner built in 1872 in Green Bay, Wis. The vessel was rated at 346 gross tons and was 145 feet long.

Within a year of her launching, the *City of Green Bay* struck an obstruction near Port Stanley, Ont. and was sent to Buffalo, N.Y. for unloading and repairs. In 1874, the

> *The City of Green Bay enjoys one of the most colorful histories of all Great Lakes vessels.*

City of Green Bay collided with the schooner *Minnie Slauson* near Chicago, Ill., with minor damage to both.

In 1877, after serving various Great Lakes ports, the *City of Green Bay* carried a variety of cargoes to and from Scotland, Argentina, Paraguay, Brazil, England, and Portugal, and was condemned in Trinidad in late 1879. The vessel was purchased and repaired by a Chicago seaman who ran the trade route between New Orleans and New England starting in 1880. Late that year the vessel returned to Chicago to serve Great Lakes commerce once again. But the *City of Green Bay* continued to flirt with disaster.

In 1881, near Chicago, the *City of Green Bay* collided with the schooner *Hattie Earl*. While the *City of Green Bay* sustained minor damage, the *Hattie Earl* required considerable repair. In a dense fog in 1883, the *City of Green Bay* ran aground on Thunder Bay Island in Lake Huron. After several days, the vessel was pumped out, lightened, and sent to drydock for repairs.

On Oct. 3, 1887, luck ran out for the *City of Green Bay*. The vessel was caught in Lake Michigan by the same storm that claimed the *Havana*. Ironically, both vessels had taken on a load of iron ore at Escanaba, Mich. and were both headed to St. Joseph. The *City of Green Bay* grounded two to three miles south of the piers at South Haven, about 180 yards from shore.

> **The City of Green Bay's crew of seven clung to the rigging while the U.S. Life Saving Service crew at South Haven attempted a rescue.**

The *City of Green Bay*'s crew of seven clung to the rigging while the U.S. Life Saving Service crew at South Haven attempted a rescue. Although lines were shot to the vessel, equipment failures and wreckage made rescue by breeches buoy impossible. By the time the life saving crew realized they needed the surf boat, it was nearly too late to save any of the crew. Only a single sailor was rescued when he fell into the water near the surf boat.

Controversy surrounded the poor rescue effort and the captain of the station was eventually discharged.

The remains of the *City of Green Bay* rest in shallow water near South Haven. The wreck is badly broken up and few small artifacts remain. This site is usually not buoyed but it can be accessed by shore or boat. Shifting sands alternately cover and expose wreckage.

Location:	Near the South Haven piers.
Loran:	32773.42/49926.61
Lat/Lon:	42 22.00/86 17.97
Depth:	12-15 feet
Visibility:	5-15 feet, less when heavy seas are running from the west.
Tips:	This is a good snorkel. Little remains to be seen.

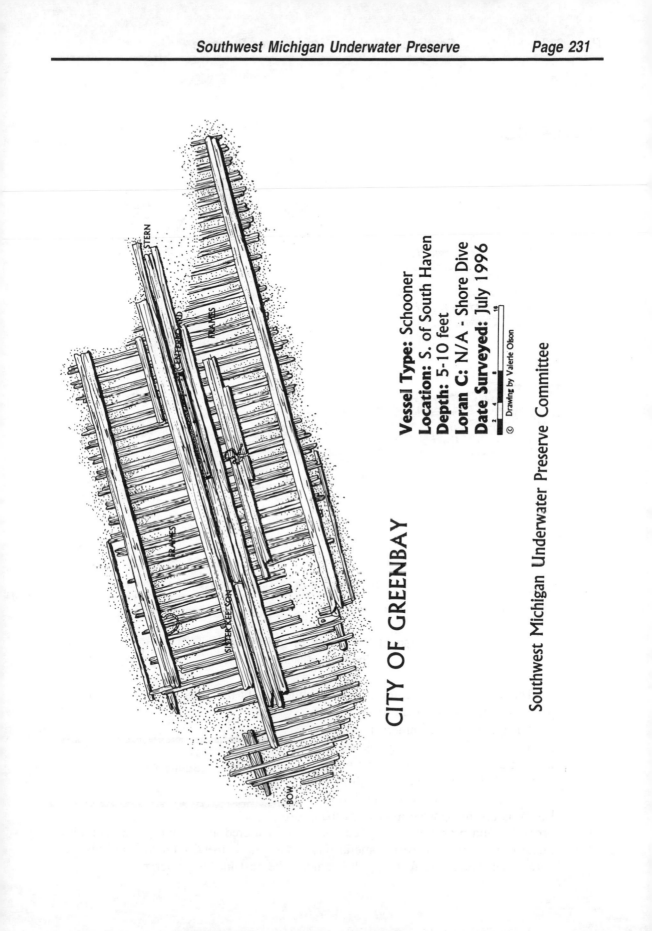

CITY OF GREENBAY

Vessel Type: Schooner
Location: S. of South Haven
Depth: 5-10 feet
Loran C: N/A - Shore Dive
Date Surveyed: July 1996

© Drawing by Valerie Olson

Southwest Michigan Underwater Preserve Committee

VERANO

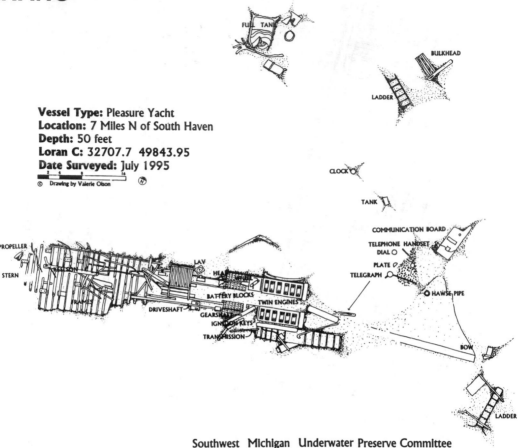

Vessel Type: Pleasure Yacht
Location: 7 Miles N of South Haven
Depth: 50 feet
Loran C: 32707.7 49843.95
Date Surveyed: July 1995

© Drawing by Valerie Olson

Southwest Michigan Underwater Preserve Committee

Site plan of the wreck of the VERANO.
By Valerie Olson

The *Verano* was a 92-foot, wooden-hulled yacht that was built in 1925. It was lost north of South Haven in 1946.

Today, mostly machinery is left to see of the *Verano*. The engines are upright and intact as well as the bow section of the vessel including the capstan. The stern is broken up but keelsons are recognized as well as the

This site is usually buoyed.

propeller and propeller shaft. Much debris is scattered and zebra mussel colonies make it difficult to discern some artifacts. The site is usually buoyed and visibility here often reaches 30 feet, which is among the best in this preserve.

Location:	About seven miles north of South Haven near the Clay Banks.
Loran:	32707.71/49843.95
Lat/Lon:	42 30.21/86 15.96
Depth:	45-51 feet
Visibility:	10-30 feet
Tips:	Bring good dive gloves to scrape zebra mussels off ship structure.

Glenn Pier

Glenn Pier is located about ten miles north of South Haven. This was once the location of a busy pier and dock that was used to load and unload lumber, tanbark, agricultural products, and passengers. The pier was deemed especially useful by local farmers who, with the aid of small lake steamers, could deliver fresh fruit and produce to Chicago in a day.

There are clear records as to when Glenn Pier was first constructed but historical accounts frequently mention the need to rebuild it almost annually. Each spring, ice conspired with the forces of waves to loosen and even break massive pilings driven into the Lake Michigan bottomland.

In 1894, frustrated by the amount of maintenance the pier required, an organization was formed to rebuild the structure and make considerable improvements. Eventually, warehouses and railroad tracks were added. At one time, the pier extended 667 feet into Lake Michigan and as many as 25 men were employed for fruit handling at the pier.

Glenn Pier became an important factor in the rapid growth of the resort industry in Glenn.

Peaches were an especially popular commodity grown in the region and one historical account tells of farmers' wagons loaded and lined up at Glenn Pier for more than a mile. Once loaded on small lake steamers and schooners, the fruit would be shipped to South Haven or directly to Chicago.

In addition to agricultural products, Glenn Pier became an important factor in the rapid growth of the resort industry in Glenn, a community 3/4 miles east of the pier. Visitors came from Chicago and other cities to enjoy the country atmosphere and clean air of the region. The pier was a convenient place to load and unload passengers coming and going to the resorts or on excursions to Holland.

Glenn Pier is located about 3/4 miles west of the community of Glenn on Hwy. A-2. The remains of the pier include several pilings on shore and broken pilings westward into the water. There are many small artifacts to be found even in relatively shallow water. These artifacts include machinery parts, tools, bottles, and other discarded items.

Access to this site is convenient with a park located on a hill and beach where the pier remains are found. A stairway helps divers access this site safely. This site is also popular among swimmers and parking can be a problem on weekends or hot weekday afternoons.

Glenn Pier is typical of many dock ruins found on the Lake Michigan shore. Pilings are broken off near the bottom and artifacts are scattered in a broad area. At this site, artifacts and ruins are likely to be found 200 yards out. It is also likely that some gamefish, such as perch, trout, and salmon, will frequent the area.

> *This site is also popular among swimmers and parking can be a problem on weekends or hot weekday afternoons.*

Divers should be aware of the potential dangers of entering and exiting this site during heavy seas. It is difficult to balance scuba equipment and a slip could cause injury or damage equipment. Also, visibility at this site is generally poor, sometimes less than two feet. Visibility is likely to be best during periods of calm seas but will be reduced to almost zero near shore during heavy seas. No current was found near shore in this area.

Location:	3/miles west of Glenn off Hwy. A-2 (Take 96 to exit 30, go south to Glenn, go west on 114th to a two track road that will get you close to shore.
Loran:	32697.51/49833.53
Lat/Lon:	42 31.22/86 15.20
Depth:	0-20 feet
Visibility:	2-12 feet

Pier Cove

The circumstances concerning the founding of the community of Pier Cove are disputed, but there is little doubt that settlement occurred around the mid-1800s and construction on the first pier began soon afterward. This was an attractive area because of a natural cove and stream found here.

Lumber and tanbark were the first products shipped from this area and commercial activity created a boom town. Mills were built for grinding grain and sawing timber and the pier underwent annual repairs and improvements.

Eventually, another pier was added but lumber production waned. About that time fruit production, particularly peaches, increased. The pier and community were virtually abandoned shortly after the turn of the century. Major remnants of the pier were still existing in 1930.

The text of a historical marker at this site provide a concise history of this site and the important role maritime commerce played:

> Surveyed in 1839, the village of Pier Cove was once hailed as "the busiest port between St. Joseph and Muskegon." Before the Civil War, Pier Cove was a bustling community and a major point for lumber distribution, with ships departing daily carrying tanbark and cordwood to Chicago and Milwaukee. With the exhaustion of the lumber supply in the late 1860s, Fennville, and Pier Cove's prosperity diminished. In the 1880s, however, fruit became a major shipping commodity. This site once overlooked the warehouse and two piers that revived the village's economy. In 1899, a freeze killed much of the local harvest and shipping at Pier Cove was reduced to passenger traffic. Commercial activity ceased in 1917.

Today, there are few remains apparent from either of the two piers at Pier Cove. Remains here are similar to the remains at Glenn Pier--pilings driven into Lake Michigan bottomland are broken and tools and various artifacts can be found. The area contains shifting sand that alternately covers and exposes artifacts.

Visibility at this site is often reduced during and shortly after heavy seas from the west. Visibility is generally 2 to 6 feet and shifting sand offers divers an opportunity for new discoveries of small artifacts such as tools, machinery, and bottles. Caution must be exercised when entering and exiting the water during heavy seas. Some gamefish may be seen near the pilings.

Location:	About 14 miles north of South Haven off Hwy. A-2. (Take US 31 to Hwy. 89, go west to 70th St. On 70th, go south to the historical marker and park.
Loran:	32667.12/49793.53
Lat/Lon:	42 35.16/86 14.29
Depth:	0-20 feet
Visibility:	0-6 feet, often 2-4 feet
Tips:	Visibility is often reduced to zero during periods of heavy seas and those periods are also difficult for entry and exiting with scuba gear. But this makes a good snorkel in calm weather.

Grand Mere Outcropping

The Lake Michigan basin was formed about 10,000 to 13,000 years ago as massive glaciers retreated from the Midwest. In their wake they left deepened and widened river valleys that eventually filled with water as natural outlets of the Great Lakes basin rose with glacial rebound.

Geologists are currently studying how the Great Lakes were created and new evidence suggests rapid climatic changes and dramatic changes in lake levels. The Grand Mere Outcropping is believed to be the result of geologic forces although the precise nature of those forces is not yet clear.

The Grand Mere Outcropping extends for approximately one mile along the Lake Michigan coast 3/4 miles off St. Joseph. The geologic feature is found in 15 to 25 feet of water and is 50 to 60 yards wide.

The outcropping appears to consists of glacial till, specifically, medium to large rocks on a hard clay bottom. A fine layer of sand/silt is found throughout the area. Some large rocks rise about 20 feet off the bottom with many rising 3 to 10 feet. The sudden drop and rise of the bottom lends an almost canyon-like appearance to this area.

A light layer of sand/silt is easily disturbed by divers' activities, which reduces visibility. But the water column clears relatively quickly-- within a few minutes.

Small fish, such as alewives, darters, perch, and sculpins, have been observed at this site and it seems likely that large gamefish, including walleye, trout, and salmon, would also frequent this site for feeding and perhaps breeding. Zebra mussels are found in irregular patterns on hard surfaces. The fine sand/silt may account for the fact that not all hard surfaces are evenly colonized by the mussels.

Divers will find this unusual geologic formation interesting because of the variety of features, including the sharp rise and fall that gives this area a canyon-like appearance. In addition, there are many crevices and areas where resistant clay has been eroded in unusual patterns. The relatively shallow depth and good visibility make this a good place for underwater photography.

Divers will find a variety of fish at this site and an underwater light will enable divers to explore crevices that host a variety of fish, crayfish, and other aquatic life. A light layer of sand/silt is easily disturbed by divers' activities, which reduces visibility. But the water column clears relatively quickly--within a few minutes--so this layer of sediments does not pose unusual threats to diver enjoyment and safety.

This area is a good place for beginning divers to become acquainted with the Great Lakes environment. There are no overhangs or strong currents and visibility generally ranges from 10 to 25 feet.It is also a good place for open water testing and similar field experiences.

Location:	About 3/4 mile offshore, parallel to the coastline running for about one mile near St. Joseph.
Loran:	33013.58/50135.37
Lat/Lon:	42 00.35/86 33.85
Depth:	15-25 feet
Visibility:	10-25 feet

Clay Banks

A variety of geologic processes are probably responsible for the clay formations found in this area. Some of these formations, because of their composition, are harder and thus more resistant to the weathering forces of underwater currents, waves, and ice. It is these resistant formations that form unusual features and offer divers an attractive site.

This site may also have scientific significanse because some Western Michigan University geologists believe weathering forces, at a time when Lake Michigan was much lower, may have created these formations. If that is true, these formations could be important clues in determining the age of the Great Lakes and the forces that formed them.

The clay banks were discovered in the 1960s by a local diver. Another local diver has been investigating this site in the last few years. Rising as much as 15 feet from the bottom, these features were originally mistaken for a shipwreck believed to be in the area.

The clay banks are coated with colonies of zebra mussels and a fine layer of sand/silt. Although the sand/silt can reduce visibility, divers practicing buoyancy control will have little problem at this site. Visibility is often 4 to 8 feet and may be as great as 15 feet during the most favorable conditions.

The clay banks are coated with colonies of zebra mussels and a fine layer of and/silt.

The bottom is resistant clay and the clay features are formed in unusual patterns that include holes as wide as two feet in diameter and four to six feet deep. These features are also called "clay cliffs" and extend over an area about 1/8 mile square and include many overhangs and shallow "tunnels."

Because of the hard clay bottom, anchoring at this site can be problematic. Divers should take special precautions and be sure the anchor is secure before beginning an extended dive. It is a good idea to leave someone capable of running the boat topside during dives to avoid conflicts with perch anglers.

Visibility can be reduced by careless divers and this site may not be suitable for large numbers of divers at a time unless they are instructed to spread out. Underwater currents here are variable but often less severe than more open areas of bottomland.

Divers will enjoy exploring the formations, which also make excellent underwater photography subjects. Gloves should be warn to protect hands from sharp mussel shells.

Location:	About 3.5 miles northwest of South Haven and about 3/4 mile from shore.
Loran:	32706.1/49840.4
Lat/Lon:	42 30.45/86 15.78
Depth:	45-50 feet
Visibility:	4-20 feet depending upon conditions.
Tips:	Spread out--do not get caught behind other divers or your visibility will be greatly reduced.

Donny's Reef

Here, massive blocks of concrete rise as much as 15 feet off a sand/clay bottom. The water column over these blocks varies from 25 to 40 feet.

Zebra mussel colonies here are impressive as they find the hard concrete surfaces to their liking. Visibility is variable and a slight current is often found at this site. Perch and other gamefish have been observed here. The site covers an area approximately 1/4 mile square about 1/2 mile from shore north of South Haven. This site is also referred to as the "Pier Dump Site" because the concrete blocks were dumped here during pier rebuilding projects.

It is the impressive concentration of zebra mussels that may offer the greatest attraction for sport divers at this site. The combination of concrete blocks and mussels give this area an almost coral-like atmosphere. A light sand/silt layer coats some areas but does not appear to be heavy enough to inhibit mussel colonization.

In addition to impressive mussel colonies, divers will find gamefish at this site. It is also a popular sport fishing site so divers should be ware of potential user conflicts.

Anchoring in this area is generally not a problem but because anchors can become wedged between concrete blocks, divers should check anchor position carefully before exiting to ensure convenient retrieval.

Location:	About 1/2 miles from shore and 1 mile north of South Haven.
Loran:	32745.51/49890.85
Lat/Lon:	42 25.51/86 17.10
Depth:	25-40 feet
Visibility:	10-20 feet

Piper Airplane

In 1998, a local group of divers arranged to move a crashed Piper Aztec airplane from deeper water to a spot six miles north of Benton Harbor in 80 feet of water.

The airplane is in excellent condition and makes an excellent dive. More information about this dive site, including location data, is available from local dive retailers.

Location:	About six miles north of Benton Harbor. This site is usually buoyed with an official mooring buoy.
Depth:	75-80 feet
Visibility:	10-20 feet

FRANCIE

The *Francie* was a Chesapeake Bay oyster dredge and this sailing vessel was originally used in the commercial fishing industry. Later, it was converted for use as a pleasure craft.

Wooden hulls tend to rot out quickly if not regularly dry docked for maintenance and the *Francie* suffered the fate of many such vessels that were past their primes. It was allowed to sink in the Grand River. Later, a group of local scuba divers raised the vessel and towed it to its present location for use as a dive site. In that way, the *Francie* continues in "service."

Location:	About two miles west of the Douglas/Saugatuck Harbor. This site is usually buoyed with an official morring buoy.
Loran:	32644.7/49724.1
Depth:	90-102 feet
Visibility:	10-20 feet

Crane & Barge

A crane and barge are found about a mile off the coast between Holland and Saugatuck. Little is known how the crane and barge happened to end up in the water but it is presumed that they were enroute to a marine construction project when heavy seas sank the barge.

Divers enjoy exploring both items in about 50 feet of water. This site is usually buoyed with an official mooring buoy maintained by local divers.

Location:	About a mile from shore between Holland and Saugatuck.
Loran:	32617.62/49714.92
Lat/Lon:	42 42.72/86 13.91
Depth:	40-50 feet
Visibility:	10-20 feet

Miscellaneous Site

A 27-foot sailboat is a popular diving attraction although it is usually not marked except with a small plastic jug. It is located at:
Loran: 32604.58/49681.93;
Lat/Lon: 42 45.73/86 14.84.

Inland Dive Sites

One might think that little inland diving occurs in this region because most inland lakes and streams are mesotrophic, that is, they have a medium amount of silt and sediments on the bottom. But there are many divers in West Michigan and many actually revel in their ability to "mud dive."

One of the most popular inland diving lakes is Gull Lake in Kalamazoo County. It offers snorklers and scuba divers alike the opportunity to observe fish life in weed beds and a variety of farm equipment, small boats, and fish shanties.

In some areas, it was not unusual for residents to dispose of unwanted items such as obsolete farm equipment and even old cars, by taking them out on the ice. When spring came, the disposal was complete. Some locals even bet on which day the ice would break.

These days, that practice is uncommon because of environmental concerns, but Gull Lake is one area where farmers' "trash" became divers' "treasure."

The maximum depth of Gull Lake is about 110 feet and most fish and weed beds can be found in 50 feet or less. A popular access site for divers is Prairieville Township Park on the north end of the lake. The beach slopes gently and offers a safe way to enter the lake.

At the southwest end of Gull Lake is another park, Ross Township Park, near the small community of Yorkville. Entry is easy over a grassy slope.

At the southwest end of Gull Lake is another park, Ross Township Park, near the small community of Yorkville. Entry is easy over a grassy slope.

Spring and fall offer the best visibility in this silt-bottom lake. Divers can expect to find a visibility range of 8 to 30 feet. Most divers enjoy aquatic life and discarded equipment and cars in only 10 to 40 feet of water.

Gull Lake is relatively close to Kalamazoo and Battle Creek. As a result, it can be crowded with boat traffic in July and August. Night or early morning diving may be a good idea, and it is always important to display a diver down flag.

Divers of all skill levels will find the trip to Gull Lake worthwhile. Also, local dive centers often conduct special diving activities in the lake so it may be worth a check to get in on the fun.

Information about this dive site is available from SubAquatics Sports and Service in Battle Creek, (616) 968-8551; or Wolf's Dive Shop, (616) 392-3300 or (616) 926-1068.

If you are seeking an off-the-beaten-path inland dive site, try Ruppert Lake, which is also in Kalamazoo County. The lake is small, 28 acres, but is filled with bass, northern pike, and small gamefish. It is found off U.S. 131 on B Avenue.

Other inland lakes of note for snorkeling or scuba diving are Pike Lake in Allegan County (32 acres, public access off 108th Avenue south of Allegan), and Clear Lake in Van Buren County (69 acres, public access off 2nd Avenue).

Getting There

Major highways serve the southwest Michigan region so access to this underwater preserve is quick and easy. Both U.S. 131 and I-94 will bring divers close to the preserve area. These major highways intersect in Kalamazoo, which is about 45 minutes from diving.

U.S. 31, which follows the Lake Michigan coastline, is a key access highway and divers should look for exits between Holland and New Buffalo to enter the preserve area.

Major airports are found at Grand Rapids, Kalamazoo, and Battle Creek.

Emergencies

On-water emergencies are handled by the U.S. Coast Guard while stricken divers who reach shore will find emergency medical services dispatched by either Ottawa, Allegan, Van Buren, or Berrien County Sheriff's Departments.

To contact the U.S. Coast Guard, which has a station at Grand Haven use vhf channels 9 or 16. To contact the various sheriff's departments, use the numbers listed below.

Divers should be aware that Bronson Hospital in Kalamazoo has recompression chambers capable of handling diving emergencies. The hospital staff is well trained in these emergencies so expert help is very close for this preserve.

Accommodations

West Michigan, especially the Lake Michigan coast, is a popular tourist destination. As a result, there are many hotels, motels, bread and breakfasts, campgrounds, and other overnight accommodations. Because of this large number, it is best to contact one of the chambers of commerce listed in Important Addresses/Phone Numbers

Do not take vacancies for granted just because there are many options in this area.

section or contact the West Michigan Tourist Association, 1253 Front St. NW, Grand Rapids, MI 49503 or by calling them at (616) 456-8557.

Do not take vacancies for granted just because there are many options in this area. Even a great many overnight accommodations fill quickly during the summer so plan ahead and make reservations.

Other Attractions

Because west Michigan is so heavily populated and also enjoys tremendous natural and cultural resources, there are many family attractions in the region.

Grand Rapids is within an hour's drive of much of the preserve area and offers visitors glimpses into the past at the Grand Rapids Public Museum on Museum Avenue in downtown Grand Rapids. Also downtown is the Gerald R. Ford Museum.

In Holland, visitors may wish to explore the Netherlands Museum, Baker Furniture Museum, or the Poll Museum of Transportation. The *S.S. Keewatin* is a former ferry turned museum ship at Douglas. In Kalamazoo there is a public museum of the general history of the area as well as an aviation museum. In South Haven, on the waterfront, visitors will find the Michigan Maritime Museum, which interprets the area's maritime heritage and will be of special interest to divers visiting the underwater preserve.

If museums are not of interest, try relaxing on one of the many public beaches all along the Lake Michigan shoreline. In Grand Haven, visitors enjoy the Gillette Nature Center, which has displays and nature trails.

Important Addresses/Phone Numbers

Ottawa County Sheriff's Dept.

(616) 846-9170

Van Buren County Sheriff's Dept.
(616) 657-3101

Grand Haven Coast Guard
(800) 492-2583

Grand Haven Chamber of Commerce
(616) 842-4910

New Buffalo Chamber of Commerce
(616) 469-5409

South Haven Chamber of Commerce
(616) 637-5171

Allegan County Sheriff's Dept.
112 Walnut St.
Allegan, MI 49010
(616) 673-0500

Berrien County Sheriff's Dept.
(616) 983-7111

Benton Harbor Chamber of Commerce
(616) 469-5409

Holland Chamber of Commerce
(616) 392-2389

Saugatuck Chamber of Commerce
(616) 857-1701

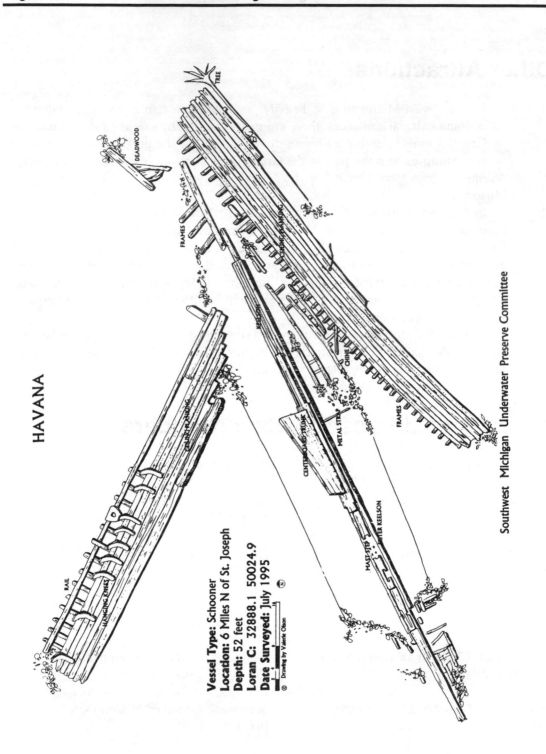

HAVANA

Vessel Type: Schooner
Location: 6 Miles N of St. Joseph
Depth: 52 feet
Loran C: 32888.1 50024.9
Date Surveyed: July 1995

Drawing by Valerie Olson

Southwest Michigan Underwater Preserve Committee

Straits of Mackinac Underwater Preserve

The dancing waves that greet tourists on their way to or from Mackinac Island have another side. When teased by winds, these waves grow to walls of water that can wrestle even the most massive vessels to the bottom of the Straits of Mackinac.

The Straits is known as a graveyard for schooners, steamers, and even modern freighters that met their doom in or near the narrow passage between the two peninsulas. Sport divers now enjoy one of the finest collections of shipwrecks in the world where the cool, fresh water of the Great Lakes preserves shipwrecks for centuries.

How did these ships come to rest on the bottom? Each has their own story, but, for many, the funnel shape of the Straits of Mackinac played an important role in their demise. The Straits acts as a natural funnel that concentrates wave and wind energy from northwesterly storms.

Ships entering the Straits from the east sometimes discovered too late that waves were much larger and more frequent in the western portion of the narrow passage. By the time the danger was recognized, it was too late or too difficult to turn around.

Such was the case for the *C.H. Johnson*, a schooner whose captain thought he could beat a September gale in 1895. With a load of stone blocks quarried from the Keeweenaw

Peninsula and bound for a bank building in Chicago, the *C.H. Johnson* was anchored in the lee of St. Helena Island west of the Straits of Mackinac. But before the storm relented, the anchor gave way and the ship with its cargo ran aground at Gros Cap Point. Fortunately, no lives were lost in the mishap, but today the remains of the hull and massive blocks host crayfish, carp, largemouth bass, suckers, rock bass, and curious scuba divers.

East of the Straits of Mackinac, near Bois Blanc Island, another schooner lies on the bottom. The *Newell Eddy* was discovered by a team of scientists from the University of Michigan in 1992. The three-masted vessel was lost in a storm on April 20, 1893. Nine lives and a cargo of corn were lost in the disaster, but today the *Newell Eddy* is one of the most intact shipwrecks in the Great

Lakes. Divers can peer into windows and doorways and see where crewmen spent their last minutes before the ship went down in 165 feet of water.

Shipping disasters in the Straits of Mackinac are not confined to the last century. In 1966, the *Cedarville*, a 588-foot steel freighter loaded with limestone, collided with another steel freighter in a dense fog. The captain of the *Cedarville* made a valiant effort to guide the

---

Some shipwrecks have been located but are still unidentified. This is the case with two shipwrecks found in the Mackinac Island Harbor.

---

stricken vessel to Mackinaw City, but it sank in 105 feet of water near the Mackinac Bridge. Ten of 35 crewmen were lost in the accident. The shipwreck lies on its side with part of the hull within 35 feet of the surface.

Some shipwrecks have been located but are still unidentified. This is the case with two shipwrecks found in the Mackinac Island Harbor. One wooden-hulled shipwreck, believed to be a schooner, lies upside down and partially buried by the east breakwall. Another, smaller sailing vessel is located on the bottom near the west breakwall. This vessel was found in the last few years and has many artifacts associated with it. Unfortunately, it lies directly in the path of the ferry route, so divers tend to avoid this site.

The Straits of Mackinac also has much more to offer than shipwrecks. An underwater survey with remote sensing equipment a few years ago revealed that

the St. Ignace and Mackinac Island harbors host a remarkable collection of small artifacts from several centuries of human activity in the region. These artifacts include tools, dinnerware, bottles, and even discarded shoes and a parasol.

What will be the next major discovery under the waters of the Straits of Mackinac? Only time will tell, but there are at least 40 major shipwrecks yet to be discovered in the area. Eventually, at least some of these shipwrecks will be found; but divers already have discovered that although these vessels were not carrying gold or silver cargoes, their wealth lies in their ability to preserve our maritime heritage for future generations.

The Straits of Mackinac Underwater Preserve is maintained by a local committee of divers. In addition to maintaining mooring buoys, the committee is responsible for creating a shore access site at the Veteran's

---

There are at least 40 major shipwrecks yet to be discovered in the area.

Memorial Park in St. Ignace and has placed interpretive materials in the park and other places in the preserve.

Each year, during the last Sunday of August, the committee sponsors a treasure hunt that often draws more than 200 divers. Prizes generally include exotic dive vacations and equipment. More information about the annual event is available by contacting the St. Ignace Chamber of Commerce at (906) 643-8717. Proceeds from the fun event are used to provide information to divers and access to wrecks.

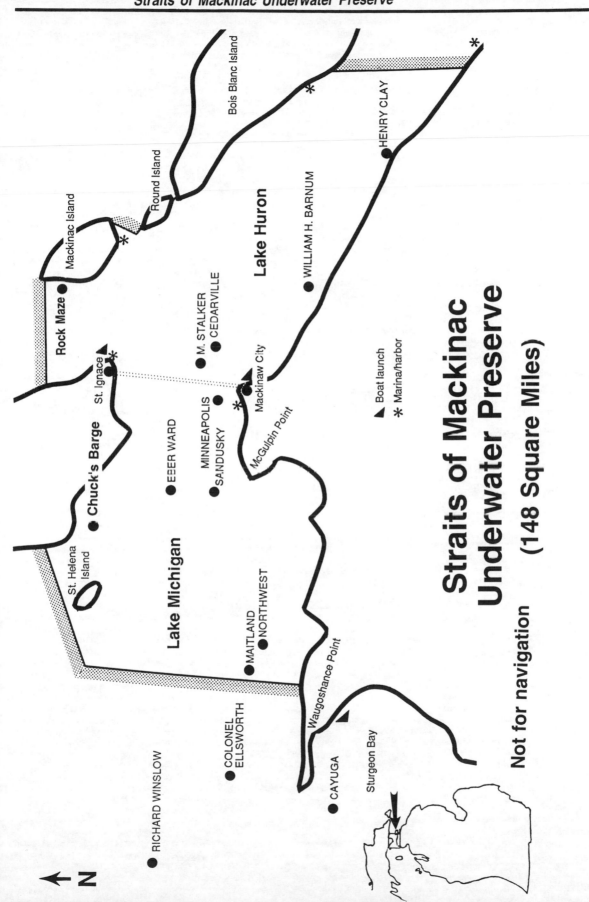

Straits of Mackinac Underwater Preserve
(148 Square Miles)

Not for navigation

▲ Boat launch
* Marina/harbor

Lake Huron

Lake Michigan

Bois Blanc Island

Round Island

Mackinac Island

Rock Maze

HENRY CLAY

WILLIAM H. BARNUM

M. STALKER
CEDARVILLE

St. Ignace

Chuck's Barge

EBER WARD

MINNEAPOLIS
SANDUSKY

Mackinaw City

McGulpin Point

St. Helena Island

MAITLAND
NORTHWEST

Waugoshance Point

COLONEL ELLSWORTH

RICHARD WINSLOW

CAYUGA

Sturgeon Bay

N

Boating

Boating in the Straits of Mackinac area is complicated by the volume of boat traffic. Specifically, the ferry services that run between Mackinac Island and the mainland and commercial shipping traffic, contribute to navigational hazards such as fog and heavy seas. In addition, autumn brings out trout and salmon anglers making this one of the busiest waterways in the U.S.

Because there is considerable boat traffic, so are there complementary boating services, such as marinas, boat launches, fuel, and pump out stations.

The marina in St. Ignace is operated by the city and owned by the Michigan Department of Natural Resources. It offers transient accommodations, gas, water, electricity, restrooms, showers, boat launch, and holding tank pumps. Similar facilities, except a boat launch, are operated by the Michigan Department of Natural Resources and found at the marina on Mackinac Island.

A marina sponsored by the Village of Mackinaw City and one in Cheboygan offer full services. Basic services are offered by marinas at Bois Blanc Island and at the Cheboygan County Marina. Diesel fuel is available by contacting local vendors who will often bring a truck to either private or public marinas for fueling.

Boat launching facilities are located at St. Ignace, Mackinaw City, and at Wilderness State Park on Sturgeon Bay in Lake Michigan.

Because the area is so popular, especially in July and August, it is best to make reservations for slip space well in advance. Most marina facilities monitor vhf channel 16. Also, commercial vessels, including passenger ferries, are not shy about rendering security calls when visibility is low due to fog or rain. Dive boats should consider the practice as common to this area to ensure safety.

Boaters should be aware that the Mackinac County Sheriff's Department out of St. Ignace operates several policing boat patrols in the preserve area. These patrols occur daily and, in addition, Michigan Department of Natural Resources conservation officers from St. Ignace and Cedarville make regular on-water patrols through the area specifically for the purpose of monitoring diving in the preserve.

Indian fishing nets have been blamed for the deaths of at least three fishermen in the St. Ignace area. The nets typically run from near the surface to the bottom and are moved

> *The big danger lies in propeller fouling in heavy seas.*

to shallow water in the autumn. During the summer, the nets could be found anywhere in the preserve although most netters avoid shipwrecks because of entanglement problems. The big danger lies in propeller fouling in heavy seas. Lean to recognize the net buoy patterns and avoid the nets to the extent possible.

With some exceptions, all major dive sites are buoyed with official mooring buoys in this preserve. Boaters will find chambers of commerce in St. Ignace, Mackinac Island, and Mackinaw City where information about other accommodations and facilities is available.

Divers' Park Shore Access

Divers' Park (VFW Memorial Park) is located on the east side of State Street (US-2) across from the St. Ignace Post Office. It is south of the Star Line Dock and north of the large curve on the hill overlooking the bay. Divers will find a gazebo, interpretive signs, and a paved parking lot. Access to the water is on the north end of the park off the gravel shore. Look for the many flags flown at this park.

> *Divers who stay south of the pilings and do not exceed 25 feet of depth will be safely out of the ferry lanes. Always display a diver down flag.*

This area is loaded with bottles, tools, hardware, and artifacts from more than 300 years of human activity in the region. This was once the site of a busy commercial dock so many unusual items can be found. Divers can also enjoy fish found in weedbeds or near pilings. The bottom ranges from sandy to silty to gravel.

Visibility is variable but is frequently 10 feet or more. Water temperature is warmest when the wind is from the east or southeast. It is often quite chilly when the wind is from the west or northwest.

This is a popular area for checkout dives, open water testing, novice divers, and anyone who likes to find and examine small artifacts.

Caution: Do not swim north of the pilings or divers risk an accident with ferries. Divers who stay south of the pilings and do not exceed 25 feet of depth will be safely out of the ferry lanes. Always display a diver down flag.

VIEW OF HARBOR • 1887

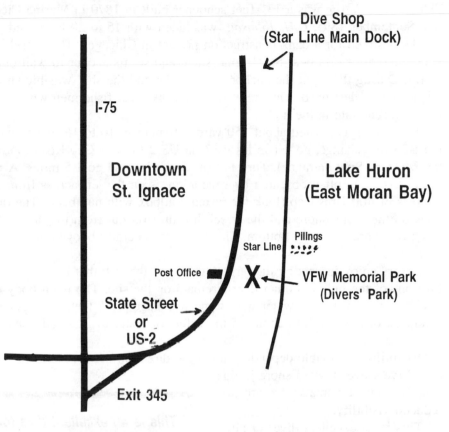

To Sault Ste. Marie

Dive Shop
(Star Line Main Dock)

I-75

Downtown
St. Ignace

Lake Huron
(East Moran Bay)

Pilings

Star Line

Post Office

X

VFW Memorial Park
(Divers' Park)

State Street
or
US-2

Exit 345

To Mackinac Bridge

Location:	Across from the St. Ignace Post Office on State Street (US-2) in downtown St. Ignace.
Loran:	31211.57/48086.14
Lat/Lon:	45 51.824/84 42.993
Depth:	0-25 feet
Visibility:	Usually 10-25 feet
Tips:	Entry with scuba equipment is easy because it deepens fast. This is a good snorkeling site.

C.H. JOHNSON

The *C.H. Johnson* was a 137-foot schooner built in 1870 in Marine City, Mich. In late September 1895, *C.H. Johnson* was laden with 15 to 20 large, red, sandstone blocks destined for a bank construction project in Chicago. The vessel encountered a storm near St. Helena Island and set its anchor to wait out the storm. During the night the anchor chain broke and the ship was blown ashore where it was destroyed. The crew was saved by local fishermen who made a heroic rescue late in the night.

This wreck is located about 150 yards offshore in 10 to 15 feet of water. From the I-75 interchange, go 4.1 miles west on US-2 to Gros Cap Road (across from the Mystery Spot entrance). Turn left on Gros Cap and go 1.5 miles. A narrow, steep driveway, often obscured by vegetation, is on the left across from the street address of 400 Gros Cap (look for rusted mailbox with number). The drive dead ends on the rocky shore and the wreck lies directly out from the drive. A turnaround area is at the bottom. The wreck is generally buoyed during summer months.

Divers enjoy inspecting the large blocks and the fish that hide between them. Portions of the hull and other debris remain on the site. The main body of the wreck lies in 10 feet of water with some wreckage at 15 feet. Divers can swim southeast of the wreck to about 15 to 20 feet of water to find additional pieces of wreckage.

Visibility is variable depending upon the direction of wind and waves. Storms that drive waves toward shore in this usually protected area will result in reduced visibility.

This is an excellent dive for all skill levels because of the interesting cargo. Although it is about 150 yards to the wreck itself, much of that can be walked or snorkeled. Walking can be difficult, however, because the water is shallow and rocks are slippery. A dive light may enable divers to see the fish that lie between the blocks more clearly.

> *This is an excellent dive for all skill levels because of the interesting cargo.*

This is a great third dive for a full day of diving and makes an excellent night dive because the fish and other aquatic life are more active then.

Report Shipwreck Thefts
1-800-292-7800

CEDARVILLE

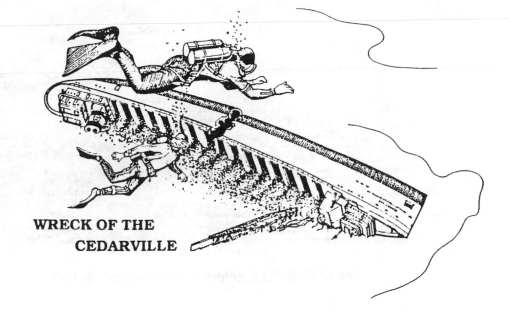

**WRECK OF THE
CEDARVILLE**

**The CEDARVILLE is one of the most
popular shipwrecks of this preserve.**
(Graphic Copyright 1981 by Chuck and Jeri Feltner)

The wreck of the *Cedarville* is one of the most popular shipwrecks not only of this preserve but of the entire Great Lakes. The 588-foot freighter was constructed at River Rouge, Mich. in 1927. It was a fairly contemporary Great Lakes commercial vessel when it sank after a collision on May 7, 1965 with the loss of ten lives. Unfortunately, the wreck has claimed the life of one diver since.

The *Cedarville* was enroute from Calcite, Mich., near Rogers City, to Gary Ind. with a load of 14,411 tons of limestone and a crew of 35.. Limestone is used in the steel-making process and is a common cargo on the Great Lakes. The *Cedarville* left Calcite in a light fog at full speed but ran into a dense fog near the Mackinac Bridge.

As the vessel approached the bridge, another ship, the *Topdalsfijord* was east bound and would not communicate on the vhf radio with the captain of the *Cedarville*. Although the captain saw the ship

Although the captain saw the ship coming on his radar, his evasive actions were unsuccessful.

The CEDARVILLE before her last voyage in 1965.

coming on his radar, his evasive actions were unsuccessful. The *Topdalsfijord* rammed the port side of the *Cedarville* between the seventh and eighth hatches, cutting a fatal gash.

The captain of the *Cedarville* made a desparate effort to ground the vessel in shallow water near Mackinaw City but the ship sank before it could reach safety. The vessel sank in about 105 feet of water about 3.5 miles southeast of the center of the Mackinac Bridge.

Today, divers will find the *Cedarville* intact and lying on her starboard side at an angle of about 45 degrees. Divers enjoy exploring the cabin areas of the stern and bow and, if sufficiently skilled, can enter the engine room through an open door on the stern's port side. Extreme caution should be exercised if exploring the interior of this wreck because of the silt and inverted condition. The cargo holds rise to within 35 feet of the surface and, they, too, can pose disorientation problems if divers are not cautious.

> *The cargo holds rise to within 35 feet of the surface and can pose disorientation problems if divers are not cautious.*

Divers will also find that many artifacts have been removed through the years and even the propeller was cut off and now lies off the stern on the bottom in 105 feet of water. This site is usually buoyed by an official mooring buoy placed by local divers.

Location:	About 3.5 miles southeast of the center of the Mackinac Bridge; from Old Mackinac Point about 2.8 miles on a bearing of 89 degrees.
Loran:	31210.7/48130.6
Lat/Lon:	45 47.13/84 40.13
Depth:	35-105 feet
Visibility:	5-20 feet depending upon currents running.
Tips:	Use extreme caution when penetrating wreck due to disorientation problems.

ANGLO SAXON and J.A. SMITH

The J.A. SMITH at dock in more productive times.

The *Anglo Saxon* was a 134-foot schooner that was built in 184 in Port Dalhousie, Ont. The vessel served the Great Lakes shipping industry for 23 years before it was stranded at the Straits of Mackinac.

The *J.A. Smith* was similar to the *Anglo Saxon* in that it was a 138-foot schooner built in 1872 in Algonac, Mich.

Both vessels were being towed by the steamer *Mattawan* and on Sept. 8, 1887, were anchored off Waugoshance Point in Lake Michigan with cargoes of cedar wood while the steamer refueled at Cheboygan, Mich. A sudden storm arose and both vessels were stranded. The *Anglo Saxon*, a Canadian vessel at the time of her loss, broke up quickly.

The *J.A. Smith* was more durable and an attempt to raise the vessel was made. During the salvage attempt, the captain of the *J.A. Smith* was killed when a steam pump broke loose. The attempt and ship were abandoned and it was later reported that the vessel burned to the waterline where she sank.

Little remains of the ships today. Wreckage is intermingled and consists only of timbers that are accessible from shore. The wrecks are located in Lake Michigan about 12.3 miles from Old Mackinac Point on a bearing of 260 degrees. This site is usually not buoyed.

Location:	About 12.3 miles from Old Macinac Point on a bearing of 260 degrees in Lake Michigan.
Loran:	31309.6/48102.8
Lat/Lon:	45 45.24/84 57.25
Depth:	10-14 feet
Visibility:	10-20 feet

CAYUGA

The remains of the *Cayuga* are located and are relatively close to the resting places of the *J.H. Tiffany* and *Milwaukee*, which were discovered relatively recently. Although these sites are remote, they offer quality diving adventures for "serious" divers. Additional information about all three vessels can be found at the maritime museum on Beaver Island.

The *Cayuga* was a 290-foot steamer that hauled a variety of cargoes on the Great Lakes. Built in 1889 in Cleveland, Ohio, she was a familiar sight to many in northern Michigan.

On May 10, 1895, the *Cayuga* was bound for Buffalo, N.Y. from Milwaukee, Wis. with a load of flour and grain. In a dense fog, the *Cayuga* collided with the steamer *Joseph L. Hurd*. Although the latter was in a decrepit condition, it managed to steam away with 15 feet of her bow missing. The *Cayuga* was less fortunate as the accident tore a large hole in her starboard hull. The ship sank in 25 minutes.

After the sinking, a series of salvage attempts were made by the Reid Towing and Wrecking Co., of Bay City, Mich., until 1900. Finally, with his company almost bankrupt, James Reid gave up the task. The wreck was relocated in the 1970s.

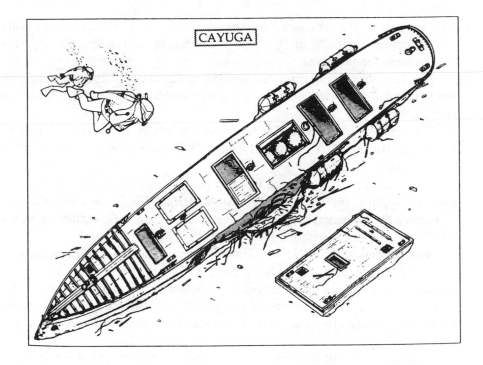

The CAYUGA as she lies today.
(Graphic Copyright 1981 by Chuck and Jeri Feltner)

The *Cayuga* today lies upright and intact with about a 40 degree list to port. All of the cabins are missing and portions of the port side midships is somewhat broken up. Still, there is much for divers to see on this double-deck wreck.

The first deck can be reached in about 70 feet of water and inside divers will find much machinery including a triple-expansion steam engine, which was very common in the late 1800s and early 1900s. Divers will also find a large gash from the collision on the vessel's starboard side. A 75-foot salvage barge, sunk during Reid's attempts, is found about 40 feet away from the *Cayuga*'s port midships.

This site is generally not buoyed.

Location:	In Lake Michigan about 3.6 miles southwest of Grays Reef Light.
Loran:	31390.4/48089.8
Lat/Lon:	45 43.07/85 11.16
Depth:	70-100 feet
Visibility:	10-20 feet

J.H. TIFFANY and MILWAUKEE

The fates of the schooner *J.H. Tiffany* and steamer *Milwaukee* were linked on a cold, autumn morning of Nov. 29, 1859 making both among the oldest wrecks in this underwater preserve.

The schooner was constructed in 1856 in Cleveland, Ohio and was 137 feet long. Typical of the schooners of the day, the ship sported only a single deck and two masts.

The steamer was built in 1853, also in Cleveland. It was 185 feet long and bound for Buffalo, N.Y. from Milwaukee, Wis. with a load of wheat when the disaster occurred.

The *J.H. Tiffany* was bound to Chicago, Ill. from Oswego, N.Y. with a cargo of rail iron when it collided with the steamer *Milwaukee* in the autumn darkness. Watching the entire event was the crew of the steamer *Free State*, which was traveliing in consort with the other steamer.

Both vessels sank quickly in about 100 feet of water. The *Free State* first rescued the crew of the *Milwaukee* and then turned her attention to the *J.H. Tiffany*. Although five lives aboard the stricken vessel were lost, five crewmen were found in the trees (masts) of the *J.H. Tiffany*. Masts sometimes protruded above the surface after a shipwreck and sailors would occasionally cling for days until rescue.

Today, divers will find the remains of the vessels less than a half mile apart. The hull of the *J.H. Tiffany* is flattened on the bottom as the result of salvage operations. The cargo and ship's machinery was recovered so there is not much for divers to explore at this site.

The site of the *Milwaukee,*however, is more interesting to divers because the remains are upright and include the ship's propeller, wheel, windlass, and other machinery. Some machinery was recovered in a salvage operation but enough remains to keep divers interested in this historic vessel.

Location:	The *Milwaukee* is located in Lake Michigan about 5.2 miles from Grays Reef Light on a bearing of 238 degrees. The *J.H. Tiffany* is located 4.8 miles from the light on a bearing of 232 degrees.
Loran:	31407.2/48077.8 (*Milwaukee*) 31402.0/48081.7 (*J.H. Tiffany*)
Lat/Lon:	45 43.50/85 14.85 (*Milwaukee*) 45 43.37/85 13.76 (*J.H. Tiffany*)
Depth:	95-105 feet
Visibility:	10-20 feet
Tips:	If you are in the neighborhood visiting the *Cayuga*, the *Milwaukee* makes a good second dive.

ALBEMARLE

The *Albemarle* was a 154-foot, wooden-hulled schooner that was built in 1867 in Buffalo, N.Y. It was hauling a cargo of iron ore when it ran into an autumn gale. On Nov. 6, 1867, the vessel ran aground north of Point Nipigon. Salvors recovered the ship's masts, anchors, cargo, and various equipment soon after the disaster.

The *Albemarle* led a short life on the Great Lakes, primarily serving the upper Great Lakes and Lake Erie, less than one season, but today it provides divers with an opportunity to learn about ship construction as the keelsons and centerboard trunk are still intact. Some ribs and hull planking are still standing at the site.

This site is usually not buoyed and lies only 100 yards northwest of the wreck of the *Henry Clay*.

Location:	In Lake Huron just north of Point Nipigon. The site is usually not buoyed.
Loran:	31188.7/48183.1
Lat/Lon:	45 42.57/84 33.50
Depth:	10-12 feet
Visibility:	10-20 feet, less if heavy seas are running.
Tips:	This site makes a good snorkel and can be reached from shore (about 150 yards).

HENRY CLAY

The *Henry Clay* was a 87-foot brig built in 1842 in Huron, Ohio. Little is known about the working life of this small sailing vessel but these vessels were once very common on the Great Lakes as they served small communities hauling package freight from the east. Cargoes such as fish, salt, and other foodstuffs were common.

Small sailing vessels such as this were once common on the Great Lakes.

This ship was stranded on Dec. 3, 1850 during a prolonged storm at the Straits of Mackinac. The crew was rescued and the *Henry Clay* was left to the forces of waves and ice.

Today, divers will find little but timbers remaining. But the wreck is only 100 yards southeast of the *Albemarle*. Both can be reached from shore and make a good snorkel.

Location:	North of Point Nipigon, about 100 yards southeast of the wreck of the *Albemarle*.
Loran:	31189.7/48183.7
Lat/Lon:	45 43.33/84 32.31
Depth:	10-12 feet
Visibility:	10-20 feet, less if heavy seas are running.
Tips:	This could be part of a good scuba dive/snorkel if visited with the wreck of the *Albemarle*.

EBER WARD

The wreck of the *Eber Ward* illustrates the fact that shipwrecks can occur on the Great Lakes even on calm, sunny days.

It was such a day on April 20, 1909 when the ship, bound for Port Huron, Mich. with a load of 55,000 bushels of corn from Milwaukee, Wis. struck an ice floe in the Straits of Mackinac.

The EBER WARD on the Great Lakes.

The ice cut a deep gash in the bow of the *Eber Ward* and the ship sank in ten minutes taking five of her crew with it. Before this fateful day, the 213-foot, wooden-hulled steamer had served the Great Lakes shipping trade for 21 years with little problem. Two years after the disaster, the load of corn was salvaged and sold to a starch works, which demonstrates the preservation qualities of the Great Lakes.

The remains of the wreck were discovered in 1980 by Chuck and Jeri Feltner, of Dearborn, Mich. Divers will find the wreck upright with a modest debris field off the stern. The gash that sank the vessel can be plainly seen on the port side near the bottom in 140 feet of water.

Although the cabins and transom are not intact, divers will be interested in seeing unusual cargo unloading machinery in some of the hatches. A lifeboat, which capsized during the sinking, is found northeast of the port stern.

Location:	In Lake Michigan northwest of Mackinaw City. This site is usually buoyed with a mooring buoy.
Loran:	31253.6/48096.7
Lat/Lon:	45 48.13/84 49.04
Depth:	130-140 feet
Visibility:	10-15 feet
Tips:	Watch for currents and use extreme caution at this depth.

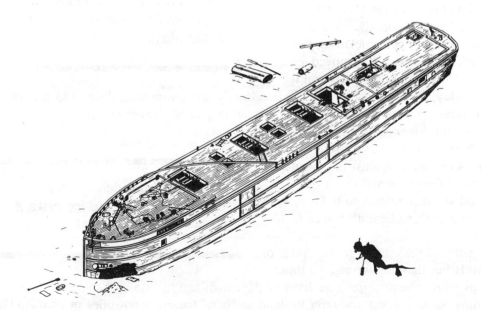

The EBER WARD today. (Graphic Copyright 1980 by Chuck & Jeri Feltner)

CANISTEO

The forces of waves and ice can be tremendous in the Great Lakes. They can take sturdy steel hulls and, over time, crush them like so much aluminum foil. It is in the shallow water where these forces are especially powerful. In water less than 20 feet deep, waves and ice are capable of moving even the most immoveable shipwreck up and down the coast. Waves and ice, unrelenting.

From the air is the best place to see how sturdy hulls have been pummeled to pieces and then moved again and again like a child's broken toy in a clumsy dance we may never understand. The *Canisteo* knows that dance. Lying in 15 feet of water, waves and ice levitated the shipwreck more than 3,000 feet into shallower water. Time marks her progress on the bottomland. Waves and ice.

The *Canisteo* was a 196-foot steamer built in 1862 in Buffalo, N.Y. She was a proud vessel that served many Great Lakes ports hauling bulk cargoes in her fragile, wooden hull. On the evening of Oct. 14, 1880, the ship met her end when it ran aground at Waugoshance Light. Only those who have traversed this narrow hallway between Gray's Reef and White Shoal know how such a navigational error can be made in the middle of the night.

While the crew sought the aid of a tug to pull off the stricken *Canisteo,* Mother Nature was readying a final knockout blow in the form of a powerful gale that broke up the ship two days after the grounding.

> *Only those who have traversed this narrow hallway between Gray's Reef and White Shoal know how such a navigational error can be made in the middle of the night.*

The bones of the *Canisteo* can be spotted easily from the air and newspaper accounts detailing the wreck show that it has moved eastward over time. Waves and ice.

Today, divers will find the *Canisteo* badly broken up with about 143 feet of her hull intact. The remainder has been ground to pieces. Waves and ice.

No machinery remains, only the keelsons and some ribs testify to the forces of nature against the ingenuity of man. Only remnants of a once-proud steamer remain to tell a story about a century beneath waves and ice.

> *It is a little melancholy, this business. Waves and ice make it so.*

Some divers refuse to dive piles of boards but they are wrong. To those of us who believe ships have lives of their own and always call ships by their full names out of respect and refer to them as "her," these are not piles of boards. They are piles of bones. It is a little melancholy, this business. Waves and ice make it so.

Location:	About .6 miles east of Waugoshance Light.
Loran:	31341.9/48070.8
Lat/Lon:	45 47.32/85 04.75
Depth:	12-15 feet
Visibility:	10-20 feet
Tips:	This site makes a good snorkel and a good second dive for novice wreck divers. But, owing to its remote location, few dive this pile of bones. If returning from the *Cayuga* or the *Colonel Ellsworth,* give it a try.

COLONEL ELLSWORTH

Some of us are lucky in life and so it was with the *Colonel Ellsworth.* The Great Lakes is a dangerous mistress that can easily lead the unwary astray. If we are lucky long enough we begin to take our good fortune for granted. And so it was with the *Colonel Ellsworth.*

The *Colonel Ellsworth* was a 137-foot schooner born in 1861 in an Euclid, Ohio shipyard. After six years on the lakes, in 1867, the ship ran aground late in the season at Thunder Bay near Alpena, Mich. She spent her winter beached on the shore and was removed the following spring.

Again in the late autumn, the *Colonel Ellsworth* ran aground again off Forty Mile Point in Lake Huron while it was hauling a full load of coal. In May 1870, the ship collided with another near Green Bay, Wis. The *Colonel Ellsworth* was thought by some to have run out of luck when it sank in 1872 on the Canadian side of Lake Erie. And in 1875 the ship pressed her luck again when it ran aground near Calumet, Mich. during a Lake Superior gale. Then in late autumn of 1895, the aging *Colonel Ellsworth* ran aground at Whitefish Point in Lake Superior and spent another winter on the beach.

Each time the ship ran into trouble the resourcefulness of the captain and her owners managed to save the small schooner. But in the late autumn of 1896, luck ran out for the *Colonel Ellsworth.* This time the ship collided with the schooner *Emily B. Maxwell* four miles northeast of Waugoshance Point. She was eastbound and headed for the Straits of Mackinac when the bow flooded and the ship sank in 85 feet of water.

> *Each time the ship ran into trouble the resourcefulness of the captain and her owners managed to save the small schooner.*

Divers will find the once-lucky vessel upright and intact. Although the cabins and the aft deck, at 70 feet, are pushed up somewhat, there is much to see here. The bow is broken up a bit and the vessel's machinery and anchors were removed. Still, some hardware remains.

Some of us are lucky in life. And if we begin to take luck for granted it is often taken away. So it is was with the *Colonel Ellsworth*.

Location:	About six miles northeast of White Shoals Light.
Loran:	31317.2/48067.7
Lat/Lon:	45 48.26/85 01.00
Depth:	70-85 feet
Visibility:	10-15 feet
Tips:	Many small artifacts remain because the wreck is remote and few divers dive it. It is usually not buoyed.

NEWELL A. EDDY

The wreck of the *Newell A. Eddy* proved that few nondivers understand how many such vessels have been wrecked on the Great Lakes. When it was accidentally discovered by a scientific research vessel in 1991, it made headlines; quite unusual for a scow schooner less glamorous than most semi-trucks on the highway.

For divers, it became a test of mettle, a challenge of how far they would go to reach the highly publicized discovery. Northeast of Bois Blanc Island in Lake Huron, the site is remote. And at 168 feet, a decompression dive, the wreck was a challenge for those who push recreational diving limits.

The *Newell A. Eddy* was constructed in 1890 in West Bay City, Mich. It was a three-masted scow schooner barge with a wooden hull 242 feet in length. Little of the history of this vessel has been reported, probably because like most scow schooners, it merely served as a cargo barge towed by steamers.

The end for the *Newell A. Eddy* came during a spring gale while the vessel was enroute from Chicago, Ill. to Buffalo, N.Y. with a load of corn. On April 20, 1893, the relatively young *Newell A. Eddy* became separated from her steamer consort as

The forces of huge waves were too much and the schooner sank taking nine lives with her.

a gale began to rage. The steamer lost its steering gear and could not come to the aid of the schooner. Both vessels were left on their own to weather the storm.

The *Newell A. Eddy* found herself at the northeast end of Bois Blanc Island and deployed an anchor, a tactic often used in heavy seas. But the forces of huge waves were too much and the schooner sank taking nine lives with her. A day after the storm, most of the stern section of the vessel washed ashore at Bois Blanc Island. The vessel was presumed lost and was not in the news again for a century.

In July 1992, the University of Michigan research vessel *Laurentian* was demonstrating side scan sonar equipment to students when it ran across a three-masted schooner with eight hatches. Research indicated that it was the wreck of the *Newell A. Eddy* and a later expedition by the university confirmed the identity.

> **Today, the Newell A. Eddy rests in 168 feet of water and rises so that it is 144 feet to the deck of the vessel.**

Today, the *Newell A. Eddy* rests in 168 feet of water and rises so that it is 144 feet to the deck of the vessel. A mast is partially erect and rises to within 78 feet of the surface. Local divers sometimes place a small marking buoy on this mast, which can be followed down to the deck. Anchorage, because of the depth, can be a problem at this site.

The stern section is broken up and the stern cabin section is missing, but the bow, including capstans and other machinery, is upright and intact. Divers enjoy exploring the bow machinery and examining the bow nameplates and the eagle figurehead.

Location:	On the northeast side of Bois Blanc Island, about .3 miles north of Raynolds Reef.
Lat/Lon:	45 46.89/84 13.75
Depth:	80-168 feet
Visibility:	10-20 feet
Tips:	Always use extreme caution when exceeding recommended recreational diving depth limits.

FRED McBRIER

The *Fred McBrier* was a wooden-hulled steamer constructed in 1881 at West Bay City, Mich. by the same shipbuilder that constructed the *Newell A. Eddy*. The *Fred McBrier* was one of many small steamers that were used to tow scow schooners.

In October 1890, the ship was downbound with a cargo of iron ore and towing two scow schooners when it was struck by the much larger steamer *Progress* west of the Straits of Mackinac. The 161-foot *Fred McBrier* sank quickly but there was no loss of life.

The wreck of the *Fred McBrier* was discovered in 1967 and many artifacts, including a one-ton anchor, were recovered from 104 feet of water.

Today, divers will find the *Fred McBrier* upright and intact. Much machinery, such as engines, boiler, and windlass, remain to offer divers an interesting exploration opportunity. But the wreck is rarely visited by scuba divers because visibility is often low and the vessel is broken in a manner that makes it confusing to dive.

Location:	In Lake Michigan, about 9 miles west of Old Mackinac Point.
Loran:	31287.8/48085.3
Lat/Lon:	45 48.11/84 55.09
Depth:	104 feet
Visibility:	2-15 feet
Tips:	Note that silt gets kicked up and reduces visibility here. Also, be sure to orient yourself carefully during the dive.

GENESEE CHIEF and LEVIATHAN

The *Genesee Chief* was originally built as a twin propeller steamer in 1846 in Carthage, N.Y. It served 17 years on the Great Lakes until 1863 when it was rebuilt into a single-propeller steamer and in 1868 burned to the waterline. Also in 1868, the vessel was rebuilt into a barge and in 1885, the *Genesee Chief* was rebuilt into a 142-foot, two-masted schooner.

The number of rebuilds on such an old, wooden-hulled vessel indicates how pressed shipowners were to get every trip they could out of the resources they had. It is interesting to note that during much of the 1800s, shipowners could usually recoup their ship expenses in abut three years. If that was the case, then the *Genesee Chief* paid for herself several times over.

In 1891 the vessel waterlogged and was abandoned in the Cheboygan, Mich. harbor. Eventually, the *Genesee Chief* and the *Leviathan* were towed to Duncan Bay and scuttled.

The *Leviathan* was a twin-propeller steamer built in 1857 in Buffalo, N.Y. It was 126 feet long and was well known in the Straits

During much of the 1800s, shipowners could usually recoup their ship expenses in abut three years. If that was the case, then the Genesee Chief paid for herself several times over.

of Mackinac area as a salvage and wrecking tug. It was stationed at Mackinac Island and Cheboygan for most of her life and was known to have pulled many ships out of trouble in the Straits.

The *Leviathan* sank at her docks in Cheboygan in 1891. It was later raised, stripped of its metal and machinery, and scuttled in Duncan Bay with the *Genesee Chief*.

Today, both vessels lie upright but are broken up in shallow water. The *Leviathan* makes a more interesting dive because her heavy timbers were more durable. The *Genesee Chief* lies about 100 yards south of the *Leviathan* at the mouth of Duncan Bay.

Location:	Both vessels are found at the mouth of Duncan Bay in shallow water.
Loran:	31156.9/48227.8 (*Genesee Chief*)
	31156.5/48228.0 (*Leviathan*)
Lat/Lon:	45 39.71/84 26.13 (*Genesee Chief*)
	45 39.65/84 25.95 (*Leviathan*)
Depth:	10-12 feet
Visibility:	10-25 feet
Tips:	The wrecks of both vessels can be seen in one dive. They are only 100 yards apart.

M. STALKER

The *M. Stalker* was a small, 135-foot, schooner that served the iron ore trade. It was built in 1863 in Milan, Ohio and had a rating of 267 gross tons.

The *M. Stalker* was slightly damaged in a gale while sitting at the Marquette iron ore docks on Lake Superior in 1869. The vessel was rebuilt in 1875 and received major repairs in 1885. Only a year later, in 1886, the *M. Stalker* was lost for all time.

It was during a November 1886 storm that the *M. Stalker* anchored off Mackinaw City to ride out the heavy seas. While at anchorage, the vessel was struck by a scow schooner towed by a small steamer. At first, the crew thought they could save the plucky *M. Stalker* (named after her captain) with steam bilge pumps, but the water rose too quickly and was soon abandoned.

The crew thought they could save the plucky M. Stalker with steam bilge pumps, but the water rose too quickly and was soon abandoned.

The wreck was discovered in 1967 and some artifacts, such as nameboards, were recovered.

The *M. Stalker* lies upright and intact although the stern section is broken up. Much machinery and large artifacts remain on the wreck. Divers can expect to find a centerboard winch, windlass, wire rigging, bilge pump, and similar items. This site is sometimes buoyed with a mooring buoy but caution must be exercised because it lies in the Mackinac Island ferry route.

The M. STALKER in an oil painting.

Location:	In Lake Huron about two miles east of Old Mackinac Point.
Loran:	31213.6/48125.9
Lat/Lon:	45 47.38/84 41.04
Depth:	85 feet
Visibility:	5-15 feet
Tips:	Visibility is often reduced on this wreck due to silt and current conditions.

MAITLAND

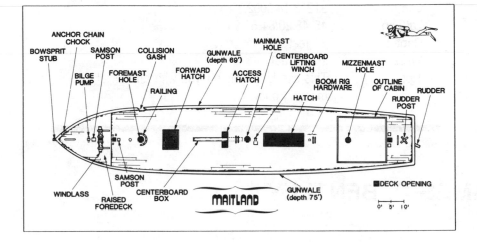

Site Plan of the MAITLAND.
(Graphic Copyright 1981 by Chuck & Jeri Feltner)

The *Maitland* was a 133-foot bark that was built in 1861 in Goderich, Ont. It was rated at 252 gross tons.

The ship was bound for Buffalo, N.Y. from Chicago, Ill. on June 9, 1871, with a cargo of corn when it was struck a glancing blow by another schooner, the *Golden Harvest.* The collision is somewhat of a mystery because visibility was good that evening and the captains took evasive actions to avoid the accident.

During the collision, the bowsprit of the *Maitland* was broken and a hole was cut into her starboard bow hull. The *Golden Harvest* did not escape unscathed. The *Golden Harvest* crew suffered two serious injuries and lost her masts. Eventually it was towed to Racine, Wis. for repairs.

Today, the remains of the *Maitland* are found in 85 feet of water. The vessel is upright and intact and divers will discover that they can penetrate the stern cabins. Many artifacts, including deck hardware, windlass and centerboard lifting winch, are found at the site.

> **The vessel is upright and intact and divers will discover that they can penetrate the stern cabins.**

The vessel sports a single deck and three mast holes (the masts were recovered). The *Maitland* is considered one of the best sites in this preserve.

Location:	About seven miles west of Old Mackinac Point in Lake Michigan.
Loran:	31273.1/48092.7
Lat/Lon:	45 48.20/84 52.29
Depth:	85 feet
Visibility:	10-20 feet
Tips:	This site is usually buoyed with an official mooring buoy.

JAMES R. BENTLEY

The *James R. Bentley* was a 178-foot wooden-hulled schooner that was built in 1867 in Fairport, Ohio.

On Nov. 12, 1878, the ship was bound for Buffalo, N.Y. from Chicago, Ill. with a load of 35,000 bushels of rye. When the ship was nearly through the Straits of Mackinac area, it struck a reef between Lighthouse Point and Bois Blanc Island in Lake Huron.

The force of the collision caused the centerboard significant damage and the vessel began to take on water. The captain and crew tried to save the stricken vessel for more than three hours but a strong northwest gale made the effort impossible. All hands escaped the wreck in a yawl and the *James R. Bentley* sank bow first.

Today, divers will find the wreck upright and intact. There are many artifacts at this site, including belaying pins, anchors, deck hardware, and windlass.

Because of its depth, and the fact that it is officially outside the preserve boundaries, this wreck is not usually buoyed.

Location:	About 10 miles east of Poe Reef Light in Lake Huron.
Loran:	31057.7/48251.1
Lat/Lon:	45 41.45/84 09.12
Depth:	150 feet
Visibility:	5-15 feet
Tips:	Visibility here is often very low due to heavy silting.

L.B. COATES and MYRTIE M. ROSS

The *L.B. Coates* was a 116-foot schooner that was built in 1874 in Saugatuck, Mich. It was considered "lost" in 1922, making this a very long-lived schooner considering that the average lifespan of such wooden-hulled vessels was only seven years on the Great Lakes.

The vessel had a variety of owners through her lifetime and probably was used to transport package goods between small Great Lakes communities. *The L.B. Coates* was eventually abandoned at the Whitehall Lumber Company dock around 1921. The wreck of the *Myrtie M. Ross* lies within 200 feet of the *L.B. Coates*. Seamen call this abandonment of a ship in shallow water "moldering". Eventually, the portions of the wreck above water degrade and end up in the water and it is impossible to tell a ship was left there decades ago.

The *Myrtie M. Ross* was a 113-foot steamer that was built in 1890 at South Haven, Mich. The little steamer hauled freight of various kinds including coal and grain. The vessel was involved in several mishaps and sank at least twice but was repaired and put back in service each time.

Finally, on Oct. 28, 1913, during a regular inspection by government officials, her boilers and hull were declared unsafe and she was refused a

Both wrecks sit upright but are completely broken up.

license to operate. She was declared abanonded in 1916 at the Whitehall Lumber Company dock.

Today, divers can visit both shipwrecks in 8 to 10 feet of water near the Little Black River near Cheboygan. Both wrecks sit upright but are completely broken up. Machinery and metal items have been removed over the years so there is little to see but large timbers. Pilings from old docks are a hazard to boaters so it is best to inspect this wreckage from shore.

Location:	About 400 feet offshore and 1,500 feet west of the mouth of the Little Black River near Cheboygan.
Loran:	31174.2/48219.0 (*L.B. Coates*) 31174.9/48218.8 (*Myrtie M. Ross*)
Lat/Lon:	45 39.85/84 29.02 (*L.B. Coates*) 45 39.90/84 28.98 (*Myrtie M. Ross*)
Depth:	8-10 feet
Visibility:	10-20 feet
Tips:	Although there is little here to justify a scuba dive, this site makes a good snorkel. Access from shore.

MINNEAPOLIS

The *Minneapolis* was a 226-foot steamer that was built in 1873 in Marine City, Mich. In its day, it was considered on the large size for a steamer. Wooden-hulled vessels of this type could only be built to a little over 200 feet because designs of the time could strengthen the hull only so much. Large arches were incorporated and either stood above decks or were part of the hull construction.

The *Minneapolis* started her first run of the 1894 season on April 1 from the Chicago River Harbor with a load of 48,000 bushels of wheat and pulling schow schooners that were also loaded with grain. Interestingly, the *William H. Barnum*, (see page 277) also started the season from this port and ended her career one day before the *Minneapolis,* at the Straits of Mackinac.

Three days into the voyage to Buffalo, N.Y., the crew of the *Minneapolis* suddenly realized that the hold was filling rapidly with water. Pumps could not keep pace with the flow and the crew of 14 managed to escape almost as the *Minneapolis* sunk from sight.

After the disaster, the crew of the *Minneapolis* surmised that ice cut into the wooden hull because iron plates protecting the bow were not secured after winter repairs. But the wreck was discovered in the early 1960s and since then divers have been unable to pinpoint a cause of the wreck.

> ***Pumps could not keep pace with the flow and the crew of 14 managed to escape almost as the Minneapolis sunk from sight.***

Today, divers will find the *Minneapolis* upright and mostly intact. Part of the bow section is broken but there are many interesting artifacts left on the wreck including a donkey steam engine amidships, 12-foot propeller, and other machinery. The smokestack is erect and rises to within 75 feet of the surface.

Because this wreck is so close to the commercial shipping lanes, it is usually not buoyed. It is found about 500 feet southwest of the main south tower of the Mackinac Bridge. Strong currents and heavy silt, which reduces visibility, make this a wreck to dive cautiously.

Location:	About 500 feet southwest of the Mackinac Bridge's main south tower.
Loran:	31226.2/48111.2
Lat/Lon:	45 48.32/84 45.54
Depth:	75-125 feet
Visibility:	2-15 feet depending upon current conditions.
Tips:	Use extreme caution when diving this wreck due to poor visibility and currents. This wreck is usually not buoyed.

The MINNEAPOLIS in more productive days.

NORTHWEST

The story of the *Northwest* is much like the story of any 18-wheeler on the highway. It was a 223-foot scow schooner that was built in 1873 in Bangor, Mich. It had a single deck and four masts with a square stern.

Although little is actually known about the working life of the *Northwest,* it is reasonable to assume that, like other scow schooners of her day, the vessel was used to haul bulk cargoes such as iron ore, grain, coal, limestone, and similar materials. Rarely, if ever, would the sails be deployed. Instead, it was likely towed by small steamers and in consort with other schooners of her ilk.

But on April 6, 1898, after a long life on the Great Lakes, the *Northwest* made a plunge to the bottom of the Straits of Mackinac. The *Northwest*'s hull was damaged by ice as it entered the Straits of Mackinac and began to take on water. The crew of the steamer *Aurora,* which was towing the *Northwest* tried to pull the stricken schooner to shallow water but the tactic did not succeed. Instead, the crew of the *Aurora* and *Northwest* could only watch helplessly from the steamer's deck as the schooner slipped away.

> *On April 6, 1898, after a long life on the Great Lakes, the* **Northwest** *made a plunge to the bottom of the Straits of Mackinac.*

The resting place of the *Northwest* was discovered by Chuck and Jeri Feltner in 1978. Today, divers will find the wreckage broken and scattered. The site is quite a mess, which makes it difficult for divers to orient themselves.

The wreck is collapsed on the port side and the transom is broken up, but there are key artifacts remaining, including a donkey steam engine and other machinery.

Some artifacts have been removed from the wreck since its discovery. These artifacts include an anchor, which is on display at Dossin Great Lakes Museum in Detroit, Mich. This site is usually buoyed with a mooring buoy.

Location:	About 6 miles west of Old Mackinac Point.
Loran:	31270.2/48102.2
Lat/Lon:	45 47.32/84 51.30
Depth:	About 75 feet
Visibility:	10-20 feet
Tips:	Wreckage lays in a confusing pattern.

RICHARD WINSLOW

The *Richard Winslow* was a 216-foot schooner that was built in 1871 in Detroit, Mich. At 885.2 gross tons, this vessel was the largest sailing ship on the Great Lakes for a time.

The *Richard Winslow* set several records for hauling cargoes of coal and grain. She spent much of her life running from Cleveland, Ohio to Chicago, Ill. with coal. In 1890, the vessel was sold and cut down to a tow barge.

The last season for the *Richard Winslow* was 1898 when, on Sept. 4, while hauling a load of iron ore from Escanaba, Mich. to Cleveland, Ohio, the schooner ran into a strong southwest gale while in tow by the steamer *Inter Ocean*. The crew of the *Richard Winslow* discovered that water was rising rapidly in the bilge and the steamer rescued the crew. The schooner sank near the White Shoals buoy.

> **The crew of the Richard Winslow discovered that water was rising rapidly in the bilge and the steamer rescued the crew.**

In 1902, the wreck was dynamited by the U.S. Corps of Engineers as a hazard to navigation. The location was discovered by sport divers in 1981 and three weeks after disclosing the location to others, both anchors were stripped from the wreck. Fortunately, one Alpena diver was prosecuted for the theft. The court decision set precedence, which is followed today in state courtrooms.

Divers will find that the *Richard Winslow* is completely broken up due to the dynamiting. Still, there remains enough machinery and other artifacts to keep divers interested. And while this wreck may not be "worth" the long haul, it may make a good second dive when visiting westerly wrecks such as the *Colonel Ellsworth* or *Cayuga*.

Location:	1½ miles west of White Shoals Light.
Loran:	31356.4/48026.4
Lat/Lon:	45 50.45/85 09.48
Depth:	30-35 feet
Visibility:	10-20 feet
Tips:	Follow an organized search pattern to find all of the artifacts associated with this wreck. It is usually not buoyed.

ST. ANDREW

The *St. Andrew* lies in the easterly portion of the Straits of Mackinac Underwater Preserve and has been more popular in recent years, especially when westerly winds blow, because it is in fairly protected water.

The vessel was a schooner that was built in 1857 in Milan, Ohio. The *St. Andrew* saw its last run on June 26, 1878, when it collided with another schooner, the *Peshtigo*, when both ships were about five miles west of Cheboygan, Mich. The vessel was loaded with a cargo of corn bound from Buffalo, N.Y. from Chicago, Ill.

Interestingly, the captain of the St. Andrew was Edward Fitzgerald, part of the sea-going Fitzgerald family and whose namesake, the *Edmund Fitzgerald*, sank in 1975 in Lake Superior.

One way the *St. Andrew* was identified was through the stepping coin. It was customary for shipbuilders to place a coin in the slot carved for the mast in a keelson. Traditionally, the coin would be minted the same year as the ship was built, or underwent a major rebuilding. The stepping coin of this wreck matches the build date: 1857.

> *Traditionally, the coin would be minted the same year as the ship was built, or underwent a major rebuilding.*

Divers will find this shipwreck upright and mostly intact. The stern section is broken up, perhaps by the force of hitting the bottom when it sank. This wreck is a good one for beginning wreck divers as there is usually no current or silt and is relatively shallow. Visibility is usually quite good here.

The centerboard is intact and divers may want to inspect the construction techniques used to make it. Watch for fishlife. This dive site is usually buoyed with an official mooring buoy.

Location:	In Lake Huron, about 11 miles southeast of Old Mackinac Point.
Loran:	31180.2/48195.1
Lat/Lon:	45 42.07/84 31.46
Depth:	55-62 feet
Visibility:	10-20 feet

SANDUSKY

The wreck of the *Sandusky* is one of the most popular shipwrecks in the Straits of Mackinac Underwater Preserve. With brig rigging, the vessel was nortoriously difficult to navigate in close quarters, which may have been a contributing factor in her demise in this area.

The *Sandusky* was constructed in 1848 in Sandusky, Ohio. It was 110 feet long, wooden hulled, and rated at 225 gross tons.

This brig left the Chicago Harbor on Sept. 16, 1856 and two days later found herself in a terrible gale. Bound for Buffalo, N.Y. from Chicago, Ill. with a cargo of grain, the *Sandusky* was unable to handle the high seas created by the Lake Michigan storm. The vessel sank about 5 miles west of Old Mackinac Point. Seven lives were lost in the disaster.

The wreck of the *Sandusky* is interesting to divers for several important reasons. First, it lies upright and intact and many of its "finer" features have survived the wrecking incident and years on the bottom. Thankfully, divers have done an excellent job protecting some of the smaller artifacts, although the wheel is now broken up. Divers will find deadeyes, a cutwater bow, a 45-foot bowsprit, two wood-stock anchors, and jib-boom.

The brig also sported a scroll figurehead (like a ram's head), one of a few on the Great Lakes. It was removed by divers who feared that others would take it. Eventually, the figurehead ended up at the Michigan Maritime Museum where it remains

Thankfully, divers have done an excellent job protecting some of the smaller artifacts, although the wheel is now broken up.

today. A replica figurehead was made and placed on the wreck in 1989.

The brig rigging of the *Sandusky* is fairly uncommon because it was a clumsy affair in close quarters. Many Great Lakes vessels eventually adopted the fore and

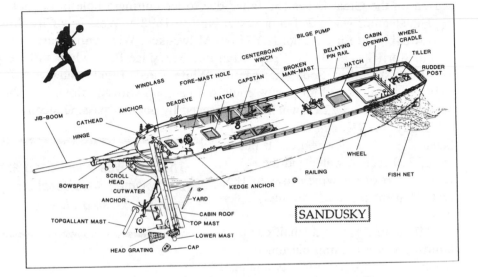

The Sandusky
Graphic Copyright 1981 by Chuck & Jeri Feltner.

aft schooner rigging, which was more maneuverable.

The wreck is also popular because it lies fairly close to Michigan's Lower Peninsula, which offers some respite from the weather, depending upon the direction of the wind. Visibility is generally good to excellent here and the wreck is usually buoyed with an official mooring buoy.

Location:	About 5 miles west of Old Mackinac Point in Lake Michigan.
Loran:	31261.8/48100.9
Lat/Lon:	45 48.09/84 50.06
Depth:	85 feet
Visibility:	10-30 feet
Tips:	This wreck is watched closely. Don't consider taking even the smallest artifact.

UGANDA

The *Uganda* was one of several wooden-hulled vessels that attempted an early season on the Great Lakes and failed due to ice cutting a hole in the hull.

The steamer was a 291-foot vessel built in 1892 at West Bay City, Mich. The ship was bound for Buffalo, N.Y. from Milwaukee, Wis. with a cargo of corn.

On April 19, 1913, the *Uganda* ran into heavy ice floes while still west of the Straits of Mackinac. Soon after passing White Shoals Light, water was discovered rising in the hold and all pumps could not keep up with the flow. The ship was abandoned and all 22 crewmen were rescued by another passing steamer.

Today, the *Uganda* remains pristine because it is rarely dived on. It lies in about 210 feet of water and the highest part of the wreck rises to 185 feet. That makes it an extremely risky dive.

> *The ship was abandoned and all 22 crewmen were rescued by another passing steamer.*

All cabins, except a small cabin amidships, are missing but much machinery and other artifacts remain.

It is interesting to note that the *Uganda* sits near the bottom of a deep trench that extends between Michigan's Upper and Lower Peninsulas. This is believed to be the remnants of an ancient river that once connected Lake Michigan to Lake Huron soon after the last Ice Age, about 10,000 years ago. The wreck of the *Eber Ward* (see page???) rests about 100 feet from the edge of this trough.

The UGANDA, note the small cabin amidships.

Location:	About four miles directly east of White Shoals Light.
Loran:	31321.7/48047.2
Lat/Lon:	45 50.30/85 03.49
Depth:	185-210 feet
Visibility:	2-10 feet
Tips:	This is an extremely risky dive. Note that because of the depth, silt, and current, visibility here is usually quite poor. This site is usually not buoyed.

WILLIAM H. BARNUM

The WILLIAM H. BARNUM as she looked about 1873.

The wreck of the *William H. Barnum* is a very popular dive site in this preserve because it is found in only 75 feet of water, visibility is generally excellent, and the wreck is upright and mostly intact.

The *William H. Barnum* was a twin-deck steamer of 218 feet and was constructed in 1873 in Detroit, Mich. The vessel was hauling a cargo of 55,000 bushels of corn from Chicago, Ill. to Port Huron, Mich. when it ran into a nasty gale on April 3, 1894. In addition, many ice floes were in the area and the *William H. Barnum* eventually damaged her bow hull on one of them.

At first the crew believed they could save the vessel, but between the damage and foul weather she began to take water on rapidly. No lives were lost in the disaster thanks to a passing steamer. Ironically, the ship was nearly out of the Straits and probably could have weathered the storm had it been a little further along.

The ship's rail is nearly complete around the vessel but the stern section has been broken up by dynamite that was used to remove the rudder in the 1960s.

Today, the vessel lies on the bottom of Lake Huron, east-southeast of Mackinaw City. There is much to see, especially in the way of machinery, and although portions of the deck have collapsed, divers can penetrate the cargo holds. The ship's rail is nearly complete around the vessel but the stern section has been broken up by dynamite that was used to remove the rudder in the 1960s. The rudder is on display at the park near the municipal marina in St. Ignace.

Massive schools of whitefish and perch have been seen here and many burbots are generally found.

Location:	About 5½ miles east-southeast of Mackinaw City.
Loran:	31205.5/48153.3
Lat/Lon:	45 44.42/84 37.53
Depth:	70-75 feet
Visibility:	10-20 feet, sometimes more depending upon currents.
Tips:	This site is usually buoyed with an official mooring buoy. Please do not anchore into the wreck. Keep an eye out for large schools of whitefish.

Chuck's Barge

This unusual vessel was discovered by Chuck and Jeri Feltner in 1982. It is a wooden barge about 200 feet long resting in 43 feet of water and rises 11 feet from the bottom. Divers can explore the interior of the barge dumping mechanisms as it lies upside down on the bottom.

While no one is certain of its identity and how it happened to come to rest about a mile southwest of St. Helena Island, rumor has it that it was lost by the Durocher Dock and Dredge Company of Cheboygan, Mich. in the 1940s. It appears, from its construction, to have been used to haul dredge spoils.

This is a good wreck to dive as a second dive or for novice wreck divers. Look for large schools of whitefish that sometimes visit this wreck. Also, burbots are often found here.

This site is usually buoyed with an official mooring buoy.

Location:	One miles southeast of St. Helena Island in Lake Michigan.
Loran:	31255.8/48074.3
Depth:	32-43 feet
Visibility:	15-40 feet
Tips:	Stump your dive buddy. Ask him or her to figure out what this is.

Rock Maze

This is a relatively new dive site discovered by local divers who noted the unusual patterns of colors in the Lake Huron water east of Mackinac Island.

What divers found is a series of breccias, or pillars of resistant conglomerates, that rise more than 30 feet from the bottom to within a few inches of the surface. While the rock is not particularly colorful, its patterns are. There are caverns and steep rock walls to explore and fish often congregate here.

While it is unlikely to have a conflict with boaters, it is a good idea to fly a diver down flag. Often, however, anglers will come near to the dive site because they believe the dive boat is involved in fishing activities.

There are caverns and steep rock walls to explore and fish often congregate here.

Location:	About 300 yards east of Mackinac Island at Arch Rock.
Loran:	41155.27/48080.01
Lat/Lon:	45 54.863/84 36.403
Depth:	0-35 feet
Visibility:	15-40 feet
Tips:	This is a good, protected dive site and is usually not buoyed, but it is easy to find. Be careful with dive boats in here!

Inland Dive Sites

Because the Straits of Mackinac area has many protected areas, there is little inland diving in this region.

In Mackinac County, there are four lakes with public access sites. They are: Bay City, Millecoquins, South Manistique, and Milakokia lakes.

In the lower peninsula, in Emmet and Cheboygan counties, there are several lakes with public access sites, but little diving activity is seen.

Divers seeking a good inland dive site in this region should look to Torch Lake in Antrim County. This lake is noted for its clear, clean water but it is deep and cold. There are several access sites on the lake and landowners may permit access on their private property. Cribs, structures to attract fish, may be found throughout the lake and can provide an interesting opportunity to interact with finny friends.

Emergencies

On-water diving emergencies in this area are generally handled by the U.S. Coast Guard Station at St. Ignace. This station monitors vhf channel 16 and can also be reached on vhf channel 9 for emergencies. The U.S. Coast Guard here has several large vessels as well as smaller, fast boats for an emergency response. In addition, the Coast Guard has access to the Traverse City Air Station for evacuation, if necessary. The telephone number for the station is (906) 643-9191.

Once on land, it is best to coordinate with the Mackinac County Sheriff's Department, which dispatches ambulances in the community. They can be reached at (906) 643-1911 or (800) 643-1911. If divers contact the U.S. Coast Guard from their boats, the Coast Guard will have emergency crews ready and waiting on shore.

The nearest recompression chamber is located at Marquette, about a 2½- hour drive from St. Ignace.

Getting There

St. Ignace is the major "host" city for the Straits of Mackinac Underwater Preserve. It is here that the St. Ignace Chamber of Commerce provides expert advice and information on diving the preserve. Also, it is from here that most resident charter operators depart. Transient charter operators generally depart from Mackinaw City because of the facilities available and the relative closeness to the wrecks.

Both communities are located on I-75, which can be accessed throughout much of the state. To reach St. Ignace, cross the Mackinac Bridge and take Exit 345A and follow Business Route US-2 (State Street) north through the city. A resident dive charter operation, which includes a small dive shop with an air station, is found at the Star Line Main Dock on the north end of the city on the waterfront.

Mackinaw City is located south of the Mackinac Bridge off I-75 at exits 337 and 338. The municipal marina is located near Shepler's ferry docks on the waterfront. Michigan Department of Transportation Welcome Centers are found at both ends of the bridge.

St. Ignace has a small aircraft airport located on BR US-2 (State Street) north of the city. Also, regular bus service (Indian Trails) serves St. Ignace and Mackinaw City.

Visitors to the area should be aware that the Michigan State Police appear to seek out nonresidents for ticketing. Also, local judges levy heavier penalties on nonresidents as well. Local business people have

> *Visitors to the area should be aware that the Michigan State Police appear to seek out nonresidents for ticketing.*

routinely complained that the practices are hurting tourism in the area but the police and judges continue to treat nonresidents more harshly; so be on your best behavior!

Additional Information:

When it comes to the shipwrecks of the Straits of Mackinac, there is only one real reference. That is the book, *Shipwrecks of the Straits of Mackinac,* by Dr. Charles E. and Jeri Baron Feltner.

The Feltners are responsible for locating many of the most popular shipwrecks in the Straits. Their book details diving conditions, but more than that, provides a fascinating history of the vessels. The Feltners, besides being among the nicest people anyone would want to meet, are known for their attention to detail and ability to write a fascinating story about one of the most interesting areas of the Great Lakes.

Shipwrecks of the Straits of Mackinac is available at or through bookstores and at many dive centers, or by ordering directly from SeaJay Publications, P.O. Box 2176, Dearborn, MI 48123.

Accommodations

Because the Straits of Mackinac annually attracts about two million visitors during the summer months, overnight accommodations exist but divers must reserve them well ahead of time.

In addition to many fine motels and hotels, the Straits area also has many private and public campgrounds. Rustic campgrounds can be found in the Upper Peninsula as part of the Hiawatha National Forest. Information about all campgrounds is available by contacting the St. Ignace Chamber of Commerce.

Other Attractions

About two million visitors come to the Straits of Mackinac region each year to enjoy the many attractions. These attractions include quaint Mackinac Island with its colonial flair, restaurants, golf courses, fine hotels, or museums. Visitors can enjoy a re-enactment at the fort on the island or the many interpretive displays and program at Fort Michilimackinac at Mackinaw City. In addition, the Mill Creek facility, which is located between Mackinaw City and Cheboygan on U.S. 23, offers visitors a chance to learn about the early logging days in northern Michigan.

Besides all the trappings of a tourist mecca, the Straits region also boosts of outstanding natural resources, such as geologic formations, rare plants, and wildlife.

In Mackinaw City proper, most attention is focused on getting tourists to Mackinac Island and back. But at Wilderness State Park, west of the community (a village, actually, and not a city), offers miles of unspoiled wilderness trails for hiking with spectacular views of the Mackinac Bridge.

At Mackinac Island, visitors can visit many historic sites that have been restored by the state. These include the fort, cemetary, and the residence of Dr. Beaumont, who was reknowned for his work on the digestive system. A butterfly house and the Grand Hotel are also found on the island.

In St. Ignace, visitors can enjoy casino gambling, which attracts large crowds. Slot machines, blackjacks, roulette, and other games of chance tempt many who venture on the north side of the Mackinac Bridge. In addition, St. Ignace offers a museum dedicated to the interpretation of the life of Father Marquette, an early missionary to the region, as well as the Fort de Baude Museum in town. Quaint shops that feature unusual, Native American crafts are also found here.

In Cheboygan, 23 miles south of Mackinaw City on U.S. 23, visitors will find shopping and historic sites in the city. Perhaps the most attractive waterfront park in the region is found in Cheboygan with an extensive playground for children and boardwalk through a wetland for adults.

In Sault Ste. Marie, Mich., about 45 miles north of Mackinac City on I-75, visitors enjoy the museum ship *S.S. Valley Camp*, which served the Great Lakes commercial shipping trade for many decades. The ship has been converted to the

largest museum ship on the Great Lakes and is highly recommended. Also in Sault Ste. Marie are unusual
restaurants that cater to groups looking for something different, such as Antlers Bar, which is located near the waterfront.

Visitors also enjoy the fine campus of Lake Superior State University, which has one of the finest collections of shipwreck furniture in the area. Many shipwrecks dove on by divers today are represented in the collection despite state efforts to discourage such collecting and use of shipwreck artifacts.

Locals enjoy long summer days at the extensive beach along US-2 west, which follows the Lake Michigan shoreline for many miles. The beach is a great place to meet others and for family outings. Visitors will also learn about National Forest Service camping facilities located in the nearby Hiawatha National Forest.

Important Addresses/Phone Numbers

Mackinac County Sheriff's Dept.
100 Marley St.
St. Ignace, MI 49781
(906) 643-1911
(800) 643-1911

St. Ignace Ambulance Service
100 S. Marley
St. Ignace, MI 49781
(906) 643-8811

St. Ignace Chamber of Commerce
480 N. State St.
St. Ignace, MI 49781
(906) 643-8717
(800) 338-6660

St. Ignace Coast Guard Station
1075 Huron St.
St. Ignace, MI 49781
(906) 643-9191

Greater Mackinaw City Chamber
of Commerce
P.O. Box 856
S. Huron Ave.
Mackinaw City, MI 49701
(616) 436-5574

Mackinaw Area Tourist Bureau
P.O. Box 658
Mackinaw City, MI 49701
(616) 436-5664

Charter Operator:

Straits Dive Center (air station/charters/equipment)
587 N. State St.
St. Ignace, MI 49781
(906) 643-7009 or call
Macomb Scuba
(810) 558-9922

Lighthouses, such as this one
on St. Helena Island west of
the Straits of Mackinac, were
of limited use to vessel battling
the vicious waves and ice of
the Straits.

Thumb Area Underwater Preserve

There are ten major shipwrecks in the 276 square miles of the Thumb Area Underwater Preserve in Lake Huron. There are also other attractions that keep divers returning to this remote but scenic area.

Although there are no major cities now located in this preserve area, the region was once busy with ships traveling between Buffalo, N.Y. and western ports such as Duluth, Minn., Milwaukee, Wis., and Chicago, Ill. Storms, accidents, and fires claimed their share of these ships.

For many years few divers visited this preserve. It was an area known to a relatively few who sought the challenges a remote diving vacation can bring. But in recent years, the area has been served well by dive charter operators and retailers who have focused on the many underwater attractions found here.

Divers can expect to find shipwrecks in a variety of conditions--from intact to scattered pieces. Sites around docks near old port communities offer divers an opportunity to explore and discover artifacts from the past. Visibility in this region is excellent with up to 30 feet of visibility not uncommon.

The Thumb Area Underwater Preserve contains many shipwrecks that

have yet to be located. When diving in this area, look for debris trails that could lead to important and exciting discoveries of new dive sites. This is especially true in the Grindstone City area.

Many divers, with the advent of technical diving, seek out wrecks such as the *Daniel J. Morrell*, a lakes freighter resting intact in 213 feet of water. Another wreck of note in this area is the schooner *Dunderberg*, which rests in 155 feet of water.

In addition to charter operators, this preserve area also has boat launches and marinas capable of serving divers who bring their own vessels. And unlike other preserves, slip space is generally available throughout the summer as there is no substantial tourist influx during July and August.

Boating

Boating in the Thumb Area is convenient. Because this is a popular sport fishing region, there are many support facilities.

Boat launches are available at Harbor Beach, Wagener County Park, Port Hope, Stafford County Park, Port Crescent State Park, Lighthouse County Park, Port Austin, and Grindstone City. Because of the location of shipwrecks, dive boats generally launch from Lighthouse County Park, Grindstone City, and Harbor Beach. The latter two are best to launch boats over 22 feet.

Marinas are located at Harbor Beach, Port Austin, and Grindstone City. Those facilities offer transient accommodations, fuel, restrooms, and other support services. Most marinas monitor vhf channel 16. Because fishing in late summer is popular in this region, it is best to reserve slips in advance during July, August, and September.

Boaters must be aware that the shipping channel passes through the underwater preserve and a watchful eye should be posted to keep track of large ships. Security calls are a practical way of avoiding problems with commercial ship traffic.

PHILADELPHIA

The *Philadelphia* collided with the steamer *Albany* in 1893. The *Philadelphia* rests in about 130 feet of water.

The *Philadelphia* was a 236-foot steamer that took the *Albany* in tow for a short time after the collision. When the *Philadelphia* started to founder, the captain attempted to make it to shallow water.

The *Philadelphia* rests on the bottom upright and intact with some penetration diving possible. Divers may be surprised to find a cook stove still upright on the deck of the ship.

Location:	About 5.5 miles northeast of Pte. Aux Barques Lighthouse.
Loran:	30786.2/49183.7
Depth:	110-130 feet.
Visibility:	10-30 feet
Tips:	This wreck is usually buoyed with an official mooring buoy. To access this wreck it is best to depart from Grindstone City.

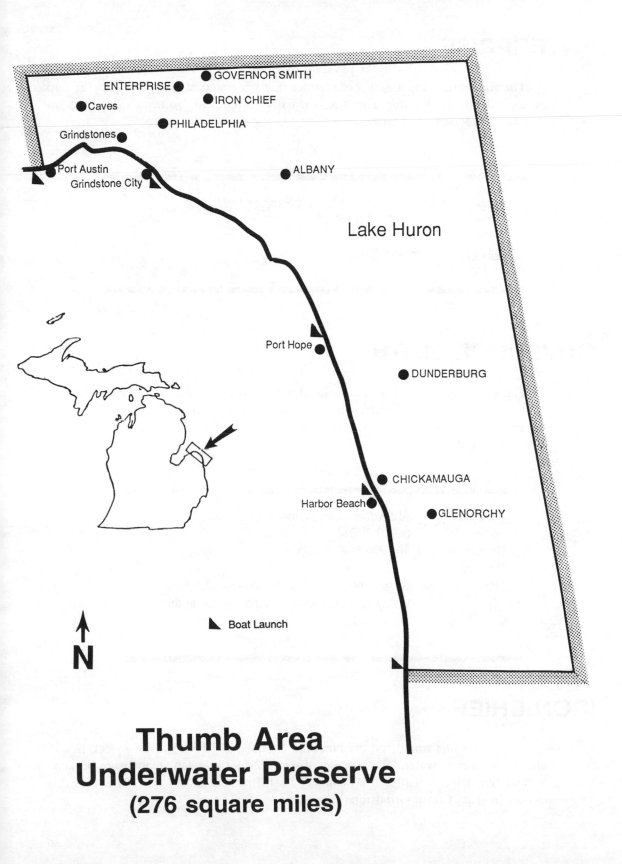

GOVERNOR SMITH

ENTERPRISE

IRON CHIEF

Caves

PHILADELPHIA

Grindstones

Port Austin

Grindstone City

ALBANY

Lake Huron

Port Hope

DUNDERBURG

CHICKAMAUGA

Harbor Beach

GLENORCHY

N

Boat Launch

Thumb Area
Underwater Preserve
(276 square miles)

ENTERPRISE

The *Enterprise* was a 120-foot steamer that was rated at 303 gross tons. It sank in about 185 feet of water. This site is usually not buoyed. To access this dive site it is best to depart from Grindstone City.

Location:	Northeast of Pte. Aux Barques Lighthouse.
Loran:	30779.8/49145.5
Depth:	180-185 feet
Visibility:	10-30 feet

GOVERNOR SMITH

The *Governor Smith* was a steamer that sank after a collision off Pte. Aux Barques in 1906. The shipwreck is scattered in deep water.

This site is generally not buoyed and to access it, it is best to depart from Grindstone City.

Location:	About four miles northeast of Grindstone City.
Loran:	30763.9/49141.3
Depth:	180-200 feet
Visibility:	5-20 feet
Tips:	Search the area for small artifacts. Debris is widely scattered. Use extreme caution at this depth.

IRON CHIEF

The *Iron Chief* foundered off Pte. Aux Barques in 1904. The shipwreck lies in about 135 feet of water. The remains of the 212-foot wooden steamer are broken up and wreckage is scattered. Machinery is still present at this site. To access it, it is best to depart from Grindstone City.

**The Thumb Area Underwater Preserve offers beautiful scenery
in addtion to a variety of underwater attractions.**

Location: About three miles northeast of Grindstone City.
Loran: 30779.0/49172.0
Depth: 125-140 feet
Visibility: 10-20 feet
Tips: This site is usually not buoyed. This wreck is sufficiently deep to warrant caution.

ALBANY

The *Albany* was a steel steamer that collided with the steamer *Philadelphia* about 12 miles off Pte. Aux Barques in 1893. The *Albany* was taken in tow by the *Philadelphia* for a short time after the collision but the *Albany* sank about eight miles northeast of the Pte. Aux Barques Lighthouse in about 150 feet of water.

The 267-foot ship was carrying a cargo of grain when it was lost. Twenty-four lives were lost in the disaster.

To access this dive site it is best to depart from Grindstone City. This wreck is usually not buoyed.

Location:	About eight miles northeast of Pte. Aux Barques Lighthouse.
Loran:	30775.5/49174.2
Depth:	130-140 feet
Visibility:	5-20 feet
Tips:	Use extreme caution at this depth.

DUNDERBURG

Little is known about the 187-foot schooner *Dunderburg*. The vessel was built in Detroit, Mich. in 1867 and served the Great Lakes shipping trade for only a year before it collided with the *Empire State*.

The *Dunderburg* was lost about four miles off Harbor Beach and rests in about 160 feet of water.

Divers will find the Dunderburg in excellent condition, sitting upright and intact. Although the stern cabins were probably blown off during the sinking, there are many small artifacts remaining. In addition, there is a wide debris field where more artifacts can be found.

There is a wide debris field where more artifacts can be found.

Divers enjoy exploring the cargo holds, which can be accessed through one of three hatches. Also, the bowsprit is intact as well as the figurehead of a reptile below the bowsprit. Divers will note a large gash in the vessel's stern starboard quarter, which resulted from the collision. Some machinery remains on deck and is interesting to investigate.

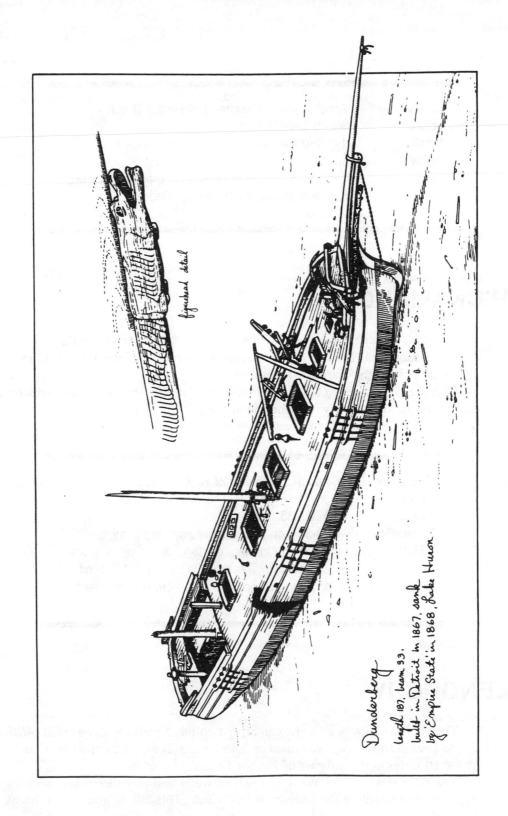

figurehead detail

Dunderberg
length 187, beam 33.
built in Detroit in 1867, sank
by Empire State in 1868, Lake Huron.

Location:	About four miles northeast of Harbor Beach.
Loran:	30740.9/49257.5
Depth:	145-160 feet
Visibility:	10-25 feet
Tips:	This site is usually not buoyed. To access this site it is best to depart from Harbor Beach.

CHICKAMAUGA

The *Chickamauga* was a 322-foot vessel that foundered one mile north of Harbor Beach in 1919. The double-decked schooner was later moved to about one-half mile east of the Harbor Beach Harbor.

Because the remains of the vessel rest in relatively shallow water, it is broken up due to the forces of waves and moving ice.

Location:	About .5 mile east of Harbor Beach.
Loran:	30785.1/49292.7
Depth:	About 35 feet
Visibility:	10-30 feet, less if heavy seas are running.
Tips:	Do not try to swim out to it, this is **not** a shore-access dive. The wreck is usually not buoyed and can be accessed best from Harbor Beach.

GLENORCHY

The *Glenorchy* was a steel steamer that collided with the *Leonard B. Miller* in 1924. The 365-foot ship was rated at 2,465 gross Tons. The collision occurred about 10 miles east-southeast of Harbor Beach.

The *Glenorchy* lies in about 120 feet of water and provides divers with the opportunity to explore the interior of the wreck. This site is usually not buoyed.

**The GLENORCHY was lost in a collision
off Harbor Beach in 1924.**

Location:	About ten miles east-southeast of Harbor Beach.
Loran:	30750.4/49314.2
Depth:	100-120 feet
Visibility:	10-20 feet
Tips:	Use fins properly to avoid visibility problems due to silt.

DANIEL J. MORRELL

The *Daniel J. Morrell* was a 603-foot steel-hulled freighter that met her match in Lake Huron on Nov. 29, 1966. It was on that day that a fierce gale blew and the *Daniel J. Morrell* was bound for Taconite Harbor, Minn. on Lake Superior empty on the last run of the season.

Well into the storm in the early morning hours, the captain of the *Daniel J. Morrell* was off the Michigan's thumb when he reported to another commercial freighter that he was considering taking refuge at Thunder Bay, near Alpena. But the huge vessel never made it.

The resting place of the Daniel J. Morrell was readily discovered off Grindstone City where it lies upright and intact on the bottom.

The *Daniel J. Morrell* was not reported missing and never issued a distress call. But a body with a life belt from the vessel washed ashore the next day. Carefully, the U.S. Coast Guard began a systematic search, and, remarkably, one crewmember survived. The crewman, Dennis Hale, spent 36 hours on a flimsy life raft in freezing water. He survived where 28 other men did not.

The resting place of the *Daniel J. Morrell* was readily discovered off Grindstone City where it lies upright and intact on the bottom. Although the wreck lies in 213 feet of water, divers frequent the site, which is usually buoyed with an official mooring buoy despite being in the commercial shipping channel.

Visiting the deep *Daniel J. Morrell* is risky business. It is 185 feet to the top of the cabins and divers explore those cabins and the cargo hold. A permit to recover the ship's safe was sought but the safe was dropped off the starboard side before it could be raised. It now lies on the bottom holding secrets that fuel speculation.

But visiting the deep carries special risks in the form of nitrogen narcosis and decompression sickness. Only the exceptionally trained and equipped should attempt such a venture and, then, only during the best of conditions.

What is in the safe? Is it worth recovering? Nothing, and probably not. A permit is required first but the likelihood of finding treasure is probably about the same as finding gold on a semi-truck on the highway. More than that, some say the *Daniel J. Morrell* has not finished taking lives and those who visit her today are flirting with disaster. This could be so.

As a result of the sinking, new regulations were created to strengthen the aging fleet of Great Lakes freighters. One must wonder what regulations will follow from the death of a careless diver.

Diving information about the *Daniel J. Morrell* is provided here not to encourage sport diving, but in the interest of being complete and honest. It is the same with the *Carl D. Bradley, Kamloops,* and a dozen other wrecks in this book. We believe no one should be restricted in shipwreck exploration and, just as in mountain climbing, people should be able to push the envelope as far as they wish. But risks are real and divers should descend with their eyes open and heads clear. Enough said.

Location:	Off Grindstone City in Lake Huron. It is usually marked with a mooring buoy.
Loran:	30761.4/49068.4
Depth:	185-215 feet
Visibility:	10-15 feet
Tips:	Be well trained and equipped. Exercise due caution.

Miscellaneous Dive Sites

Grindstones, used in manufacturing, were once produced in great quantities at Grindstone City. Discarded grindstones can be found off the Grindstone City pier. Look for fish and small artifacts among the rubble.

A reef and a series of caves are found at the edge of the reef off the Port Austin Lighthouse.

E.P. Door, depth, 180 feet, Loran: 30780.0/49145.5
Arctic, depth, 130 feet, Loran: 30748.4/49371.4
Goliath, depth, 104 feet, Loran: 30761.7/49326.1 (buoyed)

Emergencies

The Huron County Sheriff's Department monitors vhf channels 16 and 69. In the event of a medical emergency, it is best to contact that department. The sheriff's department will coordinate a rescue and it is important to give your location as closely as possible. The sheriff's department can be reached at (517) 269-6421. They are headquartered in Bad Axe.

The sheriff's department will coordinate a rescue.

If your boat is not equipped with a vhf radio, it is best to flag down a boat that does. Otherwise, use signal flares to summon help. A U.S. Coast Guard Station is located at Harbor Beach and the sheriff's department has vessels for search and rescue.

Getting There

Lighthouse County Park is the most popular port for divers because it is close to most shipwrecks. The park is located on Lighthouse Road about .5 mile from M-25. It is six miles north of Port Hope and ten miles south of Port Austin. It is also one mile south of the Huron City Museum. Travelers from the Saginaw Valley area can reach the park using M-25 or M-81 to M-53 to M-25. It is about a two-hour drive from Saginaw.

Lighthouse County Park has bathrooms but no showers. Most campsites do not have electrical or sewer hookups, although there are some that do. There is a boat launch in the park that can handle boats of up to 22 feet. The park can be reached at (517) 428-4749.

Other Attractions

Although local chambers of commerce have tried to boost tourism in this area, it is not a major industry here. Perhaps it is the remoteness that keeps tourists away, it is certainly not the scenery as this is one of the most beautiful areas in the Lower Peninsula.

For all members of your dive party (and nondivers, too), there is the museum at the lighthouse at Lighthouse County Park; admission is free. A museum featuring a pioneering community is located near Port Austin. The museum requests a modest admission fee.

There are many small, unique shops and a few theaters in the area. Personal watercraft (jetskis) can be launched at the ramp at the Lighthouse County Park.

Finally, sightseeing, especially in the Grindstone City area, is popular because of unusual sandstone formations that once made this area the primary producer of grinding and sharpening stones. Discarded stones can be found along the Grindstone City waterfront.

Accommodations

This area has many state parks and campgrounds. There are about 900 campsites in this region.

There are 18 motels and cottages in Port Austin, which offer more than 300 rooms. Port Hope has two motels and Harbor Beach as three motels. Information about overnight accommodations can be obtained by contacting the East Michigan Tourist Association or Lighthouse County Park at (517) 428-4749.

Although tourism in this region is not a major industry, it is still a good idea to make reservations early to avoid disappointments. This is especially true when the trout and salmon anglers flock to the area in July, August, and September.

Important Addresses/Phone Numbers

Huron County Sheriff's Department
120 S. Heisterman
Bad Axe, MI 48413
(517) 269-6421

U.S. Coast Guard Station
Harbor Beach, MI 48441
(517) 479-3285

Lighthouse County Park
7400 Lakeshore Road
Port Hope, MI 48468
(517) 428-4749

Port Austin Area Medical Clinic
8731 Independence
Port Austin, MI 48467
(517) 738-5191

Charters:

All Seasons Diving Company
3910 Lake George Road
Dryden, MI 48428-9709
(810) 796-2357
(air, equipment, instruction)

Bay Medical Center
Emergency Department
Bay City, MI 48710
(517) 894-3111

Greater Port Austin Chamber of
   Commerce
P.O. Box 274
Port Austin, MI 48467
(517) 738-7600

Harbor Beach Hospital
210 S. First St.
Harbor Beach, MI 48441
(517) 479-3201

Huron Memorial Hospital
1100 S. Van Dyke
Bad Axe, MI 48413

Air Station:

Fathom Four Diving
Port Sanilac, MI 48469
(810) 622-3483

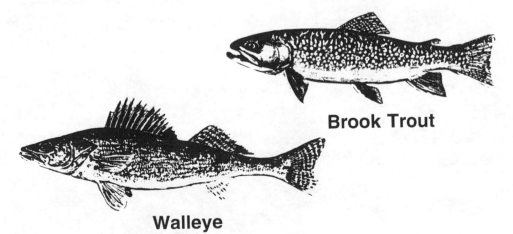

Brook Trout

Walleye

Thunder Bay Underwater Preserve

The Thunder Bay Underwater Preserve is a shipwreck diver's paradise. This is one of the most popular underwater preserves due to the large number and variety of shipwrecks found here.

The preserve is 288 square miles and contains 14 major shipwrecks. There are many wreck sites that are still being studied by maritime archaeologists. In addition, this preserve is being studied as a possible site for a National Marine Sanctuary. Ironically, a vote of county residents indicated opposition to the sanctuary proposal by a 2:1 margin.

This preserve hosts many shipwrecks because it is an area where shipping traffic must make a turn toward the northwest. If captains overestimated their ships' capabilities during northwestern gales, they sometimes found themselves in trouble. Many hidden reefs and islands contributed to navigation difficulty.

Local divers also guard the locations of certain deep wreck sites. A few fatalities and a rash of near tragedies have prompted some to rethink the wisdom of making it easy for sport divers to go beyond their capabilities. Most dive sites are buoyed throughout the summer months by local dive charter operators.

The Thunder Bay Underwater Preserve includes the Lake Huron bottomland around Alpena and east

beyond islands protecting the harbor. The eastern boundary of the preserve follows the 150-foot depth contour.

Water clarity, probably owing to the concentration of limestone and zebra

---

Water clarity is one of this preserve's greatest assets.

---

mussels in the area, is one of this preserve's greatest assets. Visibility of 40 feet or more is not uncommon. In shallow areas, however, heavy seas can disturb bottom sediments and reduce visibility to five feet.

The Thunder Bay Underwater Preserve offers divers of all skill levels an opportunity to practice their wreck diving skills. Some shipwrecks, because of condition and depth, are considered ideal for learning wreck diving basics.

Boating

Boating in the Thunder Bay area is convenient because of many support services available at Alpena and Presque Isle. Boaters must be aware, however, that the shipping channel veers relatively close to shore in the area so it is a good idea to be watchful of large commercial shipping vessels.

A navigation chart showing depths is also a good idea because some areas, especially those around islands, are surprisingly shallow and must be navigated carefully.

Boaters must use caution when anchoring in this region. The bottom is mostly limestone and secure anchorage can be difficult to obtain. Whenever possible, use mooring buoys provided at dive sites by local dive charter operators.

A marina offering transient accommodations, including fuel, is located in the Alpena Harbor. Alpena was once a busy commercial shipping center but industrial practices have yielded to sport fishing these days. Another marina is located south of Alpena at Partridge Point. This marina also offers transient accommodations, including fuel.

> *Boaters must use caution when anchoring in this region. The bottom is mostly limestone and secure anchorage can be difficult to obtain.*

A marina at Presque Isle has recently undergone expansion and upgrading. It is located about 25 miles north of Alpena and offers transient accommodations and support services.

Boat launches are located at the municipal marina and Riverfront Park in Alpena. Launches are also located at Partridge Point and at Rockport, about 10 miles north of Alpena.

A boat launch with limited parking is located at the Ossineke State Forest Campground, about ten miles south of Alpena.

It is important to remember that sport fishing is an important tourist activity in this region, especially when the trout and salmon bite best in late July, August, and September. Unfortunately, these months also correspond to the best diving period. To avoid conflicts it may be a good idea to start in late morning after anglers have already launched their boats and return in mid-afternoon before anglers return.

A vhf radio is a must in this area and electronic navigation aids are important because fog can arise suddenly and surprise even the most vigilant boater. There are simply too many shallow areas in this region to take chances.

Boaters should also be aware that the Alpena County Sheriff's Department performs on-water patrols as well as Michigan Department of Natural Resources Conservation Officers. Both agencies are capable of making safety inspections as well as enforcing underwater preserve regulations that prohibit unauthorized collecting. This is not a place to expect to bend the law.

To become familiar with this area, divers with their own boats may want to consider a dive charter their first time out.

Thunder Bay Underwater Preserve
(288 square miles)

MOLLY H./MOLLY T. HORNER/NELLIE GARDNER

The identity of this vessel has been the source of considerable debate. Locally, divers refer to this wreck as the *Molly H.* with some referring to it as the *Molly T. Horner.* But ship building and enrollment records fail to list either names. Recent research by shipwreck expert Charles E. Feltner indicates that the wreck could be that of the *Nellie Gardner,* a three-masted schooner rated at 565 tons and lost in the Thunder Bay area in 1883.

Regardless of the name, this wreck is found in shallow water (about 20 feet) north of South Point at the mouth of Thunder Bay. It is badly broken up and only timbers remain. Unfortunately, no remains of the cargo are found at the site. One account has the cargo as a load of lumber while another account, the one identifying the wreck as that of the *Nellie Gardner*, has the vessel hauling a cargo of coal.

Locals refer to this wreck as the Molly H. or Molly T. Horner but it is likely that of the Nellie Gardner.

While this is not one of the primary dive sites in this preserve, it is an interesting place for snorkeling. The broken wreckage is testimony of the powerful forces of waves and ice on the Great Lakes.

Location:	North of South Point at the southern lip of Thunder Bay.
Loran:	30893.7/48737.9
Depth:	15-20 feet
Visibility:	20-30 feet
Tips:	Look for clues about how ships of this era were constructed.

E.B. ALLEN

The *E.B. Allen* was a 275-ton schooner that was built in 1864 in Ogdensburg, N.Y. On Nov. 18, 1871, the *E.B. Allen* was bound for Buffalo, N.Y. from Chicago, Ill. with a load of grain when it ran into a dense fog. In the fog, the ship collided with the *Newsboy*, a bark. The *E.B. Allen* sank quickly but there was no loss of life.

Today, divers enjoy exploring the upright and mostly intact vessel. The windlass, chain, and rudder are intact.

When the location of this wreck was discovered in the early 1970s, it was first mis-identified as the wreck of the *Corsican*. Historical research, however, has positively identified this wreck as that of the *E.B. Allen*.

Location:	About 2.5 miles southeast of the south end of Thunder Bay Island.
Loran:	30811.6/48693.1
Depth:	90-105 feet
Visibility:	20-30 feet
Tips:	This wreck has been dived on little since the 1970s. Many small artifacts may be found on the bottom nearby the hull.

Lucinda VanValkenburg

The *Lucinda VanValkenburg* is a popular dive site in this preserve. The site features the upright and partially intact remains of a schooner that was built in 1862 in Tonawanda, N.Y. The ship was 128 feet long and rated at 301 tons.

The *Lucinda VanValkenburg* was bound for Lake Michigan ports with a load of coal when it ran into heavy seas and a dense fog on June 1, 1887. On that day the ship collided with the steamer *Lehigh*. The ship sank quickly but the crew was rescued by the *Lehigh*. There was no loss of life in the disaster but history remembers that the cook aboard the *Lucinda VanValkenburg* sustained a head injury.

Today, the *Lucinda VanValkenburg* has decks that are partially collapsed but the centerboard trunk and centerboard are upright. The damage to the wreck is the result of salvage efforts. Some artifacts, including some decking, can be seen on the bottom near the main hull structure. Part of the cargo remains at the site.

Location:	About two miles northeast of Thunder Bay Island.
Loran:	30807.3/48672.9
Depth:	65-70 feet
Visibility:	20-35 feet
Tips:	Search the bottom near the main hull structure to find decking and perhaps small artifacts.

P.H. BIRCKHEAD

The *P.H. Birckhead* was a 156-foot steamer that was rated at 568 tons. It was built in 1870 in Marine City, Mich. and served the lumber and coal trades. The vessel was once lauded for towing six barges and transporting a remarkable combined cargo of nearly 3 million board feet.

On Sept. 30, 1905, the *P.H. Birckhead* caught fire at her docks, which was not especially uncommon among wooden steamers of this class. The vessel was set adrift and burned in shallow water. No lives were lost in the disaster.

> *Although the ravages of time and the forces of ice and waves have broken up the wreck, enough remains to interest divers.*

Today, the *P.H. Birckhead*'s remains lie in only 12 feet of water near the south breakwall of the Thunder Bay River. Although the ravages of time and the forces of ice and waves have broken up the wreck, there remains a propeller, shaft, large timbers, boiler, and some of the hull structure. But because this site is so close to shore, visibility here is often reduced because wave action keeps sediments suspended in the water column.

The P.H. Birckhead at dock.

Location:	About 3/4 of a mile south of the breakwall at the mouth of Thunder Bay River in Lake Huron.
Loran:	30903.2/48651.4
Depth:	10-15 feet
Visibility:	5-20 feet, depending upon wave conditions.
Tips:	This could make a good snorkel during periods of clarity.

GRECIAN

The wreck of the *Grecian* is one of the most popular shipwrecks in the Thunder Bay Underwater Preserve.

The *Grecian* was a 296-foot steamer that was built in 1891 in Cleveland, Ohio. The ship was a workhorse of the Great Lakes and hauled a variety of bulk cargoes. The vessel was rated at 2,348 tons.

Problems for the Grecian began on June 7, 1906 when the ship, loaded with coal for the fueling station at DeTour, ran aground on a reef near the entrance to the St. Mary's River. The ship was pulled off, unloaded, and a hasty repair was made on her hull. But the repairs did not save the *Grecian*. The ship was in the tow of the steamer *Henry Bessemer*, bound for Detroit, Mich. for more durable repairs when it sank in Thunder Bay in about 100 feet of water. The disaster occurred on June 15, 1906. No lives were lost.

Many small artifacts, such as tools, pulleys, windlass, and other small machinery, are still present.

An attempt to raise the vessel failed and it remains upright and mostly intact on the bottom.

Today, divers enjoy exploring the three deck levels at the stern. The deck, which is accessible at 70 feet of water, is collapsed toward the bow as the ship is broken in the middle.

Many small artifacts, such as tools, pulleys, windlass, and other small machinery, are still present at the site. Also present are the engines, boilers, and propeller. The engines are a popular subject for underwater photography. This site is usually buoyed with an official mooring buoy.

Location:	About five miles southwest of the Thunder Bay Island Lighthouse.
Loran:	30832.7/48713.3
Depth:	70 feet to the deck, 105 to the bottom.
Visibility:	15-30 feet
Tips:	Use caution and proper equipment if penetrating this wreck.

NEW ORLEANS

The *New Orleans* was another ship that sank near Thunder Bay in June of 1906. The ship was loaded with coal headed for Chicago, Ill. when it ran into a dense fog in Thunder Bay on June 30. Suddenly, the captain of the *New Orleans* spotted the *William R. Linn* emerging from the mist.

Both captains apparently panicked as no evasive action was taken to avoid the resulting collision. The *New Orleans* took a mortal blow and sank rapidly. All hands were picked up by the *William R. Lynn*.

The pilothouse blew off the 21-year-old bulk freighter as she sank. Today, divers enjoy exploring the cargo hold and other remains. The depth to the deck of the *New Orleans* is about 145 feet; the ship rests in about 155 feet of water.

> *Both captains apparently panicked as no evasive action was taken to avoid the resulting collision.*

Location:	About ten miles north, northeast of Thunder Bay Island Lighthouse.
Loran:	30808.0/48613.7
Depth:	145-155 feet
Visibility:	20-40 feet
Tips:	The depth here makes this a relatively unpopular dive site given the condition of the remains.

MONOHANSETT

The *Monohansett* was another victim of fire. The wooden steamer was built in 1871 and was enroute to Collingwood, Ont. with a load of 900 tons of coal when it anchored in the lee of a storm behind Thunder Bay Island on Nov. 23, 1907.

While waiting the storm out, the crew discovered that the engine room was in flames. The crew of 12 managed to be rescued by the U.S. Life Saving Station at Thunder Bay Island but the fire claimed the *Monohansett*.

Because this shipwreck was weakened by fire and it sank in relatively shallow water where it is exposed to the forces of waves and ice, it is broken up into three large pieces. A variety of artifacts, including machinery, are found at the site, which is only 15 to 20 feet deep. Because this area is somewhat protected from the weather, visibility here is generally good.

Local divers enjoy this shipwreck as a snorkel and as a scuba dive because there are many fish in the area. Also, many small artifacts can be found on the bottom around the main wreckage.

Location:	About 200 yards southwest of an old dock on the southwest part of Thunder Bay Island.
Loran:	30822.6/48681.4
Depth:	15-20 feet
Visibility:	20-40 feet
Tips:	This is a good snorkel; expect to see many fish here.

WILLIAM PETER THEW

The first decade of the new century was a bad one for ships traveling through the Thunder Bay area. The *William Peter Thew* met her end on June 22, 1909 while upbound with no cargo (light). It was on that morning that the *William Peter Thew*, a wooden-hulled lumber hooker, was struck by the steel-hulled *William Livingston*.

Because steel is so much harder than wood, and the *William Peter Thew* was 25 years old, it took the worst of the blow. The ship sank quickly in about 80 feet of water. Luckily, another passing ship spotted the crew and was able to manage a rescue soon after the collision.

Today, divers enjoy exploring the engine and boilers of the *William Peter Thew*. The remainder of the vessel is badly broken up although an anchor and much chain are found at this site.

**The WILLIAM PETER THEW, foreground, was a
Great Lakes workhorse. As with many lumber hookers,
it often towed schooner barges (background).**

Location:	About two miles east of the Thunder Bay Island Lighthouse.
Loran:	30802.7/48679.6
Depth:	75-80 feet
Visibility:	15-30 feet
Tips:	This wreck is not particularly popular and is usually not buoyed.

OSCAR T. FLINT

The *Oscar T. Flint* was yet another vessel that found a home in the Thunder
Bay area soon after the turn of the century.

The ship was bound for Duluth, Minn. from Kelly's Island, Ohio with a load of
limestone and barreled salt. It was towing the barge *Redington*, which also had a
light load of limestone. The captain of the *Oscar T. Flint* decided to stop in
Alpena for minor engine repairs. Anchored about four miles from the harbor, the

**The OSCAR T. FLINT was a typical Great Lakes
bulk freighter of the late 1800s.**

ship caught fire in the bow section in the early morning of Nov. 24, 1909.

The captain barely escaped with the clothes on his back and he and the crew managed to launch two yawls. The yawls were towed back to Alpena as the *Oscar T. Flint* burned to the waterline and settled on the bottom. The 1,126-ton vessel was built in 1889 in St. Clair, Mich.

About seven feet of the hull remain on the bottom of Lake Huron and divers can explore this wreckage as well as the cargo and miscellaneous machinery on the bottom. Burbots are quite commonly found here and this is a good site for beginning wreck divers.

Location:	About 4 miles southeast of the mouth of the Thunder Bay River and about one mile offshore.
Loran:	30879.8/48671.9
Depth:	30-35 feet
Visibility:	20-40 feet
Tips:	Look for machinery around the main wreck. Burbots like to hide among the limestone cargo.

MONTANA

Fire struck again in Thunder Bay in 1914. The package freighter *Montana*, a small steamer of 236-feet, was built in 1872 in Port Huron, Mich. It served the Great Lakes package shipping trade for more than 41 years before succumbing to flames off Sulphur Island in Thunder Bay. By then, the package steamer had been cut down into a lumber hooker and hauled sawed lumber from northern ports to southern.

The fire was discovered on Sept. 6, 1941 and immediately the captain order the yawl launched. Despite heroic efforts by the captain, the *Montana* was a total loss and burned to the waterline and sank. All 14 crewmen were saved.

> **Today, the Montana provides divers with an opportunity to see old machinery in the burned out hull of the vessel.**

Today, the *Montana* provides divers with an opportunity to see old machinery in the burned out hull of the vessel. Although it burned to the waterline, much of the hull is upright and intact for divers to see. The anchor chain, windlass, capstan, boiler, rudder, and propeller remain at the site.

This is generally a "clean" site with no netting or monofilament and a good place for beginning wreck divers although divers of all skill levels enjoy it.

The MONTANA cut down as a lumber hooker.

Location:	Southwest of Thunder Bay Island.
Loran:	30855.9/48699.9
Depth:	30 feet to engine, 75 feet to bottom.
Visibility:	20-40 feet

WILLIAM P. REND

The *William P. Rend* was a 287-foot steamer that was built in 1888 at West Bay City, Mich. It was a bulk freighter rated at 2,973 gross tons. It was the *William P. Rend* (at that time named the *George G. Hadley*) that collided with and sank the whaleback steamer *Thomas Wilson* at the mouth of the Duluth, Minn. Harbor.

The *William P. Rend* had been cut down to a barge in 1916 and a year later, on Sept. 22, 1917, while hauling a cargo of limestone, the barge sank. All nine crewmen were saved in the disaster.

Today, the William P. Rend has little but her hull and cargo to offer curious divers. Still, these features attract many fish and can be interesting in themselves. A boiler, rudder post, and other machinery is still present at the site.

Location:	About 2/3 of a mile east of the Huron Portland Cement Plant.
Loran:	30891.0/48649.5
Depth:	15-20 feet
Visibility:	5-15 feet

Barge No. 1 (Colonel Sanders Wreck)

Barge No. 1 was constructed in West Bay City, Mich. in 1895. It had a rating of 1,544 tons and was 309 feet in length. It was constructed specifically for the car ferry trade but in 1910 she was converted into a lumber barge.

On Nov. 8, 1918, a strong sea was running off North Point. *Barge No. 1* was being towed by the *Matthew Wilson* when the barge suddenly broke in two. The crew aboard the barge was rescued by a passing steamer and the lumber cargo was spread over a wide area, much of it washing ashore at Thunder Bay Island. Also among the lumber cargo was a cargo of chickens. The U.S. Life Saving Station reported having a chicken barbeque the next day so this wreck is sometimes referred to as the "Colonel Sanders Wreck."

Today, the wreck is spread out over a large area but the bottom and sides are still evident. The steering mechanism is present at the stern. The remains lie in about 45 feet of water.

Location:	About 7 miles southeast of Thunder Bay Harbor.
Loran:	30865.0/48680.8
Depth:	About 45 feet
Visibility:	20-35 feet
Tips:	Although the wreck is spread out, divers may want to take time to search the vicinity for small artifacts.

D.R. HANNA

The wreck of the *D.R. Hanna* proved that even small errors in navigation can have disastrous results.

The *D.R. Hanna* was a 532-foot steel steamer that was rated at 7,023 gross tons and had a beam of 56 feet. It was built in Lorain, Ohio in 1906. The ship was bound for Buffalo, N.Y. from Duluth, Minn. with a cargo of 377,000 bushels of wheat on May 16, 1919 when it entered the Thunder Bay area. There was a fog about but not a particularly dense fog.

The captain of the *D.R. Hanna* spotted the *Quincy Shaw*, which was upbound with a load of coal and it was expected that they would pass starboard to starboard but as they neared, the *Quincy Shaw* gave one blast on her horn--the signal for a port-to-port passing.

That sent the captain of the *D.R. Hanna* scrambling. Despite evasive action, the bow of the *Quincy Shaw* crunched the *D.R. Hanna* just forward of the number four hatch. The crew of the *D.R. Hanna* abandoned ship and were picked up by the *Quincy Shaw*, which had been damaged only slightly in the mishap.

The *D.R. Hanna* sank quickly after capsizing. Today, it is found on the bottom, upside down, and no salvage attempt was made although the ship and its cargo was estimated to be worth more than $2 million at the time of its loss.

Much of the cabin area of the *D.R. Hanna* can be penetrated by divers but caution must be exercised to avoid confusion given the position of the vessel on the bottom. It rests in 135 feet of water and is usually buoyed with a mooring buoy.

The D.R. HANNA sank quickly after capsizing.

Location:	About 6.5 miles east southeast of Thunder Bay Island Lighthouse.
Loran:	30771.3/48666.4
Depth:	135 feet to bottom, 100 to wreck (bottom of hull).
Visibility:	20-40 feet

MONROVIA

The *Monrovia* is among the most popular shipwreck in the Thunder Bay Underwater Preserve for experienced shipwreck divers. This Liberian freighter was lost in the area in 1959 after serving the commercial shipping trade on the Great Lakes and oceans for only 16 years. It wrecked on its first trip to the Great Lakes.

The *Monrovia* was a 430-foot, 6,700-ton vessel that was built in Scotland in 1943. It was hauling a cargo of rolled steel to Chicago, Ill. from Antwerp, Belgium when it ran into a fog off Thunder Bay Island.

In the dense fog, the *Monrovia* was struck by the *Royalton*, a Canadian ship that was hauling a cargo of grain. The *Monrovia* took the worst of the collision and her crew of 29 quickly sought the safety of the lifeboats after the accidents.

The crew of the *Monrovia* was shortly picked up by the radar-equipped *Norman W. Foy*, which had heard the distress call from only five miles away. The *Royalton* kept on a course for Sarnia for repairs to her bow.

The *Monrovia* slowly sank in about 140 feet of water and divers enjoy exploring her superstructure, hull, cargo holds, and machinery on deck. It is upright and mostly intact and a popular dive site. But note the depth, it could be too deep for some but the deck can be accessed at about 125 feet. This site is usually buoyed with an official mooring buoy.

Location:	About 13 miles southeast of Thunder Bay Island.
Loran:	30723.5/48729.9
Depth:	About 125 to the deck and 140 to the bottom.
Visibility:	20-40 feet.
Tips:	Go slow, checking out the deck machinery could make this dive interesting enough.

NORDMEER

The *Nordmeer* is one of the most well-known shipwrecks in the Thunder Bay Underwater Preserve but relatively few divers dive it. This is because it is so remote that a special trip must be planned by dive charters that visit it. Instead, many dive charters prefer to treat divers to dives on other, more convenient shipwrecks in the preserve.

Regardless, the *Nordmeer* remains one of the best shipwrecks for diving in the preserve.

The *Nordmeer* was a 470-foot freighter that was built in Flensburg, Germany in 1954. It served its German owners for 11 short years before it grounded in the Thunder Bay Underwater Preserve on Nov. 19, 1966.

The ship settled on the bottom with only seven feet of freeboard remaining.

The *Nordmeer* was loaded with 990 coils of steel wire (valued at a million dollars) and upbound on a clear, calm evening when it struck a reef about seven miles north of Thunder Bay Island. The bottom of the German vessel was rapidly torn out and water filled all of the cargo holds and the engine room. The ship settled on the bottom with only seven feet of freeboard remaining.

About a week later salvage operations were begun to save what could be saved from the large vessel and its cargo. But on Nov. 28 a November gale began to blow and the ship quickly became a hazardous area. Eventually, several wrecking crews aboard the stricken ship had to be rescued by the U.S. Coast Guard.

Most of the cargo was recovered but the *Nordmeer* remains grounded as she was in 1966. Unfortunately, part of the superstructure has collapsed owing to years of exposure to the forces of waves and ice but that part of the ship has fallen into the water where it offers divers yet another piece of shipwreck to dive on.

Also, divers enjoy exploring the wooden barge that is found on the port side of the *Nordmeer*. This barge was used in salvage operations but sank in rough weather.

Divers often describe diving here as one of their favorite diving experiences. They remark about the light filtering in through the open cargo hatches into the cargo hold as well as fish life and machinery found at this site.

> *Also, divers enjoy exploring the wooden barge that is found on the port side of the Nordmeer.*

Slowly, the *Nordmeer* is settling into the bottom but it has only become a better wreck to dive over the years. It is very non-threatening to new divers and is a great place to learn shipwreck diving techniques and ship construction.

The NORDMEER as she looked before the disaster.

Location:	About seven miles north of Thunder Bay Island.
Loran:	30790.4/48634.7
Depth:	40 feet, but many things to see shallower.
Visibility:	20-40 feet.
Tips:	Some dive charter operators will make special trips to this wreck--ask.

The NORDMEER shortly after running aground.

Other Dive Sites

Although some local divers prefer not to divulge the exact locations of certain shipwrecks in or near the preserve, sport divers may find small buoys on historically important shipwrecks. Local divers contend that the wrecks are too dangerous to be publicized, but that lack of information has not significantly affected popularity among sport divers.

The *New Orleans* was a 231-foot wooden steamer that collide with the *William*

R. Linn and sank in Thunder Bay on June 30, 1906. It was loaded with a cargo of coal. No lives were lost in the mishap.

The *New Orleans* is located about 9.2 miles north of Thunder Bay Island in 140 to 150 feet of water. **Loran: 30808.0/48613.7.**

The *Isaac M. Scott* was one of many ships lost during the Great Storm of 1913. It foundered near Port Elgin with a loss of 28 lives. The ship was built in 1909 and was loaded with coal when it sank.

The steel steamer is upside down and half-buried in clay in about 175 feet of water, 7 miles northeast of Thunder Bay Island Lighthouse.

The *Pewabic* foundered after colliding with the steamer *Meteor* on August 9, 1865. There were 125 lives lost in the seventh-worst disaster on the Great Lakes.

The reason for the collision is uncertain because it occurred on a clear evening in relatively calm seas on August 9. The vessels were sister ships and familiar with each other's routes. The *Pewabic* was heading south with a load of passengers and copper ore from Lake Superior. The *Meteor* was headed north from Detroit, Mich. with a load of passengers.

> *The reason for the collision is uncertain because it occurred on a clear evening in relatively calm seas on August 9.*

By all accounts, the captains of both ships could see each other well in advance. Many aboard the 200-foot *Pewabic* were killed at the time of the collision. Many others were thrown into the water and clung to wreckage until they were rescued the next morning.

Artifacts from the *Pewabic* are displayed at the Jesse Besser Museum in Alpena. The ship, which was built in 1863, is intact and upright. It is located 6.7 miles at 130 degrees from Thunder Bay Island Lighthouse and lies in 140 to 165 feet of water.

The *Viator* was a 231-foot Norwegian steel steamer that collided with the *Ormidale* in a heavy fog on Oct. 31, 1935. The ship was northbound from Detroit, Mich. with a load of cod liver oil and sardines. No lives were lost in the accident.

Today, the *Viator* lies at an angle with the bow of the ship in 190 feet of water and the stern is in 250 feet. It is located 8.9 miles 112 degrees from Thunder Bay Island Lighthouse.

Two areas in the Thunder Bay Underwater Preserve provide interesting diving along limestone walls and reefs.

The Thunder Bay Island area, including nearby islands, offer divers a variety of terrain. South of the islands are reefs that support large schools of fish. The wreckage of a variety of unidentified wooden ships can also be found in the these regions.

These are good places for skin divers to explore. Boats are required to access these areas and good navigation charts are recommended because shallow water extends far into the bay.

On the southeast side of Thunder Bay Island and on the north side of South Point are limestone walls that provide divers with an interesting wall diving experience. A limestone wall can be found off Middle Island. That wall descends to 70 feet and empties into a large bowl and is a popular area for exploration.

The Misery Bay Sinkholes are fissures in limestone formations. The sinkholes are found in relatively shallow water, five feet or less, and penetrate the limestone for 80 feet or more. Diving these sinkholes is much like diving in caves and requires proper equipment, training, and skills.

Recent testing of water samples showed a concentration of hydrogen disulfide gas--a corrosive chemical that occurs naturally. Because of the concentration of this gas, most divers are avoiding this site. It is unknown what effecxt this chemical may have on expensive diving equipment.

Finally, old cribbing used to construct docks and piers can be found off Rockport, a city located just north of Alpena. Here, divers will find a shore-access dive that will treat them to many colorful gamefish in addition to the old dock ruins. The dock ruins may host old tools and other small artifacts from the area's rich maritime past.

> *Because of the concentration of this gas, most divers are avoiding this site.*

Emergencies

In the event of a medical emergency, it is best to contact the Alpena County Sheriff's Department or the U.S. Coast Guard Station at Tawas on vhf channel 16. Those agencies will coordinate on-water emergency procedures.

Generally, an ambulance will meet the injured at an arranged point and transport them to Alpena General Hospital for stabilization. If recompression is necessary, arrangements will be made by hospital staff to transport the victim to the nearest chamber. Telephone numbers are listed on the next page.

Accommodations

There are three private campgrounds and more than 400 public campground sites within an hour of Alpena. There are 32 motels, cottages and resorts in the area that can be reserved through the Alpena Area Chamber of Commerce, (517) 354-4181.

Although this area is not known as a primary tourist destination, the region is slowly making the transition from an industrial economy to a tourist economy. There are many fine accommodations as well as restaurants located on the "sunrise" side. Special dive package rates may be available at the Holiday Inn, Day's Inn, and the Fletcher Motel in Alpena but reservations must be made well in advance for groups.

Divers tend to congregate at the Owl Cafe, Courtyard Restaurant, 19th Hole, and John A. Lau's. JJ's Bar and Grill and Bogarts are two popular bars in the area that cater to divers' refreshment needs.

Inland Dive Sites

Alpena County has few inland lakes with public access sites. One that does is Long Lake, which is located off US-23 near the Rayburn Highway. There, at the Alpena County Park, there is a 5,652-acre lake with a rocky bottom. It is clear with many large boulders. It may be worth a dive if winds keep you off Lake Huron.

Another area worth investigating is found at the Presque Isle Harbor in Presque Isle County. Although this is not technically an inland dive site, the harbor is rich with fish life. It is located off Rayburn Highway on Grand Lake Road.

Other Attractions

Much of the land around the Alpena area is owned by the state and forms part of the Mackinaw State Forest. There are many campgrounds and hiking trails southwest of Alpena in the forest.

Alpena is slowly transforming itself from an industrial economy to a tourist economy and there are now several excellent golf courses in the Alpena area. In addition, the Jesse Besser Museum in Alpena interprets the industrial heyday of the region as a lumbering center. The museum also features a planetarium.

The Besser Company, a leading manufacturer of cement blocks, offers industry tours and can be contacted in Alpena at (517) 354-4111.

Important Addresses/Telephone Numbers

Alpena Co. Sheriff's Dept.
320 Johnson St.
Alpena, MI 49707
(517) 354-4128

U.S. Coast Guard Station
Alpena, MI 49707
(517) 356-1656

U.S. Coast Guard Station
Tawas City, MI 48764
(517) 362-4428

Alpena General Hospital
1501 W. Chisholm St.
Alpena, MI 49707
(517) 356-7390

Alpena Ambulance Service
430 Helen
Alpena, MI 49707
(517) 354-5412

Mich. DNR District Office
District Office-Gaylord
(517) 732-3541

Michigan State Police
2160 S. State St.
Alpena, MI 49707
(517) 354-4101

Alpena Chamber of Commerce
P.O. Box 65
Alpena, MI 49707
(517) 354-4181

East Mich. Tourist Assn.
One Wenonah Park
Bay City, MI 48706
(517) 895-8823

Thunder Bay Divers
405 E. Chisholm
Alpena, MI 49707
(517) 356-9336
(Air, equipment, charters)

White Sucker

Lake Sturgeon

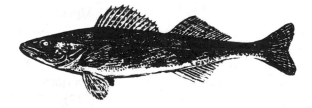

Sauger

Whitefish Point Underwater Preserve

The Whitefish Point Underwater Preserve is known for offering deep diving experiences on a variety of shipwrecks in its 376-square miles of Lake Superior bottomland.

Many of the shipwrecks in this area, despite their depth, were stripped of important artifacts in the 1970s and early 1980s. After that time, many artifacts were removed without permits and displayed at the Great Lakes Shipwreck Historical Museum at Whitefish Point.

This activity has been met with furious outcry by the sport diving community because the museum divers were given special treatment, they faced no criminal prosecution and were actually "thanked" by the Michigan Bureau of History for removing artifacts

To protest this disparity of treatment, many sport divers now boycott the museum.

---

without permits. Ironically, while this was going on in the late 1980s and early 1990s, individual sport divers were prosecuted freely.

To protest this disparity of treatment, many sport divers now boycott the museum. But in fairness, it must be

admitted that this is not the only maritime museum that has benefitted from this unofficial exemption to the law. Unfortunately, it is this attitude that has driven apart sport divers from archaeologists and put some of our most precious cultural resources in peril in the process.

Good visibility is a hallmark of this underwater preserve. Divers can expect to find 25 to 30 feet of visibility at 100 feet, with great visibility at shallower depths. And although the surface water temperature may reach 60 degrees in the warmest months, expect much cooler temperatures at even slight depths in this preserve. Unlike the Alger and Marquette preserves, there are no protected coves or bays to offer even a slight respite from the cold. Drysuits are strongly recommended and are a necessity for extended dives.

Because most of the dive sites in the Whitefish Point Underwater Preserve are deep, divers must be certain of their abilities and equipment. This is not a place for second guessing recompression tables or pressing the capability of equipment.

The Whitefish Bay area is often referred to as the "graveyard of the Great Lakes;" a title shared with at least half a dozen other areas. But the reason for so many shipwrecks in this particular area is clear--weather is notoriously unpredictable in this region.

July and early August are the best months to visit the preserve because weather patterns are most predictable.

> *July and early August are the best months to visit the preserve because weather patterns are most predictable.*

But no matter when divers visit Whitefish Bay, it should be with a boat capable of handling rough weather. For that reason, it is especially wise to use local charter services to become familiar with the region.

Unfortunately, the best diving periods coincide with the heavy black fly infestations--from mid-June to August. Swarms of black flies notoriously seek out the succulent flesh of tourists, which is one reason why this area has not

> *Plan on swatting even on the quickest boats.*

flourished as a tourist destination despite outstanding natural resources.

Even though black flies and other insect pest populations are reduced on

the water, plan on swatting even on the quickest boats.

The small community of Paradise is the primary support community for the Whitefish Point Underwater Preserve. Paradise has only recent thrived as the result of an influx of snowmobilers who keep enough business in the area to sustain motels and restaurants year around.

Air is available at two locations--Curley's Motel and Traveller's Inn--in Paradise and sometimes a charter operator can be contacted in the community. Overall, however, it is best to bring all necessary equipment before arriving and avoid disappointments with rock-solid reservations. For this reason, many divers book dive charters through

> *It is best to bring all necessary equipment before arriving and avoid disappointments with rock-solid reservations.*

their local dive centers.

Most popular dive sites are buoyed each diving season by local divers but amateur archaeologists in this area have gone to great lengths to discourage sport diving. They have stolen and/or destroyed expensive mooring systems, which causes boaters to anchor into the wrecks themselves. Sometimes there is simply no other option. Please do not contribute to the problem. Leave mooring buoys and all mooring materials in place.

Despite these conflicts, the Whitefish Point Underwater Preserve is a great place to dive. Not all wrecks are deep and the variety of shipwrecks gives the region a rich maritime heritage.

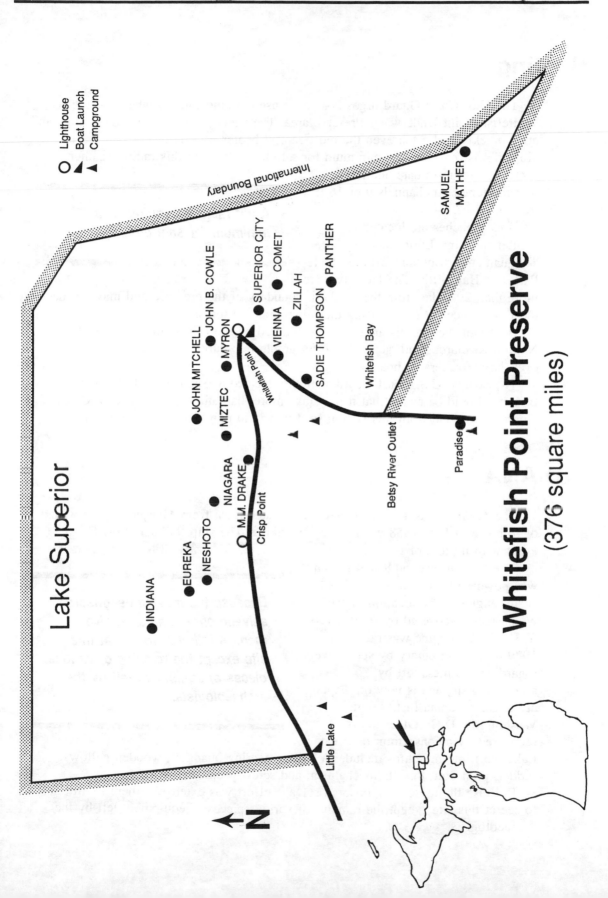

Lake Superior

○ Lighthouse
▲ Boat Launch
▲ Campground

International Boundary

INDIANA

EUREKA
NESHOTO

NIAGARA
M.M. DRAKE
Crisp Point

MIZTEC

JOHN MITCHELL

JOHN B. COWLE

MYRON

Whitefish Point

SUPERIOR CITY

VIENNA
COMET

ZILLAH

SADIE THOMPSON

PANTHER

Whitefish Bay

SAMUEL MATHER

Betsy River Outlet

Paradise

Little Lake

N

Whitefish Point Preserve
(376 square miles)

Boating

The U.S. Coast Guard urges boaters to use extreme caution when visiting the Whitefish Point Underwater Preserve area. The agency says storms and/or fog can arise quickly and catch even the most careful boater off guard. For that reason, a vhf radio is required at a minimum for safe boating. With this radio, weather forecasts are up-to-date and help can be summoned on channels 9 or 16 if trouble arises.

A vhf radio is required at a minimum for safe boating.

Boat lanuches are located at Whitefish Point, Little Lake Harbor, Tahquamenon Bay, and Brimley State Park and Bay Mills. The latter two are more than 20 miles from the southern boundary of the preserve and may not be the first choice for divers using their own boats in this area.

Boat launches in this area are administered by the Michigan Department of Natural Resources and, generally, offer ample free parking and facilities to launch even large, trailerable boats.

The nearest U.S. Coast Guard station is located at Sault Ste. Marie, Mich. Boaters should be aware that it may take more than an hour for the U.S. Coast Guard to respond from this station so it is best to play it safe on the water.

INDIANA

The *Indiana* was a steamer that was headed down from Marquette with a load of iron ore in June 1858 when it began leaking. The ship foundered off Crisp Point with no loss of life.

The *Indiana* was built in 1834 and was powered by one of the earliest steam engines. The location of the wreck was discovered by sport divers in 1975. The engine was raised in 1979 despite an outcry by sport divers regarding the mess left by archaeologists, and is now on display at the Smithsonian Institute in Washington, D.C. Other items recovered by a consortium of Great

Because the museum-sponsored salvage effort was extensive, there is little left to see at this site except the remains of various pieces of equipment left by the archaeologists.

Lake maritime museums includes a boiler, steering quadrant, wooden gallows, rudder, preheater, throttle mechanism, and screw propeller.

Because the museum-sponsored salvage effort was extensive, there is little left to see at this site except the remains of various pieces of equipment left by the archaeologists.

Location:	North of Crisp Point.
Loran:	31215.1/47520.3
Depth:	110-120 feet
Visibility:	10-30 feet.
Tips:	If you want to learn about this portion of Michigan history, travel to Washington, D.C.

EUREKA

The 330-ton, schooner-barge *Eureka* was loaded with iron ore from Marquette when the ship, which was in tow, broke her line and disappeared on Oct. 20, 1886. Unfortunately, it was not unusual for such schooners in tow to break away in heavy seas.

The 138-foot schooner sank about six miles north of the Vermilion U.S. Life Saving Service Station. Her entire crew of six was lost in the disaster. Today, the vessel is mostly broken up and there is little to see.

Location:	About six miles north of Vermilion.
Loran:	31181.2/47524.4
Depth:	About 50 feet.
Visibility:	10-40 feet

NESHOTO

The true identity of this shipwreck is uncertain but it is believed to be that of the 284-foot steamer *Neshoto*, which was built in 1889.

The *Neshoto* was carrying a cargo of iron ore when it ran aground on a reef about 2.5 miles northeast of Crisp Point on Sept. 27, 1908. The accident was caused when the crew was blinded by the dense smoke of a forest fire raging on the mainland.

The *Neshoto* swung broadside to the waves and was broken apart. The crew of 16 was saved by the Crisp Point U.S. Life Saving Sation. Today, little is left but the remnants of machinery and large timbers from the wooden-hulled ship.

Location:	About 2.5 miles northeast of Crisp Point.
Loran:	31181.2/47527.4
Depth:	15 feet
Visibility:	10-40 feet
Tips:	Although this is a shallow dive, be prepared for cold water any time of the year.

NIAGARA

The 205-foot schooner-barge *Niagara* was in tow by the steamer *Austrialasia* when it capsized in heavy seas on Sept. 7, 1887.

The three-masted *Niagara* was hauling a cargo of iron ore at the time of the disaster. The crew of nine perished. It had been built at Tonawanda, N.Y. in 1873 and had been rebuilt in 1883.

Location:	About two miles off Vermilion Point.
Loran:	31168.3/47543.9
Depth:	100-120 feet
Visibility:	15-40 feet

JOHN MITCHELL

The *John Mitchell* was headed off Vermilion Point in a dense fog when it was struck by the freighter *Mack* on July 10, 1911.

The 420-foot *John Mitchell* was carrying a load of coal and a few passengers. Although the ship sank rapidly, all but three crew members were able to make it to the *Mack* and save themselves. The *John Mitchell* was a relatively new steel-hulled bulk freighter as it was constructed in 1907 at St. Clair, Mich.

Although this wreck lies upside down on the bottom in 140 to 150 feet of water, some divers explore the cargo holds and cabin areas of the wrecked vessel.

Location:	About three miles west-northwest of Whitefish Point.
Loran:	31153.7/47545.6
Depth:	140 feet
Visibility:	15-40 feet

MYRON

The *Myron* was a 186-foot lumber hooker that was claimed by a violent storm on Nov. 22, 1919.

The *Myron* was heading east from Munising with a load of lumber and was towing the schooner-barge *Miztec*. Ice began to build and the *Myron* made a desperate race for the safety of Whitefish Point but foundered a little more than a mile west-northwest of the point.

The crew of 17 was lost. The captain was rescued by standing on the pilot house, which broke free when the ship sank.

The remains of the *Myron,* which was built in Grand Haven in 1888, lie scattered in about 50 feet of water. Divers enjoy exploring the remains of the steamer's machinery, equipment, and timbers.

Location:	About one mile west-northwest of Whitefish Point.
Loran:	31142.5/47566.2
Depth:	45-50 feet
Visibility:	15-40 feet
Tips:	This is a good dive for new wreck divers or a good second dive for the day.

JOHN B. COWLE

The *John B. Cowle* was a steel, 420-foot steamer that was headed south near Whitefish Point when it was struck by the steamer *Isaac M. Scott*, on July 12, 1909.

The *John B. Cowle*, a 4,731-ton iron ore carrier, was nearly cut in two by the force of the collision. It sank rapidly, claiming 14 lives.

The collision occurred during the maiden voyage of the *Isaac M. Scott*, a ship that later foundered near Thunder Bay in Lake Huron.

Although this is a very deep shipwreck and carries considerable risks in diving, some expert divers have penetrated the interior of this vessel, including the cabins. It is usually not buoyed.

Location:	About one mile northwest of Whitefish Point.
Loran:	31124.9/47579.2 (bow)
	31124.8/47579.3 (stern)
Depth:	180-220 feet
Visibility:	15-30 feet
Tips:	Be sure you are capable of diving at this extreme depth.

VIENNA

The *Vienna* was a wooden steamer that was struck by the steamer *Nipigon* on Sept. 17, 1892 while hauling a cargo of iron ore. The ship sank rapdily while being towed by the *Nipigon* but no lives were lost in the accident.

The *Vienna* lies in about 145 feet of water about 1.5 miles southeast of Whitefish Point. The remains are intact and upright and divers exploring the deck equipment and machinery, which can be reached at 115 feet and includes a lifeboat. Divers also explore the intact engine and the bow cabins. Most divers enjoy the bow section the most.

In recent years, this has been one of the most popular dive sites in the Whitefish Point Underwater Preserve. It is usually marked with an official mooring buoy. The remains were discovered by a scientific research vessel.

Location:	About 1.5 miles southeast of Whitefish Point.
Loran:	31135.9/476610.4
Depth:	115 feet to the deck, 145 feet to the bottom.
Visibility:	10-30 feet

PANTHER

The *Panther* was a 249-foot, wooden steamer that collided in a fog with the larger, steel-hulled steamer *James J. Hill* off Parisienne Island on June 26, 1916.

The 1,643-ton *Panther* was headed north when it was struck amidship. The ship was damaged heavily in the collision and sank rapidly. No lives were lost due to the quick thinking of the captain of the *James J. Hill.*

The remains of the *Panther* lie in about 100 feet of water. The remains are quite broken up on the bottom.

Location:	About four miles southwest of Whitefish Point off Parisienne Island.
Loran:	31105.8/47685.9
Depth:	100-110 feet
Visibility:	10-30 feet
Tips:	This has become a popular dive site in this preserve in recent years. It is usually marked with a buoy.

SAMUEL MATHER

The *Samuel Mather* was a 246-foot wooden steamer that was loaded with wheat bound for Buffalo, N.Y. from Duluth, Minn. when it was struck on its starboard side by the *Brazil* on Nov. 22, 1891. The accident occurred in a dense fog and a large gash was torn in the starboard hull of the *Samuel Mather.*

The *Samuel Mather* was about eight miles north of Point Iroquois when the accident occurred. The ship did not sink quickly and the crew was able to leave the doomed vessel in lifeboats. The *Samuel Mather* was a small bulk freighter that usually carried coal and was built in 1887.

Divers enjoy exploring the intact cabins.

The *Samuel Mather* is a very popular dive site in this preserve as it rests upright and intact and is in very good condition. Divers enjoy exploring the intact cabins, which remain probably because the vessel sank slowly allowing pressure to equalize and thus, did not "blow" off the deck. A mast can be reached at 75 feet.

Location:	About eight miles north of Point Iroquois, 15 miles southeast of Whitefish Point.
Loran:	31086.7/47734.8
Depth:	75 feet to mast, 155 feet to deck, and 180 feet to bottom.
Visibility:	10-30 feet.

M.M. DRAKE

The *M.M. Drake* was a steamer towing the schooner-barge *Michigan* when it began to take on water. The 19-year-old, 201-foot ship sank on Oct. 2, 1901 while coming to the aid of the *Michigan*. One Crew member, the cook, was lost in the mishap.

Wreckage is scattered on the bottom.

Location:	About .5 miles north of Vermilion Point.
Loran:	31167.6/47668.9
Depth:	About 50 feet.
Visibility:	10-30 feet

MIZTEC

The 194-foot schooner-barge *Miztec* was a victim of a spring storm that arose suddenly on the night of May 13, 1921.

The *Miztec* was in tow headed north out of Whitefish Bay when it ran into rough seas. The ship was hauling salt found for Duluth, Minn.

About 10 miles west of Whitefish Point, the tow line broke and the lights of the *Miztec* suddenly disappeared. Two years before, the *Miztec* survived a fierce autumn storm by anchoring in Whitefish Bay.

The remains of the vessel are broken up on the bottom.

Location:	About four miles west-northwest of Whitefish Point.
Loran:	31156.9/47561.2
Depth:	50 feet
Visibility:	10-40 feet

SADIE THOMPSON

Little is known about the incident that resulted in the sinking of the steel barge *Sadie Thompson*. It is believed by some that the barge was used in constructing the breakwall at Whitefish Point.

Today, the barge rests on its side and divers enjoy exploring the remains, which include a derrick attached to one side of the vessel.

Location:	About six miles south of Whitefish Point.
Loran:	31150.3/47619.8
Depth:	80-100 feet
Visibility:	10-40 feet

COMET

The *Comet* was a 744-ton wooden-hulled steamer that collided with the steamer *Manitoba* on August 23, 1875. The *Comet* was struck on her port bow, a fatal collision for the vessel but the *Manitoba* went relatively unscathed.

The *Comet* was bound for Buffalo, N.Y. with a load of mixed ore--iron, copper, and Montana silver--when the accident occurred near Whitefish Point. Ten survivors were picked up by the *Manitoba*.

Divers will find much of the hulll intact with twin standing arches.

Location:	About seven miles southeast of Whitefish Point.
Loran:	31111.4/47638.1
Depth:	130-140 feet
Visibility:	10-40 feet

ZILLAH

The 202-foot steamer *Zillah* was 36 years old when it ran into trouble in heavy seas about four miles south of Whitefish Point in May 1926. The vessel's cargo, limestone blocks, shifted in the heavy seas and caused the ship to slowly capsize.

The event was witnesses by two other steamers who came to the *Zillah's* aid and as a result no lives were lost in the disaster. The wreck is upright and intact.

Location:	About four miles south of Whitefish Point.
Loran:	31123.8/47624.4
Depth:	230 feet to deck; 250 feet to bottom
Visibility:	10-40 feet

SUPERIOR CITY

The *Superior City*, a powerful, 429-foot steel freighter, met her end in Whitefish Bay, about five miles south of the point, when it collided with the *Willis L. King*. There was no apparent reason for the collision as there was no fog or heavy seas, only the dimming light of early evening.

The *Superior City* took the worst of the blow and water rushed into her engine room, which caused a boiler to explode. The explosion blew the entire stern away and caused the ship to sink rapidly. Twenty-nine lives were lost in the disaster.

Today, the remains of the Superior City lie on the bottom in 260 feet of water. The deck can be reached at 215 feet. The bow of the vessel plowed into the bottom up to the pilot house. What is left of the stern is intact and divers enjoy exploring that area.

Location:	In Whitefish Bay, about five miles southeast of the point.
Loran:	31112.0/47653.3 (stern)
	31118.9/47635.6 (bow)
Depth:	215 feet to top of wreck, 260 to bottom
Visibility:	20-40 feet

J.M. OSBOURNE

The *J.M. Osbourne* has become a popular dive site at the Whitefish Point Underwater Preserve. The vessel was a new, 178-foot wooden steamer that was towing two barges on July 27, 1884. There was a dense fog and the captain of the *J.M. Osbourne* was sounding the horn of the ship at regular intervals.

Suddenly, the steel steamer *Alberta* emerged from the fog and struck the *J.M. Osbourne* on her starboard side, nearly cutting the wooden steamer in two at her boilers. The two vessels remained stuck together at first and passengers and crew from the *J.M. Osbourne* clamored aboard the *Alberta*, which was barely scathed in the accident. When the *J.M. Osbourne* finally went down, it took a cook and three other crew members with her.

The remains of the *J.M. Osbourne* were discovered in the mid-1980s and were quickly stripped for the benefit of a local museum. State officials turned a blind eye to the salvage operation.

Today, the J.M. Osbourne is upright and mostly intact.

Today, the *J.M. Osbourne* is upright and mostly intact. Divers enjoy exploring the hull, cargo holds, and cabins of the vessel. The nameboard and other key artifacts were recovered by the museum.

Location:	About 3.5 miles northwest of Whitefish Point.
Loran:	31149.5/47528.2
Depth:	145-165 feet
Visibility:	20-40 feet

ALEX NIMICK

The captain of the *Alex Nimick* was resting in Whitefish Bay on Sept. 20, 1907, when he thought it prudent to head out and attempt to make the long, unprotected haul to Munising Bay. The 298-foot, 1,968-ton wooden steamer was a competent vessel and a slight southwest wind would not keep her in the bay for long.

But a few hours later a northwesterly gale came in and the *Alex Nimick* was stopped dead and taking on water off Crisp Point. The ship made it to within 1.5 miles of Vermilion Point when it grounded and the waves quickly beat it to pieces in shallow water. Seven lives were lost in the disaster despite a quick response from the U.S. Life Saving Station at Crisp Point.

Today, the remains of the vessel are badly broken and scattered but there is enough to keep divers interested for a short time. Some machinery can be found in shallow water as well as massive timbers.

Location:	About 1.5 miles west of Vermilion Point.
Loran:	31203.3/47555.2
Depth:	15-20 feet
Visibility:	20-40 feet, less if heavy seas are running.

Inland Dive Sites

Little inland diving occurs in the eastern region of Michigan's Upper Peninsula, primarily because there are so many excellent and protected Great Lakes sites to explore. But one site worth investigating is Monacle Lake, which is located west of Brimley off 6 Mile Road, which can be accessed off I-75 south of Sault Ste. Marie.

The road follows Lake Superior and takes you through Brimley and the small reservation community of Bay Mills. Keep going west and you will pass the Point Iroquois Lighthouse (see Other Attractions) and just past the lighthouse is a road going south (left). That road will take you to Monacle Lake.

Monacle Lake sports a wonderful public access site that is operated by the Hiawatha National Forest. Because National Forest land surrounds the 146-acre lake, there are no cottages and rarely even any fishing boats.

Monacle Lake has a sand bottom, which is a function of its formation between Lake Superior north and a towering ridge of sand dunes south. There is also a small amount of gravel.

Here, divers will find a relatively shallow lake loaded with colorful gamefish, which include rock bass, bass, northern pike, and suckers. There is a convenient parking lot and extensive beach to enjoy. Don't expect to find shipwrecks here, but the fish are enough to keep divers interested. This lake also makes a good snorkel.

Emergencies

In the event of an on-water medical emergency in the Whitefish Point Underwater Preserve, it is best to contact a nearby boat for assistance on vhf channel 16. Because the U.S. Coast Guard Station at Sault Ste. Marie is more than an hour from the preserve, the most practical assistance may be from sport fishermen or other dive boats, if any are in the area.

The emergency plan for this preserve calls for injured divers to be transported to War Memorial Hospital in Sault Ste. Marie for stabilization. Hospital staff are instructed to contact the Diving Accident Network (DAN) to determine the closest available recompression chamber if that treatment is necessary.

If ground or commercial air ambulances are unavailable, a helicopter from the U.S. Coast Guard Air Rescue Station in Traverse City will be summoned for assistance to transport victims to the nearest recompression chamber.

Ambulances in this region are dispatched by the Chippewa County Sheriff's Department at Sault Ste. Marie. That department does **not** monitor vhf channel. The sheriff's department can be reached at (906) 635-6355.

In recent years, divers have had medical emergencies while diving the *Vienna*. Depsite these problems, a more practical emergency response and evacuation plan has not been developed.

Because of the depths, it is a good idea to carry a small tank of oxygen in the event a medical diving emergency occurs here. Most charter boats carry such supplies and will render aid if summoned.

Other Attractions

The Hiawatha National Forest abounds with wildlife and scenic overlooks that feature Lake Superior. The road that follows the shoreline is one of the most scenic in the Upper Peninsula and probably the state. The road has many names but can be picked up west off I-75 just south of Sault Ste. Marie as 6 Mile Road or east off M-123 near Eckerman as Lake Shore Drive.

The road takes visitors through forests and near the Point Iroquois Lighthouse, which is a free historic attraction maintained by the National Forest Service. In addition to spectacular scenery, the lighthouse stop offers boardwalks and foot paths along a sandy beach. Monacle Lake (see Inland Dive Sites) is also nearby and worth a stop if you are in the area.

At Whitefish Point there is the lighthouse and adjoining shipwreck museum but many sport divers boycott this spot in protest to the way local shipwrecks have been stripped. Visitors also enjoy Tahquamenon Falls, which are located off M-123 south of Whitefish Point. Unfortunately the black flies and other insect pests probably know you are coming so be prepared.

A better place for family activities is Sault Ste. Marie, which is an hour's drive from Whitefish Point. Here, visitors can enjoy the museum ship *Valley Camp,* this floating museum is one of the largest maritime museums in the country. There is a small fee.

Sault Ste. Marie, Michigan also offers tours of the Soo Locks, where visitors can get close-up views of large Great Lakes freighters. The city also offers casino gambling as well as many fine restaurants.

Accommodations

Overnight accommodations are available in the Paradise area. There are ten motels within 12 miles of Paradise, which is located south of Whitefish Point on M-123. Additional lodging is available in Newberry, but many divers, especially if they are traveling with their families, prefer to stay in the Sault Ste. Marie area and make the hour drive to Whitefish Point.

Because the Hiawatha National Forest and the Tahquamenon Falls State Park are in this area, there are many state, federal, and private campgrounds. There are more than 400 campsites within 10 miles of Paradise.

Getting There

Whitefish Point Underwater Preserve is located near the end of the road identified as M-123. Locals know that although the highway turns west at Paradise, the road continues north through Paradise as Whitefish Point Road.

To access M-123, continue on I-75 through St. Ignace and exit about five miles outside of town at Exit 352--Newberry. This is M-123.

The nearest airport is located at Sault Ste. Marie.

Important Phone Numbers/Addresses

U.S. Coast Guard Station
337 Water St.
Sault Ste. Marie, MI 49783
(906) 635-3273

Michigan State Police
Newberry, MI 49868
(906) 293-5151

Helen Newberry Joy Hospital
Newberry, MI 49868
(906) 293-5181

U.P. Travel Assn.
P.O. Box 400
Iron Mountain, MI 49801
(906) 774-5480

Chippewa County Sheriff's Dept.
331 Court St.
Sault Ste. Marie, MI 49783
(906) 635-6355

War Memorial Hospital
Sault Ste. Marie, MI 49783
(906) 635-4460

Paradise Chamber of Commerce
P.O. Box 82
Paradise, MI 49768

Charter Operator:
Scuba North
13380 W. Bay Shore
Traverse City, MI 49684
(616) 947-2520

St. Clair River

The St. Clair River offers a challenging dive experience. Divers must be certain they are prepared to handle limited visiblity and a strong current.

The St. Clair River is about 40 miles long and connects Lake Huron to Lake St. Clair. Because the current often prevents a buildup of ice, it is "diveable" much of the year. And don't be surprised to see groups of other hearty souls visiting this unique dive site in cold weather. It is popular, especially for those who live in southeastern Michigan and have a limited amount of recreational time.

There are nine major dive sites--all near Port Huron where the water is surprisingly clear. Although interesting "junk" can be found throughout much of the river, caution must be exercised because the St. Clair River is a busy shipping channel. Some divers prefer to hit the water in early morning to avoid boat traffic.

Visibility in the St. Clair River is usually excellent at 10 to 20 feet and sometimes more. A few days of the year, usually during the coldest months, visibility may reach 20 to 30 feet, but such water clarity is uncommon.

Divers can call the Port Huron Waste Water Treatment Plant to determine water clarity on a particular day. Divers should as for the turbidity index." Anything less than 1.0 is good. An index of 1.5 or more means less than five feet of visibility.

Another consideration to St. Clair River diving is fishing line. A dive knife is a must because there are many log jams, which attract fish -- and fishermen. Some say they enjoy river diving more than lake diving because fish are more tolerant of divers and permit closer observation.

Diving in the St. Clair River may require an orientation dive. If new to the area and this type of diving, divers should contact local dive stores to find others experienced in the stream. Club Poseiden, which provided much of the information featured in this chapter, is a cadre of experienced river divers and it is possible that one of their members may be available for orientation. Again, contact a local dive store for more information and consider specialized instruction.

The diving hazards found here are balanced by the rewards of diving in the St. Clair River. Many divers use the river as a way to maintain diving skills through the winter. And there are plenty of bottles and similar items to find and examine. Unfortunately, wrecks in the river are breaking up as a result of the force of the current.

Three shipwrecks near the head of the stream are identified as the "ghost fleet" of the river. They are covered here but support services are generally associated with the Sanilac Shores Underwater Preserve. Divers should check out that chapter for charter information.

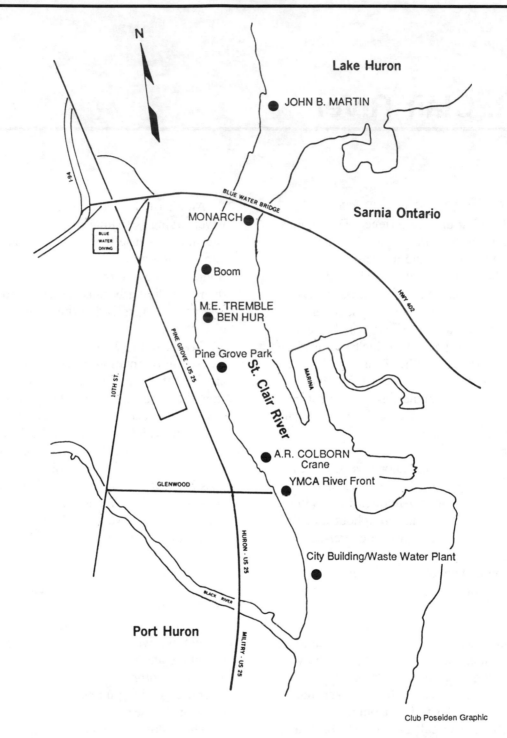

Club Poseiden Graphic

St. Clair River

Access

Except for the "ghost fleet", boats are not needed to access the dive sites in the river. The common practice is to plan entrance and exit sites and display diver down flags at those places. The current makes it impractical to drag a flag and float while diving. Divers must use their own discretion regarding the use of diver down flags at this site.

JOHN B. MARTIN

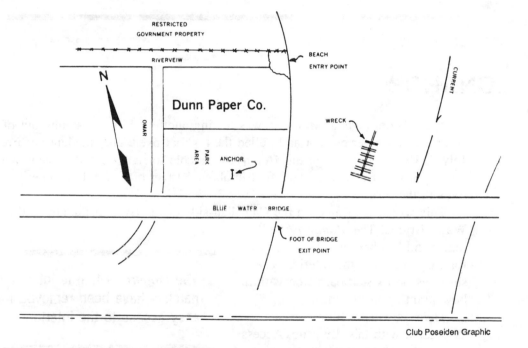

Club Poseiden Graphic

The *John B. Martin* was a 220-foot schooner built in 1873, that had been trimmed to serve as a barge. In 1900, the ship was being towed south by a steamer and had just entered the St. Clair River when it was struck by the steel steamer *Yuma.*

The *John B. Martin* sank rapidly, taking several lives and a cargo of iron ore with her. The incident occurred in about 60 feet of water, about 225 feet from the U.S. side near old Fort Gratiot.

The collision caused extensive damage. The cabin washed ashore the next day. An anchor of the *John B. Martin* was removed and is on display near the Blue Water Bridge.

The wreck is located between the bridge and a public beach at the end of Riverview Street in Port Huron. The beach is the best entrance point and most divers exit at the foot of the bridge. The wreck is broken up but the strong currents in this area make this dive hazardous. Some report that the current holds them against the crumbling hull of the wreck.

Location:	About 200 yards from the U.S. shore about 100 yards north of the Blue Water Bridge.
Depth:	60 feet
Visibility:	5-20 feet
Tips:	Because of the strong currents here, dive first with another diver familiar with this wreck site.

MONARCH

The 60-foot tugboat *Monarch* was towing another ship that swung out of control in the river current and pulled the tugboat over. The incident occurred on July 7, 1934 and although the *Monarch* was able to right herself, it had taken on too much water and sank stern first in about 50 feet of water. Four men lost their lives in the disaster.

This wreck is located on the Canadian side of the river just south of the Blue Water Bridge. The *Monarch*'s hull is intact and hatches have been removed for easy access to the interior. The ship lies on its starboard side with the bow pointing upstream.

The *Monarch*'s hull is intact and hatches have been removed for easy access to the interior.

There is usually little current associated with this dive site. Access can be gained by parking near a navigational light next to a warehouse. Look for steel stairs and a steel cable that guides divers to the wreck.

Location:	South of the Blue Water Bridge on the Canadian side of the river.
Depth:	50 feet
Visibility:	5-20 feet
Tips:	Use heavy gloves to protect hands if following the cable to the wreck.

SIDNEY E. SMITH Unloading Boom

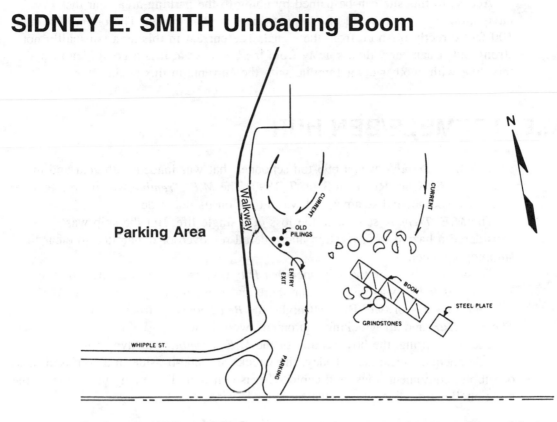

On June 5, 1972, the 356-foot steamer *Sidney E. Smith* was northbound just south of the blue Water Bridge when it lost control in the current. The ship swung crosswise in the current and was struck by a southbound freighter.

The collision caused a 20-foot hole in the bow of the *Sidney E. Smith* and the ship sank quickly. The wreck was removed from the river but a large self-unloading boom remains on the river bottom.

This dive site is interesting not only because divers can explore the boom, but because there are several large grindstones nearaby that apparently fell from a ship many years ago.

Location:	South of Blue Water Bridge, at the end of Whipple Street in Port Huron.
Depth:	50-55 feet
Visibility:	10-40 feet
Tips:	Look for grindstones north of boom and a steel plate east of the boom. Currents can be tricky in this area.

    Access to this site can be gained by going to the parking area near the navigation signal at the end of Whipple Street in Port Huron. The boom lies about 100 feet directly offshore from the signal. The current in this area is usuallly not strong but it can carry divers away from the boom area. It is a good idea to make this dive with another diver familiar with the currents in this area.

M.E. TREMBLE/BEN HUR

    The *M.E. Tremble* was a 693-ton schooner that was loaded with coal and in tow on the St. Clair River on Sept. 7, 1890. The *M.E. Tremble* was unable to steer clear of a southbound steamer and was struck on its port side.

    The *M.E. Tremble* sank with the loss of a single life. But the ship was considered a hazard to navigation and ordered removed or dynamited to clear the shipping channel.

    To salvage the ship, the schooner *Ben Hur* was brought to the site. On Nov. 8, 1890, the *Ben Hur* was moored near shore and was preparing to raise the *M.E. Tremble* in a day or two. But that night, the *Ben Hur* was struck by a passing ship. The *Ben Hur*, and all wrecking equipment, were lost.

    The next spring, the bow section of the *M.E. Tremble* was dynamited to provide adequate clearance. Today, the wrecks are side-by-side in a confused mass of rubble, equipment, logs, and cable. This is considered by many to be one of the most challenging dive sites in the St. Clair River.

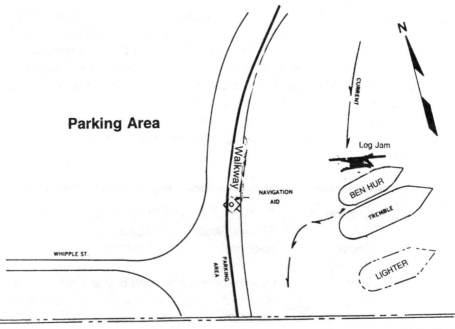

Club Poseiden Graphic

Access to this site is at the navigational signal at the end of Whipple Street in Port Huron. A steel cable leads from the signal to the *M.E. Tremble,* which lies in about 70 feet of water. Divers first encounter wreckage, the result of the dynamiting. Then, divers find the *M.E. Tremble.* North of this wreck is the *Ben Hur*, upside down.

South of the *M.E. Tremble* is another wreck, the *Lighter*, a ship that had tended cables for the *Ben Hur* during the salvage attempt. These wrecks are mostly broken up.

Because there are many cables associated with this dive site, it is easy to become disoriented and the current can sweep divers into the shipping channel. Plan to return early and keep track of your position. Guide cables once used by divers at this site have been swept away.

If divers are swept from the site, it is best to swim west toward the shore. An emergency ascent may cause divers to enter the shipping channel.

Location:	At the end of Whipple Street in Port Huron.
Depth:	60-65 feet
Visibility:	10-30 feet
Tips:	Be careful! This can be a dangerous dive in the event of disorientation and panic. The current is swift in this area.

Pine Grove Park

Pine Grove Park, located between Prospect and Kearney streets in Port Huron, is a popular recreation area. It is good for fishing and a good place for new divers.

This is a good dive site for new divers.

There is little current at this site but access to the water from the boardwalk can be difficult with scuba gear. Enter the water at the north ladder in the breakwall and exit at the south ladder in the breakwall.

Divers can find a variety of old bottles and other artifacts at this historical site.

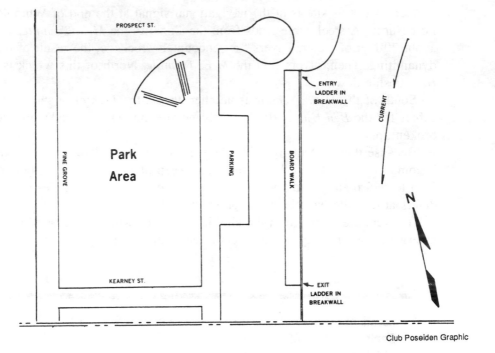

Club Poseiden Graphic

Location:	Between Prospect and Kearney streets in Port Huron.
Depth:	25-45 feet
Visibility:	10-30 feet
Tips:	Watch for anglers. Avoid fishing lines and be courteous.

A.R. COLBORN/Crane

The *A.R. Colburn* was a 129-foot wooden-hulled steamer built in 1882 in Saugatuck, Mich. The ship was used in the lumber industry until 1909. The *A.R. Colborn* changed owners, underwent major structural changes and was used for hauling salt from St. Clair, Mich. to a railhead at Courtright, Ontario.

In 1920, the ship was purchased for conversion to a tug boat but the owner died and the ship sank at her moorings. It was formally abandoned in 1922.

The engine and boiler of the *A.R. Colborn* remain, but the hull is deteriorating

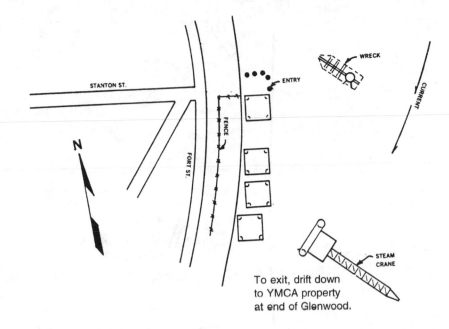

To exit, drift down
to YMCA property
at end of Glenwood.

with the current. The propeller is displayed on the campus of St. Clair Community College.

The *A.R. Colborn* lies east of an old coal dock marked by pilings. Parking is available near the intersection of Fort, Stanton, and Merchant streets in Port Huron north of the YMCA building. There is a steep bank leading to the water.

Divers will find an old steam crane south of the wreck. The origin of the crane is unknown but was probably lost off a barge or dock. The shipwreck and crane lie in about 25 feet of swift water.

For most divers, the best game plan is to dive from an area south of the U.S. Coast Guard Cutter *Bramble* slip and stay along the 25 to 30 foot depth contour past the discharge pipe area to the shipwreck.

The engine is still upright while the boiler has toppled toward the river. After inspecting the wreck, divers can then drift to the crane in 25 to 30 feet of water. From the crane there are two automobile chassis. One chassis is about 45 feet away from the slope near the YMCA area.

Another lies on the slope uncovered when a wrecker removed a vehicle that crashed through the guardrail at the end of Glenwood Street next to the YMCA. The old guardrail lies in about 15 to 20 feet. Also in the area is a large wooden rudder lying in about 38 feet of water south of the auto chassis areas. It is suspected that the rudder is from one of the wrecks on the bottom near the Blue Water Bridge.

Also in the area is a large wooden rudder believed to be left from ships that sank near the Blue Water Bridge.

Note: a white "flurry" in the water here is from a paper plant discharge north of the dive site.

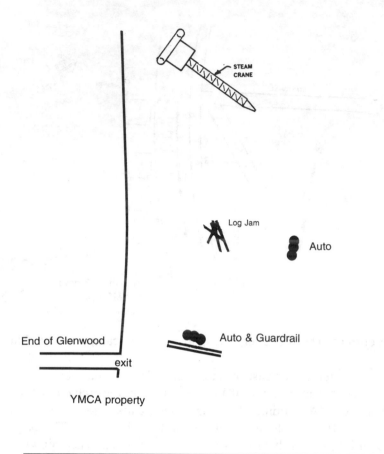

Location:	North of the Port Huron YMCA building.
Depth:	25-30 feet
Visibility:	10-30 feet
Tips:	Watch for swift water and low visibility.

YMCA River Front
City Building/Waste Water Plant

This dive site is loaded with old bottles and artifacts. A breakwall is found along the shore and divers can enter and exit at several points along the wall. The current in this area is not particularly swift during most of the year.

The northern entry point is at the north YMCA parking lot at the end of Glenwood Street in Port Huron. A convenient exit point is at the north end of the city building at a ladder built into the breakwall. Another exit point can be found at the city's waste water treatment plant south of the city building.

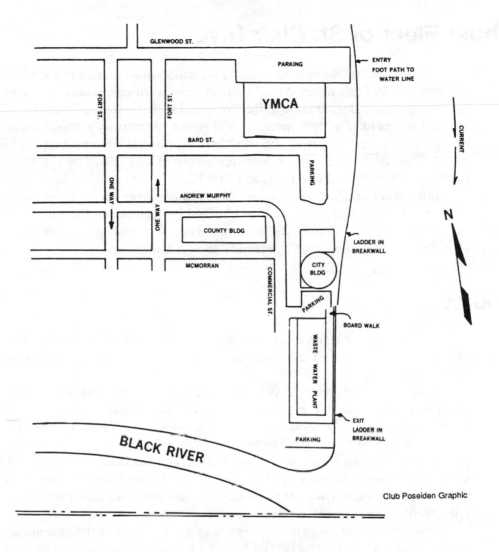

Club Poseiden Graphic

Location:	Between the Port Huron YMCA and city buildings east of Fort Street.
Depth:	25-45 feet
Visibility:	10-30 feet
Tips:	Entries and exits may be difficult due to a steep breakwall.

Ghost Fleet of St. Clair River

Four vessels, the *Yakima, Sachem, Aztec,* and *Province,* comprise the "Ghost fleet" of the St. Clair River. Actually, these were worn-out vessels that were once secured in Sarnia Bay, Ontario at the lower end of Lake Huron. They were allowed to "molder" at their mooring until seamen eventually repaired them enough to float and they were then scuttled in lower Lake Huron near the head of the St. Clair River. The remains were researched and identified by divers Jim and Pat Stayer, Tim Juhl, David Fritz, and Cris Kohl.

Unlike other St. Clair River dives, these are not shore access dives. Information about charters to these wrecks can be obtained by referencing the Sanilac Shores Underwater Preserve chapter earlier in this book. A review of the dive sites is provided here because of their proximity to St. Clair River.

YAKIMA

The *Yakima*'s big claim to fame is the fact that it was the first Great Lakes shipping vessel with electrical lights. It was a 279-foot bulk freighter that was built in Cleveland, Ohio in 1887.

On June 10, 1905, during a dense fog, the *Yakima* ran aground in the St. Clair River near Stag Island. Although serious efforts were made to release the vessel for three days, it would not budge. Finally, it was early on June 13, that the ship was discovered on fire. A passing steamer managed to save the crew of the *Yakima*, but the ship burned to the waterline. Later, the hulk was raised and towed to shallow water in Sarnia Bay and allowed to sink. After several stripping events, the hulk of the *Yakima* was finally raised one last time and towed out into lower Lake Huron where it sank on Oct. 15, 1928.

Today, the Yakima is partially intact with her keel and keelsons remaining as well as some of the machinery. Old beer bottles are also scattered at the site. The wreck provides divers an opportunity to see first hand how steamers of this class were constructed at the end of the last century.

Location:	About 12 miles southeast of Lexington Harbor.
Loran:	30775.1/49612.6
Lat/Lon:	43 10.56/82 19.38
Depth:	70 to 77 feet
Visibility:	10-30 feet

SACHEM

The *Sachem* was a 187-foot steamer that was built in Grand Haven, Mich. in 1889. The vessel served the commercial shipping trade, primarily hauling lumber on the Great Lakes, for many years before it was laid up for repairs at Roberts Landing in the St. Clair River. A kitchen accident caused the ship to catch on fire and a local fire department finally put it out after many long hours.

The *Sachem* was allowed to sink in Sarnia Bay, much like the *Yakima*. Then, in December 1928, the *Sachem* was raised again and towed to lower Lake Huron. It was set on fire again and rammed to sink her (Scuttling was generally a festive event with much drinking and other fun associated with it. Unfortunately, scuttling was not always a rational event.)

Today, the wreck of the *Sachem* is found about 14 miles northeast of the St. Clair River's headwaters. Divers enjoy exploring the stern of the vessel where they find an old-fashioned four-bladed propeller. A boiler remains in the hull but no engines are found on the wreck. Divers may note a unique hull design that is reinforced with massive timbers. This wreck is upright and has a mostly intact hull.

Location:	About 14 miles north of the St. Clair River's headwaters.
Loran:	30770.5/49618.3
Lat/Lon:	43 09.83/82 18.49
Depth:	70-77 feet
Visibility:	10-30 feet

AZTEC and PROVINCE

The *Province* was a 162-foot dredge barge that was built in Fort William, Ont. in 1911. The maritime life of this vessel was rather unremarkable until it was being towed by a steamer up the St. Clair River on Sept. 28, 1923. On that date it began to take on water. When a list was noticed by the crew, two jumped in and drowned. The other nine stayed on board and got off without incident when the vessel settled in shallow water.

The *Province* was relfoated and then allowed to sink in Sarnia Bay. Some years later, it was refloated for scuttling in lower Lake Huron. The

It hauled coal and iron as a bulk freighter and was later converted into a lumber hooker.

remains of the *Aztec* were piled on top of her for the scuttling.

The *Aztec* was a 180-foot steamer that was built in 1889 in Marine City, Mich. It hauled coal and iron as a bulk freighter and was later converted into a lumber hooker. On Nov. 8, 1923, the *Aztec* caught fire while moored in the Belle River at Marine City. The vessel was refloated and allowed to sink in Sarnia Bay after being stripped.

Both vessels were disposed of in lower Lake Huron on Nov. 2, 1936. It was an miserable end to once-pround vessels that served the commercial Great Lakes shipping trade well for many years.

Location:	About 13 miles southeast of Lexington Harbor.
Loran:	30770.5/49618.3
Lat/Lon:	43 09.83/82 18.49
Depth:	70-77 feet
Visibility:	10-30 feet

Grass Pickerel

White Bass

Inland Waters

Diving Michigan's inland waters is exciting. Inland lakes and streams offer their own brand of challenges that make them popular among skin and scuba divers of all skill levels.

One of the greatest advantages of inland diving is accessibility. Michigan

---

One of the greatest advantages of inland diving is accessibility.

---

has many lands and streams--no matter where one stands in the state, water is within six miles.

Inland lakes are generally warmer than the Great Lakes. Although they rarely offer shipwrecks for exploration, inland lakes frequently host abandoned machinery, antique bottles, abandoned fishing boats, and a variety of fishing equipment. The most interesting portions of inland waters are usually within 100 feet, so wetsuits are generally adequate during the summer.

But the water is not always warm. Thermoclines form early in the summer and frigid temperatures are common in 50 feet of water in even the hottest summers.

Game fish, such as bluegills, speckled bass, northern pike, perch, and bass are commonly seen in inland waters. In the spring, divers may come across large schools of fish in shallow water where most game fish prefer to spawn.

Because the ice forms early on inland lakes, they are frequently sites for ice diving. During the winter, sediments are undisturbed by boats and waves and the water is unusually clear. That makes winter an ideal time for underwater photography. Ice diving is a sport quickly gaining popularity among Michigan sport divers.

Ice diving involves a variety of specialized techniques and novices should seek out expert instruction in this area. Drysuits are standard for this type of diving although many hearty souls continue to use wetsuits. Brrrrrr!

The best time to dive in inland water is in the early morning--before pleasure

---

Some lakes have restrictions as to when people can water ski or speed with boats.

---

boat traffic is too heavy. On small lakes and streams, this may not be a problem any time during the day. In fact, some lakes have restrictions as to when people can water ski or speed with boats.

Some divers avoid crowds by diving at night. This obviously requires good lights and many divers say fish are less likely to be frightened during the night when approached slowly and quietly. Check out a lake nearby for convenient diving.

Higgins Lake

Higgins Lake in Roscommon and Crawford counties is popular for night diving and for divers who enjoy observing aquatic life.

There are many sunken logs that attract fish. Because Higgins Lake is popular among boaters and anglers, divers can also find a variety of items lost overboard.

Besides underwater log jams and aquatic life, Higgins Lake is popular because of water clarity. During summer months, divers can expect visibility of 20 to 50 feet.

Higgins Lake, at 9,600 acres, is one of the largest inland lakes in the state. It is also deep -- up to 135 feet in the northwest section of the lake. But there are also many shallow areas where divers can observe fish. In the southern end of the lake is a "sunken island" where a variety of game fish can be found in large schools, especially during the early summer spawning season.

There are two state parks with boat ramps and one boat launching facility on the west side of the lake to provide ample access for divers. Many divers simply explore the lake from the public access sites.

A dive shop that has undergone several management changes is located on the northwest side of the lake but it is open only sporadically so don't count on it.

It is a good idea to make reservations for overnight accommodations well in advance because hotels and motels in this area fill fast because it is a popular tourist destination during the warm summer months.

Getting There

Higgins Lake is located east of US 27/I-75 about ten miles south of Grayling. There are several communities on the lake, including Hillcrest, Sharps Corners, and Higgins Lake.

Streets circle the lake and there are two state parks, on the south and north ends of the lake. A boat launch is located on the west side of Higgins Lake near Lake City Road.

Perhaps the best way to become acquainted with the area is to simply begin diving from the various public access sites on the lake. Exploration here will be both fun and rewarding.

N

DNR Graphic

Higgins Lake

Gull Lake

Gull Lake is located in Kalamazoo County and offers skin and scuba divers an opportunity to observe fish life in weed beds and a variety of farm equipment, small boats, and fish shanties.

In some areas, it was not unusual for residents to dispose of unwanted items, such as obsolete farm equipment and even old cars, by taking them out on the ice. When spring came, the disposal was complete. Some even set up betting pools to guess on which day the ice would melt enough to give way.

These days, that practice is uncommon because of environmental concerns, but Gull Lake is one area where farmers' "trash" became divers' "treasure."

The maximum depth of Gull Lake is about 110 feet and most fish and weed beds can be found in 50 feet or less. A popular access site for divers is Prairieville Township Park on the north end of the lake. The beach slopes gently and offers a safe way to enter the lake.

At the southwest end of Gull Lake is another park, Ross Township Park, near the small community of Yorkville. Entry is easy over a grassy slope.

Spring and fall offer the best visibility in this silt-bottom lake. Divers can expect to find visibility ranging from 8 to 30 feet. Most divers enjoy aquatic life and discarded farm equipment and cars in 10 to 40 feet of water.

Gull Lake is relatively close to Kalamazoo and Battle Creek. As a result, it can be crowded with boat traffic in July and August. Night or early morning diving may be the best times for scuba diving and it is always important to display a diver down flag.

Information about this dive site is available from Sub-Aquatic Sports and Service in Battle Creek, (616) 968-8551 or Wolf's Dive Shop, (616) 392-3300 or (616) 926-1068. Some dive retailers sponsor annual charity events at Gull Lake.

Information about diving and other activities, including wildlife watching at the nearby Kellogg Bird Sanctuary, is available from the Battle Creek Chamber of Commerce, 172 W. VanBuren,
Battle Creek, MI 49017.

Getting There

Gull Lake is located ten miles northwest of Battle Creek off M-89. A system of streets circle the lake and make access easy at many points. There are two township parks where divers generally access the lake from shore.

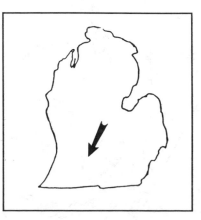

Brockway Lake

Brockway Lake is a small lake in southern Mecosta County that offers an usual diving experience.

The lake was created through mining of "marl," which was used to "sweeten" farmers' fields. As a result, there are steep walls that extend to depths of 25 feet.

In addition to steep walls, Brockway Lake is thick with vegetation, primarily lily pads, and fish life. Northern pike are abundant and divers can often observe them closely. At times, they are so secure in their weedy hideouts that they must actually be touched to "spook."

Spring in the shallows offers divers tremendous schools of sunfish, bluegills, and speckled bass. An occasional smallmouth bass may be seen in the company of these prey fish. Look for these fish around sunken logs, which are found in profusion in this lake.

Brockway Lake, which is 14 acres, is a popular fishing lake but because it is relatively small, few anglers use motors. As a result, visibility of 15 to 25 feet is not unusual. Also, there is no danger of being run over by waterskiers, but it is still a good idea to display a diver down flag.

The lake supports a variety of uncommon waterfowl spring through fall.

Access to Brockway Lake is by a public fishing site. A gravel path used to launch boats (but not really a ramp) is convenient for diver entry. The maximum depth of Brockway Lake is 30 feet. This is a good place for beginning divers and is an excellent place for snorkeling.

Getting There

Brockway Lake is in southern Mecosta County. Take US 131 to the Jefferson Road (Morley) Exit and go east about ten miles to 100th Avenue. Turn left (north) and at the first road (Three Mile Road) turn right (west). Follow the signs to the public access.

Note: A boat here is not necessary for diving. Many use both scuba and snorkel diving to explore this remote lake.

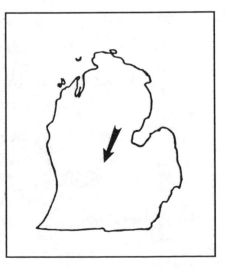

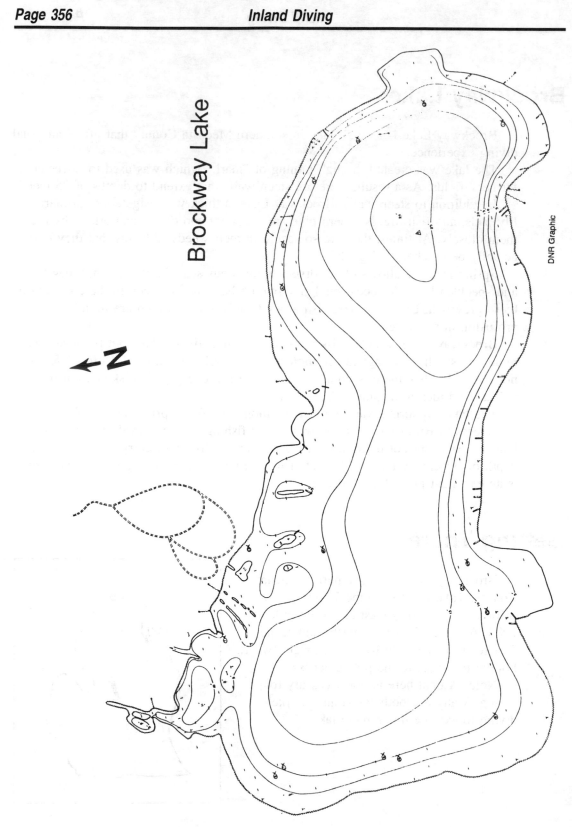

Brockway Lake

DNR Graphic

Murray Lake

When Grand Rapids area divers want a convenient, pleasureable dive, they head for Murray Lake in northern Kent County.

Murray Lake is 320 acres of fish and fun. It is an excellent dive site for beginning divers, snorkelers, and night divers.

Murray Lake is horseshoe-shaped and there is a public access on each arm. In 20 feet of water and less there is lush vegetation that attracts large schools of small game fish, particularly speckled bass, bluegills, sunfish, and small perch. Predatory fish, such as northern pike and bass, are also common.

There is no where to go wrong in Murray Lake if snorkelers and scuba divers are interested in exploration. The shore of the lake is moderately developed, but there is enough adjacent wetland to preserve habitat for an abundant fishery and wildlife.

Murray Lake is a popular ice diving site. Summer brings out water skiers so divers must use caution.

Because Murray Lake is heavily fished, divers can expect to find small wooden boats on the bottom and a variety of fishing equipment. Several

> *There is enough adjacent wetland to support an abundant fishery and wildlife.*

outboard motors that have fallen off fishing boats have been discovered by divers.

Visibility ranges from 10 to 25 feet. May and June are the best month for diving this lake because fish are congregated in large schools as they prepare to spawn and boat traffic is minimal.

In addition to two public access sites on each arm of the lake, divers can also enter the lake from the north off Five Mile Road. There is ample parking in lots at the public access sites or along the road at the north end.

Dive shops in Grand Rapids can direct divers to Murray Lake and provide information about current diving conditions.

Getting There

Divers can find Murray Lake by taking M-21 (Fulton) to Parnell Avenue (between Ada and Lowell). Go north on Parnell to Four Mile Road and turn right (east) to Murray Lake Avenue and turn left to go to Five Mile Road and the northern access site. Turn right (south) on Murray Lake Avenue and then left (east) on Lally Road and left (north) on Causeway Drive to the public access sites on each arm. Signs guide visitors to these sites.

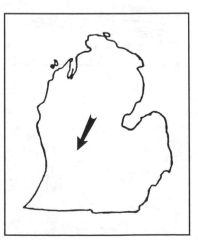

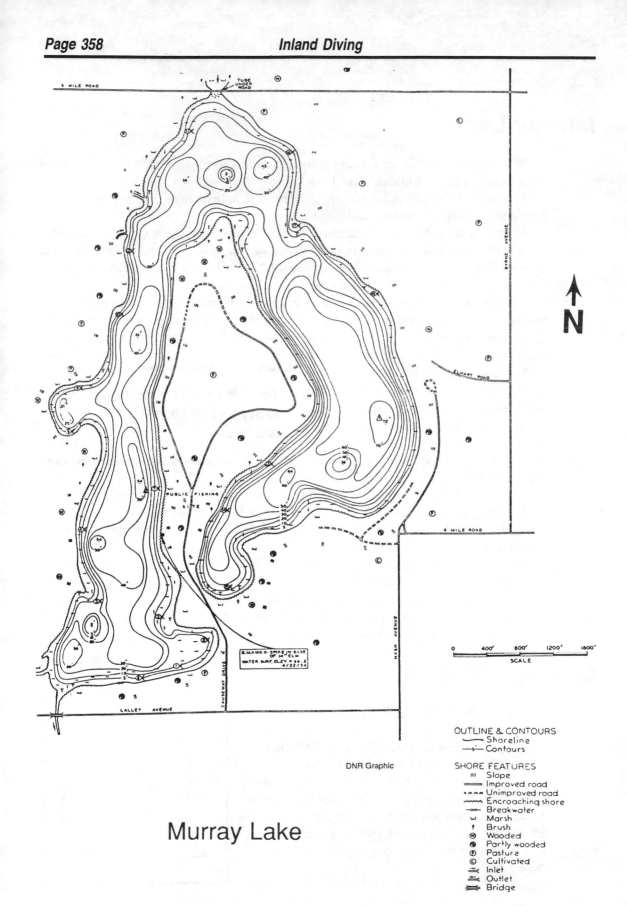

N

DNR Graphic

OUTLINE & CONTOURS
— Shoreline
—·— Contours

SHORE FEATURES
||| Slope
═══ Improved road
▪▬▪▬ Unimproved road
⌇⌇ Encroaching shore
∘∘ Breakwater
ⱳ Marsh
† Brush
Ⓦ Wooded
Ⓟ Partly wooded
Ⓟ Pasture
Ⓒ Cultivated
≋ Inlet
≋ Outlet
⊟ Bridge

Murray Lake

Baw Beese Lake

Baw Beese Lake was created with an impoundment of the St. Joseph River. The lake, southeast of Hillsdale, hosts a variety of small boats, ice shanties, and weed beds that attract small game fish.

Baw Beese Lake covers about 300 acres and has a maximum depth of 70 feet. Visibility is generally 15 to 30 feet.

Divers will find a small cabin cruiser at the northeast end of the lake in 55 feet of water.

Divers will find a small cabin cruiser at the northeast corner of the lake in about 55 feet of water. Divers will also find bottles and other discarded items on the silty lake bottom.

There are several parks on the lake that provide easy access. Streets encircle the lake making access from other points possible but divers should be sure they are not using private property without permission.

Waterskiing is popular on Baw Beese Lake so use extreme caution and display a diver down flag prominently.

Getting There

Baw Beese Lake is about one mile southeast of the city of Hillsdale. Access can be obtained from many roads off M-99, which runs through the city.

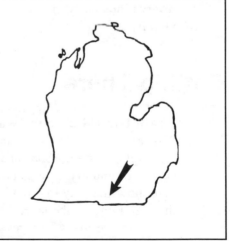

Heart Lake

Heart Lake in southern Otsego County is known for remarkable clarity, despite heavy water skiing activity during the middle of the day (waterskiing is prohibited in the early mornings and evenings).

There was once a sawmill on the south end of Heart Lake and logs were floated across the alke to the mill. Before some logs made it to the saw, however, they became waterlogged and sank. As a result, divers can find massive logs on the silty to sandy bottom.

The logs attract a variety of fish, especially smallmouth bass, trout, and small perch.

Heart Lake is divided into two sections with the easternmost section being the largest and deepest. This is where virtually all waterskiing occurs, although the lake is barely large enough. The maximum depth of this large section is about 125 feet, and a thermocline rarely exceeds 25 feet in the summer. Beyond the thermocline the water can be extremely cold.

The western section of Heart Lake is a good swim from the public access site and it is very shallow--about 20 feet maximum depth. Because it is shallow, this portion of the lake warms quickly and is often warmer than 70 degrees in late July and August. This is a good environment for snorkeling, although there are few features to interest divers in this portion of the lake. The bottom is silty and there is little vegetation to attract fish.

> **This is a good environment for snorkeling and novice scuba divers.**

The western section, however, often yields curious bottles and fishing equipment. This lake is suitable for divers of all skill levels as long as they do not goo too deep for their abilities.

There is a public access site on the south end of Heart Lake that offers plenty of parking and easy diver entry. Divers seeking overnight accommodations in July and August may find hotels and motels booked. It is a good idea to make reservations early in this area. There are many state forest campgrounds in the vicinity.

Getting There

Take I-75/US 27 to the Waters Exit (exit 270) and turn right (west) and at the stop sign, turn right (north). About one mile north of the small community of Waters there are signs that show the way to a public access site on the south end of the lake.

There are many cottages on the lake but it is generally quite peaceful.

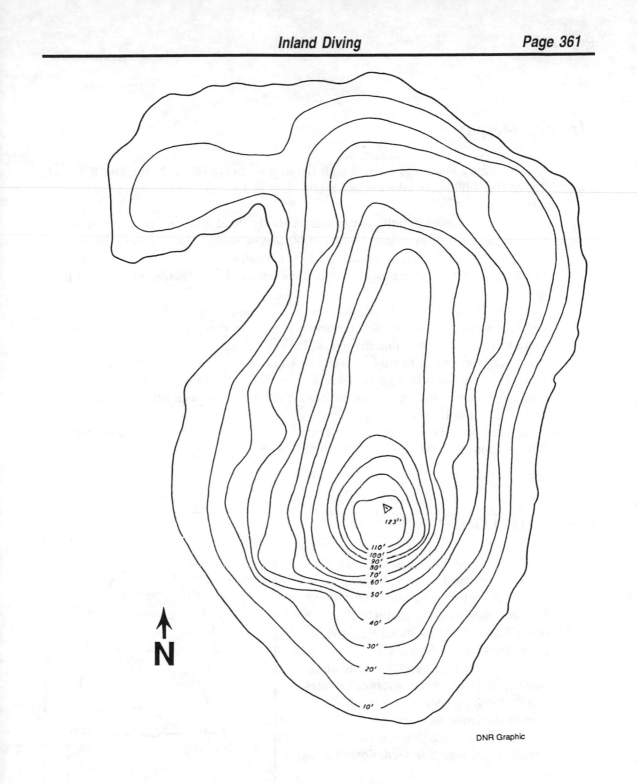

123′

110′
100′
90′
80′
70′
60′
50′

40′

30′

20′

10′

N

DNR Graphic

Heart Lake

Hardy Pond

The Hardy Pond was created with the impoundment of the Muskegon River in 1932. The 4,000-acre lake created by the dam is a popular West Michigan dive site.

Among the most popular attractions in Hardy Pond is a steel bridge that was submerged with rising water. It rests in 60 feet of water. The maximum depth of Hardy Pond is 110 feet. Visibility is limited because of sediments. Although visibility may be as great as 30 feet in some areas, divers should be prepared for less.

Hardy Pond is a popular fishing site and log jams can collect masses of monofilament fishing line. Several divers have been thankful they had a good dive knife to remove fishing line that entangled their equipment.

Divers can expect to find a variety of game fish, including walleye, around log jams. Hardy Pond offers good diving for divers of all experience levels.

Campgrounds and an access site are available at Newaygo State Park on the east side of the impoundment.

Information about diving Hardy Pond is available from the U.S. Forest Service Ranger Station at White Cloud, (616) 689-6696.

Getting There

Hardy Pond is located in Newaygo County and can be reached by taking US 131 north to the Jefferson Road-Morley Exit and then heading east. Or divers can reach Hardy Pond by traveling through the community of Newaygo on M-37 and taking Croton Drive east out of town to Muskegon Drive which eventually takes you to Newaygo State Park on the east side of the impoundment.

Divers may also enjoy diving the Croton Pond which is seen along the way.

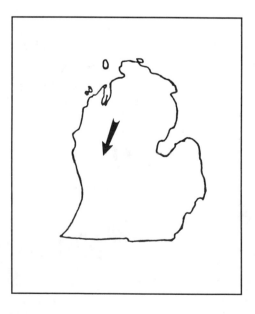

Diving Law

Laws affect virtually every aspect of our lives and diving is no exception.

Michigan, through the efforts of the sport diving community, has developed a tough set of laws designed to preserve underwater artifacts while ensuring recreation opportunities. These laws are contained in the Aboriginal Records and Antiquities Act.

In 1988, Michigan's laws were amended to provide for stiff criminal penalties for vandals or thieves who tamper with underwater artifacts. As a result, divers of future generations will be able to enjoy our underwater maritime heritage for decades to come.

The law is presented here to answer questions about what may or may not be legal activities in Michigan. Readers will note that there are specific regulations that apply to Michigan's underwater preserves. These regulations apply to all underwater preserves, but because the National Park Service has jurisdiction over a larger area around Isle Royale, these laws do not necessarily apply there. Isle Royale regulations are covered in the chapter pertaining to that area.

There is remarkably little case law to interpret these statutes. But challenges to the constitutionality of the laws have been unsuccessful and it appears as though state courts will take a firm stand to protect the interests of sport divers.

The comment is not part of the law but is provided to help readers understand the implications of the law

for sport diving. When in doubt or if specific questions arise, it is best to contact a competent lawyer.

Divers who discover what they believe may be historically significant artifacts should contact the Michigan Department of Environmental Quality or the Michigan Bureau of History (Secretary of State's office).

Divers who suspect violations of the Aboriginal Records and Antiquities Act by others should gather enough information to identify the suspects (boat registration, license plate numbers, etc.) and contact the Michigan Department of Natural Resources.

The 24-hour, toll-free hotline used to report poachers may also be used to report violations of this law. That number is **1-800-292-7800.**

There are two basic sets of laws that govern sport diving in the Great Lakes: state and federal. Federal laws include the Abandoned Shipwreck Act, which is a powerful guarantee of ready access to shipwrecks by sport divers. States cannot make a law that is more restrictive than federal law.

In this chapter, we look at both sets of laws. Note that the "comment" section of this material is not law and is provided only to help readers understand what the law says.

Abandoned Shipwreck Act
U.S.C. 43 Sec. 2101

Comment: The Abandoned Shipwreck Act purports to transfers title of shipwrecks, including Great Lakes shipwrecks, from the Federal Government to the states. The act also establishes some guidelines, which are advisory and non-binding, to the states.

One important aspect of the act is that it creates eligibility for shipwreck conservation activities for funding under the National Historic Trust Fund.

It is interesting to note that although the act states that it is the policy of Congress to guarantee access to shipwreck sites for recreational exploration, at least two sites at the Apostle Islands National Lakeshore in Wisconsin and the site of the *America* at Isle Royale have been closed by the National Park Service to sport divers for varying periods. Other dive sites have been closed permanently at Isle Royale National Park. If ever challenged, it appears as though it would make a good legal argument that such closures are in violation of federal law.

Although there is little litigation that has helped define the Abandoned Shipwreck Act, one case, *Zych v. State of Illinois*, focused on this statutory scheme. Most court decisions have fallen in favor of states' rights to shipwreck ownership. There are, however, some unresolved issues raised by salvors. Some of those arguments are particularly compelling when they involve the removal of certain artifacts for public display. Even Michigan has permitted private museums to remove hundreds of artifacts without permits. Some divers complain about the double-standard but the bottom line here is that political clout counts.

Harry Zych, a Chicago-based salvor who found the *Lady Elgin* and other important shiprecks, is noteworthy. He is one of the most colorful characters in the Great Lakes diving community. Even if you do not agree with Harry, one must appreciate his tenacity and passion. He has worked to preserve diver access to shipwrecks.

Text of Abandoned Shipwreck Act

Sec. 2101. Congressional statement of findings

The Congress finds that--

(a) States have the responsibility for management of a broad range of living and nonliving resources in State waters and submerged lands; and

(b) included in the range of resources are certain abandoned shipwrecks, which have been deserted and to which the owner has relinquished ownership rights with no retention.

Comment: This section establishes Congress' intent to delegate responsibility for most submerged cultural resources to the states.

Sec. 2102. Definitions

For purposes of this chapter--

(a) the term "embedded" means firmly in the submerged lands or in coralline formations such that the use of tools of excavation is required in order to move the bottom sediments to gain access to the shipwreck, its cargo, and any part thereof;

(b) the term "National Register" means the National Register of Historic Places maintained by the Secretary of the Interior under section 470a of Title 16;

(c) the terms "public lands", "Indian lands", and "Indian tribe" have the same meaning given the terms in the Archaeological Resource Protection Act of 1979 (16 U.S.C. 470aa-470ll);

(d) the term "shipwreck" means a vessel or wreck, its cargo, and other contents;

(e) the term "State" means a State of the United States, the District of Columbia, Puerto Rico, Guam, the Virgin Islands, American Samoa, and the Northern Mariana Islands; and

(f) the term "submerged lands" means the lands--

(1) that are "lands beneath navigable waters," as defined in section 1301 of this title;

(2) of Puerto Rico, as described in section 749 of Title 48;

(3) of Guam, the Virgin Islands and American Samoa, as described in section 1705 of Title 48; and

(4) of the Commonwealth of the Northern Mariana Islands, as described in section 801 of Public Law 94-241 (48 U.S.C. 1681).

Section 2103. Rights of access

(a) **Access rights**

In order to--

(1) clarify that State waters and shipwrecks offer recreational and educational opportunities to sport divers and other interested groups, as well as irreplaceable State

resources for tourism, biological sanctuaries, and historical research; and

(2) provide that reasonable access by the public to such abandoned shipwrecks be permitted by the State holding title to such shipwrecks pursuant to section 2105 of this title, it is the declared policy of the Congress that States carry out their responsibilities under this chapter to develop appropriate and consistent policies so as to--

(A) protect natural resources and habitat areas;

(B) guarantee recreational exploration of shipwreck sites; and

(C) allow for appropriate public and private sector recovery of shipwrecks consistent with the protection of historical values and environmental integrity of the shipwrecks and the sites.

Comment: This subsection states the reasons for the sections that follow. It also states that these resources should be open to access for sport divers, while at the same time protecting the resources. The subsection provides for "appropriate" recovery of shipwrecks and presumably artifacts. What is or is not appropriate probably lies solely within the province of each state. It is interesting to note that although some state officials have at least considered "closure" of some sites citing archeological importance, this factor is not considered in this federal regulatory scheme.

(b) Parks and protected areas

In managing the resources subject to the provisions of this chapter, States are encouraged to create underwater parks or areas to provide additional protection for such resources. Funds available to States from grants from the Historic Preservation Fund shall be available, in accordance with the provisions of title I of the National Historic Preservation Act, for the study, interpretation, protection, and preservation of historic shipwrecks and properties.

Comment: This subsection permits states to apply for funds from the Historic Preservation Fund to study, interpret, protect and preserve shipwrecks.

Section 2104. Preparation of guidelines

(a) Purposes of guidelines; publication in Federal Register

In order to encourage the development of underwater parks and the administrative cooperation necessary for the comprehensive management of underwater resources related to historic shipwrecks, the Secretary of the Interior, acting through the Director of the National Park Service, shall within nine months after April 28, 1988, prepare and publish guidelines in the Federal Register which shall seek to:

(1) maximize the enhancement of cultural resources;

(2) foster a partnership among sport divers, fishermen, archeologists, salvors, and other interests to manage shipwreck resources of the States and the United States;

(3) facilitate access and utilization by recreational interests;

(4) recognize the interests of individuals and groups engaged in shipwreck discovery and salvage.

(b) Consultation

Such guidelines shall be developed after consultation with appropriate public and private sector interests (including the Secretary of Commerce, the Advisory Council on Historic Preservation, sport divers, State Historic Preservation Officers, professional dive operators, salvors, archeologists, historic preservationists, and fishermen).

(c) Use of guidelines in developing legislation and regulations

Such guidelines shall be available to assist States and the appropriate Federal agencies in developing legislation and regulations to carry out their responsibilities under this chapter.

Comment: This section establishes a process where guidelines for developing submerged cultural resources. Congressional intent to maintain recreational access is a high priority. These guidelines are not binding, however, and states are not required to follow them when developing resource management plans.

Section 2105. Rights of ownership
(a) United States title

The United States asserts title to any abandoned shipwreck that is--

(1) embedded in submerged lands of a State;

(2) embedded in coralline formations protected by a State on submerged lands of a State; or

(3) on submerged lands of a State and is included in or determined eligible for inclusion in the National Register.

(b) Notice of shipwreck location; eligibility determination for inclusion in National Register of Historic Places

The public shall be given adequate notice of the location of any shipwreck to which title is asserted under this section. The Secretary of the Interior, after consultation with the appropriate State Historic Preservation Officer, shall make a written determination that an abandoned shipwreck meets the criteria for eligibility for inclusion in the National Register of Historic Places under clause (a)(3).

(c) Transfer of title to States

The title of the United States to any abandoned shipwreck asserted under subsection (a) of this section is transferred to the State in or on whose submerged lands the shipwreck is located.

Comment: Under these subsections, the Federal Government asserts title to all shipwrecks, and then transfers its interest to the states. This is a "housekeeping" measure designed to make state ownership less susceptible to legal challenges. One legal argument suggests that these subsections conflict with admiralty law, and thus, are unconstitutional.

(d) Exception

Any abandoned shipwreck in or on the public lands of the United States is the property of the United States Government. Any abandoned shipwreck in or on any Indian lands is the property of the Indian tribe owning such lands.

Comment: In this subsection, the United States makes an exception as to what resources on what lands are transferred to the states. This especially affects the shipwrecks of Isle Royale, which are apparently federal property.

(e) Reservation of rights

This section does not affect any right reserved by the United States or by any State (including any right reserved with respect to Indian lands) under--

(1) section 1311, 1313, or 1314 of this title; or
(2) section 414 or 415 of Title 33.

Section 2106. Relationship to other laws

(a) Law of salvage and the law of finds

The law of salvage and the law of finds shall not apply to abandoned shipwrecks to which section 2105 of this title applies.

(b) Laws of the United States

This chapter shall not change the laws of the United States relating to shipwrecks, other than those to which this chapter applies.

(c) Effective date

This chapter shall not affect any legal proceeding brought prior to April 28, 1988.

ABORIGINAL RECORDS AND ANTIQUITIES
(State Law)

P.A. 1929, No. 173, Imd. Eff. May 20
Part 761

MCL 324.76101 Definitions.
Sec. 76101. As used in this part:

(a) "Abandoned property" means an aircraft; a watercraft, including a ship, boat, canoe, skiff, raft or barge; the rigging, gear, fittings, trappings, and equipment of an aircraft or watercraft; the personal property of the officers, crew, and passengers of an aircraft or watercraft; and cargo of an aircraft or watercraft which have been deserted, relinquished, cast away, or left behind and for which attempts at reclamation have been abandoned by owners and insurers. Abandoned property also means materials resulting from activities of historic and prehistoric native Americans.

(b) "Bottomlands" means the unpatented lake bottomlands of the Great Lakes.

(c) "Committee" means the underwater salvage and preserve committee created in section 76103.

(e) "Great Lakes" means lakes Erie, Huron, Michigan, St. Clair, and Superior.

(f) "Great Lakes bottomlands preserve" means an area located on the bottomlands of the Great Lakes and extending upward to and including the surface of the water, which is delineated and set aside by rule for special protection of abandoned property of historical value, or ecological, education, geological, or scenic features or formations having recreational, educational, or scientific value. A preserve may encompass a single object, feature, or formation, or a collection of several objects, features, or formations.

(f) "Historical value" means value relating to, or illustrative of, Michigan history, including the statehood, territorial, colonial, and historic, and prehistoric native American periods.

(g) "Mechanical or other assistance" means all humanmade devices, including pry bars, wrenches and other hand or power tools, cutting torches, explosives, winches, flotation bags, lines to surface, extra divers buoyancy devices, and other buoyance devices, used to raise or remove artifacts.

(h) "Recreational value" means value relating to an activity that the public engages in, or may engage in, for recreation or sport, including scuba diving and fishing.

324.76102 Aborginal records and antiquities; right to explore, survey, excavate, and regulate reserved to state; possessory right or title to abandoned property.

Sec. 76102. (1) The state reserves to itself the exclusive right and privilege, except as provided in this part, of exploring, surveying, excavating, and regulating through its authorized officers, agents, and employees, all aboriginal records and other antiquities, including mounds, earthworks, forts, burial and village sites, mines or other relics, and abandoned property of historical or recreational value found upon or within any of the lands owned by or under the control of the state.

(2) The state reserves to itself a possessory right or title superior to that of a finder to abandoned property of historical or recreational value found on the state owned bottomlands of the Great Lakes. This property shall belong to this state with administration and protection jointed vested in the department and the secretary of state.

324.76103. Underwater salvage and preserve committee; creation, purpose, appointment, qualifications, and terms of members; vacancy; compensation; appointment, term, and duties of chairperson; committee as advisory body; functions of committee; limitation.

Sec. 76103. (1) The underwater salvage and preserve committee is created in the department of natural resources to provide technical and other advice to the department and the secretary of state with respect to their responsibilities under this act.

(2) The underwater salvage and preserve committee shall consist of 9 members appointed as follows:

(a) Two individuals appointed by the department who have primary responsibility in the department of natural resources for administering this part.
(b) Two individuals appointed by the secretary of state who have primary responsibility in the department of state for administering this part.
(c) One individual appointed by the director of commerce.
(d) Four individuals appointed by the governor with the advice and consent of the senate from the general public. Two of these individuals shall have experience in recreational scuba diving.

(3) An individual appointed to the committee shall serve for a term of 3 years. A vacancy on the committee shall be filled in the same manner as an original appointment and the term of a member appointed to fill a vacancy shall be for 3 years. Members of the committee shall serve without compensation, except for their regular state salary where applicable.

(4) The chairperson of the committee shall alternate between the representatives from the department and the department of state. The chairperson shall be designated by the department or the secretary of state, whichever is applicable from among his or her representatives on the committee. The chairperson's term shall run for 12 months, from

October 1 through September 30. The department shall appoint the first chairperson of the committee for a term ending September 30, 1989. The chairperson shall call meetings as necessary but not less than 4 times per year, set the agenda for meetings, ensure that adequate minutes are taken, and file an annual report of committee proceedings with the head of the departments of state, natural resources, and commerce.

(5) The committee is an advisory body and may perform all of the following functions:

(a) Make recommendations with regard to the creation and boundaries of Great Lakes underwater preserves.

(b) Review applications for underwater salvage permits and make recommendations regarding issuance.

(c) Consider and make recommendations regarding the charging of permit fees and the appropriate use of revenue generated by those fees.

(d) Consider the need for and the content of rules intended to implement this part and make recommendations concerning the promulgation of rules.

(e) Consider and make recommendations concerning appropriate legislation.

(f) Consider and make recommendations concerning program operation.

(6) The committee shall not replace or supersede the responsibility or authority of the secretary of state or the department to carry out their responsibilities under this act.

324.76104 Deed; clause reserving to state property and exploration rights in aborginal antiquities; exceptions; waiver.

Sec. 76104. A deed, as provided by this part, given by this state, except state tax deeds for the conveyance of any land owned by the state, shall contain a clause reserving to this state a property right in aboriginal antiquities including mounds, earthworks, forts, burial and village sites, mines, or other relics and also reserving the right to explore and excavate for the aboriginal antiquity by and through this state's authorized agent and employee. This section applies only to the sale of tax reverted land. The department, with the approval of the secretary of state, may waive this reservation when conveying platted property and when making conveyances under subpart 3 of part 21.

324.76105 Permit for exploration or excavation of aboriginal remains; exception.

Sec. 76105. A person, either personally or through an agent or employee, shall not explore or excavate an aboriginal remain covered by this part upon lands owned by the state, except under a permit issued by the department with written approval of the secretary of state. A permit shall be issued without charge. This section shall not apply to the Mackinac Island state park commission on lands owned or controlled by the Mackinac Island state park commission.

324.76106 Removal of relics or records of antiquity; consent of landowner required.

Sec. 76106. Without the consent of the land owner, a person shall not remove any relics or records of antiquity such as human or other bones; shells, stone, bone, or copper implements; pottery or shards of pottery, or similar artifacts and objects from the premises where they have been discovered.

324.76107 Permit to recover, alter, or destroy abandoned property; recovered property as property of secretary of state; prohibitions as to human body or remains; violaton as felony; penalty.

Sec. 76107. (1) Except as provided in section 76108, a person shall not recover, alter or destroy abandoned property which is in, on, under, or over the bottomlands of the Great Lakes, including those within a Great Lakes bottomlands preserve, unless the person has a permit issued jointly by the secretary of state and the department pursuant to section 76109.

(2) A person who recovers abandoned property without a permit when a permit is required by this part shall transmit the property to the secretary of state and the recovered property shall be the property of the secretary of state.

(3) A person shall not remove, convey, mutilate, or deface a human body or the remains of a human body located on the bottomlands of the Great Lakes.

(4) A person who violates subsection (1) by recovering or destroying abandoned property with a fair market value of $100.00 or more is guilty of a felony, punishable by imprisonment for not more than 2 years, or by a fine of not more than $5,000.00 or both.

324.76108 Recovery of abandoned property without permit; report; availability of recovered property for inspection; release of property.

Sec. 76108. (1) A person may recover abandoned property outside a Great Lakes bottomlands preserve without a permit if the abandoned property is not attached to, nor located on, in, or located in the immediate vicinity of and associated with a sunken aircraft or watercraft and if the abandoned property is recoverable by hand without mechanical or other assistance.

(2) A person who recovers abandoned property valued at more than $10.00 without a permit pursuant to subsection (1) shall file a written report within 30 days after removal of the property with the department or the secretary of state if the property has been abandoned for more than 30 years. The written report shall list all recovered property that has been abandoned for more than 30 years and the location of the property at the time of recovery. For a period of 90 days after the report is filed, the person shall make the

recovered property available to the department and the secretary of state for inspection at a location in this state. If the secretary of state determines that the recovered property does not have historical value, the secretary of state shall release the property to the person by means of a written instrument.

324.76109 Permit; scope; application; filing, form, and contents; additional information or documents; notice of deficient application; failure to respond; approval or disapproval of application; display of property; payment of salvage costs; recovery of cargo outside Great Lakes bottomlands preserves, administrative review; conduct of hearing; combined appeals; joint decision and order; duration of permit; issuance of new permit; transfer or assignment of permit.

Sec. 76109. (1) A permit issued under this section shall authorize a person to recover abandoned property located on, in, or located in the immediate vicinity of and associated with a sunken aircraft or watercraft.

(2) A person shall file an application for a permit with the department on a form prescribed by the department and approved by the secretary of state. The application shall contain all of the following information:

(a) The name and address of the applicant.

(b) The name, if known, of the watercraft or aircraft on or around which recovery operations are to occur and a current photograph or drawing of the watercraft or aircraft, if available.

(c) The location of the abandoned property to be recovered and the depth of water in which it may be found.

(d) A description of each item to be recovered.

(e) The method to be used in recovery operations.

(f) The proposed disposition of the abandoned property recovered, including the location at which it will be available for inspection by the department and the secretary of state.

(g) Other information which the department or the secretary of state considers necessary in evaluating the request for a permit.

(3) An application for a permit is not complete until all information requested on the application form and any other information requested by the department or the secretary of state has been received by the department. After receipt of an otherwise complete application, the department may request additional information or documents as are determined to be necessary to make a decision to grant or deny a permit. The department, or the secretary of state, shall notify the applicant in writing when the application is deficient.

(4) An applicant notified that an application for a permit may be deficient and returned due to insufficient information under subsection (3) shall, within 20 days after the date the notice is mailed, provide the information. If the applicant fails to respond within the 20-

day period, the application shall be denied unless the applicant requests additional time and provides reasonable justification for an extension of time.

(5) The department and the secretary of state shall, with the advice of the committee, approve or disapprove an application for a permit within 30 days after the date a complete application is filed with the department. The department and the secretary of state may approve an application conditionally or unconditionally. A condition to the approval of an application shall be in writing on the face of the permit. The department and the secretary of state may impose such conditions as are considered reasonable and necessary to protect the public trust and general interests, including conditions that accomplish 1 or more of the following:

(a) Protect and preserve the abandoned property to be recovered, and the recreational value of the area in which recovery is being accomplished.

(b) Assure reasonable public access to the abandoned property after recovery.

(c) Are in conformity with rules applying to activities within a Great Lakes bottomlands preserve.

(d) Prohibit injury, harm, and damage to a bottomlands site or abandoned property not authorized for removal during and after salvage operations by the permit holder.

(e) Prohibit or limit the amount of discharge of possible pollutants, such as floating timbers, planking, and other debris, which may emanate from the shipwreck, plane wreck or salvage equipment.

(f) Require the permit holder to submit a specific removal plan prior to commencing any salvaging activities. Among other matters considered appropriate by either the department or the secretary of state, or both, the removal plan may be required to ensure the safety of those removing or assisting in the removal of the abandoned property and to address how the permit holder proposes to prevent, minimize, or mitigate potential adverse effects upon the abandoned property to be removed, that portion of the abandoned property which is not to be removed, and the surrounding geographic features.

(6) The department shall approve an application for a permit unless the department determines that the abandoned property to be recovered has substantial recreational value in itself or in conjunction with other abandoned property in its vicinity underwater, or the recovery of abandoned property would not comply with rules applying to a Great Lakes bottomlands preserve.

(7) The secretary of state shall approve an application for a permit unless the secretary of state determines that the abandoned property to be recovered has substantial historical value in itself or in conjunction with other abandoned property in its vicinity. If the property has substantial historical value, the secretary of state, pursuant to subsection (5), may impose a condition to the approval of the application requiring the applicant to turn over recovered property to the secretary of state for the purpose of preserving the property or permitting public access to the property. The secretary of state may authorize the display of the property in a public or private museum or by a local unit of government. In addition to the conditions authorized by subsection (5), the secretary of state may provide for payment of salvage costs in connection with the recovery of the abandoned property.

(8) A person who discovers an abandoned watercraft that is located outside of a Great Lakes bottomlands preserve shall be entitled to recover cargo situated on, in, or associated with the watercraft, if the person applies for a permit pursuant to this section within 90 days after discovering the watercraft. If an application for a permit to recover cargo is not filed within 90 days after a watercraft discovery, subject to subsections (4) and (5) an exclusive cargo recovery permit shall be issued to the first person applying for such a permit. Only 1 permit to recover the same cargo will be issued and operative at a time. When a watercraft containing cargo is simultaneously discovered by more than 1 person, a permit shall be approved with respect to the first person or persons jointly applying for a permit.

(9) A person aggrieved by a condition contained on a permit or by the denial of an application for a permit may request an administrative review of the condition or the denial by the commission or the secretary of state, whichever disapproves the application or imposes the condition. A person shall file the request for review with the commission or the secretary of state, whichever is applicable, within 90 days after the permit application is submitted to the department. An administrative hearing conducted pursuant to this subsection shall be conducted under the procedures set forth in chapter 4 of the administrative procedures act of 1969, Act No. 306 of the Public Acts of 1969, being sections 24.271 to 24.287 of the Michigan Compiled Laws. If neither the department or the secretary of state approves the application and an administrative review is requested from both the commission and the secretary of state, the appeals shall be combined upon request of the appellant or either the commission or the secretary of state and a single administrative hearing shall be conducted. The commision and the secretary of state shall issue jointly the final decision and order in the case.

(10) A permit issued under this section shall be valid until December 31 of the year in which the application for the permit was filed and is not renewable. If an item designated in a permit for recovery is not recovered, a permit holder may, upon request following the expiration of the permit, be issued a new permit to remove the same abandoned property if the permit holder demonstrates that diligence in attempting recovery was exercised under the previously issued permit.

(11) A permit issued under this section shall not be transferred to assigned unless the assignment is approved in writing by both the department and the secretary of state.

324.76110 Recovered abandoned property; report; examination; removal from state; action for recovery; release of property.

Sec. 76110. (1) Within 10 days after recovery of abandoned property, a person with a permit issued pursuant to section 76109 shall report the recovery in writing to the department. The person recovering the abandoned property shall give authorized representatives of the department and the secretary of state an opportunity to examine the abandoned property for a period of 90 days after recovery. Recovered abandoned property shall not be removed from this state without written approval of the department and the secretary of state. If the recovered abandoned property is removed from the state without written approval, the attorney general, upon request from the department or the secretary of state, shall bring an action for the recovery of the property.

(2) If the secretary of state determines that the recovered abandoned property does not have historical value, the secretary of state shall release the property to the person holding the permit by means of a written instrument.

324.76111 Great Lakes bottomlands preserves; establishment; rules; determination; factors; granting permit to recover abandoned artifacts; limitation; intentional sinking of vessel; prohibited use of state money.

Sec. 76111. (1) The department shall establish Great Lakes bottomlands preserves by rule. A Great Lakes bottomlands preserve shall be established by emergency rule if it is determined by the director of the department that this action is necessary to immediately protect an object or area of historical or recreational value.

(2) A Great Lakes bottomlands preserve may be established whenever a bottomlands area includes a single watercraft of significant historical value, includes 2 or more abandoned watercraft, or contains other features of archeological, historical, recreational, geological, or environmental significance. Bottomlands areas containing few or no watercraft or other features directly related to the character of a preserve may be excluded from preserves.

(3) In establishing a Great Lakes bottomlands preserve, the department shall consider all of the following factors:

(a) Whether creating the preserve is necessary to protect either abandoned property possessing historical or recreational value, or significant underwater geological or environmental features.
(b) The extent of local public and private support for creation of the preserve.
(c) Whether a preserve development plan has been prepared by a state or local agency.
(d) The extent to which preserve support facilities such as roads, marinas, charter services, hotels, medical hyperbaric facilities, and rescue agencies have been developed in or are planned for the area.

(4) The department and the secretary of state shall not grant a permit to recover abandoned artifacts within a Great Lakes bottomlands preserve except for historical or scientific purposes or when the recovery will not adversely affect the historical, cultural, or recreational integrity of the preserve area as a whole.

(5) An individual Great Lakes bottomlands preserve shall not exceed 400 square miles in area. Great Lakes bottomlands preserves shall be limited in total area to not more than 10% of the Great Lakes bottomlands within this state.

(6) Upon the approval of the committee, not more than 1 vessel associated with Great Lakes maritime history may be sunk intentionally within a Great Lakes bottomlands preserve. However, state money shall not be expended to purchase, transport, or sink the vessel.

324.76112 Rules generally.

Sec. 76112. (1) The department and the secretary of state, jointly or separately, may promulgate rules as are neessary to implement this part.

(2) Within each Great Lakes bottomlands preserve, the department and the secretary of state may jointly promulgate rules that govern access to and use of a Great Lakes bottomlands preserve. These rules may regulate or prohibit the alteration, destruction, or removal of abandoned property, features, or formations within a preserve.

324.76113 Limitations not imposed by §§ 324.76107 to 324.76110.

Sec. 76113. Sections 76107 to 76110 shall not be considered to impose the following limitations:

(a) A limitation on the right of a person to engage in diving for recreational purposes in and upon the Great Lakes or the bottomlands of the Great Lakes.
(b) A limitation on the right of the department or the secretary of state to recover, or to contract for the recovery of, abandoned property in and upon the bottomlands of the Great Lakes.

(c) A limitation on the right of a person to own either abandoned property recovered after July 2, 1980 or abandoned property released to a person after inspection.

324.76114 Suspension or revocation of permit; grounds; hearing; civil action.

Sec. 76114. (1) If the department or the secretary of state finds that the holder of a permit issued pursuant to section 76105 or 76109 is not in compliance with this part, a rule promulgated under this part, or a provision of or condition in the permit, or has damaged abandoned property or failed to use diligence in attempting to recover property for which a permit was issued, the department or the secretary of state, individually or jointly, may summarily suspend or revoke the permit. If the permit holder requests a hearing within 15 days following the effective date of the suspension or revocation, the commission or the secretary of state shall conduct an administrative hearing pursuant to chapter 4 of the administrative procedures act of 1969, Act No. 306 of the Public Acts of 1969, being sections 24.271 to 24.287 of the Michigan Compiled Laws, to consider whether the permit should be reinstated.

(2) The attorney general, on behalf of the department or the secretary of state, individually or jointly, may commence a civil action in circuit court to enforce compliance with this part, to restrain a violation of this part or any action contrary to a decision denying a permit, to enjoin the further removal of artifacts, geological material, or abandoned property, or to order the restoration of an affected area to its prior condition.

324.76115 Dangers accepted by participants in sport of scuba diving.

Sec. 76115. Each person who participates in the sport of scuba diving on the Great Lakes bottomlands accepts the dangers which adhere in that sport insofar as the dangers are obvious and necessary. Those dangers include, but are not limited to, injuries which can result from entanglements in sunken watercraft or aircraft; the condition of sunken watercraft or aircraft, the location of sunken watercraft or aircraft, the failure of the state to fund staff or programs at bottomlands preserves; and the depth of the objects and bottomlands within preserves.

324.76116 Violation as misdemeanor; penalty.

Sec. 76116. (1) A person who violates section 76105 or 76106 is guilty of a misdemeanor, and shall be punishable by imprisonment for not more than 30 days, or a fine of not more than $100.00 or both.

(2) A person who violates sections 76107 or 76111 or a rule promulgated under this part is guilty of a misdemeanor. Unless another penalty is provided in this act, a person convicted of a misdemeanor under this subsection shall is punishable by imprisonment for not more than six months or fine of not more than $500.00 or both.

324.76117 Attaching, proceeding against, or confiscating equipment or apparatus; procedure; disposition of proceeds.

Sec. 76117. (1) If a person who violates this part or a rule promulgated under this part uses a watercraft, mechanical or other assistance, scuba gear, sonar equipment, a motor vehicle, or any other equipment or apparatus during the course of committing the violation, the items so used may be attached, proceeded against, and confiscated as prescribed in this part.

(2) To effect confiscation, the law enforcement or conservation officer seizing the property shall file a verified complaint in the circuit court for the county in which the seizure was made or in the circuit court for Ingham County. The complaint shall set forth the kind of property seized, the time and place of the seizure, the reasons for the seizure, and a demand for the property's condemnation and confiscation. Upon the filing of the complaint, an order shall be issued requiring the owner to show cause why the property should not be confiscated. The substance of the complaint shall be stated in the order. The

order to show cause shall fix the time for service of the order and for the hearing on the proposed condemnation and confiscation.

(3) The order to show cause shall be served on the owner of the property as soon as possible but not less than 7 days before the complaint is to be heard. The court, for cause shown, may hear the complaint on shorter notice. If the owner is not known or cannot be found, notice may be served in 1 or more of the following ways:

(a) By posting a copy of the order in 3 public places for 3 consecutive weeks in the county in which the seizure was made and by sending a copy of the order by certified mail to the last known business or residential address of the owner. If the last addresses of the owner are not known, mailing a copy of the order is not required.

(b) By publishing a copy of the order in a newspaper once each week for 3 consecutive weeks in the county where the seizure was made and by sending a copy of the order by registered mail to the last known residential address of the owner. If the last residential address of the owner is not known, mailing a copy of the order is not required.

(c) In a manner as the court directs.

(4) Upon hearing of the complaint, if the court determines that the property mentioned in the petition was possessed, shipped, or used contrary to law, either by the owner or by a person lawfully in possession of the property under an agreement with the owner, an order shall be made condemning and confiscating the property and directing its sale or other disposal by the department. If the owners signs a property release, a court proceeding shall not be necessary. At the hearing, if the court determines that the property was not possessed, shipped, or used contrary to law, the court shall order the department to immediately return the property to its owner.

(5) The department shall deposit the proceeds it receives under this section into the state treasury to the credit of the underwater preserve fund created in section 76118.

324.76118 Underwater preserve fund; creation; sources of revenue; purposes for which money appropriated.

Sec. 76118. (1) The underwater preserve fund is created as a separate fund in the state treasury, and it may receive revenue as provided in this part, or revenue from any other source.

(2) Money in the underwater preserve fund shall be appropriated for only the following purposes:

(a) To the secretary of state for the development of maritime archeology in this state.
(b) To the department of commerce for the promotion of Great Lakes bottomlands preserves.
(c) To the department for the enforcement of this part.

Note: Michigan's criminal code makes it illegal to photograph or videotape and then display images of deceased persons on Great Lakes shipwrecks. This law is actually redundant because other laws determine the disposition of such bodies.

Diver Down Flag Law

Michigan's Diver Down Flag Law
MCL 324.80155

Michigan's "diver down" flag law has come under some criticsm in recent years. Here, we attempt to straighten out misconceptions about what the law says and means.

> Any person diving or submerging in any of the waters of this state with the aid of a diving suit or other mechanical diving device shall place a buoy or boat in the water at or near the point of submergence. The buoy or boat shall bear a red flag not less than 14 inches by 16 inches with a 3½-inch white stripe running from 1 upper corner to a diagonal lower corner. The flag shall be in place only while actual diving operations are in progress. A vessel shall not be operated within 200 feet of a buoyed diver's flag unless it is involved in tendering the diving operation. A person diving shall stay within a surface area of 100 feet of the diver's flag.

The term "operate" is defined in state law: "...to be in control of a vessel while the vessel is underway and is not secured in some manner such as being docked or at anchor.

The question has been raised regarding the applicability of the diver down flag to vessels entering a diving area, specifically, dive charter vessels approaching mooring buoys on a shipwreck.

From a first read of the law, it appears as though any operation of a vessel within 200 feet of a diver down flag is illegal. Taken literally, this would mean that only one vessel at a time may use a mooring buoy(s) depending upon the location of the buoys. Also, on most wrecks, divers would be required to carry their own flags in order to enjoy the entire shipwreck.

This literal interpretation defeats the purpose of the law and yields ludicrous results. One provision of the law may

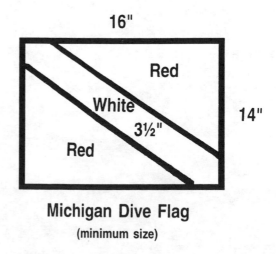

Michigan Dive Flag
(minimum size)

provide a reasonable means of interpretation. It can be argued that an approaching vessel, exercising due caution, would be "tendering" the dive operation. This interpretation is consistent with common dictionary definitions and also lends appropriate meaning to the statute.

To avoid liability, vessels approaching should contact any vessels displaying diver down flags at a dive site. Communication should be by radio or voice and the approaching vessel should attempt to determine how many and where divers may be located. Approaching vessels should exercise extreme caution and when possible drift toward mooring buoys with the engine running but in neutral. A watch should be posted to look for divers' bubbles or divers at or near the surface.

Note: A blue and white alpha flag is not a legal dive flag in Michigan waters.

To avoid liability, vessels approaching should contact any vessels displaying diver down flags at a dive site.

Location Data

Although every effort has been made to ensure accuracy, location data is only as good as the person providing it. For that reason, there may be significant errors that we were unable to detect. We recommend that divers use the following data as a reference only in their research. Note that the data below covers all the Great Lakes, not just those shipwrecks in Michigan waters.

Lake Michigan

Advance, schooner, 80 feet, 32741.0/48919.2; 43 36.72/87 49.93, Sheboygan, Wis.

Alva Bradley, schooner, 26 feet, 31798.5/48339.2; 45 02 27/85 59 26, N. Manitou Island

America, steamer, 32423.1/48498.5; 44 21.02/87 26.83, Kewanee, Wis.

A.P. Nichols, schooner, 40 feet, 32006.5/48032.3; 45 17.16/86 55.23, Door County, Wis.

Appomattox, steamer, 20 feet, 32969.3/49231.0; 43 95,54.76 52,12, Milwaukee, Wis.

Aral Dock, dock ruins, 15 feet, 31899.93/48488.80; 44 45 50/86 04 20 Manitou Passage

Atlanta, steamer, 18 feet, 32772.5/48933.5; 43 34,23.76 46.89, Port Washington, Wis.

Boaz, schooner, 15 feet, 32082.4/48093.8; 45 08.30/87 03.09, Door County, Wis.

Burton's Wharf, dock ruins, 45 feet, 31833.37/48334.08; 45 01 32/86 05 00, S. Manitou Island

Byron, schooner, 135 feet, 32736.4/48929.0; 43 36.29/87 41.28, Sheboygan, Wis.

Canisteo, streamer, 15 feet, 31341.9/48070.8; 45 47.31/85 04.86, Mackinac, Mich.

Carl D. Bradley, steamer, 380 feet, 32427.2/49190.4; 43 29.84/86 29.94, Beaver Island, Mich.

Car Ferry No. 2, car ferry, 42 feet, 33407.6/50205.7; 41 44.80/87 27.09, Chicago, Ill.

Carrington, schooner, 50 feet, 32167.4/48067.4; 45 05.58/87 19.33, Green Bay, Wis.

Cayuga, steamer, 125 feet, 31390.4/48089.8; 45 43 07/85 11 16, Mackinac, Mich.

Carrington, schooner, 50 feet, 32167.4/48067.4; 45 05.58/87 19.33, Green Bay, Wis.

Cayuga, steamer, 125 feet, 31390.4/48089.8; 45 43 07/85 11 16, Mackinac, Mich.

China Wreck, schooner, 40 feet, 33372.3/50089.2; 41 53.63/87 33.45, Chicago, Ill.

Cherubusco, bark, 10 feet, 32084.5/48090.2; 45 08.46/87 03.71, Door County, Wis.

C.H. Johnson, schooner, 13 feet, 31247.0/48061.7; 45 52.20/84 50.08, Mackinac, Mich.

Coast Guard Lifeboat Launch, 31498.2/48294.8; 45 19.14/85 15.32, Charlevoix, Mich.

Chuck's Barge, 45 feet, 31255.8/48074.3; 45 50.97/84 50.80, Mackinac/St. Helena Island

Circassian, schooner, 12 feet, 31356.6/48033.7; 45 50 09/85 09 22, Mackinac, Mich.

Colonel Ellsworth, steamer, 85 feet, 31317.2/48067.7; 4548 26/ 85 01 00, Mackinac, Mich.

Congress, steamer, 165 feet, 31834.3/48330.4; 45 01 50/86 05 44 S. Manitou Island, Mich.

Crescent Dock, dock ruins, 15 feet, 31802.15/48288.43; 45 06 57/86 03 35, N. Manitou Island, Mich.

Daniel Lyons, schooner, 95 feet, 32283.5/48329.1; 44 40.23/87 17.70, Manitowoc, Wis.

David Dows, schooner, 40 feet, 33383.6/50201.5; 41 45.91/87 23.69, Chicago, Ill.

Dock Ruins, dock ruins, 31852.59/48391.36; 44 59 86/86 07 50, S. Manitou Island, Mich.

Double Ender, sailboat, 55 feet, 31744.1/48548.7; 44 46.39/85 36.06, Traverse Bay, Mich.

Dredge 906, dredge, 55 feet, 32995.7/49328.9; 42 48.11/87 47.14, Milwaukee, Wis.

Eber Ward, steamer, 135 feet, 31253.6/48096.7; 45 48 13/84 49 04 Mackinac, Mich.

Edward E. Gillen, tug, 73 feet, 32981.4/49283.8; 43 01.63/87 49.09, Milwaukee, Wis.

Elizabeth II, Pleasure craft, 60 feet, 31497.6/48296.4; 45 18.83/85 13.52, Charlevoix, Mich.

EMBA, schooner, 165 feet, 32949.6/49271.6; 43 03.91/87 44.95, Milwaukee, Wis.

Empire Dock, dock ruins, 12 feet, 31895.46/48482.05; 44 46 25/86 04 00;, Empire, Mich.

Erie L. Hackley, steamer, 110 feet, 32209.4/48058.1; 45 03.87/87 27.17, Green Bay, Wis.

Eureka, steamer, 30 feet, 31181.2;47527.4; 46 50.13/85 10.78, Whitefish Bay, MI

Fleetwing, schooner, 25 feet, 32041.1/48006.2; 45 17.25/87 02.99, Door County, Wis.

Flora M. Hill, steamer, 37 feet, 33375.4/50077.0; 41 54.28/87 35.22, Chicago, Ill.

Floretta, schooner, 180 feet, 32576.4/48732.4; 43 57.24/87 32.20, Manitowoc, Wis.

Flying Cloud, schooner, 15 feet, 31816.47/48403.46; 44 56 18/85 57 40, Manitou Passage, Mich.

Forest, schooner, 40 feet, 32006.5/48032.3; 45 17.16/86 55.23, Door County, Wis.

Francisco Morazon, steamer, 15 feet, 31859.2/48339.3; 44 59 07/86 08 09, S. Manitou Island, Mich.

Frank O'Connor, steamer, 65 feet, 32078.7/48115.9; 45 06.82/87 00.76, Door County, Wis.

Frank W. Wheeler, steamer, 40 feet, 33228.7/50278.9; 41 44.60/86 52.11, Michigan City, Ind.

Fred McBrier, steamer, 92 feet, 31287.8/48085.3; 45 48 11/84 55 09, Mackinac, Mich.

General Taylor, 10 feet, 44 53.68/86 04.56, Manitou Passage, Mich.

George F. Williams, steamer, 20 feet, 33338.8/49970.2; 42 02.63/87 40.11, Chicago, Ill.

George's Wreck, 12 feet, 31265.2/48127.3; 45 45.28/84 49.16, Mackinac, Mich.

Glen Haven Dock, dock ruins, 15 feet, 31840.71/48401.69; 44 55 30/86 01 30, Glen Haven, Mich.

Grace Channon, schooner, 32963.2/49388.1; 42 55.77/87 36.12, Milwaukee, Wis.

Hattie Taylor, schooner, 106 feet, 32701.0/48885.6; 43 40.88/87 39.30, Sheboygan, Wis.

Havana, schooner, 52 feet, 32888.1/50021.9; 42 11.96/86 26.00, St. Joseph, Mich.

H.D. Moore, schooner, 22 feet, 27999.70/48514.17; 45 02.01; 86 04.45, S. Manitou Island, Mich.

Headland Wreck, steamer, 15 feet, 31252.3/48119.0; 45 46.69/84 47.59, Mackinac, Mich.

Helvetia, schooner, 165 feet, 32650.7/48824.2; 43 47.42/87 36.43, Sheboygan, Wis.

H.P. Baldwin, schooner, 80 feet, 32487.3/48597.3; 44 10.91/87 29.10, Indiana Harbor

Illinois, barge, 35 feet, 33403.1/50128.4; 49.94/87 34.39, Chicago, Ill.

Illinois, dredge, 70 feet, 32995.7/49329.1; 42 48.09/87 47.12, Milwaukee, Wis.

Iowa, steamer, 35 feet, 33373.9/50087.3; 41 53.69/87 33.91, Chicago, Ill.

Ironsides, steamer, 120 feet, 32525.3/49494.5, 43 02.89/86 19.16, Grand Haven, Mich.

Island City, schooner, 140 feet, 32908.5/49138.1; 43 14.39/87 50.73, Pt. Washington, Wis.

J.A. Smith, schooner, 12 feet, 31309.6/48102.8; 45 45 24/84 57 25, Mackinac, Mich.

J.B. Newland, schooner, 10 feet, 31803.34/48338.13; 45 02 30/86 00 00 Manitou Passage, Mich.

J.D. Marshall, steamer, 32 feet, 33329.3/50309.3; 41 39.99/87 04.31, Gary, Ind.

J.E. Gilmore, schooner, 40 feet, 32006.5/48032.3; 45 17.16/86 55.23, Door County, Wis.

J.H. Guthwaite, steamer, 31187.3/48184.3; 45 42.93/84 33.46

J.S. Crouse, steamer, 22 feet, 31840.71/48401.68; 44 55.30/86 01.30, Glen Haven, Mich.

James McBride, brig, 15 feet, 31864.87/48408.68; 44 53 68/86 04 56 Glen Haven, Mich.

Jenny Bell, schooner, 125 feet, 32176.1/48013.3; 45 09.04/87 25.11, Green Bay, Wis.

J.H. Tiffany, schooner, 103 feet, 31402.0/48081.7; 45 43 37/85 13 76, Mackinac, Mich.

Josephine Dresden, schooner, 10 feet, 31802.15/48288.43; 45 06.57'; 86 03.35, N. Manitou Island, Mich.

Kate Kelly, schooner, 54 feet, 33053.5/49467.3; 42 46.67/87 43.38, Kenosha, Wis.

Keuka, barge, 18 feet, 31495.6/48304.4; 45 18.40/85 14.34, Charlevoix, Mich.

Lakeland, steamer, 180 feet, 32219.0/48274.2; 44 47.57/87 11.48, Door County, Wis.

Louisiana, steamer, 20 feet, 31975.7/47964.9; 45 24.10/86 55.24, Door County, Wis.

Louisville, steamer, 60 feet, 33365.9/50205.5; 41 46.23/87 20.47, Gary, Ind.

Lumberman, steamer, 65 feet, 33026.4/49400.0; 42 52.17/87 45.40, Kenosha, Wis.

Maitland, bark, 84 feet, 31273.1/48092.7; 45 48 20/84 52 29, Mackinac, Mich.

Material Service Barge, barge, 33426.3/50201.4; 41 44.40/87 30.54, Chicago, Ill.

McMillan and Pitt, dredge, 80 feet, 32632.7/48746.5; 43 53.52/87 40.31, Sheboygan, Wis.

Memorial, memorial, 30 feet, 31385.84/48305.21; 45 22.744/84 57.222, Petoskey, Mich.

Meridian, schooner, 45 feet, 32084.1/48030.2; 45 12.81/87 08.57, Green Bay, Wis.

Mike's Wreck, schooner, 40 feet 33376.49/50087.42; 41 53.73/ 87 34.16, Chicago, Ill.

Milwaukee, steamer, 96 feet, 31407.2/48007.8; 45 43.58/85 14.90, Mackinac

Milwaukee, car ferry, 125 feet, 31407.2/48077.8; 45 43.50/85 14.85 Milwaukee, Wis.

Minch, steamer, 40 feet, 32326.3/49029.9; 43 45.76/86 27.81, Pentwater, Mich.

Minch, 40 feet, stern--32327.1/49030.7; 43 45.67/86 27.87, Pentwater, Mich.

Minneapolis, steamer, 125 feet, 31226.2/48111.2; 45 48.32/84 43.54, Mackinac, Mich.

Montauk, schooner, 35 feet, 31769.59/48270.62; 45 09.55; 85 59.48, N. Manitou Island, Mich.

Muskegon, steamer, 25 feet, 33266.1/50293.6; 41 42.66/86 56.28, Michigan City, Ind.

Mystery Wreck, schooner, 70 feet, 31489.8/48302.1; 45 18.83/85 13.52, Charlevoix, Mich.

Niagara, steamer, 55 feet, 32800.1/48988.5; 43 29.30/87 46.48, Sheboygan, Wis.

Nicole, schooner, 55 feet, 31853.3/47917.2; 45 34.56/86 38.67, Green Bay, Wis.

Norland, steamer, 60 feet, 32999.9/49320.7; 42 58.43/87 48.64, Milwaukee, Wis.

Northerner, schooner, 135 feet, 32874.7/49091.7; 43 19.00/87 49.41, Sheboygan, Wis.

North Avenue Wreck, schooner, 30 feet, 33375.9/50070.4; 41 54.68/87 35.98, Chicago, Ill.

North Tug, tug, 50 feet, 33329.3/50309.3; 39.99/87 04.31, Chicago, Ill.

Northwest, schooner, 75 feet, 31270.2/48102.2; 45 47.32/84 51.30, Mackinac, Mich.

Novadoc, steamer, 15 feet, 32365.4/49063.5; 43 41.79/86 31.01, Pentwater, Mich.

Ottawa, schooner, 20 feet, 32395.6/46144.6; 46 52.85/90 46.26, Door County, Wis.

Pathfinder, schooner, 10 feet, 32473.5/48552.3; 44 14.72/87 30.65, Manitowoc, Wis.

Pickard's Wharf, dock ruins, 12 feet, 31773.72/48296.53; 45 07 15/85 58 30, N. Manitou Island, Mich.

Pipeline, pipeline to power co., 40 feet, 44 46.24/85 37.47, Traverse Bay, Mich.

Pilot Island Tug, tug, 35 feet, 32009.7/48034.4; 45 16.82/86 55.60, Green Bay, Wis.

P.J. Ralph, steamer, 45 feet, 31839.47/48333.50; 45 01.10; 86 06.00, Glen Haven, Mich.

Platte Dock & Cribs, dock ruins, 10 feet, 31936.77/48495.76; 44 43.40/86 09.40, Empire, Mich.

Port Oneida Dock, dock ruins, 10 feet, 31807.43/48397.08; 44 57.10/85 56.45, Glen Haven, Mich.

Poverty Island Wreck, unknown, 31875.6/47943.5; 45 31.19/86 40.44, Poverty Island, Mich.

Pride, schooner, 40 feet, 31975.1/47963.4; 45 29.77/86 38.76, Door County, Wis.

Prins Willem V, steamer, 90 feet, 32979.6/49286.8; 43 01.53/87 48.50, Milwaukee, Wis.

Rainbow, schooner, 20 feet, 33397.5/50098.5; 41 52.05/87 36.60, Chicago, Ill.

Rhone, schooner, 40 feet, 31889.7/47964.4; 45 28.91/86 41.02, Door County, Wis.

Richard Winslow, schooner, 25 feet, 31356.4/48026.4; 45 50.45/85 09.48 Mackinac, Mich.

Rising Sun, steamer, 13 feet, 31799.6/48386.8; 44 58.23/85 55.97 Manitou Passage, Mich.

R.J. Hackett, steamer, 30 feet, 32057.7/47938.8; 45 21.42/87 11.00, Green Bay, Wis.

Rockaway, schooner, 70 feet, 42264.4/86184.5, South Haven, Mich.

Roen, steamer, 110, 31885.0/47967.8; 45 28.71/86 40.20, Door County, Wis.

Rosinco, yacht, 195 feet, 33088.9/49586.3/ 42 37.50/87 37.62, Kenosha, Wis.

Rouse Simmons, schooner, 168 feet, 32437.4/48550.7; 44 16.64/87 24.81,
 Manitowoc, Wis.

Sailboat, sailboat, 33383.4/50201.2; 41 46.08/87 23.53, Chicago, Ill.

Salvor, barge, 25 feet, 32467.0/49355.8; 43 15.60/86 22.18, Muskegon, Mich.

Sandusky, brig, 83 feet, 31261.8/48100.9; 45 48.09/84 50.06 Mackinac, Mich.

S.C. Baldwin, steamer, 80 feet, 32487.3/48597.3; 44 10.91/87 29.10, Sheboygan,
 Wis.

Sebastopol, steamer, 15 feet, 33008.7/49300.8; 42 59.26/87 52.03, Milwaukee, Wis.

Selah Chamberlain, steamer, 70 feet, 32670.6/48827.9; 43 46.22/87 34.43,
 Sheboygan, Wis.

Sidney O. Neff, steamer, 15 feet, 32233.2/48015.2; 45 05.56/87 34.69, Green Bay,
 Wis.

Silver Lake, schooner, 210 feet, 32637.5/48819.5; 43 48.37/87 34.66, Sheboygan,
 Wis.

Southern Tug, tug, 50 feet, 33360.8/50086.7; 41 54.23/87 31.84, Chicago, Ill.

St. Albans, steamer, 180 feet, 32951.7/49268.9; 43 03.98/87 45.56, Milwaukee,
 Wis.

State of Michigan, steamer, 75 feet, 32453.8/49263.4; 43 23.29/86 27.89, White
 Lake, Mich.

Stormer Dock, dock ruins, 10 feet, 31784.39/48316.15; 45 05 00/85 58 59, N.
 Manitou Island, Mich.

Supply, schooner, 12 feet, 31769.77/48285.03; 44 58 23/85 58 50, N. Manitou
 Island, Mich.

Tacoma, tug, 35 feet, 33417.7;50178.9; 41 46.16/87 31.50, Chicago, Ill.

Three Brothers, steamer, 42 feet, 31839.3/48339.3; 45 00 55/86 05 59 S. Manitou
 Island, Mich.

Tramp, tugboat, 50 feet, 31724.4/48504.8; 44 51.04/85 36.11, Traverse Bay, Mich.

T.S. Kristee, steamer, 32105.1/48720.8; 44 18.34/86 18.44, Manistee, Mich.

Uganda, steamer, 210 feet, 31321.7/48047.2; 45 50.30/85 03.49 Mackinac, Mich.

Unknown, schooner, 30 feet, 33355.1/50033.9; 41 57.97/87 36.20, Chicago, Ill.

Unknown, schooner, 65 feet, 33331.4/50083.3; 41 55.56/87 27.38, Chicago, Ill.

Unknown, schooner, 33360.3/50036.9; 41 57.57/87 36.75, Chicago, Ill.

Unknown, schooner, 33375.9/50070.4; 41 47.42/87 36.90, Chicago, Ill.

Unknown , schooner, 31803.0/48328.0; 45 03.17/86 00.66, Manitou Preserve,
 Mich.

Unknown, schooner barge, 43 feet, 33372.0/50091.2; 41 53.51/89 33.19, Chicago,
 Ill.

Unknown, steamer, 40 feet, 33263.8/49759.4; 42 18.92/87 49.29, Chicago, Ill.

Unknown Manitowoc Wreck, 35 feet, 32487.9/48579.9; 44 12.09/87 30.69,
 Manitowoc, Wis.

Unknown Schooner, schooner, 10 feet, 32658.8/48762.7; 43 51.13/87 43.24,
 Sheboygan, Wis.

Unknown Schooner, schooner, 70 feet, 45 18.83/85 13.52; 31489.8/48302.1;
    Charlevoix, MI
Unknown Tug, tug, 30 feet, 33359.8/50084.0; 41 54.44/87 31.96, Chicago, Ill.
Unknown, tug, 33446.7/50230.2; 41 41.79/87 30.83, Chicago, Ill.
Unknown, tug, 33325.4/49977.7; 42 02.71/87 37.13, Chicago, Ill.
Unknown Tug, tug, 32009.7/48034.4; 45 16.61/86 55.85, Door County, Wis.
Vernon, steamer, 200 feet, 32461.6/48598.9; 44 12.07 87 24.73, Manitowoc, Wis.
Volunteer, steamer, 15 feet, 33007.4/49304.1; 42 59.11 87 51.49, Milwaukee, Wis.
Walter B. Allen, schooner, 158 feet, 32637.3/48798.0; 43 49.83/87 36.53,
    Sheboygan, Wis.
Walter L. Frost, steamer, 12 feet, 31859.1/48339.4; 44 59.65/86 08.68 S. Manitou
    Island, Mich.
Wells Burt, schooner, 42 feet, 33325.5/49977.8; 42 02.70/87 37.14, Evanston, Ill.
W.H. Wheeler, steamer, 33228/7/50278.9; 41 44.60/86 52.11, Michigan City, Ind.
William T. Graves, steamer, 10 feet, 31802.80/48330.75; 45 02.95/86 00.44,
    Manitou Passage, Mich.
William Home, schooner, 165 feet, 32582.5/48732.4; 43 56.94/87 33.21
    Manitowoc, Wis.
William Stone, schooner, 10 feet, 31270.7/48128.2; 45 44.90/ 84 30.05 Mackinac,
    Mich.
Winfield Scott, schooner, 10 feet, 31968.5/48000.2; 45 21.74/86 51.38, Door
    County, Wis.
Wings of Wind, schooner, 40 feet, 33357.6/50064.2; 41 44.94/87 33.48, Chicago,
    Ill.
Wisconsin, steamer, 85 feet, 32213.4/48040.1; 45 04.94/87 29.30, Green Bay, Wis.
Wisconsin, steamer, 130 feet, 33147.4/49634.042 31.93/87 42.55, Kenosha, Wis.
W.L. Brown, steamer, 80 feet, 32261.6/48096.844 48.09/87 32.91, Green Bay, Wis.
Wrecked Plane, airplane, 33428.9/50205.5; 41 44.04/87 30.54, Chicago, Ill.
WWI Airplane, 35 feet, 33408.4/50161.9; 41 47.60/87 31.76, Chicago, Ill.

Lake Huron

Albany, steamer, 150 feet, 30775.5/49174.2; 44 05.36/82 42.02, Thumb Preserve,
    Mich.
Albemarle, schooner, 12 feet, 31188.7/48183.1; 45 42.57/84 33.50; 45 42.99/84
    33.75, Mackinac, Mich.
Alberta M., steamer, 20 feet, 30659.91/48268.62; 45 54.92/83 05.26, Georgian
    Bay, Ont.
Algomah, steamer, 10 feet, 31228.0/48127.6; 45 46.88/84 43.27, Mackinaw City,
    Mich.
Anglo Saxon, schooner, 13 feet, 31309.6/48102.8; 45 45.24/84 57.25, Mackinac,
    Mich.
Arabia, schooner, 100 feet, 30202.9/48669.8; 45 18.70/81 40.46, Tobermory, Ont.

Arctic, 136 feet, 30748.90/49370.90, Lexington, Mich.

Atlantic, steamer, 40 feet, 29661.86/48743.11; 45 20.02/80 15.39 Parry Sound, Ont.

Aztec, steamer, 77 feet, 30770.5/49618.3; 43 09.83/82 18.49, Lexington, Mich.

Bentley, schooner,, 160 feet, 31057.7/48251.1; 45 41.44/84 09.15, Hammond Bay, Mich.

Burlington, steamer, 23 feet, 30709.10/48264.53; 45 53.53/83 13.34, Georgian Bay, Ont.

Carbide Barge, barge, 90 feet, 30839.5/48707.5; 44 58.60/8313.25, Alpena, Mich.

Cedarville, steamer, 110 feet, 31210.7/48130.6; 45.47 13/84 40.13 Mackinac, Mich.

Charles A. Street, steamer, 15 feet, 30818.2/49413.1; 43 35.50/82 27.50 Sanilac, Mich.

Charles S. Price, steamer, 65 feet, 30799.3/49622.7; 43 09.17/82 21.80 Sanilac, Mich.

C.H. Johnson, schooner, 14 feet, 31247.0/48061.7; 45 52.20/84 50.08, Mackinac, Mich.

Checotah, schooner, 116 feet, 30761.3/49413.4; 43 36.08/ 82 28.16 Sanilac, Mich.

Chickamauga, schooner, 35 feet, 30785.1/49292.7; 43 50.86/82 37.42, Thumb Preserve, Mich.

City of Cleveland, steamer, 30256.2/48587.4; 45 28.20/81 50.73, Tobermory, Ont.

City of Genoa, steamer, 64 feet, 30805.1/49624.9; 43 08.78/82 22.31, Sanilac, Mich.

Colonel A.B. Williams, schooner, 85 feet, 30779.1/49407.4; 43.36 72/82 30.80, Sanilac, Mich.

Daniel J. Morrell, steamer, 210 feet, 30761.4/49068.4, Thumb Preserve, Mich.

Diver's Park, park, 25 feet, 31211.57/48086.14; 45 51 824/84 42.993, St. Ignace, Mich.

D.R. Hanna, steamer, 90 feet, 30771.3/48666.4; 45 05.08/83 05.21, Alpena, Mich.

Dunderburg, schooner, 155 feet, 30740.9/49257.5; 43 55.63/82 33.41, Thumb Preserve, Mich.

E.B. Allen, schooner, 110 feet, 30811.6/48693.1; 45 00.96/83 09.87, Alpena, Mich.

Eliza H. Strong, steamer, 30 feet, 30847.0/49570.4; 43 15.77/82 30.66 Sanilac, Mich.

Enterprise, steamer, 185 feet, 30779.8/49145.5; 44 08.76/82 43.99, Thunder Bay Preserve, Mich.

F.B. Gardner, schooner, 55 feet, 30802.4/49446.8; 43 31.63/82 31.77 Sanilac, Mich.

Forest City, steamer, 160 feet, 30158.0/48675.1; 45 19.04/81 33.51, Tobermory, Ont.

F.T. Barney, schooner, 160 feet, 30984.1/48390.7; 45 29.27/83 50.51, Rogers City, Mich.

Genesee Chief, schooner, 10 feet, 31156.9/48227.8; 45 39.71/84 26.13, Mackinac, Mich.

Glenorchy, steamer, 120 feet, 30750.4/49314.2; 43 48.35/82 31.82, Thumb
Preserve, Mich.

Goshawk, schooner, 50 feet, 31049.3/49055.5; 44 14.96/83 24.95, Tawas Point,
Mich.

Governor Smith, steamer, 190 feet, 30763.9/49141.3; 44 09.48/82 42.07, Thumb
Preserve, Mich.

Grecian, steamer, 105 feet, 30832.7/48713.3; 44 58.12/83 11.98, Alpena, Mich.

Henry Clay, bark, 10 feet, 31189.7/48183.7; 45 43.33/84 32.31 Mackinac, Mich.

Iron Chief, steamer, 135 feet, 30779.0/49172.0; 44 05.59/82 42.59, Thumber
Bay Preserve, Mich.

Islander, steamer, 10 feet, 31158.9/48231.3; 45 39.29/84 26.35, Mackinac, Mich.

Jacob Bertschy, steamer, 10 feet, 30861.7/49181.4; 44 03.40/82 53.10, Thumb
Preserve, Mich.

James R. Bentley, schooner, 150 feet, 31057.7/48251.1; 45 41.45/84 09.12,
Mackinac, Mich.

J.H. Outhwaite, steamer, 30 feet, 31187.3/48184.3; 45 42.28/84 33.18 Mackinac,
Mich.

John Breden, schooner, 51 feet, 30823.4/49595.7; 43 12.26/84 27.91, Lexington,
Mich.

Landbo, steamer, 8 feet, 31167.7/48227.8; 45 29.39/84 27.91 Mackinac, Mich.

Laura H. Lee, steamer, 5 feet, 45 55.40/83 06.76, Meldrum Bay, Ont.

L.B. Coates, schooner, 6 feet, 31174.2/48219.0; 45 39 85/84 29 02, Mackinac,
Mich.

Leviathan, steamer, 12 feet, 31156.5/48228.0; 45 39 65/84 25 95, Mackinac, Mich.

Lottie Wolf, schooner, 18 feet, 29501.9/48914.3

Lucinda Van Valkenburg, schooner, 70 feet, 30807.3/48672.9, Alpena, Mich.

Mackinac Island Harbor Wreck, schooner, 52 feet, 31180.1/48110.1, Mackinac
Island, Mich.

Mapledawn, steamer, 30 feet, 29655.3/48931.5; 44 51.52; 80 14.50, Christian
Island, Ont.

Marquette, schooner, 40 feet, 29620.0/48917.0, Tobermory, Ont.

Mary Alice B, tug, 92, 30790.8/49520.5; 43 22.34/82 26.31, Sanilac, Mich.

Mary E. McLachlan, schooner, 35 feet, 31454.5/46053.0, Ontario

Michigan, barge, 15 feet, 29637.7/48912.7; 44 54.58; 80 12.15, Hope Island, Ont.

Molly T. Horner, schooner, 18 feet, 30893.7/48737.9, Alpena

Monohansett, steamer, 20 feet, 30822.6/48681.4, Alpena, Mich.

Monrovia, steamer, 130 feet, 30723.5/48728.9, Alpena, Mich.

Montana, steamer, 70 feet, 30855.9/48699.9, Alpena, Mich.

M. Stalker, schooner, 85 feet, 31213.6/48125.9; 45 47.38/84 41.04 ,Mackinac,
Mich.

Myrtie M. Ross, steamer, 10 feet, 31174.9/48321.8; 45 39.90/84 28.98, Mackinac,
Mich.

Nellie Gardner, schooner, 18 feet, 30893.7/48737.9, Alpena, Mich.

Newell A. Eddy, schooner, 168 feet, 45 46,89/84 13.75, Cheboygan, Mich.

New Orleans, steamer, 150 feet, 30808.0/48613.7, Alpena, Mich.

New York, steamer, 118 feet, 30761.0/49411.9; 43 36.23/82 28.24, Sanilac, Mich.

Nordmeer, steamer, 40 feet, 30790.7/48634.7, Alpena, Mich.

North Point Wreck, schooner, 15 feet, 30846.3/48688.4, Alpena, Mich.

North Star, steamer, 100 feet, 30787.3/49508.1; 43 23.97/82 26.50, Sanilac, Mich.

Ontario, barge, 12 feet, 31426.7/46178.0, Penetanguishene, Ont.

Oscar T. Flint, steamer, 35 feet, 30879.8/48671.9, Alpena, Mich.

Perseverence, schooner, 65 feet, 45 42.08/84 26.34, Cheboygan, Mich.

Persian, schooner, 175 feet, 31055.1/48246.2, Forty Mile Point, Mich.

Peshtigo, steamer, 13 feet, 31176.8/48108.8; 45 51,09/84 35,99, Mackinac Island,
    Mich.

P.H. Birckhead, steamer, 12 feet, 30908.2/48671.9, Alpena, Mich.

Philadelphia, steamer, 130 feet, 30786.2/49183.7, Thumb Preserve

Portsmouth, steamer, 15 feet, 30847.6/48588.2, Alpena, Mich.

Province, barge, 77 feet, 30770.5/49618.3; 43 09.83/82 18.49, Lexington, Mich.

Queen City, steamer, 51 feet, 30831.1/49622.4; 43 09.18/82 25.77 Lexington,
    Mich.

Regina, steamer, 80 feet, 30801.5/49535.0; 43 20.46; 82 29.90 Sanilac, Mich.

Rock Maze, 35 feet, 41155.27/48080.01; 45 51.863/84 36,403, Straits of Mackinac,
    Mich.

Sachem, steamer, 77 feet, 30769.2/49617.6; 43 09.90/82 18.36, Lexington, Mich.

Scanlon, barge, 15 feet, 30870.2/48669.1, Alpena, Mich.

Sea Gull, steamer, 15 feet, 31123.7/48158.4; 45 48.41/84 24.65 Mackinac

Spectacle Reef Wreck, schooner, 70 feet, 31038.1/48210.5, Mackinac

Sport, tug, 49 feet, 30824.9/49569.2; 43 15.98/82 27.93, Sanilac, Mich.

St. Andrew, schooner, 61 feet, 31180.2/48195.1; 45 42.07/84 31.46, Mackinac,
    Mich.

Stag Island Wrecks, barges, 30910.1/49748.9, Sanilac Preserve, Mich.

Sweetheart, schooner, 30 feet, 30834.0/49671.6, Sanilac, Mich.

Thomas Cranage, steamer, 25 feet, 29593.6/48906.0; 44 56.39; 80 05.27, Georgian
    Bay, Ont.

Thomas Kingsford, dredge, 14 feet, 31341.0/48069.0, Mackinac, Mich.

Unknown, schooner, 52 feet, 31180.4/48110.2, Mackinac Island, Mich.

Waubuno, steamer, 15 feet, 45 07.15 80 09.58, Tobermory, Ont.

Wawinet, yacht, 25 feet, 29501.9/48970.7--44 49.30; 79 05.54, Penetanguishene,
    Ont.

William H. Barnum, steamer, 75 feet, 31205.5/48153.3;45 44.42/84 37.53,
    Mackinac, Mich.

William P. Rend, steamer, 20 feet, 30891.0/48649.5, Alpena, Mich.

Wood Barge, barge, 50 feet, 30865.0/48680.8, Alpena, Mich.

Yakima, steamer, 77 feet, 30775.1/49612.6; 43 10.56/82 19.38, Lexington, Mich.

Lake Superior

Albert Miller, steamer, 20 feet, 32242.9/48166.7, Munising, Mich.

Alex Nimick, steamer, 20 feet, 31203.3/47555.2, Whitefish Preserve, Mich.

Algoma, steamer, 100 feet, 31738.3/46177.8, Isle Royale, Mich.

America, steamer, 80 feet, 31909.2/46082.3, Isle Royale, Mich.

Basswood Quarry, cribs, 20 feet, 23406.7/46170.1, Apostle Islands, Wis.

Charlotte, schooner, 20 feet, 32435.2/46173.3, Apostle Islands, Wis.

Chester A. Congdon, steamer, 200 feet, 31717.4/46147.8, Isle Royale, Mich.

Chicago, steamer, 90 feet, 47 43.84/85 57.91, Michipicoten Island, Ontario

City of St. Joseph, barge, 30 feet, 31777.6/46581.4; 47 28.15/88 06 .82, Keweenaw
     Preserve, Mich.

City of Superior, steamer, 10 feet, 47 28.43/87 51.73, Copper Harbor, Mich.

Colorado, steamer, 35 feet, 46553.2/41825.1;47 25.46/88 18.02, Eagle River, Mich.

Comet, steamer, 230 feet, 31111.4/47638.0, Whitefish Preserve, Mich.

Cumberland, steamer, 80 feet, 31935.9/46068.9, Isle Royale, Mich.

Edmund Fitzgerald, steamer, 555 feet, 46 59.9/85 06.6, Whitefish Point, Mich.

Elma, schooner, 10 feet, 46 27.54/86 42.91, Munising, Mich.

Emperor, steamer, 170 feet, 31712.1/46150.0, Isle Royale, Mich.

Emperor, steamer, bow, 170 feet, 31711.8/46150.6, Isle Royale, Mich.

Eureka, steamer, 50 feet, 31181.2/47527.4, Whitefish Bay, Mich.

Fedora, steamer, 10 feet, 32403.3/46153.5, Apostle Islands, Wis.

Fern, tug, 30 feet, 31825.1/46553.2;47 25.46/88 18.02, Eagle River, Mich.

Fin McCool, barge, 20 feet, 32423.3/46171.5, Apostle Islands, Wis.

Gale Staples, steamer, 15 feet, 31474.0/47421.1, Munising, Mich.

Gazelle, steamer, 20 feet, 47 27.45/88 09.28, Eagle Harbor, Mich.

George, schooner, 15 feet, 31604.5/47430.6, Munising, Mich.

George M. Cox, steamer, 100 feet, 31934.6/46069.8, Isle Royale, Mich.

Glenlyon, steamer, 100 feet, 31808.3/46188.5, Isle Royale, Mich.

H.D. Coffinberry, steamer, 10 feet, 32395.6/46144.6, Apostle Islands, Wis.

Henry Chisholm, steamer, 140 feet, 31935.9/46068.9, Isle Royale, Mich.

Henry Chisholm, steamer, engine, 140 feet, 31936.0/46068.0, Isle Royale, Mich.

Herman H. Hettler, steamer, 40 feet, 31632.2/47431.4, Munising, Mich.

Hermit Quarry, cribs, 20 feet, 32381.5/46171.0, Apostle Islands, Wis.

Indiana, steamer, 116 feet, 31215.1/47520.3, Whitefish Bay, Mich.

James Pickands, steamer, 30 feet, 31824.4/46553.3;47 25.53/88 17.88, Eagle River,
     Mich.

J.M. Osborne, steamer, 165 feet, 31149.5/47528.2, Whitefish Preserve, Mich.

John B. Cowle, steamer, 200 feet, 31125.1/47579.4, Whitefish Bay, Mich.

John Mitchell, steamer, 140 feet, 31153.7/47545.6, Whitefish Bay, Mich.

Kamloops, steamer, 260 feet, 31786.1/46124.4, Isle Royale, Mich.

Kiowa, steamer, 40 feet, 31499.6/47425.0, Munising, Mich.

Langham, steamer, 105 feet, 31758.3/46676.0;47 22.29/ 87 55.57, Bete Grise, Mich.

Lucerne, schooner, 20 feet, 32434.6/46234.9, Apostle Islands, Wis.

Manhattan, steamer, 35 feet, 31648.3/47438.1, Munising, Mich.

Mary E. McLachlan, schooner, 35 feet, 31454.5/46053.0, Schreiber, Ont.

Mary M. Scott, schooner, 15 feet, 46 27.54' 86 36.37, Munising, Mich.

Mesquite, USCG cutter, 110 feet, 31714.8/46713.1; 47 22.29/87 55.57, Keweenaw Preserve, Mich.

Miztec, schooner, 50 feet, 31156.9/47561.2, Whitefish Bay, Mich.

M.M. Drake, steamer, 50 feet, 31167.6/47569.3, Whitefish Bay, Mich.

Monarch, steamer, 150 feet, 31702.5/46171.2, Isle Royale, Mich.

Myron, steamer, 55 feet, 31142.9/47566.5, Whitefish Bay, Mich.

Neshoto, steamer, 15 feet, 31181.2/47527.4, Whitefish Bay, Mich.

Niagara, schooner, 100 feet, 31168.3/47543.9, Whitefish Bay, Mich.

Noque Bay, schooner, 12 feet, 32351.3/46184.6, Apostle Islands, Wis.

Ontario, steamer, 40 feet, 48 45 20/87 31 99, Rossport, Ont.

Ottawa, steamer, 25 feet, 32395.6/46144.6, Apostle Islands, Wis.

Panther, steamer, 100 feet, 31105.8/47685.9, Whitefish Bay, Mich.

Pretoria, schooner, 55 feet, 32288.0/46141.1, Apostle Islands, Wis.

Roswell G. Flemington, steamer, 220 feet, 63214.4/74954.3; 44 69.20/83 75.34, Serling, Ont.

Sadie Thompson, Barge, 114 feet, 31150.3/47619.8, Whitefish Preserve, Mich.

Sagamore, whaleback steamer, 65 feet, 31072.9/47771.8, Sault Ste. Marie, Ont.

Samuel Mather, steamer, 170 feet, 31086.7/47734.8, Whitefish Bay, Mich.

Scotia, steamer, 15 feet, 47 25 87/47 42 29, Keweenaw Point, Mich.

Sevona, steamer, 20 feet, 32388.1/46032.9, Apostle Islands, Wis.

Sitka, steamer, 15 feet, 31474.0/47421.1, Munising, Mich.

Smith Moore, steamer, 95 feet, 31642.2/47438.1, Munising, Mich.

Steven M. Selvick, tug, 60 feet, 31629.3/47427.0; 46 29.53; 86 35.03, Munising, Mich.

Stockton Quarry, cribs, 20 feet, 32367.8/46170.8, Apostle Islands, Wis.

Strathmore, steamer, 40 feet, 47 44.64/ 85 57.36, Michipicoten Island, Ontario

Superior, steamer, 15 fcct, 46 33.45/86 24.91, Munising, Mich.

Superior City, steamer, 270 feet, 31112.0/47633.5, Whitefish Preserve, Mich.

Thomas Wilson, whaleback steamer, 70 feet, 32605.3/45820.1, Superior, Wis.

Tioga, steamer, 35 feet, 31824.4/46553.3;47 25.53/88 17.88, Keweenaw Preserve, Mich.

Transport, barge, 30 feet, 31777.6/46581.4; 47 28.10/88 06.58 Keweenaw Preserve, Mich.

Traveller, steamer, 20 feet, 47 27.57/88 09.12

Vienna, steamer, 148 feet, 31135.9/47610.4, Whitefish Bay, Mich.

Unknown Barge, barge, 20 feet, 32431.7/46170.8, Apostle Islands, Wis.

U.S. Forest Service Dock Weedbed, 30 feet, 31657.56/47437.91; 46 26.704; 86 39.867, Munising, Mich.

Wasaga, steamer, 35 feet, 47 28.25/87 52.94, Copper Harbor, Mich.

W.C. Moreland, steamer, 35 feet, 47 24.84/88 19.73, Eagle River, Mich.

William L. Moreland, steamer, 20 feet, 31832.9/46551.1, Keweenaw Preserve, Mich.

Zillah, steamer, 250 feet, 31123.6/47624.3, Whitefish Preserve, Mich.

Lake Ontario

Bateau Channel Wreck, steamer, 15 feet, 44 15.53/76 20.23, Howe Island, Ont.

Battersly Island Wreck, schooner, 20 feet, 44 33.11/ 75 43.34, St. Lawrence, Ont.

Chippewa, steamer, 65 feet, 44 56.03/ 75 03.43, Morrisburg, Ont.

Chrysler Park Wreck, steamer, 65 feet, 44 56.03/75 03.43, St. Lawrence, Ont.

Comet, steamer, 85 feet, 44 08.34/ 76 35.15, Simcoe, Ont.

Conestoga, steamer, 28 feet, 44 46.46/ 75 23.36, Cardinal, Ont.

Eastcliff Hall, steamer, 65 feet, 44 55.29/ 75 06.04, Morrisburg, Ont.

Fred Mercur, steamer, 45 feet, 45 02.03/ 74 37.18, St. Lawrence, Ont.

George A. Marsh, schooner, 85 feet, 44 07.69/ 76 36.26, Simcoe, Ont.

Grenadier Island Wreck, schooner, 18 feet, 44 24.14/75 53.13, Mallorytown, Ont.

Grenadier Island Wreck, steamer, 20 feet, 44 24.57/ 75 51.00, Mallorytown, Ont.

Henry C. Daryaw, steamer, 85 feet, 44 31.34/ 75 45.50, Brockville, Ont.

Ida Walker, schooner, 12 feet, 44 00.57/ 77 36.22, Presquile, Ont.

John A. MacDonald, schooner, 8 feet, 44 00.36/ 77 40.30, Presquile, Ont.

John B. King, schooner, 90 feet, 43 33.46/ 75 42.43, Brockville, Ont.

Julia B. Merrill, schooner, 60 feet, 43 37.05/ 79 26.80, Kingston, Ont.

Juno, steamer, 12 feet, 43 53.01/78 80.02, Bowmanville, Ont.

Keystorm, steamer, 100 feet, 44 25.48/ 75 49.20, Mallorytown, Ont.

Lillie Parsons, schooner, 83 feet, 43 33.23/ 75 43.09, Sparrow Island, Ont.

Quinte, steamer, 10 feet, 44 10.35/ 77 02.30, Deseronto, Ont.

Rothesay, steamer, 30 feet 44 41.58/75 31.40, Prescott, Ont.

Sligo, schooner, 67 feet, 43 36.64'/79 27.27, Kinston, Ont.

Unknown, schooner, 18 feet, 44 24.14/ 75 53.13, Grenadier, Ont.

Unknown Schooner, schooner, 20 feet, 44 33.11/ 75 42.43, Brockville, Ont.

Wolfe Islander II, ferry, 80 feet, 4413.55/ 76 24.98, Kingston, Ont.

Lake Erie

Amherst Islander I, ferry, 12 feet, 44 15.53; 76 20.23, Howe Island, Ont.

Armenia, schooner, 40 feet, 43817.2/57073.6, Cholchester, Ont.

Case, steamer, 34 feet, 41 48.72/82 51.82, East Sister Island, Ont.

Charles B. Packard, steamer, 40 feet, 43808.0/57053.1, Colchester, Ont.
Coal Schooner Wreck, schooner, 72 feet, 44269.2/57975.8, Pt. Stanley, Ont.
Conemaugh, steamer, 20 feet, 43835.7/57163.1, Pt. Pelee, Ont.
David Stewart, schooner, 32 feet, 43858.0/57160.2, Pt. Pelee, Ont.
F.A. Meyer, steamer, 80 feet, 43911.8/57406.1, Erieau, Ont.
Frank E. Vigor, steamer, 90 feet, 43941.9/57464.5, Erieau, Ont.
George Dunbar, steamer, 44 feet, 43729.6/57076.4, Pelee Island, Ont.
George Stone, steamer, 45 feet, 43820.03/57135.26, West Lake Erie, Ont.
George Worthington, schooner, 40 feet, 43800.0/56994.4, Colchester, Ont.
Grand Traverse, steamer, 40 feet, 43795.9/56975.1, Colchester, Ont.
H.A. Barr, schooner, 80 feet, 44118.3/57803.2, Erieau, Ont.
Jay Gould, steamer, 40 feet, 43829.2/47202.6, Pt. Pelee, Ont.
Jorge B., tug, 36 feet, 43851.2/57184.0, Pt. Pelee, Ont.
Light Wreck, schooner, 76 feet, 43942.0/57414.4, Erieau, Ont.
Little Wissahickon, schooner, 80 feet, 43919.4/57454.9, Erieau, Ont.
Lycoming, steamer, 30 feet, 44073.0/57566.4, Erieau, Ont.
Merida, steamer, 80 feet, 44159.2/57843.9, Pt. Stanley, Ont.
Nimrod, schooner, 70 feet, 44279.7/58053.2, Pt. Stanley, Ont.
Philip Minch, steamer, 42 feet, 43741.6/57106.2, Pt. Pelee, Ont.
Robert, tug, 50 feet, 44044.0/57510.6, Erieau, Ont.
Specular, steamer, 40 feet, 43795.5/57128.5, Pt. Pelee, Ont.
Tasmania, schooner, 40 feet, 43786.8/57140.1, Pt. Pelee, Ont.
Unknown, 80 feet, 43942.0/57414.4, Erieau, Ont.
Valentine, schooner, 80 feet, 43931.2/57475.9, Erieau, Ont.
Wesee, steamer, 22 feet, 41 51.00/83 00.10,
Willis, schooner, 70 feet, 43897.4/57349.8, Erieau, Ont.

Glossary

Nautical terms represent a language that may be unfamiliar to most sport divers. But to share information about the underwater world and to learn about maritime archaeology, it is useful to have an understanding of basic terminology. These definitions are provided for that purpose.

a -- A prefix for "on" or "in." It is used commonly, aback, aboard, astern, etc.

about -- A turning around.

adrift -- Anything that floats unfastened.

aft -- Behind; toward the after or stern part of a vessel.

afterbody -- That portion of a ship's body aft of the midship section.

aground -- Wholly or partially resting on the bottom.

air port -- An opening in the side of the deckhouse of a vessel for light and ventilation.

alongside -- By the side of.

amidships -- Generally speaking, the middle portion of a vessel.

anchor -- A metal hook specifically designed to take hold of the bottom in relatively shallow water. Anchors are of many shapes and sizes and may weigh a few pounds to tons.

apron -- Knee joining or bridging stem and keel.

arch -- A structure running from bow to stern to provide support; common on early, wooden-hulled Great Lakes steamers.

astern -- Behind.

athwart, athwartships -- Across.

avast -- The order to stop or pause in any exercise.

aweather -- Toward the weather side; the side upon which the wind blows.

aweigh -- Spoken of an anchor when it has been lifted from the bottom.

backstays -- Ropes stretched from a mast to the sides of a vessel, some way aft of the mast, to give extra support to the masts against falling forward.

backstay lever -- A device for slackening or tightening running backstays.

bail -- To remove water from the bilge.

ballast -- Weight deposited in a ship's hold when she has no cargo, or too little to bring her sufficiently low in the water for proper navigation.

bar -- A ridge of sand.

barge -- A general name given to most flat-bottomed craft.

barkentine (bark or barque) -- A three-masted sailing vessel, square rigged on the fore and mainmasts, and fore and aft rigged on the mizzen.

batten -- A long strip of wood.

beacon -- A navigation light.

beam -- The width of a vessel at her widest part.

bearing -- The direction or angular distance from a meridian, in which an object lies.

beat -- To "beat to windward" is to make progress in a sailing vessel in the direction from which the wind is blowing.

becket -- Loop or eye for attachment.

belay -- To make fast; as, to belay a rope.

belaying pin -- A moveable pin or bolt of wood or metal to which lines are belayed.

below -- To "go below" is equivalent, on shipboard, to going downstairs.

bends -- Also called decompression sickness, the appearance of tiny nitrogen gas "bubbles" in sport divers' blood from a too-rapid ascent.

bent -- The condition resulting from the bends; a diver is "bent" when experiencing the bends.

berth -- A bed or bunk on board ship; a place for a ship to tie up or anchor is sometimes called a berth.

between decks or 'tween decks -- Any place below the main deck on a ship of more than one deck.

bilge -- That part of the hull of a ship inside and adjacent to the keel.

bilge keel -- Fins of wood or steel approximately paralleling the keel but built into and projecting from the ship at about where the bottom and the sides might be said to join. They are intended to minimize the rolling of the ship.

bilge water -- Water that collects in the bottom of the ship. As this is always at the lowest part of the hull, oil and other impurities are always a part of the bilge water, with the result that its odor is generally offensive and it is very dirty.

billet head -- A wooden scroll used in place of a figurehead.

billy -- Light, portable rope and pulley system that can be used anywhere.

binnacle -- The fixed case and stand in which the steering compass of a vessel is mounted.

bitts -- Posts of metal or timber projecting from the deck to which lines may be made fast.

block -- A pulley used on board ship.

bob stay -- A stay or rope made fast to the stempost of a ship at the cutwater and leading to the end of the bowsprit.

boiler casing -- Walls forming a trunk leading from the boiler room to the boiler hatch to protect deck spaces from heat.

bollard -- A short, think post on a pier for tying up ships.

booby hatch -- An access hatch from the weather deck protected by a hood from sea and weather.

boom -- The spar at the foot of a fore and aft sail.

boomkin -- Extension over the stern of a sailboat to take backstays and/or sheets.

bottomlands -- Land below Great Lakes water.

bottomland preserve -- An area designated by the State of Michigan to recognize unusual natural features or collection of historical artifacts such as shipwrecks. Special rules apply regarding the removal of artifacts from bottomland preserves. Synomonous with "underwater" preserve.

bow -- The front end of a vessel.

bowsprit -- The spar projecting from the bow of a ship and to which the fore stays are led from the foremast. It is generally decorative on power boats.

bowsprit shrouds -- Horizontal wires supporting the bowsprit against thwartship motion.

brace -- Ropes on a square-rigged ship leading to the ends of the yards and used for the purpose of setting the yard at the proper angle to the mast.

brail -- A rope leading in from the leech of a fore-and-aft sail to the mast, used to gather in the sail.

breadth (molded)-- The greatest breadth of the vessel measured from the heel of the frame on one side to the heel of a frame on the other side.

breaker -- A small water barrel.

breakers -- Waves that curl over and break because of shallow water.

breakwater -- An artificial bank or wall of any material built to break the violence of the sea and create a sheltered spot.

breasthooks -- Knees attaching stringers at the bow.

bridge -- A high platform extending from side to side of the ship, which usually supports a pilothouse.

bridles -- Several lines leading from a larger line to distribute the strain on an object to which they are attached.

brig -- A vessel with two masts (fore and main) both of them square rigged.

brigantine -- Same as a brig except that it has a fore and aft mainsail.

brightwork -- Varnished wood.

broach -- An involuntary swing to parallel with the waves.

bulkhead -- A partition of almost any material.

bulk freighter -- A freighter designed to carry a variety of bulk cargoes, such as grain, fruit, lumber, etc.

bulwarks -- A parapet around the deck of a vessel, serving to guard passengers, crew, and cargo from the possibility of being swept overboard.

bumboat -- A small harbor boat allowed to visit ships in port and supply sailors with various articles.

buoy -- A floating marker intended to serve as a guide or warning.

burbot -- A harmless but interesting freshwater fish of the cod family. It frequents shipwrecks and can be distinguished by a single barbel below its lower lip. Burbots, also called lawyerfish, have been known to grow in excess of 30 inches but most are about 20 to 24 inches in length.

butt -- End-to-end joints, sometimes against a special piece of material employed just at such joints and called a butt block.

buttock -- The rounding part of a vessel's stern.

cabin -- A habitable apartment on shipboard.

cable -- The rope or chain by which a ship's anchor is held.

calking (caulking) -- Stuffing the seams of wooden ships with oakum.

camber -- The athwartship curvature of a deck.

can buoy -- A buoy which shows above water the form of a cylinder.

canaler -- A vessel built to pass through the Welland and St. Lawrence River canals. These dimensions were roughly 133 to 140 feet long with a beam of 26 feet.

capsize -- To turn over.

capstan -- A kind of windlass sometimes found on ships and used principally for raising and anchor.

cargo hatch -- A large opening in the deck to permit loading of cargo.

carling -- Short support between beams.

carvel-built -- Built with the external planks edge to edge, meeting flush at the seams, flush sided.

casings -- The walls or partitions forming trunks above the engine and boiler spaces to provide air and ventilation and enclosing the uptakes.

catboat -- A small sailing boat with one mast and a single sail which is generally similar in shape to the mainsail of a sloop.

cat ketch -- Two-masted boat carrying only one sail on each mast and having mast sizes and locations proportioned to a ketch.

cat schooner -- A boat carrying only one sail on each mast and having mast sizes and locations proportioned to a schooner.

cat yawl -- A boat carrying only one sail on each mast and having mast sizes and locations proportioned to a yawl.

ceiling -- Inside planking of the hull of a vessel.

centerboard -- A moveable sheet of metal or wood sometimes used by small sailboats. It extends through the keel and presents a large surface to the water and tends to eliminate lateral motion while the boat is under sail. A kind of folding keel.

centerboard pennant -- Line for centerboard raising or lowering.

centerboard pin -- Pivot for a centerboard.

centerboard trunk or well -- Watertight enclosure of the centerboard.

chain plate -- A fitting at the sides of a hull to which shrouds are attached.

channel -- A ledge or narrow platform bolted to and projecting from the outside of a vessel's hull to spread the rigging.

chart -- A map of the sea and coast projections for use by navigators.

cheek knee -- Strips along the top and bottom of the trail boards.

chess tree -- A timber in which a sheave is set, bolted to the topsides of a square-rigged vessel at a point convenient for hauling down the main tack, the tack leading to the inside of the bulwark.

chine -- The line at which sides and bottom of a hull meet.

chock -- A fitting for guiding rope to a cleat or bitt.

clamp -- A longitudinal support member for deck beams.

cleat -- A prolonged fitting to which ropes are fastened.

clinker -- A method of small boat building in which the covering planks overlap.

clipper -- A fast sailing ship developed in the first half of the 19th Century. Generally, clippers were full-rigged ships and were popular for about 50 years.

coaming -- A water-stopping strip around a deck opening.

companionway -- The entrance to a ladder to flight of stairs leading from one deck to the one below.

compass -- A magnetized instrument that points approximately in the direction of the magnetic pole.

cotter pin -- Small retaining pin through a larger pin or bolt at right angles.

counter -- The under part of the overhang of the stern.

cradle -- Framework for hauling or storing a boat.

crosstrees -- The arms extending laterally near the head of a mast at right angles to the length of the vessel and to the extremities of which the topmast shrouds are stretched for the purpose of giving support to the topmast.

cuddy -- A small cabin usually on a sailboat.

cutter -- A sailing boat with one mast carrying staysail, jib, fore and aft mainsail, and sometimes a topsail; a large U.S. Coast Guard vessel.

cutwater -- That portion of the stem of a vessel that cleaves the water as she moves ahead.

davit -- A light crane mounted on a ship's side and used for hoisting and lowering boats.

deadeye -- A round block of lignum-vitae in which there are three holes, through which is rove the lanyard.

deadlight -- A porthole that does not open (fixed glass).

deadhead -- A piece of floating wood.

deadwood -- Solid area of a vessel below and aft of garboard and stern rabbet.

deck -- The covering of the interior of a ship, either carried completely over her or only over a portion. Decks correspond to the floors and roof of a flat-topped building.

deckhouse -- A cabin above the deck.

decompression sickness -- See "bends."

derelict -- A ship adrift at sea without her crew.

dinghy -- A small open boat used as a tender for a yacht.

dock -- An artificially constructed basin for the reception of vessels. It may be a wet dock, which ships lie while loading and unloading, or a dry dock, in which they are repaired after the water is pumped out.

down Lake Michigan -- In the 1800s, Chicago was considered the head of Lake Michigan so travel was "down" to the Straits of Mackinac.

draft -- The depth beneath the surface of the water of the lowest point of a ship's keel.

draft marks -- The numbers on each side of a vessel near the bow and stern to indicate the distance from the number to the bottom of the keel. Also called "Plimsoll marks" after George Plimsoll, a British naval architect who developed the practice.

drag -- A vessel's resistance to motion because of shape and friction. Also, slipping of anchor.

driver -- The fore-and-aft sail on the mizzenmast of a square-rigged ship. It is sometimes called the "spanker."

drouge -- A sea anchor.

drysuit -- A diving suit that permits sport divers to remain dry while underwater. Insulation is provided by clothing worn beneath the suit.

electrolysis -- Natural decomposition of metal by an electrical current.

engine bed -- Vertical members supporting dead weight, thrust and torque of the engine.

ensign -- The flag carried by a ship as the insignia of her nationality.

entrance -- That part of the bow that cuts the water.

eye -- A fixed, closed loop at the end of a rope.

fathom -- A nautical measure equal to six feet.

fid -- A bolt of wood or metal which holds the heel of a topmast.

fife rail -- A plank or rail in which a group of belaying pins is kept.

figurehead -- A decorative carving below the bowsprit.

flam -- Cross-sectional curvature of a hull above the water, always convex on outside of topsides.

flare -- A concave bulge spreading outward at the bow of a ship.

Flemish horse -- A short footrope at the end of a yard.

floor -- The inside bottom of a hull.

fluke -- The point area of an anchor.

footrope -- A rope slung underneath the yard, bowsprit, or jib boom on which the crew stands when furling a sail.

fore and aft -- An expression signifying those sails which, when at rest, lie in a line running from bow to stern of a vessel.

forecastle -- Forward cabin.

foredeck -- Deck at the bow of a vessel.

forefoot -- The point at which the stem joins the keel.

foremast -- The mast nearest the bow of a vessel having more than one mast, except on yawls, ketches, and other sailboats where the mast nearest the bow is larger than the mast farther astern.

forepeak -- Below-deck area at the bow of a boat.

foresail -- On a square-rigged ship, the lowest square sail on the foremast. On a schooner, the sail stretched between the boom and the gaff on the foremast.

forestay -- Stay running from lowest forward position on mast to forward deck.

forward -- The forward part or the forepart; the vicinity of the bow of a vessel.

founder -- To sink.

frames -- Athwartship structural members that give shape to the hull.

freeboard -- That portion of a vessel's side which is free of the water.

freighter -- A ship engaged in carrying freight.

full-rigged ship -- A ship carrying three masts, each mounting square sails.

funnel -- The smokestack or chimney connected with the boilers of a ship.

gaff -- The spar at the top of some fore and aft sails, such as the mainsail or foresail of a schooner.

galley -- The kitchen of a ship.

gangway -- A narrow platform or bridge passing over from one deck of a vessel to another.

garboard strake -- The plank just above the keel.

gear -- Any part of the working apparatus of a vessel, as the gear of the helm, which consists of the tiller, the chains, the blocks, and all other necessary parts.

gig -- A small boat carried on shipboard and meant for use when in port.

gimbals -- The brass rings in which a compass is mounted, and which permit it to remain horizontal despite the motions of the ship.

gollwobbler -- Over-sized sail on a schooner going forward from the top of the mainmast. Also called maintopmast queen staysail.

gooseneck -- The ring at the mast end of a boom.

ground -- To run a ship into water so shallow that she rests on the bottom.

ground tackle -- The gear connected with and including the anchors of a ship.

gudgeons -- Fittings on the transom that accept the pintles of a rudder.

gunkholing -- Exploring in shallow water.

gunwale -- The top of any solid rail along the outside of a vessel.

gusset -- Knee or bridge reinforcing two members attached to one another by end-to-end joint.

guy -- A steadying rope, as the "guy" of a spinnaker, which serves to keep that sail forward.

gybe -- The swinging over of a fore and aft sail when the wind, accidentally or intentionally, has been brought from one side of it to the other around its free edge. This is sometimes a foolish and dangerous maneuver.

gyro compass -- A direction indicator not dependent on the earth's magnetic field, works on inertial stability.

hail -- To call.

hair rail -- The top member of two or three curved timbers, extending from either side of the figurehead to the bow or cathead, to brace the head or projecting stem.

halyard -- A rope (sometimes a chain) by which a sail, flag, or yard is hoisted.

hatchway -- An opening in the deck of a vessel through which persons or cargo may descend or ascend.

hawsepipes (hawsehole) -- Short tubes through which the anchor cable or chain passes from the forward deck to the outside of the bow.

hawser -- A cable or heavy rope used for towing and for making fast to moorings.

head -- Toilet.

head sails -- All the sails set between the foremast and the bow and bowsprit of a sailing ship. These are the fore staysail and the inner, outer, and flying jibs.

heave to -- To stop dead in the water.

heel -- To lean to one side.

helm -- Used interchangeably with the word "tiller." Theoretically, every rudder is equipped with a helm or tiller, although actually tillers are seldom used except on small boats.

Hermaphrodite brig -- A two-masted sailing ship with square sails on the foremast and fore-and-aft sails only on the main. This type is often incorrectly called a brigantine.

highfield lever -- A lever used to take up slack quickly in a wire such as a backstay.

hog -- A hull bottom distorted by being lower at the ends than at the middle.

hold -- The inner space in a vessel in which the cargo is stowed.

hounds -- An area of a mast at which a gaff rides.

horses -- Footropes.

hull -- The hull is the body of a vessel, exclusive of rigging or equipment.

hull speed -- The maximum practical speed of a displacement hull of a given length and design.

hypothermia -- The cooling of the core body temperature.

inboard -- A boat with engines inside the hull (opposite of outboard).

jackstaff -- A short flagstaff at the bow.

jaws -- The horns at the end of a boom or gaff, which keep it in its position against the mast.

jib -- One of several triangular headsails of a sailing vessel.

jib-boom -- A spar running out beyond the bowsprit for the purpose of carrying other jibs.

jigger -- The fourth mast from the bow in a ship carrying four or more masts. The second from the bow in a yawl or ketch.

jolly boat -- A boat corresponding to a dinghy.

jumper -- Wire stays passing over a short strut and having both ends attached to the same spar.

kedge -- A small anchor carried by large vessels for use in shallow water or for use in keeping the main anchor clear.

keel -- The backbone of a ship. It is a strong member extending the entire length of the center of the bottom, and from it the ribs are built at right angles.

keel cooler -- A heat exchange system of pipes inside or along the keel to cool fresh water for the engine.

keelson -- An addition to the keel inside the boat. It rests upon the keel and strengthens it.

ketch -- A sailing vessel with two masts and with fore-and-aft sails.

king plank -- The center plank of a deck, notched to receive ends of curved deck planks.

knee -- A right-angled timber acting as a bracket between horizontal and vertical members.

knightheads -- Upright timbers inside of and on either side of the stem; the bowsprit sits between them.

knot -- A nautical mile per hour, about 1.1 miles per hour (a nautical mile is about 6,075 feet).

lanyard -- A short piece of rope used as a handle or to secure an object.

lapstrake -- Same as clinker built.

lashing -- Binding with light line.

launch -- A small vessel propelled by some kind of motor and generally used for pleasure; or to put a new vessel in the water.

lawyer fish -- See "burbot."

lazarette -- The enclosed storage space at the stern in the hull.

lazy jacks -- Ropes leading down vertically from the topping lift to the boom to hold the sail when taking it in.

lead -- A leaden weight attached to the end of a line to measure the depth of the water.

lee -- The lee side of a vessel is the side opposite that against which the wind blows. A lee shore is a shore on the lee side of a ship, and is therefore to be feared for the force of the wind tends to blow the ship ashore. "Under the lee of the shore," however, is an expression meaning in the shelter of a shoreline from which the wind is blowing.

leeway -- Sideward travel of a ship off her course.

leg-of-mutton -- A triangular sail sometimes used on small sailboats.

leeward -- On the lee side.

length between perpendiculars -- The length of a ship measured from the forward side of the stem to the aft side of the stern post at the height of the designed water line.

lifeboat -- A boat carried for the purpose of saving lives in case the ship which carried it is wrecked.

lifeline -- Rope or wire fence around a vessel; short portable rope for crew member's individual safeguard.

lift -- A line running diagonally from the masthead to the end of a yard, which takes the weight of the yard.

light board -- A board used to support and shield running lights.

lighthouse -- A structure erected ashore or in shallow water and equipped with a powerful light to act as a warning and navigational aid.

line -- A small rope.

list -- To lean to one side.

LOA -- Length overall. The distance from the foremost part of the stem to the aftermost part of the stern.

log -- A record of events.

lunch hook -- A small anchor used for short stops in good weather.

LWL -- Length at the waterline.

martingale -- The rope extending downward from the jib-boom to the "dolphin striker." Its duties are those of a stay or brace.

mast -- A long piece or system of pieces of timber or metal placed nearly perpendicularly to the keel of a vessel to support rigging, antennas, halyards, etc.

masthead -- Top of a mast.

maststep -- Socket or support for the bottom of a mast.

mayday -- Prefix to a radio call for help.

messenger -- A weight sent down an anchor rope to improve anchor holding ability.

midships -- Pertaining to the middle of a vessel.

mizzen -- Generally, the third mast from the bow of a ship carrying three or more masts is called the "mizzenmast." The sails set from this mast have the word "mizzen" prefixed to their names.

moor -- To moor is to make a ship fast to a mooring which is a kind of permanent anchor to which a buoy is attached.

moulded depth -- The vertical distance from the top of the keel to the top of the upper deck beams at the side of a vessel (taken at the middle of the length).

muck out -- An instance of no or reduced visibility resulting from the disturbance of fine silt underwater.

mushroom -- An anchor shaped like a mushroom.

narced -- Feeling the effects of nitrogen narcosis.

navigation -- The science which enables seamen to determine their positions at sea and lay down courses to be followed.

nitrogen narcosis -- "Rapture of the deep," a feeling of euphoria or drunkenness resulting from excess nitrogen absorbed into divers' blood. Usually occurs at depths of 100 feet or more.

nun buoy -- A buoy which shows above water in the shape of a cone.

oakum -- A substance to which old ropes are reduced when picked to pieces. It is used in calking the seams of boats and in stopping leaks.

outboard -- A boat with an engine(s) outside the hull (opposite of inboard).

packet -- A small passenger or mail boat.

paddlewheel -- A large wheel sometimes used by steamboats and on which flat boards are so arranged that when the wheel turns the boards come in contact with the water, thus propelling the boat.

painter -- A rope attached to the bow of an open boat by which the boat may be tied.

pan -- Prefix to a message concerning safety of ship but not an actual distress; a radio emergency call less urgent than a mayday.

parcel -- To protect a line from wear by covering it with another material.

parrels -- Rollers on lashings about mast or boom that allow lashings to be raised or lowered without jamming.

partners -- Short structural members to support the mast where it goes through the deck.

peak -- The upper end of a gaff. Also, the uppermost corner of a sail carried by a gaff.

peak halyards -- The halyards or ropes by which the peak is elevated.

pier -- A long, narrow structure of wood, steel or concrete built from the shore out into the water and generally used for the transfer of passengers and goods to and from ships.

pile (spile) -- A vertical post driven into the bottom as a mooring for ships.

pilot -- One qualified and licensed to direct ships in or out of a harbor or channel.

pilothouse -- A house designed for navigational purposes.

pintle -- The fitting on a detachable rudder that fits into the gudgeon.

pitch -- The up and down movement of a ship in response to seas.

poop -- An extra deck on the after part of a vessel.

pooped -- Inundated by a wave coming over the transom.

port -- The left-hand side of a vessel when one is facing the bow.

porthole -- An opening in the side of a vessel. The term generally refers to the round windows common on most ships.

pram -- A small boat with a square bow.

prevailing wind -- The normal wind for a particular place.

propeller -- A device that, when mounted on the end of a shaft outside the stern of a vessel and below the water line, moves the ship through the water when turned. Also used to refer to a boat so equipped.

prow -- The cutwater of a ship.

punt -- A small, flat-bottomed boat, generally square ended.

purchase -- The use of mechanical power.

quadrant -- A quarter-circular fitting at the top of a rudder post.

quarter -- That section of a ship's side slightly forward of the stern.

quartering -- Running at an angle to the sea.

quay -- An artificial landing place, generally of greater area than a pier.

rabbet -- A groove in a structural member into which another fits and is fastened.

rabbit boat -- A steamer with a covered hold and exposed freight deck with machinery, crew quarters, and pilot house located at the stern.

reef -- A low ridge of rock usually just below the surface of the water.

reeve -- To pass a wire, chain, or rope through a hole or pulley.

ribs -- The members which, with the keel, form the skeleton of a vessel.

riding lights -- The lights a ship is required by law to carry at night while under way.

rig -- The manner in which the masts and sails of a vessel are fitted and arranged in connection with the hull.

rigging -- The system of ropes on a vessel by which her masts and sails are held up and operated.

roadstead -- A place of anchorage at a distance from the shore.

rode -- Anchor line and chain.

ROV -- Remote-operated vehicle; "robot" controlled from the surface to explore underwater with the use of video.

rub rail -- A molding, usually metal, around the hull that acts as a bumper.

rudder -- A flat, hinged apparatus hung at the stern of a ship, by the movement of which the ship is steered.

run -- The after part of a vessel at the water line where her lines converge toward the sternpost.

running lights -- The lights a ship is required by law to carry at night while under way.

sag -- Distortion in a hull.

sail -- A sheet of canvas or other material which, when spread to the wind, makes possible the movement of a vessel.

saloon (salon) -- The main cabin of a vessel.

Samson post -- A bitt at the bow used for making fast.

scantling -- A piece of timber used in ship construction.

scarf -- A joint made between two members by tapering and overlapping.

schooner -- A fore-and-aft rigged vessel with two or more masts, the foremost of which is the foremast.

scow -- A large, flat-bottomed boat without power and of many uses.

scuba -- Self-contained breathing apparatus. The tank, regulator and accompanying equipment that permits divers to remain submerged for extended periods.

scuppers -- Openings in the bulwarks of a ship to carry off any water that may get on the deck.

scuttle -- To intentionally sink a vessel.

seam -- The space between two planks in the covering of a vessel. It is in the seam that the calking is placed.

seamanship -- The art of handling ships.

seiche -- Extreme fluctuation in depth in the Great Lakes.

shaft (shafting) -- The cylindrical forging used for transmission of rotary motion from the engine to the propellers.

sheer -- The straight or curved line that the deck line of a vessel makes when viewed from the side.

sheer strake -- The topmost plank in a hull.

sheet -- The rope attached to a sail so that it may be let out or hauled in as required.

shoal -- A shallow place in the water.

shrouds -- Strong ropes forming the lateral supports of a mast, often wire rope.

sister frame -- A partial frame fastened to the side of a broken or weak frame.

skeg -- A member running out from the keel to support the rudder post.

skiff -- A small open boat.

skin diving -- Diving with mask, fins, and snorkel but without scuba.

sleepers -- Bracket-like members connecting the transom to the structural members.

sloop -- Sailing vessel with one mast, like a cutter but having a jib stay, which a cutter has not. A jib stay is a support leading from the mast to the end of the bowsprit on which a jib is set.

smokestack -- A metal chimney or passage through which the smoke and gases are led from the uptakes to the open air.

sole -- The bottom or floor of a cabin.

sounding -- Determining the depth of water and the kind of bottom with the lead and line.

spanker -- The fore-and-aft sail set on the mizzenmast of a square-rigged ship, sometimes called the driver.

spar -- A spar is any one of the timber members of a vessel's gear.

spinnaker -- A racing sail of immense spread reaching from the topmast head to the end of a spinnaker boom which is a spar set out to take it.

spreaders -- Compression struts from masts used to increase effective support from rigging by holding rigging wires further away from the mast than they would otherwise be.

spring line -- A docking line running aft from the bow or forward from the quarter.

squall -- A sudden and very strenuous gust of wind or a sudden increase in its force.

square-rigged -- That method of disposing of sails in which they hang across the ship and in which they are approximately rectangular in shape.

stanchion -- A post supporting a rail.

standing rigging -- Ropes or wire ropes that permanently support the spars, such as shrouds and other stays, and are not moved when working the sails.

starboard -- The right-hand side of a vessel to a person facing the bow.

statute mile -- The unit of land distance (5,280 feet).

stays -- Supports made of hemp or wire rope supporting spars, or, more especially, masts.

staysails -- Sails set on the stays between the masts of a ship or as headsails.

steamers -- Vessels powered by steam engines.

steering gear -- Mechanism used to transfer torque to rudder.

steeve -- The angle the bowsprit makes with the horizontal.

stem -- The foremost timber of a vessel's hull.

stern -- The rear end of a vessel.

sternpost -- An upright timber joined to and erected above the after end of the keel to which the rudder is hung.

stock -- The crossbar in the shank of an anchor.

stoke hold -- That compartment in a steamship from which the fires under the boilers are stoked or tended.

stopwater -- A dowel in the center of a joint to prevent leakage.

stove -- Smashed in by a collision.

stow -- To stow a cargo is to pack it into a ship so that it will not shift as the vessel pitches and rolls.

strake -- A length of hull planking.

stringer -- A sturdy fore and aft structural member in the bilge.

strut -- A fitting for supporting the extended propeller shaft.

studding sails -- On square-rigged ships, narrow supplementary sails are sometimes set on small booms at the sides of the principal square sails.

superstructure -- A structure built above the uppermost complete deck; a pilothouse, bridge, galley house, etc.

swell -- An undulating motion of the water, always felt at sea after a gale.

tack -- To change the course of a vessel from one direction or to tack to another by bringing her head to the wind and letting the wind fill her sails on the other side, the object being to progress against the wind.

taffrail -- The sternmost rail of a vessel, that is, the rail around the stern.

tail shaft -- The aft section of the shaft which receives the propeller.

tender -- A small vessel employed to attend a larger one or to attend an underwater operation.

thermocline -- That point between two layers of water that differ significantly in temperature.

throat -- That part of a gaff that is next to the mast, and the adjoining corner of the sail.

throat halyard -- The rope that elevates the throat.

thwart -- Athwart means across, and in a boat the seats are called the thwarts because they are placed athwart or across the boat.

tiller -- The handle or beam at the top of the shaft to which the rudder is attached, and by which the rudder is turned. It is in use only on comparatively small vessels.

tonnage -- The measure of a ship's internal dimensions as the basis for a standard for dues, etc.

top -- In square-rigged ships, the platform built on the masts just below the topsails, and to which the sailor climbs.

topgallant mast -- In a mast built up in sections, the topgallant mast is the third section above the deck.

topmast -- In a mast built up of two or more parts, the topmast is the second from the deck.

topping lift -- A line from boom end to mast head.

topsail -- The second sail from the deck on any mast of a square-rigged ship.

topgallant sail -- The third sail from the deck on any mast of a square-rigged ship, except when the ship is equipped with lower and upper topsails, in which case the topgallant sail is the fourth.

topsail schooner -- A schooner, which on the foremast, spreads a square topsail.

trail board -- A curved board extending from the figurehead to the bow, often carved or embellished.

tramp -- The name usually given to merchant freighters that have no regular routes.

transom -- The outside stern of a hull.

transverse -- At right angles to the ship's fore-and-aft center line.

trawler -- A vessel usually driven by power and used in fishing, it tows a heavy net called a trawl.

trestle trees -- Short timbers running fore and aft on either side of a mast that rest on the "hounds." They support the "top platform" and cross trees.

trick -- The time allotted to a man to be at the wheel or on any other duty.

trim -- The attitude of a vessel with respect to the water's surface.

trip(ping) line -- Light line used to release snaps on spinnaker pole; light line used to raise an anchor from fluke end.

truck -- The very top of the mast.

trunk -- The upper part of a cabin rising through the deck.

trysails -- Small sails used in bad weather when no others can be carried, or occasionally, for rough work.

tug -- A small, powerful vessel used to assist larger ships about protected waterways. Tugs are also used to tow or push barges or almost anything that can float. The term is also used to refer to certain fishing vessels.

twin screw -- A ship equipped with two propellers.

up Lake Michigan -- In the 1800s, Chicago was considered to be at the head of Lake Michigan, thus sailors went "up the lake to Chicago.

underwater preserve -- See bottomland preserve.

Underwater Salvage and Preserve Committee -- An advisory group of state (Michigan only) officials and citizens that offers guidance on the development of bottomland preserves and the issuance of salvage permits. State officials routinely ignore committee recommendations so the group is powerless.

underway -- A ship afloat that is not tied or anchored.

unship -- To take away or remove from a secure position.

vail (vale or bale) -- Strap around boom to which sheet attaches and allows a pulley block to swing in the direction of the load.

vang -- Tackle used for controlling a boom.

vessel -- A general term for all craft larger than a rowboat.

vhf -- Very high frequency.

waist -- That part of a vessel between the beam and the quarter.

wake -- The track a vessel leaves behind her on the surface of the water. The surface turbulence left by a ship in motion.

wale -- A stake of planking running fore and aft on the outside of the hull, heavier than the regular planking.

watch -- Tour of duty.

weather -- A nautical expression applied to any object to windward of any given spot; the "weather" side of a vessel is the side upon which the wind blows. A vessel is said to have "weathered" a gale when she has lived safely through it.

weather helm -- The tendency of a ship to head into the wind.

wedges -- Tapered pieces under the stern of a powerboat to keep it from squatting.

weigh -- To lift the anchor from the bottom.

well -- A depression sometimes built in the decks of yachts or sailboats which is not covered by a deck. It is also called a cockpit and is for the convenience and protection of passengers and crew. Also, an opening leading to the lowest part of the bilge in which the depth of bilge water may be measured.

well found -- A fully equipped ship.

wetsuit -- A suit of neoprene foam or other material designed to permit a layer of water to remain between the suit and a diver. The suit offers insulation and prevents water from circulating.

whaleback -- A Great Lakes steamer with a rounded, steel hull, built by Capt. Alexander McDougall in Superior, Wisconsin.

wharf -- A loading place for vessels.

wheel -- The wheel by which a ship is steered.

winch -- A hoisting or pulling machine fitted with a horizontal single or double drum.

windjammer -- A slang expression for a person who prefers sails to engines.

windlass -- An apparatus in which horizontal or vertical drums or gypsies and wildcats are operated by means of a steam engine or motor for the purpose of handling heavy anchor chains, hawsers, etc.

windward -- That side of a vessel or any other object upon which the wind is blowing is the windward side.

wind sail -- A tube of canvas with wings of canvas at the top so arranged as to direct fresh air below decks; a temporary ventilator.

wing and wing -- Running before the wind with jib on one side and the main on the other.

work -- Structural parts that have loosened sufficiently to move against each other.

worm -- To wind a rope in a spiral.

wreck -- The destruction of a ship; the ship itself or the remnants of it after the disaster.

wreckage -- Goods or parts of a ship cast up by the sea after a shipwreck.

wreck raper -- One who illegally removes historical artifacts from shipwrecks. Also called "scurvy dogs."

yacht -- A pleasure boat, usually large and elaborate.

yard -- A spar suspended from a mast for the purpose of spreading a sail.

yardarm -- The crosspiece near the top of a mast.

yaw -- To deviate from the true course.

yawl -- A sailing vessel equipped with two masts, the main and the jigger.

zebra mussel -- A clam-like organism introduced into the Great Lakes from discharged ships' ballast water.

Great Lakes Rigs

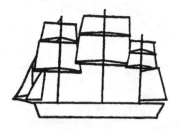

Full-Rigged Ship

Grand Haven Rig

Brig

Barque

Two-Masted Schooner

Schooner Barge

Recompression Chambers

Recompression (hyperbaric) chambers are divers' best friends when decompression sickness arises. These chambers are becoming more common, especially with the development of underwater preserves and more applications for the technology.

Fortunately, decompression sickness is uncommon. But when divers attempt especially deep or repeated dives, it should be a primary concern. Strict adherence to decompression tables can avoid problems, but even with these tables or diving computers that calculate decompression stops, there are no guarantees for safety.

Perhaps the best advice is to avoid problems by knowing limitations and planning dives carefully. It is always better to err on the side of safety than to take chances.

Play it safe by knowing the symptoms of decompression sickness and treating what may appear to be even minor cases. In a U.S. Navy diving manual, the most frequent decompression errors were listed as: failure to report symptoms early, failure to treat doubtful cases, failure to treat promptly, failure to recognize serious symptoms and failure to treat adequately.

In general, it is best to transport ill divers to the nearest hospital emergency room. There, divers can be stabilized for transportation to a decompression chamber, if necessary.

The Divers Alert Network (DAN),
which is based at Duke University in Durham, North Carolina, can provide information about treating such injuries to emergency room personnel. DAN can also assist in arranging transportation to the nearest recompression chamber.

Each Michigan underwater preserve and Isle Royale have an emergency procedure to handle diving accidents. Those procedures are outlined in the chapters covering those areas. If an accident occurs outside of those areas, contact the local county sheriff's department or the U.S. Coast Guard for assistance.

The U.S. Coast Guard Air Station in Traverse City conducts air rescue and emergency evacuation operations throughout the Great Lakes. They can transport divers to recompression chambers if no other emergency transportation is available. But it is best to first contact local officials to determine if such emergency transportation is needed.

For on-water assistance, contact the nearest U.S. Coast Guard Station on vhf channel 16.

Again, it is best not to wait until a full-blown emergency has arisen before taking action. Instead, recognize decompression sickness early and treat promptly until expert assistance is obtained.

Also, be sure to recognize the needs of other divers and watch them for signs of decompression sickness.

1. Bronson Methodist Hospital
Kalamazoo, Michigan 49007
(616) 341-7654 or
(616) 341-7778

2. Marquette General Hospital
Marquette, Michigan 49855
(906) 225-3560

3. St. Lukes Hospital
Milwaukee, Wisconsin
(414) 649-6577

4. Hennepin County Hospital
Minneapolis, Minnesota
(612) 347-3131

5. Henry Ford Hospital
Detroit, Michigan
(313) 982-8100

EMERGENCY NUMBERS:

U.S. Coast Guard
Traverse City Air Station
(616) 922-8214

Divers Alert Network (DAN)
Duke University
Durham, North Carolina
(919) 684-8111 or
(919) 684-2948

Index